LECTURES ON THE PHILOSOPHY OF RIGHT, 1819–1820

Lectures on the Philosophy of Right, 1819–1820

G.W.F. HEGEL

TRANSLATED WITH AN INTRODUCTION
AND NOTES BY ALAN BRUDNER

UNIVERSITY OF TORONTO PRESS
Toronto Buffalo London

© University of Toronto Press 2023
Toronto Buffalo London
utorontopress.com

G.W.F. Hegel: Vorlesungen über die Philosophie des Rechts
(Vorlesungen: Ausgewählte Nachschriften und Manuskripte, Band 14)
(2000) Felix Meiner Verlag, Hamburg

Excerpts from: Georg Friedrich Wilhelm Hegel, Philosophie des Rechts: Die Vorlesung von 1819/20 in einer Nachschrift. Herausgegeben von Dieter Henrich. © Suhrkamp Verlag Frankfurt am Main 1983. All rights reserved by and controlled through Suhrkamp Verlag Berlin.

ISBN 978-1-4875-0621-6 (cloth)   ISBN 978-1-4875-3354-0 (EPUB)
                                 ISBN 978-1-4875-3352-6 (PDF)

Library and Archives Canada Cataloguing in Publication

Title: Lectures on the philosophy of right, 1819–1820 / G.W.F. Hegel ;
   translated with an introduction and notes by Alan Brudner.
Other titles: Vorlesungen. English
Names: Hegel, Georg Wilhelm Friedrich, 1770–1831, author. | Brudner, Alan, translator.
Description: Translation of: Vorlesungen über die Philosophie des Rechts
   (Vorlesungen : ausgewählte Nachschriften und Manuskripte, Band 14). |
   Includes bibliographical references and index.
Identifiers: Canadiana (print) 2023013520X | Canadiana (ebook) 20230135250 |
   ISBN 9781487506216 (cloth) | ISBN 9781487533526 (PDF) |
   ISBN 9781487533540 (EPUB)
Subjects: LCSH: Philosophy.
Classification: LCC B2908 .B78 2023 | DDC 193 – dc23

Cover design: Liz Harasymczuk
Cover image: © SZ Photo / Bridgeman Images

We wish to acknowledge the land on which the University of Toronto Press operates. This land is the traditional territory of the Wendat, the Anishnaabeg, the Haudenosaunee, the Métis, and the Mississaugas of the Credit First Nation.

University of Toronto Press acknowledges the financial support of the Government of Canada, the Canada Council for the Arts, and the Ontario Arts Council, an agency of the Government of Ontario, for its publishing activities.

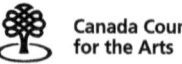

Contents

Acknowledgments vii

Translator's Introduction ix

Note on the Translation lvii

Introduction 3

First Part: Abstract Right 17
First Section: Property 21
    A. Taking Possession 25
    B. Use of the Thing 29
    C. Alienation of Property 34
Second Section: Contract 38
Third Section: Wrong 46
    A. Innocent Wrong 48
    B. Fraud 49
    C. Force and Crime 50

Second Part: Morality 61
First Section: Intention and Responsibility 64
Second Section: Purpose and Welfare 68
Third Section: The Good and Conscience 75

Third Part: Ethical Life 101
First Section: The Family 111
    A. Marriage 112

B. The Family's Wealth   126
   C. The Education of Children and the Dissolution of the
      Family   128
Second Section: Civil Society   133
   A. The System of Needs   136
      A. 1. The Nature of Need and Its Satisfaction   136
      A. 2. The Nature of Labour   139
      A. 3. Capital   142
   B. The Administration of Justice   150
      B. 1. Justice as Law   152
      B. 2. The Existence of Law   155
      B. 3. The Court   159
   C. The Police and the Corporation   167
      C. 1. The Police   168
      C. 2. The Corporation   178
Third Section: The State   185
   A. Internal Public Law   195
      A. 1. The Internal Constitution for Itself   199
         a. The Princely Power   203
         b. The Executive Power   218
         c. The Legislative Power   223
      A. 2. External Sovereignty   236
   B. External Public Law   239
   C. World History   240
      C. 1. The Oriental Realm   245
      C. 2. The Greek Realm   246
      C. 3. The Roman Realm   247
      C. 4. The Germanic Realm   248

Appendix 1   251

Appendix 2   254

Appendix 3   257

Appendix 4   260

Appendix 5   265

Index   269

Acknowledgments

I am grateful to the Faculty of Law of the University of Toronto for a grant in aid of this project and to Daniel Quinlan of the University of Toronto Press for shepherding the manuscript through to publication. I also wish to thank Jutta Brunée, Markus Dubber, Tatjana Hörnle, and two anonymous reviewers for helpful advice on the translation.

Translator's Introduction

I

At the newly founded University of Berlin, in the winter semester of 1819/20, during a period of turmoil in Germany mingling liberal demonstrations against the restoration of autocracies with chauvinist riots against Jewish emancipation, and as state watchdogs sent to universities to root out subversives looked on, Georg Wilhelm Friedrich Hegel gave his third course of lectures on the philosophy of Right.[1] The lectures began on 25 October 1819, a week after the Carlsbad Decrees, squelching the reform movement in the German Confederation, came into force in Prussia; and they ended on 17 March 1820, seven months before *Outlines of the Philosophy of Right*, Hegel's great book on natural law and the state, appeared in print.

One auditor of the 1819/20 lectures was a Swiss law student named Johann Rudolf Ringier, who went on to become a judge of the high court of a Swiss canton and later an elected member of the Federal Diet of Switzerland. Ringier transcribed Hegel's lectures, and his notes ended up in a private library in Basel, where they were discovered in 1997. Edited by Emil Angehrn, Martin Bondeli, and Hoo Nam Seelmann, Ringier's notes were published in 2000 by Felix Meiner as *Vorlesungen*

---

1 The previous two courses were given in 1817/18 (Heidelberg) and 1818/19 (Berlin), the next three in 1821/2, 1822/3, and 1824/5 (Berlin). A seventh course, begun in 1831, was interrupted by Hegel's death. The Heidelberg lectures of 1817/18, based on the *Encyclopaedia of the Philosophical Sciences*, have been translated into English; see G.W.F. Hegel, *Lectures on Natural Right and Political Science*, edited by the staff of the Hegel Archives, trans. J. Michael Stewart and Peter C. Hodgson (Berkeley: University of California Press, 1995; henceforth LNRPS).

über die Philosophie des Rechts, Berlin, 1819/20,[2] making up volume 14 of G.W.F. Hegel, *Vorlesungen: Ausgewählte Nachschriften und Manuskripte*.[3] This is a translation of that volume.

As is well known, Hegel's custom was to publish outlines of his philosophical system as a teaching aid for his courses. These outlines consist of terse, tightly packed, numbered paragraphs that Hegel would hand out to his students and then flesh out in lectures. Because the printed books take the form of outlines never meant to stand alone, the lectures that supplement them are widely acknowledged to be as important as the books for understanding Hegel's philosophy, with the caveat that they come from the hand of Hegel's students rather than from the teacher himself. That is why the editors of Hegel's posthumously published collected works included the oral elaborations taken down by students as *Zusätze* or additions to the paragraphs Hegel wrote.

However, the lectures presented here are unlike any others Hegel gave on the philosophy of Right, either before or after *Outlines* appeared. These lectures are not supplementary to a published text, as the previous ones were to part 3, section 2 of the *Encyclopaedia of the Philosophical Sciences* and as the subsequent ones were to *Outlines*. They are an independent and self-contained presentation of Hegel's legal and political philosophy.[4] No doubt, they borrowed from the manuscript of *Outlines* that Hegel had almost finished, but we can surmise that, since they preceded the book, they also contributed to it. In any case, the 1819/20 lectures are not "additions" to a printed "outline." They stand on their own. Indeed, since they are neither an outline nor a supplement to an outline, we can say that they are the *only* version of Hegel's mature political thought that stands on its own.

They are also the only version that reads like a book. Whereas both the *Encyclopaedia* and *Outlines* exhibit the style of a formal treatise, with staccato paragraphs appended by remarks, the 1819/20 lectures form a

---

2 G.W.F. Hegel, *Vorlesungen über die Philosophie des Rechts, Berlin, 1819/20*. Transcribed by Johann Rudolf Ringier, ed. Emil Angehrn, Martin Bondeli, and Hoo Nam Seelmann, vol. 14 of G.W.F. Hegel, *Vorlesungen: Ausgewählte Nachschriften und Manuskripte* (Hamburg: Meiner, 2000; henceforth Angehrn, Bondeli, Seelmann).
3 G.W.F. Hegel, *Vorlesungen: Ausgewählte Nachschriften und Manuskripte*, 17 vols. (Hamburg: Meiner, 1983–2007).
4 Hegel's correspondence suggests that he meant to have *Outlines* or a part thereof published in time for the 1819/20 semester, but that uncertainty as to the reach of a new Prussian law of censorship upset his plan: *Briefe von und an Hegel*, ed. Johannes Hoffmeister, 4 vols. (Hamburg: Meiner, 1952), 2:213, 220; and Angehrn, Bondeli, Seelmann, xiii–xiv.

continuous, flowing discourse much like Hegel's lectures on the philosophy of history, the philosophy of art, the philosophy of religion, and the history of philosophy. By virtue, therefore, of both the fullness of their content and the fluidity of their form, these lectures can be studied separately from *Outlines*, in comparison with which they offer an arguably more accessible and certainly more engaging articulation of thoughts at the same stage of development. As Dieter Henrich puts it, the lectures of 1819/20 make "Hegel's political theory appear ... with a freshness, concreteness, and transparency that is achieved by no other text of his philosophy of Right."[5]

Ringier's notes are not the only ones we have of Hegel's 1819/20 lectures on the philosophy of Right. We also have notes taken by an anonymous student that, strangely enough, turned up in the Lilly Library of the University of Indiana in 1969.[6] Edited by Dieter Henrich and published by Suhrkamp in 1983 as *Philosophie des Rechts: Die Vorlesung von 1819/20 in einer Nachschrift*, these notes are written in sentences that are generally better constructed than Ringier's, but that omit detail that Ringier included, particularly in the lectures on private law. The smoothness of their prose led Henrich to suspect that the unknown student's notes were rewritten after the lectures, possibly by someone who had not heard them, whereas Ringier's notes were, by their style, structure, and level of detail, quite evidently written contemporaneously with the lectures.

Having two sets of notes for the same course of lectures is felicitous. It compensates to some extent for the deficiency of having Hegel's lectures indirectly from students, for it allows a translator to consult one set to clarify or expand the other, thereby approximating more closely the lecturer's own discourse. Still, what is presented here is not a composite. Blending the two sets into something no one wrote hardly seems the right road to authenticity, and so I have steered clear of that approach. Instead, I have taken as the main text to be translated the Ringier manuscript edited by Angehrn, Bondeli, and Seelmann, but have supplemented the translation with the Henrich edition of the earlier-found manuscript where it amplifies or clarifies Ringier's, where it diverges from Ringier's, or where it supplies material missing from Ringier's.

---

5 G.W.F. Hegel, *Philosophie des Rechts: Die Vorlesung von 1819/20 in einer Nachschrift*, ed. Dieter Henrich (Frankfurt am Main: Suhrkamp, 1983), 38.
6 Dieter Henrich, the editor of these notes, tells us that they were acquired by the Lilly Library in 1896 from a New York publisher, Lemcke and Buechner, with ties through its Leipzig office to the German book market: Henrich, ed., *Philosophie des Rechts*, 300.

Most of the supplements appear in footnotes, but some are inserted (within square brackets) into the text, where they fill small gaps left by Ringier, and five long gap-fillers appear in the appendices. The supplements are indicated by the abbreviation UN (for unknown note-taker) and by the page in the Henrich edition where they occur.

II

The editors of Ringier's notes explain the importance of the 1819/20 lectures in the following way:

> The interest [of the 1819/20 lectures] owes to the fact that in these lectures Hegel carries out the decisive redrafting of his legal philosophy, which, in contrast to the earlier statements, represents the political turning point to which the printed legal philosophy of 1820 bears witness and which has so durably shaped the picture we have of Hegel.[7]

The witness to a turning point referred to by the editors cannot be Hegel himself, for here is his own description of the relation between *Outlines* and the previous presentation of his philosophy of Right:

> This compendium is an enlarged and in particular a more systematic exposition of the same fundamental concepts which, in relation to this part of philosophy [i.e., the philosophy of natural law and the state], are already contained in a book of mine designed previously for my lectures – *The Encyclopaedia of the Philosophical Sciences* (Heidelberg, 1817).[8]

Readers of that sentence might be puzzled as to how it describes a turning point. On its face, the sentence announces an "enlarged" and "more systematic" exposition of the fundamental ideas about natural law and the state that Hegel had previously set forth in the *Encyclopaedia*'s section on Objective Mind. There is no suggestion of a revision of the ideas, or of Hegel's understanding of how they relate to the existing political order in Prussia or in the rest of Germany. Nevertheless, the thesis that Hegel's teaching on the state took a sharp turn to the right in *Outlines* has gained wide currency ever since the appearance in 1973 of

---

7 Angehrn, Bondeli, Seelmann, xii–xiii.
8 G.W.F. Hegel, *Outlines of the Philosophy of Right*, trans. T.M. Knox, ed. Stephen Houlgate (Oxford: Oxford University Press, 2008; henceforth *Outlines*), 3.

Karl-Heinz Ilting's edition of Hegel's Berlin lectures on the philosophy of Right.[9]

With the lectures as a basis for comparison, Ilting argued that Hegel changed crucial parts of *Outlines* under pressure of Prince Metternich's restoration of the pre-Napoleonic order in the German states and, in particular, in fear of the enforcement of the Carlsbad Decrees, which had already struck close to home. Meant to suppress the nationalism that, brewing in universities, had erupted in the murder of August von Kotzebue, a German playwright turned Russian agent, by a member of a radical student society, the decrees covered the German states under a blanket of surveillance and censorship. With the assassination as pretext, they ordered the dissolution of unauthorized student societies, the censorship of the press and academic publications, the supervision and control of research and teaching by government monitors placed in universities, and the summary removal and blacklisting of professors considered dangerous to the state. One of the first victims of these measures was Wilhelm Martin de Wette, a biblical scholar and a colleague of Hegel's in Berlin. Less than a month before the start of the 1819/20 term, de Wette was fired under an executive order for writing a letter of condolence to the mother of Kotzebue's murderer, saying that her son's conscientious conviction justified his action. For this he was also banished from Prussia for life.[10]

Emblematic of Hegel's turn in reaction to these events, argued Ilting, are his remarks in *Outlines* on monarchy, the French Revolution, and the mission of political philosophy. Whereas, Ilting stated, the lectures delivered both before and after Metternich's crackdown view the

---

9 G.W.F. Hegel, *Vorlesungen über Rechtsphilosophie*, ed. Karl-Heinz Ilting, 4 vols. (Stuttgart: Frommann-Holzboog, 1973–4); for a shredding of Ilting's biographical evidence for this thesis, see Hans-Christian Lucas and Udo Rameil, "Furcht vor der Zensur? Zur Entstehungs- und Druckgeschichte von Hegels Grundlinien der Philosophie des Rechts," *Hegel-Studien*, no. 15 (1980): 63–93.

10 Besides de Wette, three students mentored by Hegel came under investigation by the Prussian police for suspected ties to or sympathies with the *Burschenschaften*, the student societies. One was arrested and held for nine months until Hegel bailed him out; another was imprisoned incommunicado but surreptitiously visited by Hegel (with other students) from a rowboat on a river that ran past the prisoner's cell window. Both arrests occurred in the July preceding the 1819/20 term. Because of his close association with these students, Hegel himself came under suspicion, something he knew while praising Napoleon and deprecating the Restorationists in these lectures; see Terry Pinkard, *Hegel: A Biography* (Cambridge: Cambridge University Press, 2000), 437–8, 442–5, 449–50.

ideal monarch as the titular head of a republic who merely assents to decisions independently made by accountable organs of government, *Outlines* justifies a true monarch who exercises discretionary and non-responsible power both domestically and externally.[11] Whereas, during the reform period in Germany, Hegel chided the reactionary nobility for having "slept through" the twenty-five years since the Revolution, in *Outlines* he attacks the Revolution for isolating the abstractly universal side of freedom and annihilating everything concrete in its name.[12] And while the preface to Hegel's first (pre-Carlsbad) Berlin lectures emphasized philosophy's struggle against a status quo having no support but tradition, the preface to *Outlines* sees philosophy's task as justifying the same status quo to rational thought.[13] Add to this the fact that Hegel's correspondence shows that he completed *Outlines* while mindful of the censor,[14] and the picture Ilting wants us to see comes into discomfiting focus: that Hegel presents his liberal-progressive doctrines in lectures, while posing as a traditionalist in print.

The editors of Ringier's manuscript argue that the importance of the lectures of 1819/20 (of which Ilting had no record) lies in their confirming Ilting's hypothesis of a rightward turn by Hegel immediately following the issuance of the Carlsbad Decrees. Yet they do not claim that Hegel said one thing in these lectures and another in print, but that, in the overheated political climate of the time, he strategically took regressive positions in both places, so that neither can count as a fully reliable source of his political thought. From this point of view, the chief interest of the 1819/20 lectures, according to Ringier's editors, is that they show Hegel working out the compromises with state power that appear later in his book. In support of this reading, the editors bring forward three pieces of evidence from the lectures: Hegel's critique of natural Right doctrine in the opening sentences of his introduction and of the Part called Abstract Right, his negative judgment of the French Revolution, and his defence of monarchy.[15] Let us consider whether

---

11 Ilting, ed., *Vorlesungen*, 1:28–32.
12 G.W.F. Hegel, "The Proceedings of the Assembly of Estates of the Kingdom of Württemberg," in *Hegel's Political Writings*, trans. T.M. Knox, with an introductory essay by Z.A. Pelczynski (Oxford: Clarendon Press, 1964), 282; and *Outlines*, paras. 5, 272.
13 I have argued elsewhere that Ilting overstates the difference between the two prefaces; see Alan S. Brudner, "The Significance of Hegel's Prefatory Lectures on the Philosophy of Law," *Clio* 8, no. 1 (1978): 41–8.
14 "Brief an Creuzer," 30 October 1819, in *Briefe von und an Hegel*, 2:220.
15 Angehrn, Bondeli, Seelmann, xiv.

Hegel's remarks on these subjects do in fact support the editors' implicit characterization of the 1819/20 lectures as an unseemly genuflection to power. I'll argue that they do not, but that the lectures show a different kind of change in Hegel, one consistent with both the authenticity of *Outlines* and the integrity of its author.

The Critique of Natural Right

Ringier's editors discern a shift from Hegel's critical conception of natural Right in the first Berlin lectures of 1818/19 to one that equates natural Right with state law just one year later.[16] From a liberal exponent of natural Right as a standard by which to evaluate positive laws and institutions, Hegel supposedly becomes a conservative foe of natural Right doctrines that juxtapose natural Right to the state. Among the passages in the 1819/20 lectures that might be taken to support this judgment, the following three stand out:

> Right on its own is the abstract Concept. The State is the realization of [the Concept of] Right. Right in the abstract is often called natural Right. Considered so, the state is viewed not as the realization of Right but as a misfortune for Right – a harsh fate by which the natural right of the human being is limited and offended. Right is viewed in such a way that a condition of abstract Right becomes a lost paradise – one that must nevertheless remain a goal to be recovered from the state …[17]
>
> The task of science is to specify the existential side through which Right comes to its realization; to begin with, however, it is to recognize what true Right is. This knowledge seems all the more needed now, when the whole world has seized upon this subject. Most people have an opinion and firm convictions about this matter and, against the real world, claim that the Right in thought should be realized. This demand counts as something absolute because it is something inwardly sacred. It is especially philosophy that should specify the Concept of Right and how reality must be [arranged] so as to correspond to the Concept. [This is so because] thoughts are necessary to the knowledge of Right. The most common view is that everyone can draw the knowledge of Right immediately from his breast and head without speculative reflection. [From this point of view,] if philosophy should deliver the Concept, then it should be an arsenal of reasons by which to combat and improve reality. [The Concept] is therefore [said to be]

---

16 Angehrn, Bondeli, Seelmann, xiv.
17 This translation, 3.

an ideal of reality, one in which all injustice is returned to balance. And, as is thought, this ideal is all the more excellent the further removed from reality it is. Such insipid ideals have then also been purveyed to the many ...[18]

The term natural Right should be banished because it does not denote anything. It is said that abstract rights are absolute, and this is meant as though the reality of these rights is to be found in a natural condition. Condition generally implies immediate reality. The actuality of Right is not an immediate condition. The Right must be rational, that is, brought forward through the rational Mind. Here belong the fictions detrimental for *philosophy* about a golden age, about a paradise, as if this condition ever existed. For just that reason, such conditions are not to be longed for. This is something powerless and opaque. Thus, there can be no discussion at all about such a state of nature.[19]

It is evident even from these passages taken alone that the target of Hegel's remonstrations is not critical natural Right as such but the particular conception of natural Right that places it in a condition logically prior to the state – in a so-called state of nature wherein human beings are dissociated atoms. Hegel's opposition in the 1819/20 lectures to this type of natural Right doctrine is nothing new in his philosophical development; it can already be found in his *Natural Law* essay of 1802–3, where it is linked to a critique of a political union characterized by "dominion" on the state's side and "absolute subjection" on the individual's.[20] Crucially, moreover, Hegel's critique of this particular conception of natural Right is made *for the sake of* natural Right. This is so in the sense that the natural Right doctrine that Hegel opposes necessarily leads to a political sovereign whose legislative determinations of natural Right are unimpeachable, there being no alternative to unaccountable authority conceivable at this standpoint but the moral anarchy of the state of nature. As a consequence, the logical space between natural Right and positive law either disappears (Hobbes) or becomes practically irrelevant (Kant); natural Right effectively means whatever

---

18 This translation, 3–4.
19 This translation, 17. Ringier's editors could have found the same idea expressed in the 1818/19 lectures: "Right in the state of nature is fictitious; it is supposed to be the true Right, and it is opposed to the state; the latter is considered the result of an unfortunate necessity. The state of nature is much more that of the barbarity of the natural will, of appetite. Paradise means a zoo" (Ilting, *Vorlesungen*, 1:240; my translation). See also LNRPS, para. 2.
20 G.W.F. Hegel, *Natural Law*, trans. T.M. Knox (Philadelphia: University of Pennsylvania Press, 1975), 63–6.

the sovereign says it means. Also vanishing, therefore, is the distinction between the natural lawyer and the legal positivist; for if natural Right dissolves into positive law or is irrelevant to the obligatoriness of law, then law is co-extensive with the commands of the sovereign. Equally, Hegel's critique of an individualistic source of political authority is made for the sake of the individual. A state grounded in the surrender of a determination of natural Right independent of the legislator's leaves the individual legally defenceless against the legislator.

What conception of natural Right does Hegel put forward instead? The answer is: the same one he put forward in the *Encyclopaedia* and in the Heidelberg (1817/18) and first Berlin (1818/19) lectures based thereon. There is no turn. His first two sentences in the 1819/20 lectures are: "Right on its own is the abstract Concept. The State is the realization of Right."[21] The Concept, we know, is a whole composed of a collective agency on one side and an individual agency on the other, a whole fixed inside self-consciousness considered as a mind-body union writ large. Their natural union within one self-consciousness grounds a non-burdensome duty on each side to defer to the other's end-status for the sake of its own. Thus, the individual is naturally bound to acknowledge a united will as the source of its own rational worth in bringing the union to reality; the united will is naturally bound to respect the individual agent as that through whose free devotion and service it obtains objective confirmation as the common good. Each side depends for validation on the other's free will, but since the other is internal to itself and reciprocally deferential, dependence is reconciled with freedom. As the structure of a political relation, the Concept's union of distinct but complementary wills exists materially in the state, but not in any state. From his youth, Hegel discerned that structure in the Greek idea of the *polis*, best exemplified in democratic Athens in the years between the Persian and Peloponnesian Wars.[22]

However, apart from his earliest fragments and sketches, this Concept of political Right was never conceived by Hegel as an ideal in the philosopher's mind by which to judge and improve existing states. His polemic in the 1819/20 lectures against those who conceive natural Right as "an arsenal of reasons by which to combat and improve reality"

---

21 The first sentence of the introduction to the 1818/19 lectures is similar: "Natural right has for its object the rational Concept of Right and its realization, the Idea of Right" (Ilting, *Vorlesungen*, 1:237; my translation). See also LNRPS, para. 1.
22 G.W.F. Hegel, "Tübingen Essay," trans. H.S. Harris, in *Miscellaneous Writings of G. W. F. Hegel*, ed. Jon Stewart (Evanston: Northwestern University Press, 2002), 67–9.

is again nothing new. At least from the *Phenomenology of Spirit* onward, his consistent position may be described in a nutshell as follows.

Taken alone, the Concept, by virtue of its both containing and (as *one* self-consciousness) not containing the differentiated individual, is self-contradictory. It is not actually the bi-personal whole that it is in its nature. It is one-sided vis-à-vis the truly differentiated individual – here, the separate or insular individual who acts only for itself. Consequently, when the *polis* enforces its law against this individual, the supposed natural law enjoining civic virtue looks more like a human convention violently repressive of nature. With as much right as his accuser, the lawbreaker can claim that nature is innocently lawless and the *polis* guiltily artificial, that he has a natural liberty to act in any way he pleases. Any attempt to reassert the Concept in the face of this challenge would have to wilfully suppress the principle of individualism expressed therein, while perhaps sublimating it in the philosopher's love of the Concept's beauty, now removed from all possible existence. That was Plato's response to individual egoism, but Hegel has a different one.

The Concept taken alone is inadequate to its nature. Double-sided in nature, it is one-sided in fact. Its self-inadequacy means, however, that a bond of complementarity connects the Concept with the separate ego, for the Concept lacks the fulfilment of its nature in this ego's freely attesting to its normative authority; while the separate ego lacks the Concept, whose need for its free attestation first gives rational and objective support to the natural right that the ego alone merely asserts. So, because the Concept's inwardness is *under*-differentiated compared to its implicit nature, it stretches to include a separate, individual self-consciousness within an extended nexus that Hegel names the Ethical Idea. This now truly bi-personal bond linking the ego's unilateral worth-claim with the validator it inwardly lacks generates an ethical energy in separate egos as real and demonstrable as any force in nature. It moves the mutually indifferent into relations of mutual respect for the sake of gaining recognition for the right-claim of each to act as *it* pleases; and it drives them into a political union for the sake of making these ethicized claims an objective reality in a lawful condition under a public sovereign.

Because of the ego's insularity, however, these relations are heteronomous and crushing. The force of the Idea's demand that unilateral worth-claims become recognized truths pulls the insular ego into legal and political relations that must press on its natural egoism as a burdensome yoke, expose its welfare to the actions of other egos indifferent to it, and subject its legal rights to the interpretation and might of the absolutist civic sovereign that is correlative to the egoism of modern society. Here, the Ethical Idea, inherently the harmony of civicism and individualism of which the model *polis* was the truncated embryo, splits into a private sphere for abstractly selfish individuals on one side and a public sphere for abstractly reasonable humans on the other, individual self-consciousness having unhappily broken into these fragments of itself.

However, beneath this tale of woe lies a deeper story. That story is about the Concept's receiving confirmation from the separate ego for its normative authority as the structure of valid worth-claims. Out of its own mouth, the insular ego proves the naturalness of the Concept's law of mutual recognition. Concomitantly, the objective mind-world becomes suffused with laws no longer given by taboo, custom, or tyrannical power, but generated from thought as determinations of equal freedom and reciprocal duty that free egos can endorse. This occurs through the insular ego's spontaneous move, for the sake of its own agency, into institutional relationships (e.g., property, contract, a transparent legal process) reflecting the Concept's structure of mutual deference between free agents. This process continues until such Concept-confirming institutions have so permeated the public and private sides of civil society as to make their inherent complementarity a factual one, thus preparing the ground for their reunification in one double-sided (hence Concept-fulfilling, Idea-mirroring) State. At that point, philosophy's task is just to disclose this rational story to our minds, calling forth the civic reverence that completes it, not to judge whether the state satisfies the subjective Concept of a thinker detached from it.

Accordingly, there is no *volte-face* in Hegel's deprecating, post-Carlsbad, a natural law standard juxtaposed to the state. Even for the author of the 1798 essay on "The Spirit of Christianity and Its Fate," to measure the existing state against the Concept is already to contradict the Concept, for the judge then opposes the form of Right to a public reality, turning Right into his opinion thereof and any action to impose it into a case of unilateral violence.[23] So, Hegel's tirade against political radicals in the 1819/20 lectures and then again in the preface to *Outlines* may have been music to the ears of the authorities, but it was in no sense a change of position intended to placate them.

Nor was it an abdication of critical reason to the authority of the given order. As far back as the 1802 essay known as "The German

---

23 G.W.F. Hegel, *Early Theological Writings*, trans. T.M. Knox (Philadelphia: University of Pennsylvania Press, 1971), 281–8.

Constitution," Hegel grappled with the dilemma of the philosopher faced with an unjust political reality but forbidden by the Concept to oppose ideal justice to existence. His solution was to urge the adoption of only those features of the Concept-fulfilling State that were already demanded by the thought of the age and that could thus be introduced by organic reform to a people ready for them.[24] So, in "The German Constitution," written before the Napoleonic export of French ideas to Germany, Hegel advocates nothing but a common sovereign for the German principalities from a standpoint no more advanced than that of Machiavelli and Hobbes.[25] At that standpoint, all that belongs to the state's essence is a unified authority possessed of coercive and fiscal power. By contrast, in 1817, after the principles of the Code Napoléon had been adopted in much of western Germany, Hegel published "The Proceedings of the Assembly of Estates in the Kingdom of Württemberg," in which he criticized the Württemberg nobility's clinging to its historic privileges from the Kantian standpoint of rational law systematically grounded in the equal rights of persons.[26] Read out of context, these occasional writings can appear derivative, but they are not derivative in the usual sense if they are intentionally derivative for an original purpose. Hegel's aim here is to reconcile critical idealism with respect for the objective Reason in history by adopting pre-Hegelian positions already widely accepted and by advocating only those institutions of the Concept-fulfilling State that a people's ethical development has prepared it to receive. By adhering to this constraint, Hegel takes up a critical standpoint, not against the state delivered by history, but on the step of the state's developmental ladder that its own vanguard consciousness has already attained.[27]

The 1819/20 lectures exhibit something similar. The difference is that, as in *Outlines*, Hegel is here writing and speaking as a political scientist rather than as a publicist and essayist. And so (with an exception I'll come to), rather than criticize, opine, and advocate, Hegel

---

24 This thought reappears in the introduction to the 1819/20 lectures; see this translation, 9. "The realm of Right, the realm of Mind, know that only that which is present to a universal consciousness, to the Mind of a people, can come into existence. Philosophy would regard as incongruous the wish to give institutions to a people that the people did not bring about itself, that are not timely."
25 *Hegel's Political Writings*, 143–242.
26 *Hegel's Political Writings*, 254, 281ff.
27 This conception of critical reason as an objective phase of the historical process to which the critic must adhere reappears in the preface to the 1818/19 lectures. See Ilting, *Vorlesungen*, 1:37: "The philosophy of Right remains neither with abstraction nor with

understands, in light of the modern "right of self-consciousness," legal and institutional features of the intellectual present that were modelled in France and Britain but missing in Germany, thereby silently indicating the gap between German life and what the normative standpoint of the age required. So, for example, he describes an administration of justice characterized by universal rights of freedom as specified in determinate and knowable laws, *habeas corpus* (which he calls the right to stand in court), impartial and transparent court proceedings, and the right to a jury trial, all of which stood in glaring contrast to the Metternichian reality around him. Who among his audience could have failed to hear Hegel's implicit criticism of an internal security apparatus operating outside the scrutiny of courts, reading private correspondence, arresting for non-defined offences against public order, and detaining people indefinitely without trial?[28] So, the critical method of the 1819/20 lectures differs from that of the occasional essays, but the goal is the same: to link political criticism to the historical state's process of self-criticism, thereby avoiding an abject surrender to power, on the one hand, and violence against the public order, on the other. It was because they were oblivious to this mean between critical idealism and content-indiscriminate historicism that Hegel distanced himself from both the political radicals and conservatives of his day.

Is Hegel a Legal Positivist?

There is one other passage in the 1819/20 lectures that, while not expressly critical of any natural Right doctrine, seems at first blush to

---

the historicist viewpoint when the latter is not conformable to the Idea. It knows that the kingdom of Right can arise only through a progressive development and that no stage of this development can be overleaped. The juridical order, however, is based only on the universal Mind of the people, so that the constitution stands in a necessary connection with the existing concepts. Accordingly, if the Mind of the people has advanced to a higher stage, then the constitutional moments that were related to earlier stages no longer have stability; they must collapse and no might can hold them. Thus, philosophy knows that only the rational can occur, however much the external, particular appearances seem to contradict it" (my translation).

28 See Donald Emerson, *Metternich and the Political Police* (Dordrecht: Springer, 1968), 31–56, 176–89. Sometimes Hegel's criticism is less subtle. In a passage with no parallel in *Outlines*, he warns against an administrative state's becoming a "police state" excessively intrusive into private affairs (where "the police must know what every burgher is doing at every hour"), leaving his audience to hear the allusion to Metternich's secret police and to the centralized domestic spy agency set up by the Carlsbad Decrees; see this translation, 170.

show Hegel collapsing natural Right into positive law. It occurs in his discussion of the administration of justice:

> Accordingly, justice must be posited. What has obligatory force as justice, has [such force] insofar as it is the law. Therefore, if one asks, What is justice, the answer is: what the law says.[29]

The corresponding paragraph in *Outlines* reads as follows:

> Due to [the] identity of being-in-itself and posited being, the only right that is binding is what is law.[30]

Neither of these statements is incompatible with a critical natural law position. What Hegel is saying is that justice in itself becomes binding only when it is rendered determinate in positive law. This is so because, without determination by a public authority, what abstract justice demands in particular cases is left to private opinion. Everyone is free to act as he or she believes is appropriate. Once the justice Concept has been fleshed out in positive law, the answer to the question, What is justice? is: what the law says. That is no more than a tautological truth. A determination of justice is justice determined. However, in contrast to Hobbes, Hegel acknowledges a continuing logical space between justice and positive law, for he goes on to say: "It can happen that the law is at variance with what is inherently just."[31] So, the "identity" or connection of which Hegel speaks in *Outlines* (para. 212) between justice in itself and justice as posited can be broken. This can occur because the legislator erred in translating natural law into positive law, or because the legislator misconceived natural law, or considered itself unbound by natural law. The important question, then, is whether Hegel's philosophy of law commits him to the view that positive law at variance with natural law is binding. If it does, then Hegel shares with Kant the legal positivist's position that the justice of a law is one thing, its validity or obligatory force another – a position the Prussian authorities would certainly have applauded.[32]

---

29 This translation, 154.
30 *Outlines*, para. 212.
31 This translation, 154; cf. *Outlines*, para. 212.
32 I. Kant, *The Metaphysics of Morals*, trans. Mary Gregor (Cambridge: Cambridge University Press, 1991), 130 [319]. The following discussion assumes that legal positivism is partly the thesis that the obligatoriness of enacted law is independent of its justice, and it tries to explain the limited sense in which Hegel accepts that thesis.

The answer to that question is not simple. To my knowledge, Hegel does not directly address the issue of whether unjust law is valid either before or after the promulgation of the Carlsbad Decrees.[33] He does, of course, criticize, both before and after the decrees, and in both its atheistic and pious forms, the claim of the private conscience to determine valid law for itself. With that claim, he argues, the moral conscience turns evil at the height of its certainty of goodness. However, Hegel's critique of an anarchistic conscience (and of contemporaries whom he sees as embodying the type) is no proof of his legal positivism, for one can both affirm that law at variance with natural law is invalid and deny that the private conscience can be the judge of this variance. The proposition *lex injusta non est lex* is compatible with the rule of law only if the abstract precepts of Right form part of a legal constitution and if a separate organ of the body politic, adhering to a rational and legally fixed method, judges whether a legal provision unjustifiably infringes one or more of them.

More indicative of Hegel's position on the validity of unjust law is his conceding, both in the lectures and in *Outlines* (paras. 3, 212), a distinctive role for the positive science of jurisprudence alongside the philosophy of law. Whereas, he says, the object of legal philosophy is law derived from the Concept of Right, that of jurisprudence is law given by positive authority, whether that law is derivable from the Concept or not, or, indeed, whether it is consistent with the Concept or not. Positive jurisprudence "has authority for its principle and has to keep to what is historically present" (UN173). The fact that Hegel grants scientific standing to a separate discipline whose object is law that is "historically present" strongly suggests that he considered law at variance with natural law to have some kind of validity just by virtue of its having been posited by a power recognized as a legal authority.

Nevertheless, Hegel is not a legal positivist. This is so because, for legal positivism, the thesis that a law's validity is conceptually independent

---

However, if by *legal positivism* is understood Hans Kelsen's thesis that the only law knowable by science is the set of generally obeyed directives that attach a detriment to non-compliance and that are enacted in accordance with a constitution arbitrarily presupposed as being normative (so not objectively normative), then there is no issue to discuss here, for *Outlines*, para. 3, flatly contradicts that thesis; see Hans Kelsen, *Pure Theory of Law*, trans. Max Knight (Berkeley: University of California Press, 1967), chaps. 3, 5.

33 T.M. Knox's original translation of *Outlines*, para. 212 ("positive law has obligatory force in virtue of its rightness") settles the question against legal positivism, but it is now recognized as an incorrect translation; *Hegel's Philosophy of Right*, trans. T.M. Knox (Oxford: Oxford University Press, 1967), para. 212.

of its moral content is unqualifiedly true. It is simply true, says the positivist, that the injustice of a law does not inherently disqualify it from being a law. Of course, a legal sovereign might make conformity with basic principles of justice a requirement of legal validity, but that would be a contingent choice. There is no necessary connection between legal validity and justice, and for the legal positivist, that statement is free of any condition that might relativize it. From this it follows that legal validity is an either-or proposition. If a command meets a legal system's criterion of validity, then it is a valid law, full stop. There is no standpoint from which it could be regarded as valid in a relative sense but invalid in truth. No doubt, there is a standpoint outside law from which a command might be judged morally wicked, though legally valid, but there is no standpoint internal to law from which a law valid in one sense could be judged legally invalid in another.

For Hegel (or, rather, for his philosophy of law, for Hegel says nothing directly on point), legal positivism's thesis is only relatively true, while a law can likewise be valid in a relative sense while being invalid inherently or in truth. Specifically, legal positivism is true only for the historical period during which despotic or untrammelled authority is valid given a certain stage of human self-knowledge. For example, the Roman emperor's despotic authority was valid for the stage of human education at which the exemplary human being was a valour-displaying *dominus*, for *domini* could secure their dominions from each other only by transferring their unbridled freedom to a ruler, who then became – quite legitimately – the supreme *dominus*. Hence, whatever laws the emperor chose to enforce were also valid for that stage, even if they allowed creditors to kill defaulting debtors or regarded children as their father's slaves for as long as the father lived. What pleased the prince had the force of law.

By contrast, despotic authority is no authority at the highest stage of human education, at which beings who live within the element of self-consciousness have learned what the true end of their development is. That end is freedom, both personal and civic, *inside* the known sovereignty of the Ethical Idea. Within that Idea, a people's united will is enjoined to respect the private rights of separate persons as confirming the naturalness of the Concept's law of mutual deference; while the individual is enjoined to serve the united will as the only solid foundation of its private rights. With that Idea in view, the philosophy of law accepts only those laws of which the end point of humanity's education approves, sifting what is durable from each stage (e.g., Roman property law) and discarding what is not (Roman family law). It is because political authority develops from despotism to constitutionalism as human beings progressively learn their true nature (concept) that Hegel can concede space to a positive jurisprudence oriented to authority in a generic sense, whether that authority is historically relative or absolute, and to law as posited by authority, whether that law survives the process of human education or not. Just as the empirical natural sciences can always stand beside the philosophy of nature, so positive jurisprudence can always stand beside the philosophy of Right.

However, the same cannot be said of legal positivism. The latter is not an empirical science of law but a philosophical position about the nature of law. Its position is that the obligatory force of a sovereign's command is for all time and for all conditions conceptually independent of its justice. For Hegel's philosophy of law, that position is false. In the constitutional State whose citizens know themselves as free actualizers of the Idea's sovereignty, commands must meet a test not only of formal pedigree but also of valid content. They must be congruent with the Ethical Idea, which is to say that they must serve a common good while respecting private rights of equal liberty, property, and contract. At that stage of human cultivation, legal positivism is passé. The conceptual independence of law and justice that was true for the low grade of human self-knowledge at which despotism was necessary and seemed fixed is true no more. Correspondingly, some laws (for example, the *paterfamilias* law) that were actually valid at that grade were always *inherently* invalid from the standpoint of humanity's true concept and become invalid actually when that concept is known and takes over from inferior self-understandings.

Accordingly, the transition from despotism to constitutionalism is not simply a move from one de facto criterion of legal validity to another, as the legal positivist might claim. That a law must now meet a substantive criterion of validity is no mere contingent choice of a sovereign that positivism can accommodate. Rather, it reflects a change from an exclusively formal criterion of legal validity inadequate to free human nature to the formal/substantive one congruent therewith. But that is a critical natural law position, albeit an historicized and nuanced one, for it says (1) that, though not all valid law is just law, only just law is valid absolutely; and (2) that unjust law is valid for a time only by virtue of its having been posited by a despotic authority that is relatively justified for a stage of human development looked back on from the consummate stage as necessary.

That historicized conception of natural law is also the one that Hegel held from the end of his sojourn as a tutor in Frankfurt. Leaving aside his earliest manuscripts on *The Life of Jesus* and "The Positivity of the Christian Religion," there is no turn from an extreme natural law position (*lex injusta non est lex*) to the moderate and historicized one we see in the 1819/20 lectures. Already in "The German Constitution," Hegel treats the feudal constitution as invalid, not simply because it is incongruent with the principle of equal freedom under rational law (i.e., unjust), but because the spirit that once animated it has departed, leaving it in the same condition as fruit fallen from a tree, whose shade "cannot save it from decomposition and from the power of the elements to which it now belongs."[34] It is only because it no longer belongs to *any* concept that the German constitution can be judged in light of the new "spirit of the world" demanding a rational organization of the state.[35]

Hegel's Judgment of the French Revolution

Hegel discusses the French Revolution twice in the 1819/20 lectures. I reproduce the passages below:

> When we reflect on the will, we notice that it is the pure abstraction, pure thought. I can make myself empty, purified of all content. We go from one object to another. I can give up everything, renounce all bonds to which I am attached, can give up the whole extent of the bonds of my existence; this too I can renounce (with death). This is the moment of complete indeterminacy, universality. If I say to myself, "I," then I have fled the world to this pure light, where all difference has been subsumed. This is the moment of lawless freedom. Mind knows itself as free, that it can renounce everything. You can lay hold of him how and where you want, [still,] he flees into his inwardness. It is the freedom of the understanding that holds fast to one moment [of freedom] ... From that freedom of the understanding emanates the fanaticism of freedom, which proceeds to negate everything determinate, which sees all particularity as something foreign, [and] which always wants to posit the particular as separate from the universal. Where someone appears particularized to him, he sees it as contemptible. Every individual is contemptible; although he appears this way [i.e., virtuous] now, he could also be different. This fanaticism was the moment of the French Revolution, as it set freedom as an aim that found its reality only in the negation, the annulling of particularity. It wanted a conscientious political condition. However, as soon as a condition comes into existence, differences emerge ... Then fanaticism will not allow anything to become real ...[36]

---

34 *Hegel's Political Writings*, 143.
35 *Hegel's Political Writings*, 146–8.
36 This translation, 15n45.

Furthermore, if one were to say that the powers [of the state] must hold bars [against each other], then they oppose each other externally. But then the unity of the whole is missing, and this [unity] precisely constitutes the essence of the State. The Mind of a people has a reality [in its constitutional powers]. If these powers are opposed to each other without unity, then the organism of the state does not work. Yet it must work [the state must function]. This necessity entails that unity must be manufactured ... Nothing can happen but that one power throws the others overboard. [UN234: The history of the French Revolution provides the decisive example of this.] The legislative body made itself the government, and one committee administered everything. This was Robespierre's period of terror. After that, the opposite occurred. [UN234: The five Directors stepped to the head of the executive.] The result was different. [When] the legislative power opposed the government, the government cleaned out the legislature and established unity. So it goes with such inventions. [UN234: Where such an artifice is devised, the end is always that one power overthrows the other.][37]

The first passage contains no thought not already expressed in the chapter on "Absolute Freedom and Terror" in the *Phenomenology of Spirit*, the work of Hegel's most thoroughly imbued with the revolutionary ethos of the Napoleonic era.[38] What Hegel is attacking in this passage is not the ideas of the French Revolution themselves; on the contrary, he says out loud that, for all its vacillations between legislative and executive supremacy, the Revolution bore two simple thoughts belonging to "the true content of the public will: the termination of feudal power and the rule of law."[39] Rather, he is attacking the peculiarly French grasp of how these ideas relate to past history and to the social world facing the enlightened intellect. His discussion of the Revolution in the *Phenomenology* throws light on what he is saying in the lectures.

To the French revolutionaries, the human world confronting them in the late eighteenth century was a world bereft of reason, its hierarchical social structure and autocratic government the outcome of blind power struggles throughout a meaningless history, yet propped up by a

---

37 This translation, 199–200.
38 G.W.F. Hegel, *Phenomenology of Spirit*, trans. A.V. Miller (Oxford: Oxford University Press, 1977), paras. 582–95.
39 UN260. Because the Napoleonic Code abolished feudalism and actualized the rule of law, Hegel openly praises it despite the Restoration's university monitors, while making fun of the nationalist students who burned it at the Wartburg Festival; see this translation, 153–4.

supernaturalist religion opaque to reason. Because it discerned no trace of reason in the feudal and monarchical world facing it, revolutionary thought located reason solely in the mind of the solitary individual detached from political society. This individual it considered fixed in its detachment, having no political nature to fulfil. As a consequence, the self-interested or particular will was identified with the idiosyncrasy, selfishness, and vainglory of this individual. This meant that the particular will had to be expelled from the concept of the reasonable will, which was thus equated with the will that was abstractly and purely general, that willed only what all free and equal persons could will for themselves. As the only genuinely public will, this abstractly general will was alone entitled to rule.

However, in order to rule, the general will must determine itself in positive legislation and executive orders, both of which moments necessarily re-engage a particular will – a will that lays down something not generally valid or necessary. Yet the particular will as such is just what the revolutionaries considered selfish and corrupt. In the name, therefore, of an abstract purity of will, they first annulled everything the executive laid down in a kind of perpetual revolution; nothing could stand firm. Subsequently, the legislature absorbed all government into itself, but then the general will fell apart, for in issuing decrees applying to some but not others, it ceased to impose reciprocal obligations to which equal citizens could assent. Because, moreover, to exist is to be concerned with self, the logically rigorous actualization of the general will's primacy was ruthless state killing on a mass scale, the one sustained executive action of which the Revolution proved capable. So, the equation of reasonableness with the abstractly general will, itself consequent on the apparent foreignness to reason of the objective world, led to a fanaticism of destruction and terror.

The more reasonable alternative to the French Revolution had already been adumbrated by Hegel in the 1817 *Encyclopaedia*.[40] Drawing a lesson from Plato, Hegel attributes the failure of free thinking to establish a stable constitution to its need to attack a superstitious form

---

40 *Hegel's Philosophy of Mind*, trans. A.V. Miller (Oxford: Clarendon Press, 1971), para. 552: "It is nothing but a modern folly to try to alter a corrupt moral organization by altering its political constitution and codes of law without changing the religion – to make a revolution without having made a reformation, to suppose that a political constitution opposed to the old religion could live in peace and harmony with it and its sanctities." See also G.W.F. Hegel, *The Philosophy of History*, trans. J. Sibree (New York: Dover, 1956), 453.

of religion, in opposition to which free thought becomes one-sided – something finitely human and distinguished from truth in the most objective sense. This, Hegel believes, is what occurred in France. The Enlightenment *philosophes* perceived the world as reason-forsaken because the religious belief in an objective purpose took the form of a mind-suppressing subservience to Catholic dogma and papal despotism. Rejecting Catholicism for enlightened autonomy meant rejecting purpose in the world and retreating into the purposiveness of the self. France's misfortune was that it lacked a Protestant Reformation and hence a free relation to the source of purpose in the world witnessed by religion. Germany, however, went through a Reformation, and so its rulers could spontaneously adopt the valid ideas of the French Revolution as the gradual unfolding of the Christian freedom already achieved in the church. Germany could thus have the valid content of the Revolution without the revolution. That content is precisely incorporated by Hegel into the evolving just State in the lecture on the administration of justice and in the corresponding paragraphs of *Outlines*: the equal rights of humans qua humans, a civil and penal code concretizing these rights, and impartial and transparent courts to apply them. *Pace* Ringier's editors and Ilting, there is no evidence in the 1819/20 lectures or in *Outlines* of Hegel's resiling from the positive judgment of the French Revolution's content expressed in the "Württemberg Estates" essay; nor is there anything new in his negative judgment of its revolutionary form.[41]

The second passage quoted above contains a critique of the mixed, checks-and-balances constitution of liberal republicanism that Hegel had already criticized in the *Natural Law* essay of 1802–3.[42] No one familiar with the body of Hegel's writings will be surprised by it. The argument, moreover, is powerful. Because classical liberalism begins its justification of state power from atomistic individuals, it must locate sovereignty in a general will abstracted from a particular will equated with partiality and selfishness. This means that it must place sovereignty in the state power uniquely expressive of a general will – the law-making power. But this leaves the executive outside the sovereign, hence outside the only body considered qualified to govern legitimately. As a consequence, the state splits into mutually hostile governing organs: on one side, a legislative assembly jealous of its sovereignty and

---

41 Hegel expresses disapproval of the revolutionary form in the "Württemberg Estates" essay itself; see *Hegel's Political Writings*, 281–2.
42 Hegel, *Natural Law*, 85–8.

distrustful of the executive, yet (as a general will) conceptually unable to issue case-specific orders; on the other, an executive charged with applying laws to cases, but lacking legitimacy for the discretion necessarily involved in doing so. Because, further, the sovereignty created by the surrender of individual powers of Right-determination is absolute, it is inherently dangerous. It is vulnerable to abuse by members of the legislature. It must therefore be externally checked by the executive, which, lacking the legitimacy of a general will, must be checked in turn by the assembly, itself given to faction. The result, as France's First Republic showed (and as other republics have shown since), is a war between the executive and the legislative assembly paralysing government and ending in dictatorship. Hegel describes this downward arc of liberal republicanism, not in order to ingratiate himself with the powers of the Restoration, but in order to make the case for the organic constitution he counterposes to the checks-and-balances one. So, let's now turn to that subject. The following subsection discusses Hegel's actual teaching on constitutional monarchy in the 1819/20 lectures. Section III describes the constitutional monarchy that his account of majesty objectively requires.

Hegel's Qualified Constitutionalism

If Hegel feared the Prussian government's monitor, he did not show it in his 1819/20 lectures on royalty. In the fullest discussion of the "princely power" (*fürstliche Gewalt*) that we have from him, Hegel justifies a prince who is far from the autocrat that Frederick William III of Prussia was.[43] Indistinguishably from the head of state who, in the pre-crackdown (1817/18) Heidelberg lectures, merely says, "I so will it," this one only wills into force the legislative and executive judgments of state organs independent of him.[44] Indeed, the prince of the 1819/20 lectures is *more* constrained than that of the Heidelberg lectures, where Hegel has him deciding "one way or another" based on considerations put before him by a council of ministers, which must flatter him to obtain the decision it desires.[45] In the 1819/20 lectures, by contrast, the prince is (domestically) a cipher. There is no need to educate him, because the constitution's wisdom does not need him to be wise; nor

---

43 "Monarch" is a misnomer for Hegel's head of state, for domestically, the *Fürst* does not rule alone.
44 LNRPS, para. 138.
45 LNRPS, para. 140.

does its stability depend on his being loved. All that matters is that the prince have a name and that he sign it, signifying "nothing further than that [the bill or executive order] comes into existence."[46]

So, even under the eye of Frederick William's spies, Hegel sets forth an ideal prince who has little involvement in the domestic life of the State. Administrators and judges speak in his name, but they hew to their role without royal interference, as do the private sector's deputies in the legislature. This mutual independence of powers embedded within a totality of which the prince is only a part – the part that formally resolves – is what Hegel calls constitutional monarchy. The latter is distinguished from monarchy in the traditional and strict sense in that it is not opposed to aristocracy and democracy, but rather contains all three elements within an articulated whole whose aim and product is the rule of Law.[47] This, says Hegel, is the constitution that "epitomizes modern times," the only one in which "freedom come[s] into its right."[48] He could hardly have intended to mollify the forces of the Restoration when he said publicly in a lecture hall, "Wishing back the feudal state is like wishing old age for a child."[49]

Of course, Hegel does not commit professional suicide by criticizing the Prussian monarchy or state directly. But he finds ways to criticize it indirectly. At one point, he warns in general terms against the despotic use of the sovereign's police power, leaving his audience to hear the allusion to Carlsbad.[50] At other times, he finds a target that his students would have understood as a surrogate for the prohibited one. In one lecture, for example, he disparages Prussia's surveillance state by characterizing the intrusively watchful state advocated by J.G. Fichte as a "giant galley."[51] In another, he implicitly condemns Prussia's monarchy by explicitly condemning autocracy in Turkey. There, the pasha, who exercises judicial power, is subordinate to the sultan. This organization, Hegel says, rests on a misunderstanding that "must be supplanted."[52]

It must be admitted, however, that the merely formal nature of the prince's power applies, according to Hegel, only in domestic affairs. In the state's relations with other states, Hegel's prince retains the freedom

---

46 This translation, 206.
47 The aristocratic element is present in the civil service, judiciary, and upper chamber, the democratic element in the representative assembly.
48 This translation, 203.
49 This translation, 203.
50 This translation, 170.
51 This translation, 170.
52 This translation, 200.

of action he has relinquished internally.[53] Yet this is not a position that Hegel suddenly adopted in the wake of the Carlsbad Decrees. In the lectures both before and after the events of September 1819, Hegel contends that interstate relations are reserved for the princely power.[54] The reason for this is that, without an impartial court to adjudicate disputes, relations with foreign states are not governable by objective Right; nor are they amenable to advance regulation by general laws. Rather, these relations reflect ad hoc decisions to enter into (peaceful or hostile) transactions with foreign states in furtherance of whatever policy the national interest momentarily favours. As the official through whom the state resolves, the prince alone makes these naked, a-legal decisions. His doing so is not quite the affront to constitutionalism and civic freedom that his unilateral action in domestic affairs would be, because his transactions with other states create no law binding on his subjects. Whatever obligations he incurs bind only the state in international law.

Nevertheless, even within this sphere (and against the Restoration), Hegel approvingly anticipates the modern evolution of the royal prerogative in external relations into an executive prerogative consistent with constitutional government. The key idea here is the same distinction between the form and content of a decision that underlies the organic division of powers between the council of ministers and elected legislature, on the one hand, and the prince, on the other. The council and legislature propose a content; the prince says, "I so will it." Similarly, in external relations, the council proposes, and the prince assents. This division of function, Hegel argues, reconciles the majesty of the prince as the State's very own will with responsible and constitutional government.[55] Were the prince involved in the content of the decision, strict constitutionalism would require that he be responsible for the action's wisdom to the assembly, for his actions towards foreign states would greatly affect his subjects' welfare even if they would not bind their will. And yet the prince's majesty precludes his accountability to any body external to himself. The solution that preserves both majesty and constitutionalism is to have the council of ministers propose the content and be responsible for it, while the prince merely adds the form of assent. Though the executive requires no legal authorization for its actions on the world stage, it is still accountable to the assembly for the

---

53 This translation, 216. As far as I can tell, *Outlines* does not explain this difference. The lectures do.
54 Ilting, *Vorlesungen*, 1:339, 2:797, 4:738.
55 This translation, 217–18.

wisdom of its acts *ex post*. Thus, the prince retains his majesty while his government is responsible for its foreign dealings to the elected representatives of the governed.

However, this solution works only if the prince's choice is shackled. If the prince retains a discretion to accept or reject his ministers' advice, then constitutionalism requires that he be responsible to the assembly for the manner of its exercise, which requirement would be incompatible with his majesty. If, however, the prince's choice is constrained, then he bears no responsibility for it; only those who proposed the content he was duty-bound to accept are accountable to the people's representatives, and so we have both majesty and accountability. Hegel's princely power is majestic but imperfectly constitutional because his prince retains a freedom to reject his ministers' advice in foreign affairs, yet he is unaccountable for his choice. Thus, civic freedom ultimately depends on the character of the prince, on whether he is disposed to follow his ministers' counsel or deliberate and act on his own. Hegel favours royal deference to executive expertise in foreign matters for prudential reasons, but he stops short of finding a duty. Indeed, he expects the prince, as head of state, to take over the reins in a national emergency (which, presumably, is for him to declare) and to choose and dismiss his cabinet as he sees fit.[56]

The question is why. Hegel's answer is tentative. He seems unsure whether princely discretion in foreign affairs is constitutionally fixed or merely a feature of his time. Quoting from King Lear ("You have that in your countenance which I would fain call master"), he wonders aloud whether, notwithstanding the fact that human beings are destined for autonomy under rational law, there is a side of them that residually calls for submission to a prince's will.[57] His answer is that interstate relations require a-legal decisions and that these decisions fall to a head of state whose representation of sovereignty and independence of faction preclude accountability. Yet this is not his complete answer, for he goes on to say that the separation of the formal (for the prince) from the substantive (for the accountable ministry) aspects of a diplomatic decision reflects "an advanced education and development"; and he thinks it no longer practically possible, given the estates' role in taxation, for a prince to wage an unpopular war.[58] In the end, he leaves as a question – a subversive question – whether "there is something in human beings

---

56 This translation, 215.
57 This translation, 216.
58 This translation, 240.

that compels them to submit to a prince, or whether this is really to be considered a necessary *evil*."[59]

Even with his concession to princely discretion in foreign affairs, Hegel's prince was far ahead of Prussia's monarch on the road to full constitutionalism; for Prussia's monarchy recognized no separation between the monarch's function and that of the ministerial council in either foreign or domestic affairs. Friedrich Wilhelm III ruled. Hegel, moreover, was not afraid to indicate the shortfall. In a veiled reference to Britain, he tells his students that ministerial responsibility for the substance of decisions formally made by the prince has been introduced elsewhere and represents an advanced stage of constitutionalism.[60] Any astute listener would have heard the rebuke of the Prussian monarchy.

III

Dieter Henrich, the editor of UN's notes of the 1819/20 lectures, argues in his introduction that Hegel's statements on the princely power, though consistent across his writings and lectures in confining the prince's domestic role to enacting the judgments of independent organs of government, are nevertheless ambiguous as to whether royal assent is automatic or discretionary. He also claims that Hegel sometimes emphasizes the constraints on the prince and sometimes his freedom, and that, in contrast to *Outlines*, which emphasizes the freedom, the 1819/20 lectures accentuate the constraint.[61] Henrich believes that this ambiguity is built into Hegel's metaphysical conception of the princely power as uniquely the power of decisive will within the State's organic division of powers mirroring the distinct elements of the free Will's Concept. Against this thesis, I'll argue that, though there may be ambiguity in the way that Hegel articulates his theory of the princely power, there is none in the theory itself. That theory requires the hands-tied prince whom we see in the 1819/20 lectures on internal public law and who puts paid to the suggestion that Hegel shaped his account of the prince to please the authorities.

In both his lectures and *Outlines*, Hegel makes the bold claim that hereditary succession to the head of state's office is required by the concept of Law.[62] That concept, regarded as it independently presents

---

59 This translation, 216; emphasis added.
60 This translation, 218.
61 Henrich, *Philosophie des Rechts*, 24–30.
62 This translation, 208, 211; and *Outlines*, para. 280.

itself, undistorted by reflexive thinking from an atomistic starting point, contains three logically interconnected elements or moments. The first is universality. Stated in the most general terms, Law is the universal medium wherein the outward freedom of each is reconciled with the equal outward freedom of all. Only as so understood is Law distinct from inward-looking morality, on one side, and the strongest interest's posing as an obligatory norm, on the other. Of course, Hegel's freedom is a complex concept having several sides, but for present purposes we can bracket the different dimensions of outward freedom – freedom from things, freedom from external force, freedom from fortuity, freedom *in* dependence on another's freedom – that he aims to integrate within a common life sufficient for freedom. More concrete but still within the sphere of universality are the particular laws of general application whereby the concept of Law is specified for particular types of human relationship – for proprietors, contractual parties, debtors and creditors, family members, and so forth. Only as so specified can Law regulate the variety of human relationships in accordance with equal freedom.

The second element of Law's concept is particularity, by which is meant the application of general laws to discrete situations or disputes so as to arrive at judgments applying narrowly to a few. The thought here is that Law would not be Law if it remained something ethereal, if it were not made determinate in particular laws and if cases in the world were not subsumed to these laws. The same thought underlies Law's third moment: that of decision. This is the part of judgment where the practical reasoning involved in applying the general concept of Law to relationship-types and in subsuming cases under particular laws issues in a definite conclusion capable of being enforced against conduct so as to bring existence under the rule of Law.

This third element in Law's concept generally goes unnoticed in constitutional thought. We are accustomed to thinking of Law's realization as a tree divided into a legislative branch, an executive branch, and a judicial branch, the occupiers of each making decisions within their respective jurisdictions. One strains to name another constitutional theorist who thinks of decision as a separate limb of government occupied by someone who is neither legislator, administrator, nor judge. Hegel, however, assimilates the judiciary to the executive as the moment of subsuming cases under laws *intellectually*, and he makes the third moment one whereby the other two materialize in an act of *will* concluding an insufficiently determinative practical reasoning. This moment gives existential force to legislative and executive judgments, which, apart from acts of will, are but exercises of thinking. Law would not be Law if thinking about what laws best realize equal freedom or about how such laws apply to cases did not end in a decision having effective force in the world. Yet as an act of will, the decision marks a transition from the practical reasoning it terminates, hence a distinct moment of Law's realization.

It is important to see that the moment of decision carries an inescapable element of subjective arbitrariness. That is because judgments are, colloquially, judgment *calls*. No decision concluding an exercise of judgment is strictly necessitated. There is always an element of ungrounded discretion in deciding this rather than that. The ancients, Hegel reminds us, did not know that this element belonged to rational Law because they did not know that justice contains a drive towards outward realization; they thought of it simply as a beloved object that moves the lover but that, being self-sufficient, is itself unmoved. For them, accordingly, the undetermined decision that concludes deliberation belonged to nature, whose fiat was revealed by signs – in animal entrails or the flight of birds – as far removed from the finite sphere of self-consciousness as self-consciousness could imagine.[63] For moderns, by contrast, the decisional locus is the individual subject through whom Law perforce becomes realized. The arbitrariness is not in nature but in the subject. After all the reasons are marshalled for this conclusion and for that, the decision comes down to: I am persuaded by this. So, an element of subjective arbitrariness belongs to the concept of Law inasmuch as that concept involves a moment of undetermined decision giving force to an otherwise merely possible determination of Law.

Now, to these three moments of Law's concept correspond the three powers of the State. To the moment of universality belongs the law-making power; to the moment of particularity belongs the executive power; and to the moment of decision corresponds the princely power. Why a prince? Why not a committee or an assembly or even a president? Hegel's answer is this: The third moment of Law's concept is the moment of ungrounded, hence subjective, will. Among the several conclusions made eligible by a weighing of considerations or by an interpretation of a statute, I choose this one. Yet this one is not determined by the common good or by the statute, and so my reason for choosing it must lie in me. *Me* is a form of the first-person singular. The subjectivity of decision is that of a single person. Hence it is institutionally expressed in a way truest to its nature if it is expressed through one person. This person is a prince rather than an elected or appointed

---

63 This translation, 207.

president because the transcendence or majesty of a particular will that belongs essentially to Law's concept requires that it be independent of contingent choice, and succession by birth is that independence.[64] Observe, however, that the monarch's (for at this point the prince is a monarch) decision presupposes the other two moments of Law's concept; he or she does not merely will a personal preference in a perfunctory or capricious way. The decision is a *conclusion*, albeit a discretionary one, resulting from the application of a universal to a particular. In other words, the decision, while ungrounded, is not unprincipled.

So far, we have three state offices – a legislative office, an executive office, and a decisional office – all occupied by one person: the monarch. Let us call her Elizabeth I. Elizabeth I may have counsellors and magistrates, but she appoints and dismisses them at pleasure; they have no independence of her. They are simply her aides. We can see, though, that insofar as all state powers contained in the concept of Law are wrapped up in Elizabeth I, the concept of Law is self-contradictory. Inherently, the monarch's arbitrary subjectivity is just the residual arbitrariness necessarily involved in Law's acquiring existential force, in its being the Law. Or we can say that, inherently, the monarch's arbitrary subjectivity is pure, for it is only a logical moment of Law's concept. As yet, however, it is just the arbitrary subjectivity of this natural individual – Elizabeth Tudor – hence something impure. After all, Elizabeth Tudor is not contained in the concept of Law; it could just as well have been Jane Grey.

Now, this self-contradiction in the abstract concept of Law is the impetus for the unfolding of the constitution that fulfils the rule of Law or in which the rule of a natural person or persons disappears in the rule of an impersonal Law. Initially, Elizabeth I merely asserts that her arbitrary fiat is nothing but that belonging to the concept of Law – that her arbitrary fiat is pure. In order that this claim be confirmed, she must divest her natural person of legislative and executive powers, keeping, as Elizabeth II, only the formal power of willing into force judgments made and tested for general agreement elsewhere. For their part, those who make legislative and executive judgments must confine themselves to the intellectual side of judgment, while putting the volitional side on one who, because she does nothing but will their

---

64 Peter Steinberger argues that a lottery would do just as well: *Logic and Politics: Hegel's Philosophy of Right* (New Haven, CT: Yale University Press, 1988), 226. But hereditary monarchy is already a lottery – a natural one. Any other form would be open to suspicion of manipulation.

ratified judgments into force, *and because she has no discretion to do otherwise,* purifies the decision of anyone's natural will. Accordingly, the constitution that realizes the rule of Law will consist of the ensemble of proofs necessary and sufficient for converting Elizabeth's claim that her decision is nothing but Law's decision into an objective truth. That is the Law concept–centred narrative that, in contrast to the individualistic narrative of liberal republicanism, integrates all parts of the constitution into a coherent whole.

For our present purposes, we need not develop in full detail all the proofs of Elizabeth's claim of purity.[65] Suffice it to say that they comprise all the institutions of a modern constitutional state: an independent and strictly meritocratic executive and judiciary, an assembly where the heads of the executive submit bills for the approval of the subjects' elected representatives, and an expert body independent of both the executive and the assembly that reviews the bills they jointly put forward for conformity with a priori determinations of universal freedom. What is important to notice here, however, is that there is no proof that Elizabeth II's will is Law's will without Elizabeth Windsor's being constrained to assent to bills and orders (1) designed by expert civil servants whose discipline to Law's rule is achieved by their professional education, a secure livelihood, and scrutiny by the assembly and courts; (2) confirmed as serving the freedom of all by elected representatives of societal groups so intertwined in their economic fortunes as to have a stake in the general interest; and (3) reviewed for their consistency with the first principles of public Right by an independent body qualified for the task.[66] Nor is there such proof without Elizabeth Windsor's being constrained to assent to advice on foreign matters given by a ministerial council responsible to the representative assembly. If Elizabeth retains a discretion to refuse assent, she is her own person, not Law's.

Accordingly, regardless of any equivocation one may find in the way that Hegel presents his theory of the prince across its various iterations, there is no room for equivocation in the theory itself. The theory rules

---

[65] For this, see Alan Brudner, *The Owl and the Rooster: Hegel's Transformative Political Science* (New York: Cambridge University Press, 2017), 256–73.

[66] Observe that, in the constitutional monarchy understood by Hegel, the review of legislation by a second chamber or special court fits seamlessly into the whole. There is no longer a tension between judicial review and the parliamentary supremacy belonging to republicanism. In an atypical concession to historical facticity, Hegel gives this reviewing role to a chamber filled by a hereditary aristocracy (see this translation, 231–2), but the qualifications he prescribes for this body – independence and expertise – are better met by a constitutional court.

out princely discretion. Elizabeth must sign. At the same time, there is indeed a double-sidedness to the head of state that can be mistaken for equivocation, but that is really the coherent paradox involved in the transition from Law's rule as concept to Law's rule as fulfilled concept. As concept, Law decides through a singularity – a majesty. As a majesty, Elizabeth alone commands, and so no one can command her to assent. She can only be advised. As a fulfilled concept, however, Law decides through a majesty-in-council-in-parliament – a constitutional majesty. As a constitutional majesty, Elizabeth must forthwith follow the advice. Advice to Elizabeth (II) that Elizabeth (Windsor) has no liberty to refuse is paradoxical but not incoherent and certainly no stranger to us. It is exactly how the British constitution reconciles the concept of majesty with the duty of a majesty that is fulfilled *as such* only as limited to a formality.[67]

IV

The chief interest of Hegel's 1819/20 lectures on the philosophy of Right is not that they foreshadow the compromises with state power that Hegel supposedly made in *Outlines*. It is that they present Hegel's fully developed legal and political thought with a liveliness and concreteness absent in *Outlines*. They also provide a unique opportunity to see Hegel in action, so to speak, during the most fraught months of the Restoration, thereby allowing us to test the image of political docility drawn by commentators from Rudolf Haym to Ringier's editors.[68] Lastly, the 1819/20 lectures foreshadow the retreat from Hegel's optimism about the present that we see in the melancholy preface to *Outlines* but that is nowhere evident in the text itself. In doing so, they suggest a withdrawal of Hegel's claim made at the end of *Outlines* that, in the Germanic realm, the rational has become actual. Let me elaborate.

In paragraph 360 of *Outlines*, Hegel's historical optimism – his conviction that the Concept of justice is powerfully immanent in world history – is matched by a Panglossian optimism about the present age, in which he sees history's completion. In the Germanic realm, he believes, the Concept of justice has become fulfilled in the constitution

---

67 Hegel's doctrine of the prince shows us that a ceremonial, non-partisan head of state need not be understood as a liberal republic's fantasy of constitutional unity. We can understand it as the culmination of a progress to the real unity of a Law State of which a republican body is one organ.
68 See Rudolf Haym, *Hegel und seine Zeit* (Berlin, 1857; repr., Hildesheim: Olms, 1962), 357–91.

of the post-revolutionary State, so that the type of State that now exists mirrors the Idea. "The present world," he writes, "has discarded its barbarity and unrighteous caprice, while the realm of truth has cast off its otherworldliness and arbitrary force, so that the true reconciliation which discloses the State as the image and actuality of Reason has become objective."[69] With this consummation, the philosopher of justice need not instruct the State in light of a standard of justice and rationality transcending it; he need only comprehend the justice and rationality of what is.

However, in the preface to *Outlines*, written in the shadow of Carlsbad and after the main text had been completed, Hegel backtracks. The tone is more sombre – realistic. Here, the reason why philosophy does not instruct the state is not that the state has become just and there is no need for instruction but that it has become moribund and it is too late for instruction. Dusk has fallen on it, and so philosophy, with no colourful world to paint, is left to paint in shades of grey. In this situation, philosophy's task cannot be to disclose the state as the "image and actuality of Reason," for that would be to falsify reality and bring discredit to philosophy. Its task instead is to apprehend the state as something *inherently* rational – as evincing a vein of intelligible necessity beneath the dross belonging to temporal contingency. Or, to employ Hegel's own metaphor, philosophy's modified aim is to recognize "the rose in the cross of the present" – that is, the rose of the Idea in the cross of a state still torn between the old and new worlds and of a society newly split between owners of capital and the class dependent on them for the means of labour and subsistence.[70]

The 1819/20 lectures foreshadow this retreat, identify more elaborately and poignantly than *Outlines* does the defect in the modern state that the next historical stage must remedy, and even indicate in a way more explicitly prescriptive than *Outlines* what a remedy would look like. In doing these things, the lectures delivered at the height of

---

69 *Outlines*, para. 360.
70 Hegel's real attitude towards the political condition existing at the time he gave the 1819/20 lectures can be gleaned from a contemporaneous letter he wrote to his friend Friedrich Creuzer: "I am almost fifty years old and have spent thirty of these years in these constantly restless times of fear and hope. I was hoping that for once we might be done with fear and hope. Now I see that things continue as ever, indeed, as it seems in one's darker hours, that they are getting ever worse" (*Briefe von und an Hegel*, 2:219; my translation). We do not know why Hegel nevertheless left paragraph 360 unchanged. One possibility is that he left it to show what a completed science of the State would look like, while indicating in the preface that this consummation was yet to be.

political repression in Germany decisively refute the suggestion advanced by Ringier's editors that, for fear of the Prussian authorities, Hegel turned from a philosophical critic of the status quo to its apologist. Let us consider the three points in turn.

The Retreat Foreshadowed

Hegel's retreat in the preface to *Outlines* from the satisfaction with the present displayed at the end of the text is subtly foreshadowed in two lectures where a sentence one expects to be spoken in the indicative mood is instead voiced in the conditional mood or in the form of an ought. According to UN's notes (uncontradicted by Ringier, whose notes leave a gap here), Hegel said the following in the introduction to his lectures:

> Yet insofar as philosophy considers something intellectual, it [engenders] a separation, for [the Mind apprehended by thought] is something other than the Mind of the real [world]. The separation gains a more precise determination, one that we see when philosophy [first] emerges. It occurred when Mind in the form of thought stood over against the form of external reality. We see this emerge in Plato, Socrates, [and] Aristotle at the time when Greek life was declining and the world Spirit [was moving] to a higher consciousness of itself. In a duller way, we find this repeated in Rome, as the earlier, peculiarly Roman life ended and a different one [infused with Christianity] took shape. Descartes appeared because the Middle Ages were spent. The concentration of spiritual life [in thought] eventually arises where thought and reality are not yet one. When this concentration developed into a difference [between thought and reality], when individuals became free and the life of the state split apart, then the great [philosophical] minds emerged. Philosophy emerged as the self-sundering Spirit. When it painted its grey on grey, the divorce between body and soul had [already] occurred. Philosophy is not what causes the fracture; it has already occurred [and] philosophy is its symptom. How is this fracture to be understood? We could think that ... Spirit abandons the existing reality as a corpse [in order to bring into existence] a state of the world where free philosophy and the education of the world agree. On this view, philosophy *would* give up its supposed opposition [to the world], and this is its true goal. For in [philosophy] lies the moment of reconciliation; it *ought to* overcome the separation between the different [philosophical and worldly] consciousness[es].[71]

---

71 Appendix 1, 251; emphasis added.

So, in *Outlines*, paragraph 360, the world *has* discarded its barbarity and unjust arbitrariness, while philosophy *has* abandoned its otherworldliness, so that the reconciliation between philosophy and the world *has become* a reality in the State that mirrors Reason. In the lectures, by contrast, philosophy's giving up its opposition to the world is only an aim that ought to be realized. Philosophy *ought* to overcome the separation between the philosophical and the worldly consciousness.[72]

The other place where the 1819/20 lectures prefigure Hegel's reassessment of political reality in the preface to *Outlines* is the beginning of his treatment of the police power and the corporation. He has just discussed the administration of justice, where the general and the particular will merge, but only in a law for abstract persons operating as an external restraint on the particularism of concrete individuals in the system of needs or market. In the corresponding move to the corporation in *Outlines*, Hegel says that "in accordance with the Idea, particularity itself makes this universal ... the end and object of its own willing and activity. In this way the *ethical returns* to civil society as something immanent in it."[73] Observe that the verbs in both sentences take the form of the indicative. In the 1819/20 lectures, by contrast, Hegel switches to the conditional:

> The second part [of civil society] dealt with justice, but only as something abstract. Over against it stood the particularistic welfare [of individuals]. The third [part] is then the higher ground, which unites both [in the idea of the well-being of all]. This *would be* the stage of the Idea – the union of the particular and the universal Will.[74]

The conditional "would," entailing the thought "if it existed," implies a state of affairs that does not yet exist.

---

72 In UN's notes, the same shift is reflected in Hegel's reformulation of the famous *Doppelsatz* that appears in the preface to *Outlines*: "What is rational is actual; what is actual is rational." In the lectures (UN51), this becomes: "What is rational becomes actual; what is actual becomes rational." However, Ringier's notes contradict UN's on this point, and we do not know who heard correctly. Ringier wrote, "What is rational is actual and vice-versa." Either formulation is compatible with Hegel's retreat, however. Both say that Reason actualizes itself such that existence is actual (i.e., realizes its inner potential) only as rational.
73 *Outlines*, para. 249; emphasis in original.
74 This translation, 167; emphasis added.

The Reason for the Retreat

Part of the reason for Hegel's altered judgment of political reality is doubtless the post-1815 restoration of absolute monarchies in Germany and their efforts to create an administrative despotism or "police state" meant to suppress liberal voices demanding the rule of Law and responsible government. However, it was not only that. In *Outlines*, towards the end of his discussion of civil society, Hegel describes, in a cursory way, the blemish of *modern liberal* society – namely, the ownership of the means of labour by one class, such that non-owners form a new dependent class whose members grow poorer inversely as society grows richer.[75] The criticism, however, is but a prelude to reconciliation. To justify philosophy's satisfaction with the present world without which its historical optimism would lack scientific warrant, Hegel points, again in a Panglossian way, to the private "corporation" as having removed the blemish. With no evidence beyond the declining craft and merchant guilds of the pre-capitalist era, he discusses this entity as if it were an existing *post*-capitalist institution in which the maladies he has diagnosed have been overcome. According to the author of *Outlines*, the corporation *has* abolished the worker's dependence on owners of capital as well as the widespread poverty consequent on treating labour solely as a means of production for the capitalist.[76]

In the 1819/20 lectures, Hegel is no Pangloss. Here, at considerable length and with more passion than he shows in any other post-Jena writing on civil society, he elucidates the connection, given the way modern industry is organized, between wealth accumulation, on the one hand, poverty, unemployment, and moral degradation, on the other. He even characterizes the relation between the owner of capital and the labourer as an iteration of the master-slave structure that Marx and Kojève-influenced French Marxists had to extrapolate from the *Phenomenology of Spirit*.[77] The upshot is that any force that Marx's

---

75 *Outlines*, paras. 243–4.
76 *Outlines*, paras. 250–5.
77 See appendix 3, 257–8. The implicit justification for this characterization comes earlier. In speaking of alienability, Hegel says that alienating the totality of one's product is tantamount to slavery or serfdom because one then alienates one's productivity as such (this translation, 34–5). The wage earner (e.g., a domestic servant) who is paid just enough to replenish his power is distinguished from the serf, Hegel says, only by the temporal limit of his contract. By itself, therefore, being paid a subsistence wage from one's product does not distinguish the wage earner from the serf

critique of Hegel's philosophy of Right as evincing both a "false positivism" and a "merely apparent criticism" may once have had is now gone.[78]

The shift in Hegel's orientation from witness to freedom to critic of unfreedom first occurs in his lecture on the "system of needs." Here Hegel discusses the division of labour and the mechanization of specialized tasks made possible by it. In *Outlines*, only the positive side of this development appears: the thoroughgoing socialization of work and the liberation from necessity-driven toil that allows agents to work for mental or self-formed ends. In the 1819/20 lectures, the negative side of a division of labour among atomistic producers – the side that Hegel emphasized in Jena – returns to the foreground. Here socialization means external dependency, and the mind's liberation for self-realizing work turns round into the mindless repetition of a single operation. Inherently, the tool mediates between the mind and nature, turning natural material to mentally formed ends. As a machine, however, the tool makes the mind superfluous, subordinating it to nature's powers. Hegel writes:

> However, in this sphere [of the Ethical Idea's glimmering], much is also lost. The labourer becomes more dependent, more apathetic. All variation ends and becomes a repetition of the same thing, resulting in mental stupor. Also, the human being becomes more dependent. In many cases, he finds himself abandoned [to chance], no matter how hard-working he tries to be. Because production has become so simple, no concrete mind is necessary, and the human being can leave his work to the machine. Thus, the culminating point of extreme mechanization involves an inversion: the human being can walk away from it. The machine has become so far removed from the tool that the active mind no longer directs [the work]; rather, everything is left to natural powers. Yet, the human being has reason to be proud of the tool. It is the middle term [between human agency

---

and does not count as retrieving part of one's product. Only self-externalizations are products, and things made just to live are not self-externalizations. If the wage earner is then faced with a choice between starvation and lifetime work for a subsistence wage, then the line between wage earning and serfdom becomes vanishingly thin. For the impact of Hegel's master-slave analysis on Kojève-influenced French Marxists, see Alison Stone, "Hegel and Twentieth-Century French Philosophy," in *The Oxford Handbook of Hegel*, ed. Dean Moyar (Oxford: Oxford University Press, 2017), 697–717.

78 Karl Marx, *Economic and Philosophical Manuscripts of 1844*, ed. Dirk Struik, trans. Martin Milligan (New York: International Publishers, 1964), 184.

and nature]. In tools, the human being mediates [its self-activity] with external work.[79]

Hegel then describes, much more extensively than in *Outlines*, the necessary connection between extreme wealth and extreme poverty once handicraft gives way to mass production using means of labour owned and controlled by individual profit-seekers. The large-scale production and distribution of generic products puts artisans out of work and forces them to work for wages kept at subsistence levels in order to maximize the capital-owner's profits. Moreover, success in accumulation enhances competitiveness, so that small businesses fall to larger ones, their owners likewise reduced to subsistence wage earners. The result of this proletarianization of work is that the social surplus over life's necessities to which everyone in the division of labour contributes accrues only to a few. The many toil for survival in mindless tasks for the sake of the self-determined activity of others. As wealth increases on one side, misery deepens on the other. No longer is poverty tied to indolence, disability, or ascetic choice; it is now a social artefact – the obverse side of wealth expansion, where capitalists lawfully capture the entire surplus product of labour. So altered, says Hegel, poverty is a social wrong rather than a mere misfortune.[80] It issues from a relation of domination and subordination akin to that between feudal master and serf, a kind of relation condemned as unjust by modernity's own norm of equal self-determination. Like the feudal relation, moreover, this one corrupts both master and servant, for it engenders in both a shamelessness in wrongdoing. The servant thinks of law as the master's law, and the master agrees.

> Just as, on the one hand, poverty is the root of vulgarity, of disrespect for Right, so, on the other hand, does the attitude of vulgarity likewise appear in wealth. The rich man considers everything as being for sale to him, because he is conscious of himself as the power of the particularity of self-consciousness. Thus, wealth can lead to the same mockery [of Right] and shamelessness to which the poor rabble descend. The disposition of the master of slaves is the same as that of the slave.[81]

---

79 This translation, 141–2. In the Heidelberg lectures of 1817/18, the negative side of mechanization is treated as a step in the restoration of human freedom through the replacement of mechanical by creative labour (LNRPS, para. 101).
80 This translation, 174.
81 Appendix 3, 257.

In *Outlines*, too, Hegel tells us that, because modern poverty is a social wrong, it produces in the poor a resentment and disrespect for law that turns them into a rabble. However, in the 1819/20 lectures, he goes further. He presents the creation of a rabble of paupers ("the worm in civil society") not only as a psychological and sociological fact, but also as something objectively subversive of civil society's legitimacy such that the poor are justified in civil disobedience.[82] "Duties exist," says Hegel, "only if rights exist."[83] But since the poor cannot access the administration of justice or hire adequate counsel to defend them in court, their rights might as well be non-existent. They are also excluded from all other benefits of civilized life – from higher education, health care, the fine arts, even the consolations of religion, for church attendance requires fine clothes. As a consequence, the criminal's "infinite judgment" denying his duty to obey the law, a judgment that came forward in abstract Right as a mere logical possibility, acquires in modern society a relative sociological justification.[84] In this way, says Hegel, the extremes of wealth and poverty "constitute the ruination of civil society."[85]

The inability of the proletarian poor to see their own freedom in the law not only subverts the civil society in history. It also bars the door to the just State at the end of history, for this State requires not only that notional citizens be able to see their freedom in the law, but also that determinate individuals actually revere the State as the ground of their particular well-being. The institutions evolved within civil society are supposed to foster this sentiment, yet with the creation of a pauper class, they do just the opposite. Hegel writes:

> Not only is there an external distress [UN194: that weighs on the poor], but a quite different conflict arises: the conflict between the soul and society. The poor feel themselves scorned. All around them, there is satisfaction, and they have nothing; they must go hungry. Here, the [civic] consciousness that civil society is precisely supposed to raise gets smothered.[86]

The contrast with the roseate picture painted in *Outlines*, paragraph 360, could not be starker.

---

82 On this point, see also Henrich, *Philosophie des Rechts*, 20.
83 This translation, 174. See also this translation, 108–9.
84 Hegel suggests an alternative justification for civil disobedience. The right of necessity that permits a taking of property to save life in an emergency also applies where the necessity is ongoing. See appendix 3, 257.
85 Appendix 3, 258.
86 This translation, 174.

The Prescription

In *Outlines*, Hegel makes no overt prescription. The task of philosophical science is to understand, not to prescribe. Yet, in treating a condition that is non-ideal as the image and actuality of Reason, Hegel sometimes embellishes what is with what he thinks ought to be. For example, in 1820, a welfare system involving the mutual assurance of autonomy in the face of chance rather than unilateral transfers to the starving was barely on the horizon; yet that is what Hegel describes as part of the model state of his time. In an ideal world, the orientations of the political scientist and the metaphysical idealist merge harmoniously; the scientist/idealist can passively disclose the reasonableness of what is. In a non-ideal world, these orientations fall apart. The scientist must only observe, but the metaphysical idealist cannot observe what is not there; he can only advocate. To hold science and idealism together, Hegel occasionally blurs the distinction between description and prescription, dissembling the latter as the former. He portrays the existing state as exhibiting a feature of the ideal one it does not have. This ploy has always exposed Hegel to the accusation of having falsified the reality to which he purports to submit (false positivism) and of having given idealism's imprimatur to a non-ideal condition (false idealism).

In the 1819/20 lectures, there is no dissemblance. Having been explicitly critical of modern industrial organization, Hegel is now explicitly prescriptive. As in *Outlines*, he first considers the expedients that civil society uses to alleviate poverty, explaining in terms that bring T.R. Malthus to mind why none of them work.[87] Direct transfer payments to the destitute are counterproductive because they encourage idleness and erode self-esteem. Helping the jobless find productive work only produces a cycle of overproduction and unemployment, because the mass of consumers, having been kept at subsistence wages, lack the money to buy the product. Colonization, whether by settlers spontaneously seeking an escape from their condition or pursuant to a state's policy of acquiring markets for its surplus, is merely a palliative.[88]

---

87 Malthus preceded J.M. Keynes in emphasizing effective demand over savings as the key driver of economic growth; see Thomas Robert Malthus, *Principles of Political Economy*, 2nd ed. (London, 1836), bk. 2, chap. 1, sections 9, 10. The first edition of *Principles* appeared in 1820.

88 To this context belongs also international trade, which Hegel celebrates, not as alleviating proletarianization and poverty (which free trade might exacerbate), but as educating parochial peoples to a consciousness of universal humanity; see this translation, 176–7.

As in *Outlines*, the solution Hegel puts forward is the cooperative fellowship (*Genossenschaft*) or private corporation. Public ownership of the means of production never occurs to him, perhaps because his critique of a bureaucracy that overreaches as a "need-state" invasive of privacy and stifling to individual enterprise also applies to it.[89] Both regimes violate the Ethical Idea's structure of unity-in-difference in the same way – by submerging difference. In any case, the solution to the proletarianization of labour cannot be to turn everyone but state officials into proletarians. The remedy must instead abolish the proletariat, and this is what Hegel's corporation purports to do. In *Outlines*, however, this solution is presented as a fait accompli, and its visionary character is almost completely obscured. So tersely and matter-of-factly is the corporation described in *Outlines* that commentators have often mistaken it for a resuscitated guild, so nothing really novel; and this has fed the myth that Hegel has no solution to the modern form of servitude beyond an escape into the notional realm of equal citizenship or into one of the forms of the contemplative life.[90]

In the 1819/20 lectures, however, we begin to see what Hegel has in mind. It is nothing less than a proposal for industrial democracy anticipating the worker-management co-determination councils that arose in Germany in the 1950s.[91] To be sure, Hegel's corporation resembles the medieval guild in some respects – in its training of novices and care for members' orphans, for example. But whereas the guild was an association of independent merchants or artisans, Hegel's corporation would include everyone engaged in a particular trade or profession and put them on an equal footing as co-producers. All members would work for the corporation, which in turn would aim at the welfare of each, and officers of the corporation would be elected by its members.[92] This would abolish the class hierarchy between profit-seeking capitalists and wage-earning proletarians in an "ethical society" whose members would all share in fair proportion the surplus over life's necessities that the corporation produces.

---

89 This translation, 170.
90 Shlomo Avineri, *Hegel and the Modern State* (Cambridge: Cambridge University Press, 1972), 98–9; and Allen W. Wood, *Hegel's Ethical Thought* (Cambridge: Cambridge University Press, 1990), 247–55.
91 Also of interest in this context is the Mondragon group of business cooperatives in present-day Spain; see "Co-ops in Spain's Basque Region Soften Capitalism's Rough Edges," *New York Times*, 16 November 2021.
92 UN254

As an ethical society, the corporation would, Hegel says, amount to a second family. Its difference from the first would be that recognition would here take the form not of love based on sheer existence, but of honour based on education and accomplishment.[93] Its similarity to the first would lie in the intentionality with which the collective and the individual good would each be sought through action for the other. This would distinguish the corporation from institutions where the same fusion of interests occurs unconsciously, but for that reason haphazardly: the arms-length contract between narrowly self-interested persons and the free market more generally. In the corporation, the collective would take each individual's well-being as its conscious object, guaranteeing his or her livelihood, while the individual would work purposely for the whole, aiming at its economic success, helping out colleagues in distress, and so forth. The corporation would thus replicate the Concept's intimate reciprocity within the private sector, setting the stage for the dialectical unification of public and private sectors in the political constitution.

In the 1819/20 lectures, the counterfactual character of Hegel's corporation is clear from the way in which he advocates it as something that ought to materialize.[94] The welfare system that he describes already secures the individual's welfare against contingencies of a general sort that affect everyone; what is needed to complete this system, Hegel says, is an institution knowledgeable about the specific situation of individuals joined in a particular trade or profession. Throughout the discussion, Hegel uses the language of "should" rather than that of "is." "The interest of the particular individual should not be a selfish interest," he says, "but should rather become something secure and generally recognized as a right; it should have objective reality."[95] In the following passage, Hegel advocates the corporation against what he sees as modernity's exaggerated valuation of individual self-reliance:

> Against all this, modern times have raised [the principle of] self-reliance, the self-reliance of the particular individual. Everyone wants to stand on his own feet. It is said that everyone can freely chase what he can, whatever pleases him. At this viewpoint, it is forgotten that [in civil society] subsistence [or] acquisition is not something done in isolation, that it

---

93 This translation, 179, 181.
94 In the Heidelberg lectures, too, Hegel strikes a prescriptive note with respect to the corporation; see LNRPS, para. 121.
95 UN202.

rather relates to the broader society. This is how everyone abandons himself to chance. Thus, reasonableness consists in this, that [subsistence] not remain a matter of chance, that it rather, for starters, be lasting, and [secondly,] that it not be contingent but fixed, so that, if someone comes back from illness, etc., he will be helped. Everyone has a claim that civil society have concern for him. If he says he wants to rely on himself, then he is, on the one hand, correct and, on the other hand, incorrect. [Making a living] is always dependent on external circumstances. Everything is [exposed to] chance. It is therefore baseless to want to rely only on oneself.[96]

However, the most striking illustration of the contrast between Hegel's passive understanding in *Outlines* and his critical idealism in the 1819/20 lectures is his return to the corporation at the end of the lectures, where he discusses the Germanic phase of world history. Precisely at the point where *Outlines* climaxes with a celebration of history completed, the lectures close with a rumination on history unfinished, its "destiny" still to be reached. And what remains to be achieved is the corporation. The medieval guilds, Hegel says, became ossified in positive law, resisted central authority, and imposed fetters on economic liberty. As a consequence, they were smashed by national sovereigns and by the French Revolution. The task now is to transform them into tight cooperatives, remove their barriers to entry, and bring them back so reformed on the ground of state sovereignty, no longer merely ready to hand and covered in dust, but understood as an organic part of a just polity.[97]

Hegel's switch to advocacy in his lectures on the corporation is not out of line with what he had done in the past. Recall how, in his occasional essays, he reconciles advocacy of change with respect for public order and the objective Reason in history. He urges only those reforms demanded by the thought of the age and for which the people are thus mentally and ethically prepared. So here. Though no model of Hegel's corporation existed in his lifetime, still, the principle of modernity is the universal right of human beings to self-determination. The master-servant structure of industrial organization violates that principle and, Hegel says, is the source of modernity's "bad conscience."[98] Its replacement can thus be accomplished without violence. This is even truer now than it was in 1820, owing to two developments that have occurred in industrial organization over the last two hundred years:

---

96 This translation, 180–1.
97 This translation, 249, 250n904.
98 Appendix 3, 258.

the separation of ownership and control in the shareholder-owned but independently managed enterprise, and the growth of labour unions and collective bargaining. The first allows the change to occur without expropriations; the second makes the move to industrial democracy an incremental one.

V

So far, I've discussed the importance of the 1819/20 lectures for understanding better Hegel's social and political philosophy. However, these lectures also throw new light on his philosophy of law in that they extend and clarify the condensed and often cryptic statements in *Outlines* on the natural law of property and contracts.

Hegel calls the natural law pertaining to property and contract abstract Right. It is abstract in two senses: one, it rests on an abstract conception of the moral agent as nothing but a negative free will – a will that is not determined by natural laws and not attached to any particular want or object of want; two, it presupposes an individual free will isolated from the large ethical life wherein it is truly embedded, hence from the obligations (familial, professional, political) belonging to that life. The moral agent considered in these impoverished but necessary ways is called a legal person. Abstract Right is a teleological account of how this person progressively gives objective reality to its claim of end-status by achieving a property in things valid against the world.

In *Outlines*, however, this teleology does not jump out from the text. It has to be put together with the aid of other Hegelian sources, in particular, the early, unpublished drafts of the philosophy of Spirit written in Jena. Those drafts told a story of the agent's realizing its end-status vis-à-vis natural objects by satisfying its needs through self-active labour, by turning nature to its ends through tool-making and agriculture, by unilateral acts of acquisition and exclusion, by risking its life for the excluder's recognition of its lordship, and, finally, by gaining an objective property through the mutual recognition of equals in contractual exchange. Unilateral possession and use were necessary steps towards annulling a thing's independence, but the possessor's indifference to the self-realization of others left his ownership as something merely asserted and imposed. Only in contractual exchange was a valid property achieved and thus too a perfect mastery of the object.[99]

---

99 Leo Rauch, *Hegel and the Human Spirit: A Translation of the Jena Lectures on the Philosophy of Spirit (1805–6) with Commentary* (Detroit: Wayne State University Press, 1983), 99–127.

In *Outlines*, by contrast, the relations of persons (universals) to things (particulars) distinguished as possession, use, and contract are presented as exemplifying three different kinds of judgment – positive, negative, and infinite – that belong to the doctrine of the Concept in Hegel's Logic.[100] It seems that the primary objective is to exhibit property concepts as tracking the movement of logical ones rather than to connect them as steps in a teleological narrative about the realization of personality's end-status. To be sure, Hegel tells us (in para. 39) that end-status is initially something the person subjectively claims in the face of nature's independence, and that personality "is that which acts to overcome this restriction and to give itself reality" by making the external world its own. However, it is easy to gain the impression that this mastery of things in the world is acquired simply by acts of possession, that first possession is property, and that contract is the exchange of things already owned. No mention is made of the defect of unilateralism in first possession, and so we do not see how contract within a system of exchange cures this defect so as to give an objectively valid property.

In the 1819/20 lectures, all this is much clearer. Possession is an incomplete property, because it lets the object stand independently of the person and because it is property only in the opinion of the possessor.[101] Use is a better property because it annuls the object's independence, yet it is still defective because of its unilaterality and because the person is dependent for proof of its end-status on the very material object whose independence it must annul. The problem to be solved, says Hegel, is how to detach oneself from the object, thus displaying one's independence of it, while remaining, indeed *becoming*, its owner. The solution is the contract of exchange, whereby one alienates the material object to another will, while becoming the recognized owner of its non-material value. That the possessor first becomes a full owner through exchange is clear from the following passage:

> The process by which I am – remain – an owner in ceasing to be one and because of that become an owner [in an objective sense] – that is the transition to contract. That I am an owner is the enduring moment. The

---

100 *Outlines*, para. 53; and *Hegel's Logic*, trans. William Wallace, 3rd ed. (Oxford: Clarendon Press, 1975), paras. 172–5.
101 "Possession is not objectively confirmed [as property] and is distinct from property"; this translation, 41.

generality of this determination [of ownership] presents itself as a general Will, not the will of a plurality. This can also be understood from the [other] side: in [unilaterally acquired] property I have given my [freedom] an existence; but because I have this [property] only in my individual opinion, this moment is mere externality [without objective confirmation]. The genuine reality of positive freedom [requires] that I look at the existence of my freedom in [another] will. By virtue of that, this [other will] is identical with my being: [this unity of wills] is the positive identity in which I view myself [as an owner]. This is therefore the ground and element for my will's existence.

The further thing, then, is that I have property, but mediated through the will of another. This mediation requires closer consideration. It is no longer the same relationship [as possession and use]; it is rather that I have property through the will of another. Thus, contract is a rational moment [in the development of property]. I seek the other's agreement, wherewith [the thing] is my property.[102]

Accordingly, the 1819/20 lectures make clear that, for Hegel, the contract institution is not a legal place for the exchange of things that are owned apart from exchange; rather, it is itself the social constitution of property through a bilateral recognition occurring against the backdrop of a competitive market conferring social recognition on the successful bidder for the object. First possession does not constitute property in an absolute sense; it gives the possessor only a better claim than non-possessors, but that claim does not ripen into a right *simpliciter* until the object is alienated in return for a social recognition of ownership. The right gained through a promissory exchange no longer depends on possession, and it defeats any possessory one. Thus, a finder of an object has a possessory right good against everyone except the person to whom the former owner promised the object in a valid contract, though that person never possessed it.

Hegel is also clearer in the 1819/20 lectures than he is in *Outlines* about what the object of full ownership is. It is neither the material thing one brings to the contract nor the thing one receives in exchange for it. It cannot be the former, because this is precisely the unilateral possession that one alienates. It cannot be the latter, for if pre-contractual ownership was imperfect owing to the possessor's dependence on the thing, it does not become better by exchanging one dependency for another. Since dependence on things is incompatible with mastery of things,

---

102 This translation, 38–9.

the latter (mastery) is fully accomplished only by alienating a material thing in return for recognition of one's ownership of its non-material value – of the rate at which it will exchange for other things. This coheres with Hegel's general conception of realized freedom. If, as he tells us, the free will's progress to freedom involves sublimating immediate or natural volitions in those for objects generated by the free will itself, then substituting a value reflecting a common will for the thing sensuously wanted is part of that progress.[103] Accordingly, what the free agent isolated by abstract Right can finally and absolutely own is the exchange rate agreed to by the parties to a contract:

> A real contract occurs when something else is added, namely, when I [the alienator] will also to be an owner or to remain an owner. I cease to be an owner and yet remain one, and by virtue of that become one [objectively]. This is the rational side of contract, the universal and enduring [element in the transaction]. This universal and enduring [element] is value. This value remains with me; only the quality, the character of the possession, changes hands. That I remain an owner of value is really the point of contract.[104]

The fact that what the person truly owns is the exchange rate of a commodity has important implications for how we understand contractual rights, obligations, and remedies.[105] Contrary to what Kant thought, a contractual right is never a right to control another's will to perform the contract, for that, argues Hegel, would amount to mastery over a person;[106] nor is it a right to the specific thing promised, for, absent an autonomously formed attachment to it such as that of a stamp collector to a rare stamp, that would amount to bondage to a thing. A contractual right is rather a right only to a noumenal object in which the qualitatively different things exchanged are identical and that endures

---

103 See *Outlines*, para. 21, and this translation, 11–12.
104 This translation, 40–1. See also this translation, 58: "Just as in exchange I remain an owner of the thing while receiving different things, so here [in punishment]. One has to take an [equal] value." It is difficult to reconcile with these passages other statements Hegel makes to the effect that what the contracting party acquires at contract formation is the "thing" promised; see this translation, 42. How can I "remain" the owner of something I never owned?
105 For a full elaboration of these implications, as well as a demolition of the arguments against a disjunctive contractual obligation, see Jennifer Nadler, "Freedom from Things: A Defense of the Disjunctive Obligation in Contract Law," *Legal Theory* 27, no. 3 (2021): 177–206.
106 *Outlines*, para. 40.

throughout the movement of things from one pair of hands to another. That object is value – in other words, the exchange rate reflecting a union of minds. But the right to a certain exchange rate can be respected in either of two ways: by performing the promise or by paying the promisee the difference between the contract price and the market price for a substitute at the time performance came due. Thus, on Hegel's theory of the object of a contractual right, the contractual obligation is normally disjunctive. Only if, in light of an autonomously formed project of the promisee, there is no substitute for the thing promised does ownership of the exchange rate require specific performance.

A disjunctive obligation to perform or compensate might seem to contradict the morality of promising, which requires that, excusing conditions aside, promises be kept. But that is not so. As Hegel explains, contractual obligations are enforced as proprietary, not as moral, and what the promisee finally owns is just an exchange rate.[107] The imperfect moral duty to keep promises remains what it is. If the objection is that a disjunctive obligation implies a permission to run roughshod over a primary right if one is willing to pay the cost of the remedial one, the response is that there is no such implied permission. The promisee's primary right is to an exchange rate. Compensating him for nonperformance respects that right as fully as performance does.

Nevertheless, Hegel does not himself draw from his theory of property the implication that the contractual obligation is normally disjunctive. Despite stating that what remains with the alienator is only the value of the thing alienated, he says that failing to deliver to him the specific thing promised in exchange violates the alienator's property. This is so, he argues, because ownership of the "thing" (not of the thing *or* its equivalent) was already transferred by the agreement, so that the promisor is now withholding what belongs to another.[108] Yet this view collapses the distinction between breach of contract and tort

---

107 This translation, 42.
108 This translation, 42; cf. *Outlines*, para. 93. Hegel also says (this translation, 116) that the spiritual union of marriage without the sexual union is like a contract without performance, suggesting that the noumenal and sensuous sides are as inseparable in contract as they are in marriage. This, however, cannot be an apt analogy. Abstract Right differs from the marriage relationship precisely in that its free agent is expected to be capable of detachment from any and every object of desire, whereas marriage is the "immediate ethical substance" – the noumenal still enmeshed in the natural. In abstract Right, sensuous dependence is a defect that persists as a moment in possessory rights but that is overcome in the executory contract – in what Hegel calls "ideal exchange." While Hegel is doubtless an expert witness concerning what concrete determinations absolute idealism requires, he is not an infallible one.

and implies a crime of knowingly breaching a contract without more that neither common- nor civil-law jurisdictions have seen fit to recognize.[109] The fact that Hegel held this view should not be conclusive of its being correct for his philosophy, for there is no evidence that he turned his mind to whether a disjunctive contractual obligation is implied in his theory of what independent agents can finally own; nor is this the only place (his thoughts on women and the prince are others) where a conventional opinion leads him away from the direction in which his philosophy objectively takes us. Whether or not Hegel saw it, his theory of what a free agent can conclusively own offers a right-based argument for a disjunctive contractual obligation that almost all legal scholars think can be defended only in terms of the social utility of economically efficient breaches.[110]

Furthermore, that theory has great explanatory power, at least for the common law that Hegel thought was so muddled. It accounts for settled features of the common law of contract that are plainly inconsistent with a right to performance and with the idea that failure to perform is by itself a legal wrong. In particular, it explains why the remedy for breach is not specific performance unless the defendant shows that monetary compensation would be adequate, but monetary compensation unless the plaintiff shows that it would be inadequate; why the remedy for breach is monetary compensation even if the thing promised is particularized (a used Toyota) rather than generic (a new Toyota), so that it is impossible to characterize the damage remedy as another way of giving plaintiffs the things they were promised; why, unless an autonomously formed attachment (for example, to a family heirloom) colours the thing promised as admitting no substitute, there is no injunction against an anticipated breach of contract as there is against an anticipated trespass; why, unlike tortfeasors, those who breach a contract may normally keep their gains from the breach; and why an intentional breach of contract is not a property crime.[111] When understood with the aid of the 1819/20 lectures, Hegel's theory of contract yields an understanding of the contractual obligation that, though it will unsettle many jurists, provides the best account of the law by which roughly a third of the world's countries live.

---

109 Canada punishes a wilful breach of contract if it was probable that death, serious bodily harm, destruction of property, or public harm would result and if the breaching party either knew or had reasonable cause to believe this: *Canadian Criminal Code*, R.S.C. 1985, c. C-46, s. 422(1).
110 But see Nadler, "Freedom from Things."
111 For all this, see Nadler, "Freedom from Things."

Note on the Translation

Translating Hegel's philosophical vocabulary into English presents challenges almost as formidable as that of comprehending Hegel's ideas. Partly, this is because a literal translation of some technical expressions would only produce a jargon forbidding to non-specialist readers; partly, it is because the same German term often means different things in different contexts, and failing to signal the difference risks conflating concepts and distorting the philosophy.

The latter problem occurs especially with the terms *Geist*, *Begriff*, *Idee*, *Recht*, *Willkür*, *Wille*, *allgemeiner Wille*, and *Staat*. Sometimes *Geist* refers to the finite mind of the individual, sometimes to the finite but ideal-type mind of an epoch, the family, a people, or humanity, and sometimes to the infinite mind of a divinity. Where it refers to the finite mind of the individual, I translate *Geist* as "mind," where to the finite but ideal-type mind of an epoch, the family, a people, or humanity, as "Mind," and where to an infinite Mind, as "Spirit."

Where *Begriff* means the general form of just relations without the determinate content belonging to the Idea, I translate it as "Concept"; where it refers to the specific excellence of a particular kind of being (e.g., a free one) or of a particular institution or activity, I translate it as "concept."

Where *Idee* denotes the Concept developed into a system of concrete determinations of the Concept, I render it as "Idea"; where, synonymously with *Vorstellung*, it means an ordinary mental conception, I translate it as "idea."

Where *Recht* means the justice of laws or of political and social institutions, I translate it as "Right," "Law," or "justice"; where it means an individual person's valid claim to respect for its free will, I translate it as "right."

Where the context shows that *Willkür* is meant in a pejorative sense, I translate it as "arbitrary will" or "caprice"; where it is used in an ethically neutral sense (as in "contracts proceed from the parties' *Willkür*" or "It must lie within the State's *Willkür* to remove the civil servant from office"), I translate it as "free choice" or "discretion."

Where *Wille* refers to the individual person's or the individual moral subject's free will, I render it as "will"; where it denotes the reasonable will of individuals regarded in their natural immediacy or the reasonable will of a politically united people, I translate it as "Will." Where *allgemeiner Wille* refers to the reasonable will of individuals viewed in their natural immediacy, I translate it as "the general Will"; where it refers to the reasonable will of a politically united people, I translate it as "the universal Will"; and where (rarely) it refers to the common will embodied in an agreement between two free wills, I translate it as "the general will."

Where *Staat* denotes a people's self-conscious unity that mirrors in existence (*Dasein*) the Idea of Right, I translate it as "State." Where it refers to the patriarchal states of ancient China and Persia, the Greek *polis*, the Roman state, the feudal state, or the state relative to modern civil society, I translate it as "state."

Where possible, I have translated Hegel's technical expressions with a non-technical English equivalent. For example, *an und für sich* is usually rendered as "inherently and actually" rather than as "in and for itself."

A different problem arises with the terms *Vorsatz* and *Absicht*, which occur thematically in the Part called Morality. Both can be rendered as "intention," but Hegel uses *Vorsatz* to denote intention in a broad sense that includes both purposely aiming at an outcome and knowing that an outcome will result from an action aimed at another purpose, whereas he uses *Absicht* to denote intention in the narrow sense of purpose. The problem is that T.M. Knox, Stephen Houlgate, and H.B. Nisbet all translate *Vorsatz* as "purpose" and *Absicht* as "intention" – so exactly the converse of the translation I believe is correct – making my offering an outlier.[1] Outliers bear a burden of justification.

The justification is straightforward. It is that, in the lectures of 1819/20, Hegel explicitly tells us how he is using *Vorsatz* and *Absicht*. Ringier's notes contain these passages:

---

1 See *Outlines*, 115, 118; and G.W.F. Hegel, *Elements of the Philosophy of Right*, ed. Allen W. Wood, trans. H.B. Nisbet (Cambridge: Cambridge University Press, 1991), 143, 147.

The subject who is a particular [individual] also has a particular content. This is what *Absicht* means in the context of action.[2]

When I do something, I must have an interest in it. I have [my interest] in different ways when, through the action, my insight [into the value of the action for me] crystallizes ... If the interest evinces a content, then it is called *Absicht*. *Absicht* is precisely the more specific content that one puts into the external form of the deed. The *Absicht* counts for me as what is really the essential thing [in my action]. My knowledge that [an action will produce] something [or] my desiring it, is called general *Vorsatz*.[3]

So, *Absicht* refers to a specific content of the will, whereas *Vorsatz* refers to intention in a "general" sense that includes both desiring an outcome and knowing that it will result. Moreover, this usage is corroborated by UN's notes, according to which Hegel said, "With crime it is enough if it is proved that someone had the *Vorsatz* for a certain action."[4] The word "enough" indicates that *Vorsatz* is less, not more, specific than *Absicht*.

Lastly, rendering *Vorsatz* as general intention and *Absicht* as intention qua purpose makes better sense of the text. The first two sections of Morality are titled *"Der Vorsatz und die Schuld"* and *"Die Absicht und das Wohl."* Knox, Houlgate, and Nisbet translate these titles as "Purpose and Responsibility" and "Intention and Welfare," respectively. Yet in the first of these sections, Hegel says that one of the rights of self-consciousness is to be held responsible only for deeds that lay in its *Vorsatz*. The translation of *Vorsatz* by Knox et al. requires us to ascribe to Hegel the proposition that one is responsible only for outcomes one produces purposely, a proposition not only counterintuitive but also contradicted by Hegel himself. As a being capable of thought, Hegel says (*Outlines*, paras. 118, 120), a human is responsible for consequences that a thinking agent in its shoes would have foreseen as inevitable, whether or not it produced them purposely. This, he says, is "the right of objectivity" over one's action. Moreover, just as general intention fits better with responsibility than purpose, so does purpose go better with welfare than general intention. "The individual," Hegel says, "has the right to make its welfare its *Absicht*..."[5] Reading *Absicht* as intention is fine here as long as intention means only purpose. Treating it as a

---

2 This translation, 68.
3 This translation, 69, 70–1.
4 This translation, 71n248.
5 This translation, 69.

concept wider than purpose (as Knox et al. do) has Hegel speaking nonsense. I do not act for my welfare or self-interestedly if I merely expect satisfaction as a collateral benefit of acting with indifference to my interests. For all these reasons, I translate the two titles as "Intention and Responsibility" and "Purpose and Welfare."

The editors of Ringier's notes organize them in accordance with the Part, Section, and Subsection titles of Hegel's *Outlines*, enclosing within square brackets those titles not found in Ringier's manuscript. In this, I have followed their lead. I have also drawn the benefit of their editorial work in deciphering Ringier's abbreviations and in correcting his grammatical slips. In addition, I have incorporated, with due credit, a few of their editorial notes. However, I have not considered it important to reproduce the punctuation or paragraph breaks of the German edition. Since neither comes from Hegel's hand, I felt free to punctuate in a way that made Ringier's notes most readable in English, and to begin and end paragraphs where it seemed most natural to do so. Moreover, because the text is a transcript of lectures hurriedly taken down by a student, I exercise a degree of editorial agency that would be inapt for a text written by Hegel himself. In particular, I frequently insert connectives to bring out the sense of Ringier's often elliptical notes, and, where Ringier's rendering leaves Hegel's point unclear, offer a suggestion as to what was meant. All interventions of mine are indicated either by intra-textual square brackets or by footnotes clearly marked as expressing a thought of the translator.

Intra-textual numbers following "UN" refer to page numbers of the Henrich edition; intra-textual numbers standing alone refer to the pages of the Angehrn, Bondeli, and Seelmann edition.

LECTURES ON THE PHILOSOPHY OF RIGHT, 1819–1820

[Introduction]

[3] Right on its own [*für sich*] is the abstract Concept. The State is the realization of [the Concept of] Right. Right in the abstract is often called natural Right. Considered so, the state is viewed not as the realization of Right but as a misfortune for Right – a harsh fate by which the natural right of the human being is limited and offended.[1] Right is viewed in such a way that a condition of abstract Right becomes a lost paradise – one that must nevertheless remain a goal to be recovered from the state. Thus, Right is considered (1) as an abstract universal, and (2) in its realization. In essence, Right is the Idea, the Concept, the universal, but not as something [only] subjective but also as realized as a State. Right is the holy on earth, incapable of being injured. In its inwardness, the holy is inviolable;[2] [but] set forth in reality, it can be infringed.

The task of science is to specify the existential side through which Right comes to its realization; to begin with, however, it is to recognize what true Right is. This knowledge seems all the more needed now, when the whole world has seized upon this subject. Most people have an opinion and firm convictions about this matter and, against the real world, claim that the Right in thought should be realized.[3] This demand counts as something absolute because it is something inwardly sacred.[4] It is especially philosophy that should specify the Concept of

---

1 Translator: Ringier added "favoured" (*bevorteilt*). The UN wrote only "offended."
2 UN46: Only when it is in heaven or thought is the holy incapable of being injured. But the Right on earth can be violated, attacked.
3 UN46: This investigation is especially needed nowadays, when everyone thinks he has the Right in his conviction, which he wants to have fulfilled.
4 UN46: The failure of fulfilment counts as something outrageous that one must oppose.

Right and how reality must be [arranged] so as to correspond to the Concept. [This is so because] thoughts are necessary to the knowledge of Right. The most common view is that everyone can draw the knowledge of Right immediately from his breast and head without speculative reflection. [From this point of view,] if philosophy should deliver the Concept, then it should be an arsenal of reasons by which to combat and improve reality. [The Concept] is therefore [said to be] an ideal of reality, one in which all injustice is returned to balance. And, as is thought, this ideal is all the more excellent the further removed from reality it is. Such insipid ideals have then also been purveyed to the many.

On the one hand, one demands from philosophy that knowledge of the Concept of Right be a weapon with which to fight against the [objective] Concept; on the other hand, we can say that Right and the State belong to Spirit. [The latter] is their ground; its freedom is the foundation of the State, which is just the realization of Spirit. [The State] is the way in which Spirit knows itself. The existing state is based on developed or undeveloped thoughts as well as on the confidence of those who belong to it. If, for example, all citizens changed their conceptions of their constitution at once, the question arises: what would remain? Nothing but a soulless skeleton that would already be crumbling. It cannot be entirely a matter of indifference to the state what conceptions its members predominantly hold of Right and its reality.

Philosophy as science does not concern itself with opinions. Opinion [*Meinung*] is only mine [*das Meinige*]; someone else can have a different one. Philosophical knowledge is an absolute; [it is] knowledge of the Absolute. It thus seems that philosophy still makes demands of reality from [the standpoint of] an absolute authority. Certainly, [philosophy] is not a [positive] science of reality that takes up the Right from what is given in reality. The positive science of law has as its criterion that which is [legally] valid. Inasmuch as philosophy [by contrast] draws its determinations from the inner Concept [of Right], it can appear to make absolute claims against reality. Reality might conform to [the determinations of] philosophy or it might not, because [philosophy's] vocation is thought, the Concept; so, [philosophy] seems at first, indeed, to stand over against reality to the extent that the need arises for us to compare it with reality.

The first point [is that] we have to consider what the end of the philosophy of Right is and what its relationship to reality is so that its nature and goal within science [as a whole] might better emerge. We begin with Plato's notorious position (*Republic*, V). Unless either philosophers rule or kings philosophize and philosophy and rule unite, there will be no end of maladies for the human race.[5] Here is expressed the [5] supreme presumptuousness of philosophy. Because philosophy knows the truth and [because] government is based on ideas and knowledge of the state's well-being, it must also be the director. We must examine this more closely. We must stand at a still higher standpoint with respect to the relationship between philosophy and reality. Plato's position assumes that philosophy apprehends the truth – specifically, in the form of the Concept. If [philosophy alone] understood the truth, then the truth [would issue] from a peculiar happening, from an understood mental image, not from feeling.[6] [But] philosophy does not have a monopoly on truth. To be sure, it apprehends the truth, but it is not the only form of doing so. In recent times, indeed, it came to be ["]known["] that one cannot know the truth – a conviction that, if it could take root more firmly, would destroy in human beings a consciousness of the Divine and of the truth. So, the first proposition of Plato's we adopt with the latter more precise determination.[7]

Secondly, in that [proposition of Plato's] lies the assumption that this truth is merely an ought-to-be opposed to reality. Against that [view], we must defend and affirm the true Idea of philosophy. The true Idea is the substantial, the inner nature itself – no empty figment but rather the most powerful thing, that which alone is mighty. It would be an empty, irreligious conception [of the Divine] were the Divine not powerful enough to provide existence for itself, were the truth merely beyond the blue sky or in subjective thoughts, [something] merely inward. We concede divinity to nature, but we think that the Idea of God is forfeit [to us], abandoned to the opinion, caprice, [and] contingency of humans. The Idea is quite simply the omnipresent Absolute – not an indifferent spectator but an omnipotent animating presence, so that reality is only the body, the Idea the soul without which the body cannot exist at all. In apprehending the Idea through philosophy, we apprehend the real itself, that which is, not that which is not.

If the Platonic republic had not been inherently deficient, it would necessarily have come to reality. That is why those who infer from reality [6] the [Platonic] idea's unreality are not entirely wrong, but in the

---

5 Plato, *Republic* 473c–d.
6 UN47: If this is understanding, thinking, then the truth from other forms [of apprehension], for example, from feeling, is also truth.
7 Translator: Hegel adopts Plato's proposition that the truth apprehended by philosophy ought to rule with the more precise determination that philosophy has no monopoly on truth.

sense that reality is the mirror of the true [Idea].[8] Hidden from them, [however, is the truth] that the world can be understood only through the Idea; how humanity looks at the world is how the world looks back at it.[9] Viewed with Reason, it is rational; [viewed] with reflexive detachment [*Reflexion*], it presents a distorted image. In the philosophy of Right, we have regard for what is, not for what is nothing. In philosophy, we contemplate the realm of Mind together with the world of external nature; philosophy considers the realm of Mind and its reality.

With regard to the content of the Platonic idea, it has certainly expressed what appears to us as the idea of [Greek] reality. [Plato] brings the principle of Greek ethical life to consciousness; Plato captured the truth about the Greek Mind just as it existed in Greece.[10] Everywhere [in his work] the Platonic form of ethical life confronts us. Action and the individual are details that have to do with externality and that are subordinated to a thoroughgoing Mind; they are located only on [Mind's] surface, and the Mind of this ethical life is the soul, the inner principle. Motion is on the surface; that is where one gets buffeted about by passions that destroy things or bring one down to existence – to the play of existents. Mind exists only amid particular circumstances. Here it must make its way through.[11]

However, in the development of the cosmos, this ethical life cannot last, cannot remain in this beauty and purity; it has to step out into bifurcation. Plato sensed the beginning of this bifurcation. In his time, the driving force of world history emerged. The further principle of bifurcation that is necessary to the higher Idea of ethical life appeared to him only as a destructive force, because it had not yet been cultivated and returned to harmony. So, it had a destructive effect, and Plato was acquainted with it [only] in that aspect; and so he sought to manage it by not allowing a higher principle to befall his state, by instead eradicating it, the way the Spartans suppressed the passions, prohibited money, only to cause greed [7] to break out inwardly all the more

---

8 Translator: not in the sense meant by them that the Idea as such is unreal.
9 UN48: They just haven't held the mirror of reality in the right way, haven't looked at it in the light of Reason, for that is how the world, too, appears rational.
10 UN48: Plato understood the reality of his world; the principle of ethical life in the form of simplicity, this is the Greek Mind, Greek ethical life; this was veritably just as Homer, Herodotus, [and] Sophocles, the poet of Greek ethical life, depict.
11 Translator: Perhaps this refers to the distinction between Plato's *Republic* and Plato's *Laws*, the former depicting the absolutely best but impossible city conformable to pure Mind, the latter concerned with the best possible city having regard to the concessions that Mind must make to existence.

perniciously.[12] The principle [in question] is that of singularity, of subjective consciousness; it too is in ethical life, but embedded. Plato had already foreseen it, but he wanted, not to resolve it, but to eradicate it by dissolving the picture of the family and everything consequent thereon. That is why he seems to have hold, not of a reality, but only of reality in the form of an ideal, of something unreal, for it was [indeed] the form of the Greek Mind.

The truth is not the one that exists as the living present Mind [of an epoch]. For that reason,[13] the state sets up an ideal type [for an epoch]. [The ideal state for an epoch] is the Mind known to philosophy. Therefore, every philosophy stands essentially in time. [It] knows the inherent and actualized Being, the present [instantiation of the] eternal truth, which is neither in the future nor in the past. But it[14] is no abstraction; it is rather a concrete whole, for the [worldly] embodiment is the reality [of the concept]. A specific instance of the Mind of the time[15] is the highest mode of [that] Mind, of its concept, the mode in which the Mind understands itself, is conscious of itself. To be sure, this concrete whole has a dual aspect as belonging (1) to philosophy, and (2) to the external shape of existing reality. In its existence, Mind is this multicoloured carpet that has these or those crossing purposes. Philosophy considers, not this aspect, but rather the motley crowd [insofar as it has] returned to simple thoughts, without the aims of individuals, without interests, to the system of its simple life.[16]

---

12 UN48: As the Spartans prohibited money because it gives rise to evil inclinations, only to have greed break out inwardly all the more perniciously, so Plato wanted to dissolve the principle of ethical self-consciousness that created bifurcation; no property, no family was to count in his state.
13 Translator: "for that reason," i.e., because the true state for any epoch is not an empirical state.
14 Translator: "but it," i.e., the inner concept of a particular epoch.
15 Translator: for example, Athens.
16 UN48: Philosophy should not overshoot its time; she stands in it, she understands the present. The eternal truth is not something in the past or in the future. This inherent and realized truth [*an und für sich Wahre*] is not without [concrete] form and shape; it is rather a concrete whole, a particular [historical] mode of Spirit; this current mode of Spirit, which distinguishes itself from other shapes is the highest mode of the [epoch's] concept, of its self-understanding. This concrete whole is double, partly belonging to philosophy, partly belonging to the external shape of the empirically existing reality. This Mind in empirical existence is the colourful carpet, where a crowd of interests and purposes cross, struggle against each other. This shape philosophy does not consider. This detritus, led back to thought, is the object of philosophical consideration, Mind [as] a system of its simple life.

In religion, it is said that world events are tools in God's hands; that is, He brings everything forth. His purposes are unintentionally executed by those who seek to carry out theirs, and precisely in this acting. [UN49: We can express the relationship with more precision in the following way.] The true Mind, the substantial, is, on the one hand, the essential universal principle, what the genus is to animals. Among animals, the genus acts through instinct, in which the genus announces itself, makes itself known. Moreover, in order that this inward nature be revealed in them, [the animals] must also be individuals that belong to the genus.[17] On the other hand, they [qua humans] are discrete singulars that make up the existing reality of Mind.[18] The universality of Mind fills them, and yet the singular also has its right, forms its particular purposes. The universal, however, is in the genus. The general interests also count as something essential. The passions that [8] seek their satisfaction are the actuating force of the universal. The truth by itself is lethargic; it does not effectuate itself. The doer is the subjective, the realizer, which the abstract universal takes on. The real world is the simple drama that the universal thoroughly penetrates as the [unconscious] end of the individual, [of] the will of individuals qua discrete singulars, who are the actors. This is necessary for the realization of the Idea; otherwise, the powers and purposes of the Idea, which have their own prior right, would lack realization.[19]

But secondly,[20] the universal makes itself invincible [in the drama of individual purposes]; it executes itself therein. If philosophy contemplates the truth, then it cares nothing for this side,[21] but exalts only the simple, the substantial. It leads the manifold back to simplicity. If we were to look at the outline of a fine drawing through a microscope, it

---

17 Translator: "that belong to the genus," i.e., that have their being as instances in which the genus expresses itself.
18 Translator: Here UN shows that Hegel made a transition from non-human animals to humans, one that Ringier does not record. UN wrote (49): "The human being does not act from instinct, which is why the discrete singular asserts its worth. The [two things, the universal and the particular] come together [in the] community. [Individuals] have their particular purposes, and even these purposes are partly particular to individuals, partly common to the kind, the universal. Here belong the passions that seek their satisfaction. They show that human beings seek [the satisfaction of] their particularity in the universal. This is the actuating force of the universal."
19 UN49–50: The real world offers the double aspect that the ends of individuals appear there, the will of individuals, which [at the same time] are the realizers [of the] universal. This external side is absolutely essential.
20 Translator: The first point is that individuals with their particular purposes are the actors.
21 Translator: "for this side," i.e., the external side consisting of individual purposes.

would look uneven and with rough irregularities. For the eyes alone, it is beautiful. *Worldly consciousness is such a microscope*, for which only details are visible. The naked eye[22] leads the hurly-burly of reality back to the simple reality, [UN50: to the still spaces that are] free of those particular interests. Thus, philosophy does not float its history beyond [world] events but rather contemplates their substantial nature. Philosophy is that which reflects the enduring being of reality. The realm of Right, the realm of Mind, know that only that which is present to a universal consciousness, to the Mind of a people, can come into existence. Philosophy would regard as incongruous the wish to give institutions to a people that the people did not bring about itself, that are not timely. [Philosophy] gives the assurance that what is timely necessarily occurs.[23]

Spirit is the ground of Right. There is no Right higher than the Right of the universal Spirit. But this Right is no abstract thought: what is rational is real and vice versa, but [the real is rational] not in the details and particulars that can bewilder and confuse.[24] A detail always misses, fails to meet, Reason's Right. Rational contemplation rises above holding as something so important what is [9] contradictory in the details. The object of the philosophy of Right is, accordingly, to recognize the basis, the inward nature, of the real world – the systematic edifice of Spirit, but in its simple aspect, in the element of thoughts. In this respect, philosophy has the same relationship to the State as [religion has] to the Church; the object for both [philosophy and religion] is the truth, but in its simple spirituality, in the form of its eternal validity. The Divine felt in this form [by religion] is present in the world[25] as realized Spirit. Philosophy is nothing but the [worldly] shape of religion. Relative to religion, the goal [of philosophy] is nearer.[26] Religion has for its object the truth in the form of its eternal validity [...][27]

---

22 Translator: "the naked eye," i.e., philosophy.
23 UN50: [Philosophy] acknowledges the Right belonging to the present, for in the multicoloured fabric of exotic interests ... lies the universal. [Philosophy] respects reality as the realm of Right; it knows that in the real world only what belongs to a people's concept can have validity. It would be nonsense to force on a people institutions into which it did not enter itself. What is timely for the inward Spirit happens certainly and necessarily.
24 UN51: What is rational becomes real, and what is real becomes rational.
25 Translator: "in the world," i.e., in the State.
26 Translator: The goal of philosophy is nearer than the goal of religion because, for philosophy, the divine Kingdom is a State.
27 Translator: The editors of the Ringier manuscript tell us that, from this point, several pages of the manuscript are blank. See appendix 1 for the corresponding pages of UN's manuscript from the Henrich edition.

The relationship of negativity to itself is the negation of oneself.[28] The negative is the indeterminate. The free will can will nothing but itself. Itself is its only content, purpose, and object. If we enquire about the content [of the free will], then we are enquiring about a particularization. The *I* that is my object and end must have particularity within itself, that it might have a content. This just means that the will is not *abstract* but rather *concrete*. The [concrete universal] is therefore [the free will's] substance. Furthermore, the content is my own: *the I itself*. To begin with, the determinations [of the will] are an unmediated in-itself, and I find these determinations in me, they are mine. It is this substance that is distinguished from me considered as an abstract [will]. The mind, [to be sure,] is itself the system of its volitions; nevertheless, this content has [to begin with] the form of immediacy, and for that reason, it does not have the form adequate to [mind]. This form [of immediacy] is unsuited to the nature of mind. The content must be made fitting [to mind], not just with respect to its content but also with respect to its form.[29] It must in addition have the form of mine. This form of mine is the universal.

Initially, the form of universality is built into the content of the will. When we say we have impulses and inclinations, these are nothing else [but universals]. These impulses are natural. The contents of these drives are entirely ours. We know ourselves in these impulses. At first, this content, these determinations, [10] appear singly. We say that they were implanted in us, that is to say, they are our own, immanent. It also means that they came from outside. Impulses are so called insofar as we still have them [as they initially appeared]. These impulses are not moments of a system, but miscellaneous [things] side by side. The human being is thus [to begin with] the collection of these impulses, a mere aggregate, [UN62: as empirical psychology presents them]. These impulses are for that reason powers that rule our lives, but we feel ourselves ruled, and that is why they have a foreign quality for us. I find myself free in my impulses insofar as my own essence wills them, but also unfree and, indeed, the more they take the form of *passion*, the more passive I am.[30] Passions are just like the sickness of the body, where the life force has thrown itself onto [UN62: one part of the organization].

---

28 Translator: For me to relate to nothing but my abstract ego is to treat as nothing my determinate individuality.
29 Translator: Not only must I have the desire (e.g.) to acquire property and to marry, but I must also desire these things reflectively as requirements of my freedom.
30 *je mehr es Leidenschaft ist (ich leide dabei)*.

I (the abstract I) will and *I* [this particular I] will, but [the distinction] between these two I's is still unclear. We will consider this relationship only briefly. I relate myself to my essential nature. At the same time, I as the universal stand over [the I as particular]. This, my formal subjectivity, which can pass from one particular [content] to another, is the standpoint of arbitrary will [*Willkür*] in general. Thus, the arbitrary will is this: to be able to choose, and this I can do because I am an abstract subject that can take or leave the concrete [possibility]. This will is the natural will in general; its system is a natural one, driven by nature. This is of no concern to us here. The [utilitarian] system of felicity remains with this merely natural will, where one has to choose among inclinations and impulses in order to be happy. There is thus an opposition here.[31] There is also a split here. This will be overcome in such a way as to overcome the form of naturalness [in the content]. [The content of the will's volitions] will thereby become a rational system. Therefore, the task is to raise impulses and inclinations to mere moments of a unity. This elevation is elevation in accordance with the concept [of freedom]. The elevation of impulses to moments [of a whole] must occur in the individual [through education].

Education, culture, discipline consist in this, that the natural will is put aside in the whole and these impulses [11] gain their rational boundaries (one is reminded of the body and the particular parts – their physical behaviour).[32] Discipline first brings forth the interest [in cultivation]; it strips off the natural will. Impulses brush aside the form of naturalness. This occurs first of all through obedience (he who has not learned to obey cannot command either). Self-will must raise itself to the substantial. [This is the sense in which] the fear of the Lord is the beginning of wisdom. [UN63: The fear is that I felt my negativity as a natural being.] The natural in me has trembled; as a consequence, nature has become fluid, unstable. The lack of character in people arises just from this, that they did not have to obey. The lack of character in people is the result of a lack of discipline.

There is a crudeness, an immediacy in impulses. Insofar as impulses are side by side, they often collide. This collision stems from their particularity. The main thing is that the truth of the impulse lies [not in its immediacy but] in its essential nature. One can call this transition

---

31 Translator: The opposition is between the form of agency and the nature-given content.
32 Marginal note: Only where one system [of the body] fully limits another such that none dominates is there complete harmony, perfect health.

[from immediacy to mediation] the purification of impulse. There are two ways of looking at [impulses]. [From one point of view,] impulses are essential determinations of the will [UN63: and should be satisfied]. [From another,] impulses and inclinations are not there in their true form, which is why [some think] they must be extirpated – precisely because they have the form of immediacy. However, the mind is not an abstraction, but rather an inwardly organized system. To root out this content, to make mind into an abstraction, is what one might call monkish. It is also well said [from the first point of view] that the human being is by nature good; he has his natural inclination. There is an old saying: humans took the material from the passions to the gods. [From the second viewpoint,] however, the mind is not in its true form [when its volitions take] the form of impulses. This form of immediacy is what makes for a separation between the [Angehrn, Bondeli, Seelmann: for-itself] and the in-itself of the will; and then this concept [of the in-itself] is my entire purpose.[33] About property [and the family] one can say: we have the [natural] urge to acquire it, to live in the family. But if one grasps these things in that way, then these determinations [of the will] are merely found. The matter [of the will] is not given to the will from outside; rather what is given to it is only the inward, the self-determined. [UN64: The system of rational determinations of the will are the particular stages that we have to consider in this science.] The free will desires nothing else than to be free. Therefore, the will desires [only] itself. Considered superficially, this can be understood as self-interest. But the will desires its essential nature [*Wesen*].

There is another misconception to notice. When one speaks of the *free* will, this is, as it were, only a [subjective] will, but when the will is [a free will only] in its concept, it is only in itself.[34] Only insofar as it is an object for itself [in the world], is [the will] a *free* will. If its object is not itself, it is the dependent will. If one asks what is best for human beings, the answer is that they be *free*; but this is different from arbitrary will.[35] The subject is the free will [in] form as well as [in] content – this is the truth, but it is the abstract truth. Here the difference [between subject and object] has not attained its due. The realization of freedom is alone the truth. As a system of [rational] determinations, it is a system of necessity. Here freedom becomes necessity and necessity freedom.

How does the elevation of the particular to the universal occur? This is necessary. This occurs through thinking. The free will has (the free will)

---

33 Translator: "is my entire purpose," i.e., it dominates my will.
34 Translator: here "only in itself" seems to mean "only inherently or potentially a free will."
35 Translator: "different from arbitrary will," i.e., different from the freedom to do as one pleases.

as its object only through thinking. One can say of the slave: he does not grasp his self, that is why he is a slave. He knows himself only as a finite being. He lives in dependence, in finitude. This is where the absolute value of education comes in; the educated man does everything in a universal way.[36] Originality withers away. What withers, [however], is only crudity. Duties contain just what natural drives contain.[37] To regard barbaric people as splendid is error, and the same is true of the Middle Ages. So, too, when a man decides something from his idiosyncratic opinion, solely from his heart. Here belongs also bigotry, which thinks it possesses through feeling what can come only from thinking. With just as little right people say that a cunning and clever person has understood much. This person has the finite [individual] for its aim. A greater mind has also a greater will. Our universal standpoint is: That which the free will wills is freedom. The existence of the inherently and actually free will is the Right.[38]

[Division of Subject Matter]

[13] The first sphere is formal Right. The immediate idea is the will that the free will wills.[39] The idea of freedom is [here] only formal; it has to determine itself, but all these determinations have reality only through their being determinations [of the will]. The human being is thus an absolute end for itself; it is self-determining. It is not constituted in such a way that its concept would lie outside it. Everything else is a means, inherently selfless. Accordingly, this idea [of freedom] is, to begin with, formal. The free [will] relates itself to itself. The difference [between universal and particular] is not yet internal to it. The positing of difference has a double form: outwardly [in the world] and inwardly [in natural appetite]. The free [will] that is for itself constitutes the foundation of abstract Right.

The second [sphere] is that [in which] difference is posited [within the free will], that is to say, the initial immediacy is overcome. The stage

---

36 Translator: "in a universal way," i.e., in accordance with the duties embedded in institutional roles.
37 Translator: "Duties contain just what natural drives contain," i.e., the content of duty is the content of natural desire raised by thought into a rational system of volitions ordered to freedom. See G.W.F. Hegel, *Outlines of the Philosophy of Right*, trans. T.M. Knox, ed. Stephen Houlgate (Oxford: Oxford University Press, 2008; henceforth *Outlines*), para. 19.
38 Translator: The potential for freedom actualized in existence through the State is the Right.
39 Marginal note: Right is sacred because it is a substance of the free for the free.

[distinguished by] this relationship is the moral standpoint.[40] The relation of the will to itself is then the subjective will; what is true for us is then true for the will itself.[41] By thinking the concept [of the free will], we are, so to speak, ahead [of the will we are observing]. The second [step] is the positing of difference, and this is just the moral standpoint [UN65: which is concerned with intention and insight]. Initially, in [abstract] Right, intention counts [in crime] – insight not yet. Here [at the moral standpoint], however, [insight] certainly does [count]. What we call urges and inclinations come to the fore at the moral standpoint. The Good, the Idea [of the Good] in general, the realized Idea, is something that only ought to be. The universal Good stands over both [urges and inclinations]. At the moral standpoint, one arrives only at an ought.

The third [step] is that this subjective moral will overcomes this [opposition between ought and is] and returns to the Concept. This is then ethical life. Here the Good not only ought to be [realized], but is [realized], not only ought to have an [objective] content, but also does. The other aspect [of difference] is outward difference.[42] That is, the Will is the Idea in itself. The Concept must also have reality.[43] At the stage that we have [before us, whether of abstract Right or of morality], we have to consider that stage also as Idea [that is,] not only as concept but also as [outwardly] configured in the way that it is there [before us].[44] Accordingly, we have not only a row of concepts [of freedom], but also a row of [existential] formations [14] of the Concept. In these formations we envision things [as they are] for the first time. If one speaks of the Concept, it can appear remote. But *philosophy* overcomes this remoteness. Our life and our existence are really imbued with this Idea precisely because the Idea is the truth. We prevail in existence solely within these forms of the Idea; it is very wrong to disregard the little things of daily life, for these contain precisely the Idea. The existence that the Idea gives itself is the existence of the Concept, and, as existence, it is something distinct from the Concept. But in this existence, the Concept specifies itself. If one begins with the Concept, then [the Concept's] existence is not [a series of] applications of the Concept [to a pre-existing

---

40 Translator: "this relationship," i.e., the relationship between free will and its content such that the content is no longer natural or immediate but rather self-determined.
41 Translator: "What is true for us is then true for the will itself," i.e., what is true for the philosopher, namely, that the will determines itself inwardly, is then known by the will whose development the philosopher is observing.
42 Translator: as distinct from the difference within the Concept.
43 Marginal note: The ultimate [realized] Idea constitutes the end point.
44 UN65: All the stages [of thought] that we specify are to be considered in their realized existence. These existences or formations fall within our everyday consciousness.

material]. Here the particular does not come from outside [the Concept]. Particularity is posited through the Concept itself.

Abstract, formal Right constitutes the first part [of the philosophy of Right].[45]

---

45 UN58: The will has been further considered (1) as the will in itself or in and for itself. Therein are contained moments. When we reflect on the will, we notice that it is the pure abstraction, pure thought. I can make myself empty, purified of all content. We go from one object to another. I can give up everything, renounce all bonds to which I am attached, can give up the whole extent of the bonds of my existence; this too I can renounce (with death). This is the moment of complete indeterminacy, universality. If I say to myself, "I," then I have fled the world to this pure light, where all difference has been subsumed. This is the moment of lawless freedom. Mind knows itself as free, that it can renounce everything. You can lay hold of him how and where you want, [still,] he flees into his inwardness. It is the freedom of the understanding that holds fast to one moment [of freedom]. He cannot be coerced to do anything [for he can renounce attachment to the body]. Not so the animal, which is a subjective life, but cannot differentiate itself from the particularity of its existence. From that freedom of the understanding emanates the fanaticism of freedom, which proceeds to negate everything determinate, which sees all particularity as something foreign, [and] which always wants to posit the particular as separate from the universal. Where someone appears particularized to him, he sees it as contemptible. Every individual is contemptible; although he appears this way [i.e., virtuous] now, he could also be different. This fanaticism was the moment of the French Revolution, as it set freedom as an aim that found its reality only in the negation, the annulling of particularity. It wanted a conscientious political condition. However, as soon as a condition comes into existence, differences emerge ... Then fanaticism will not allow anything to become real. The freedom of the understanding likewise appears in Stoicism, as well as in the Indian Gymnosophists [yogis], who retreat into unity with the Divine in empty speculation, absorbing all external thoughts and existence. So also arose the monks of the Middle Ages; they could not find themselves in reality, so went inward. (2) [The second moment of the will is] that I go forward to difference, to determinateness; I make myself determinate. Here there are various oppositions to overcome. The infinite first steps out into the finite. Empty universality, the indeterminate is already something other than what it meant to be, [for it is] a finite, one-sided abstraction. The indeterminate is itself the determinate, because it stands opposed to the determinate, as does the universal to the singular, the infinite to the finite ... The will steps out into particularity; this is the moment of finitude ... The will gives itself a shape. We call this content purpose ... These are determinations in the will ... From this follows the transition to limitation – that is, [the will] specifies its first moment [which was pure possibility] as [the definite thing] it is. The exemplary will wills only particular objects. (3) The third [moment] is the truth of both of these, the unity of both moments, finitude and infinitude posited as identical, so that the particular is posited as itself universal, in that I have this particular [purpose] as mine. I posit this determinateness as identical with me, join it with me; I decide, I make up my mind; this is the concrete Concept. I step into existence, realize a possibility on whose content I am dependent, on which I have decided; it is my purpose. This is a speculative Concept. If we speak philosophically, we cannot avoid speculation. The results are: (a) in limitation to remain unlimited (b) in particularization to remain universal (c) in negation to be at the same time positive. This is the negation of negation, the sublation of the limit. This is the true infinite ...

[FIRST PART]

[Abstract Right]

[15] The term *natural right* should be banished because it does not denote anything.[46] It is said that abstract rights are absolute, and this is meant as though the reality [*Realität*] of these rights is to be found in a natural condition. Condition generally implies immediate reality. The actuality [*Wirklichkeit*] of Right is not an immediate condition. The Right must be rational, that is, brought forward through the rational Mind. Here belong the fictions detrimental for *philosophy* about a golden age, about a paradise, as if this condition ever existed. For just that reason, such conditions are not to be longed for. This is something powerless and opaque.[47] Thus, there can be no discussion at all about such a state of nature. We have to consider abstract Right in contrast to morality.

The will that is free for itself is the will that in its freedom relates itself immediately to itself. In this liberation, the relationship is simple. For that reason, it is the relationship of Being or of immediacy. The pure self-relating negativity is the singular will. The free will, which is free for itself, is what we call the person, personality. Person [and] individual are distinct from each other. The person is the atom. Of course, the individual is also the atom, but it contains the further [idea] that there are differences within it. Individuality is in itself the infinitely determinate. By contrast, the person is the singular insofar as it is free for itself.

---

46 UN67: Abstract Right is the part of science that is usually called natural right ... This appellation should be abandoned. It is an erroneous opinion, as if natural rights could be valid in a state of nature.
47 UN67: It is no confirmation of the Substantial to think of all need and tension as being submerged in a general peace. To remain in such a condition with its thoughts is weak and ignoble, for it is the object of Spirit to be with itself in its opposite.

Personality is the highest thing in human beings;[48] it is that I am a *This* and that in these determinations I conduct myself as a free being. Personality is [the individual's] highest worth. In personality I know myself simply as a free being. Right in general can be expressed [so]: Be a person and [let] others be their persons.[49] He who has rights is a person. The slave, which [16] has no rights, is not a person. Human beings are by nature unlike. The equality of all human beings lies in personality.[50] Exquisitely, this thought has become universal in the world through Christianity. God has become a man; the identity of both consists in this, that the man died, [was resurrected,] and thereafter human beings become blessed. Implied therein is that every individual has the capacity to acquire a portion of blessedness. Once this idea is established, slavery must disappear. In the caste distinctions of India, matters stand otherwise; with them, natural determination is insurmountable. Everything special about humanity, all that the latter [uniquely] is, is only the second thing against the first. Caste distinction is absolutely first. If one knows this [about India], one can assert that, in India, neither Right nor ethical life had force, nor did true science blossom.[51] Now, for us, natural determinacy is subordinate; it is inherent in this sphere [of nature] that so and so can be thus but can also be otherwise. The Idea must bring forward the moment of naturalness itself. The abstract is absolute equality. We go further. When we contemptuously speak of someone as this "person," [the insult] has its basis in the fact that this expression denotes abstraction.

The first right is that I as a person can exist.[52] But person and right are something abstract. I am not only a person but also a concrete individual. Particularity runs in all directions. We have needs, urges, and inclinations. This particularity is not contained in formal Right. It is of no interest [to formal Right]; this Right makes no distinction between persons; rather [differences are] put aside. [The saying] "Let justice

---

48 Translator: Contrast G.W.F. Hegel, *Phenomenology of Spirit*, trans. A.V. Miller (Oxford: Oxford University Press, 1977), 292: "To describe an individual as a 'person' is an expression of contempt."
49 UN67: Be a person and treat others as persons.
50 UN67–8: When it is said that the first axiom of freedom is that human beings are all equal, this is indeed quite correct. Only [i.e., with this qualification] humans are not equal by nature but simply in freedom.
51 UN68: One needs to know only this one feature about India ... to understand that true science and ethical life could not have materialized there.
52 *Das erste Recht ist, daß ich als Person da sein kann.* This can also mean: "The first right is that I as a person can be here [where I stand]."

be done, though the world perish" [UN68: is to be understood in the following sense]. Strict Right has no regard for the welfare of human beings.

Because context is concrete, a right is only something possible [to act upon]. To action pertain still further [considerations and] contents. Accordingly, a right means a permission, a power; it is only a possibility. For that reason, one can say that a right is only in one person [against another]. The relationship to another is a negative relation; there are no legal mandates [in abstract Right], only legal prohibitions. No doubt, the proposition is often put positively,[53] but it is [17] positive only in expression; in truth, [the obligation] is always negative.[54] Persons are these abstract, self-oriented [*für sich seienden*] singulars. Many teachings [about freedom] have issued from the standpoint of personality. However, it has been forgotten that this is only the abstract [side of freedom]. It is only this abstract immediacy. For that reason, it is also an error to have wanted to ground the state on an original contract [proceeding UN69: from that point of the will]. One usually understands by the universal Will the will of all individuals; however, this is the bad universal and much more the all [than the universal].

The standpoint of personality has been rightly made to count [in Right, for] let us not forget that freedom has the form of universality. [But] it is a fundamental mistake, one that has caused confusion and that many drag around, to think it is the [whole] truth [about freedom].[55] The second [side] is particularity, which does not concern us here. The third is the moment of the singular, the enclosed singularity, the exclusive singularity. Because the person does not have difference within itself, difference falls outside it. This [the outside] is then the sphere of appearance.[56] The [logical] relation is that, since the person is [considered to be] the absolute in itself, everything else falls outside it.

The first [step] is: the person makes a sphere of freedom for itself. This is possession, property. Directly giving oneself existence is the first – property in general. The second [step is]: by giving myself an existence, I am at the same time [UN69: for] another. I have actuality

---

53 Translator: For example, respect the freedom of others.
54 Translator: Do not interfere with the freedom of others.
55 UN69: It is a fundamental mistake, one which has led to great confusion, to regard abstract personality as the ultimate and highest [principle].
56 Translator: It is a sphere of appearance because it is where things make a show of independence.

[*Wirklichkeit*] only through being an object for myself.[57] Indeed, the relation of person to person [completes] the relation to property. By virtue of realizing myself [in things], I am in a relationship to things that are the property of another, that have [another's] will in them.[58] Property acquisition occurs only through the mediation of the will of another – [this second step is] Contract.

The third [step is]: that I as a person am for myself and distinguished from others and at the same time identical with others. Generality enters here and, on the other side, a [single] person. This double relation is essentially my own;[59] this constitutes the stage of wrong in general – namely, on one side [there is] the [18] general and on the other, the particular.[60] Therewith [are] force, crime, and wrong posited. [These steps are so far] anticipated in an historical manner; [this overview is] an advance statement of what the object itself will bring about.

---

57 Translator: "only through being an object for myself," i.e., only through being an object for myself in property recognized by another.
58 UN69: I now step into a relationship to things that are the property of another. My relationship to such things is essentially mediated through the will of another. This second stage is contract.
59 Translator: "is essentially my own," i.e., the double relation to oneself and to others is the inner doubling of self-consciousness, which is universal on one side and particular on the other.
60 UN69: Here occurs the conflict between the general and the particular.

[First Section]

[Property]

The person's vocation is to have property. That is why the person is regarded [by the Romans] as a certain[61] status. Here belong the status of freedom and the status of slavery. From our point of view, [UN69: freedom is not at all a status and] slavery has already disappeared.[62] Slavery belongs to a barbaric, unjust state. To persons appertain as well the relationships of the family. Family rights are not purely juristic relationships.[63]

Freedom in general [UN70: shows itself first in the immediate form of singularity]. That the person is a singular individual [*eine einzelne*] flows from the concept of freedom – from the free being that wills its freedom.[64] The concept [of freedom] must posit itself in existence. The concept [of freedom] realized is the Right. This totality [of concept and reality] does not merely fall within our way of looking at the matter, but is rather the [objective] basis of the free will's being free. [The free will] is the will that overcomes its subjectivity and gives itself existence. This existence is to begin with likewise abstract or immediate.[65] The existent [in which freedom is realized] is something mediated; it embodies freedom. But property is the person self-posited in existence; [the person] is objective to itself; it develops itself into an object.[66]

---

61 Translator: Here I take UN's *gewissen* over Ringier's *gewussten*.
62 Translator: Perhaps Hegel is alluding here to the British and US ban on the Atlantic slave trade in 1807. Obviously, slavery itself had not disappeared by 1819.
63 UN70: [The family occupies] a higher ground [than the juridical], namely the ethical relationship.
64 Translator: Hegel elaborates this point in his discussion of the prince (see this translation, 205ff.).
65 Translator: Perhaps unilateral acquisition is meant here.
66 Translator: *sie spinnt sich in einem Gegenstand an*. This expression is also found at UN70. Henrich doubted whether it could be Hegel's [UN338], but here it is also in Ringier's notes.

What is the interest [that drives] the human being to give itself property? The interest is twofold: the first is an empirical interest to satisfy needs. In this respect, property is subordinate [to need]; it is prudent to have it. The other side is the rational side. The human being must have property not primarily to satisfy needs. In property [rather,] freedom gives itself existence. The interest of reason has worth on its own.[67] When I give myself existence, I am on the one hand this free individual, but on the other hand also a person. At this stage, the person stands [19] in a relationship to other external things. The method for making things ours is of no concern to us here. We comport ourselves to things as an external power against them.[68] Implied by this externality is that we [as physical beings] are also immediately external [to our free wills]. By virtue of our body's belonging to nature, it does not yet belong to our freedom. We must first become its master, make it our own. The same is true of mental skills; only through cultivation does the mind become the existence of external freedom. Abstractly considered, our body and our mind are [only inherently][69] the existence of freedom. In its immediacy, the free will has a relationship to the external [world].

The second thing is that I am a free being.[70] In that I know myself as a free being, I can abstract from everything else. Nothing else has validity for me. Personality alone has [this] further [annihilating] significance. I am a free being for myself; the freedom of the mind is the universal in which everything else is nugatory. That freedom is the absolute foundation and that everything else is nugatory is [a proposition] belonging to the preceding *philosophy*.[71] In that I know and will myself as a free being, everything else is null. If I as a human being come into contact with external things, their independence vanishes against my freedom. The expansion of freedom is pure – [it occurs as] in a pure ether without resistance.[72] What resists me is [only] the external [physical] side, which is one-sided. The fact that external things are right-less shows that only

---

67 UN70: But further, it is the interest of reason to have property because in property freedom gives itself existence. The Concept thus becomes Idea.
68 UN71: External things are powerful against us, and we likewise comport ourselves as a power against them.
69 Translator: Here I take UN's *an sich* over Ringier's *schon*.
70 Translator: The first is that I exist as a singularity.
71 Translator: If "everything else" refers only to unfree beings, then the preceding philosophy is likely Kant's and Fichte's; if it refers also to the state and law, then Friedrich Jacobi is probably meant; see this translation, 90–1.
72 UN71: Herein lies the human being's absolute right of appropriation over all external things.

a person can resist them.[73] For the will, matter is not impenetrable. It is only [impenetrable] for sensibility. Hence, [things] are selfless against freedom. They are mere matter, to which freedom first gives a soul by making them its own; their soul is then precisely the will.

That the thing is in my use constitutes possession;[74] [the thing] is property because the free will turns it into its object. In this possession, the particular interest [of the possessor] then comes in. So, considered abstractly, there can be no property without possession and no possession without property.[75] Property is not by virtue of the will alone, but also by virtue of the will's giving itself existence [in possession]. Possession is essentially property. The substance is merely an abstraction if it has no accidents. The accident is [20] empty without [the substance]. Property and possession can also be separated.[76] I can be an owner and another can rightfully or wrongfully be in possession. Insofar as the possession is separated [from the owner, property] has existence but no longer sensible immediate existence; [it now has an ideal existence]. The [ideal] existence must hold everywhere [against all], and so there enters a new element of existence, namely, the recognition of the other. The possession of another person's thing already indicates that real possession should return to the owner. The positive science [of law] also speaks of the right arising from possession – from lapse of time. The right arising from possession [of what belonged to another] appears here alongside other ways of acquiring property; here possession is a particular [mode of acquisition]. Actually, however, it is quite general [UN72: because possession occurs in all other types of ownership relation]. It must [therefore] be dealt with first (*detenere quid*

---

73 Translator: Since animals also resist the power of other animals, this must mean that only a person has a unilateral right to resist an animal such that the moral equivalence of forces that exists between animals does not exist between animals and persons. UN71: If I as an individual subject come into a fight with external things, this relationship disappears entirely into my freedom.

74 Translator: This is an odd formulation, since for Hegel use is a moment of property distinct from possession. There is no echo of this in UN.

75 Translator: "considered abstractly" may mean considered apart from contract, for contract transfers ownership separately from transferring possession. UN71: Possession and property are really only two sides of one and the same thing; possession is the external side of property considered as a substance.

76 UN71: This separability seems to contradict the [previously] expressed identity. [The contradiction is resolved so.] If the possession is separated from property, then property no longer has an immediate sensible existence, rather the existence must be ideal. This ideal existence exists in the recognition of another, as in civil society property in general is mediated through the recognition of others.

animo dominii).⁷⁷ Other determinations of the possessor are not relevant here, for example, that prohibitions apply to him or that the owner can vindicate [his right against him].

A *thing* is something over which I have power, both physical and moral. The definition of a *thing* also presents difficulties. For according to the definition [just given], scientific and scholarly talents would also be *things*. Now, these are not called things. It is now said: we understand by *things* only external things. The equivocation arises because the understanding imagines determinateness only as external existence. [Yet] the determination of thingness is a general moment; so, arts and sciences are indeed things, that is, I can make them *things*, I can communicate them, etc. [so externalize them]. The reverse is also true; what I otherwise call a thing I can make through my will no longer a thing [if by thing we mean something external], for example, when I have something as [my] property. To say that something has thingness is to say [according to the conventional understanding of thingness] that it has an external existence. [But] if I possess it, then both the external and the internal sides are present [for it is now mine]. I can also make the I itself into a thing when I make myself a slave. Something that is mine is a thing, and at the same time, its being mine makes it not a thing [not external]. Here too the concept [of a thing as something external] contains contradiction in itself.⁷⁸

[We now consider] more precisely the relationship between possession and property. Because [the thing] has an external side, it must [by signs] appear as the thing of a person. We have [21] now to consider these determinations [of ownership]. [The first is] *taking into possession* – that is, the placing of a will into something. The second is that this thing is posited as negative. The possession is at the same time the manifestation of the thing's nullity. It is then use in general. The process of use is the second aspect [of property], by which it is determined that what one uses is something personal. The third is the infinite judgment, that I am reflected into myself from the thing.

---

77 Translator: to hold with the intention to own – a civil (and common) law way of acquiring a property right.
78 UN72: A thing is not a fixed reality that forms an enduring existence merely for itself. Contrariwise [to externalizing what was inward], something [external] in which I have placed my will is no longer merely a thing but rather something at the same time inward, subjective. The I is the most inward, and yet I can also make that into a thing if I become a slave and thereby alienate my freedom, my ego. Accordingly, a thing is actually both something external and something internal.

[A. Taking Possession]

Taking possession involves the following three determinations. [First,] I am a person – this is the immediately free being, [the subject] of development. The first immediate thing is life in general. The second [determination of taking possession] is that the mind joins [its life]; and the third is [the unity of both] that I as an immediate person am a [physical] organism, and this is my general existence, the possibility of all particularity. One can ask if I take [my body] into possession. [The answer is yes.] If I have a will, then I also will to have my body; I can also will not to have it.[79] I have an entire [physical] compass only because I will [to have it]. The body constitutes my immediate existence. Existence is being for another; in my body I am there for another as a free being. It follows from this that I cannot be used as a beast of burden.[80] A Mister Rehberg has claimed that if someone forces [another] physically, he does not attack [his] freedom, [because] one cannot [physically] reach the supersensible.[81] It is just this sophistry of the understanding that separates concept and existence. Whoever attacks my body attacks my freedom as such.[82] That is why what strikes at property is not punished in the same way as an attack on my body.

The second determination [of taking possession][83] is that mind possesses itself, that is to say, is powerful over itself. Mind is free not by virtue of merely being free but by virtue of making itself free.[84] If I practise something, for example, [a piece of] music, we have conceptions [before our minds], and the body does the drill without one's thinking about the body. The same is true of the mind. The human being [22] is

---

79 UN73: As an immediate person I have an organic body. This is immediately mine, and it seems laughable to enquire about the right to take possession of the body. I have an organic body only because I will to have it, and if I do not will to have it, then I do not have it. The animal cannot kill itself, cannot mutilate itself. In that respect [by continuing to live], we put our wills into our bodies.
80 UN73: From the fact that I am free in my body it follows that my body cannot be used as the body of an animal.
81 August Wilhelm Rehberg (1757–1836). For a discussion of his work, see Frederick C. Beiser, "August Wilhelm Rehberg," in *Stanford Encyclopedia of Philosophy* (Spring 2020 Edition), ed. Edward N. Zalta, 11 January 2007, https://plato.stanford.edu/archives/spr2020/entries/august-rehberg/.
82 Translator: as distinct from a particular embodiment of my freedom.
83 Translator: The first was the person as free immediately, in its body, apart from activity.
84 UN73: Mind is that which, through its activity, posits outwardly, makes objective, what it [inherently] is.

inherently mind, but this is merely (real) possibility; involved in [mind] is [the demand] that it make itself objective. Crucially, the human being must take its mind into possession. Plato said it well: The human being learns nothing [new].[85] As a free being, the human must take possession of itself. Self-consciousness must grasp itself as free. Everything depends on whether the human being has possession of itself or not – so, whether slavery is permitted or not. The human being must make itself what it ought to be; it is not instinctual like animals, which do not grasp themselves as free [but] exist as unfree. They have a slavish disposition who are whatever befalls them.

[Our] existing for each other is in the first place external, [the] sensuous in general. If we imagine this to be a state of nature, then what falls within [this picture] is that human beings bring themselves to recognize each other. The wars of barbarous peoples are about this. This is demonstrated in their struggling with each other, each putting the other's life at risk. Each thereby shows the other that he treats life as something nugatory. He demonstrates that he posits his [brute] existence as something negative. But this occurs in abstract times. Right is then this: that everyone is recognized as a free being. However, it should not only matter that I am not a slave in the eyes of others but also that I am not a slave through [what I do] myself. Thus, there is always something rightful about another's making me a slave. I could have died [instead of allowing myself to be a slave]. That no one should enslave another is only a moral demand.[86] But this demand is only a thought. It is good but not real. It is [in] the state, in which we are recognized, that I am a free being. According to abstract Right, it is thus: Insofar as I am free, I should be regarded as such. Accordingly, the human being must first of all take possession of its mind, of its freedom.[87]

---

85 Plato, *Meno* 81c–86c.
86 Translator: This statement is also in UN's notes (see n. 87), so it cannot be doubted that Hegel made it. It is difficult to reconcile with his earlier statements (see this translation, 18, 21) that slavery belongs to an unjust state and must disappear once the Christian idea is established. The moral demand would seem to be the internal, self-regarding one. The juristic demand, rooted in the objective equality of individuated humans in Spirit, is that no one put another to a choice between slavery and death (to the proof of his inner freedom). Human trafficking laws embody this demand. Hegel has no doubt that someone who seizes another's body commits a crime even if the other has not internally made his body his own; see *Outlines*, para. 48.
87 UN73: The human being must take possession of his mind. The dispute, the antinomy, over slavery turns on this. The human being, insofar as he is free only in an

PROPERTY 27

The third determination is the taking possession of external things. This is the absolute [right of] appropriation. In this regard, various determinations related to [this right] need to be mentioned. There are external things. As particulars, these external things do not concern us [as philosophers] – so how a particular thing is taken into possession depends on its [23] nature (for example, [chemical] elements cannot be taken into possession). A general determination [of the right of appropriation] would be: how much anyone may take into possession. The idea that comes to mind is that there should be equality here. [But this idea ignores the distinction between what reason determines and what is given over to chance.] The rational element in possession is *that* I take possession.[88] The other [non-rational side] is particularity, and these instances [of taking possession] are indeterminate. This is just the field of inequality; here belong abilities, powers, contingencies. Here inequality is nature's rationality. This is already shown by the following: if one wants to divide up the earth, then one individual will get this stone, another understanding, etc.[89] [Equalization] would be an infinite progression. [But the incommensurability of things is not the only problem.] Think of the fully concrete differences of individuals. The particularity of individuals would then be juxtaposed to the manufactured equality, and this would make everything unequal again; one already sees here the emptiness of such a determination of the understanding.

---

immediate [or inherent] sense, is not yet free. No injustice befalls the human being who is free only in an immediate sense if he is made a slave. He exists only as a natural will. Defenders of slavery rely on the fact that those who let themselves be made slaves are not free for themselves. Human beings cannot tell simply by looking at each other whether they are really free. In order to be recognized as free, I must also demonstrate that I am free in my existence. The point of the wars between barbarous people is just to demonstrate their freedom in existence. The state is where everyone is recognized by others as free without being required to give evidence of one's external freedom. The injunction to treat no one as a slave is quite right. However, just as valid is the injunction against being a slave. It can always be said that one could have escaped slavery by [risking] death. To make no one a slave is not a juristic but a moral requirement. The juristic claim refers only to the freedom that manifests itself in existence and ceases to apply where this existence of freedom does not manifest itself.

88 UN74: The rational element in possession is that I put my freedom into external things.
89 UN74: The earth is itself something quite unequal, and this shows the unfeasibility of a completely equal distribution. [Translator: The thought seems to be that the denominator is made up of incommensurable things (stones and understanding), so that an arithmetic division into equal fractions is conceptually impossible.]

Whoever first takes something into possession is the owner (*primus occupans*).⁹⁰ Occupation can take several forms. The thing is not mine just by virtue of my willing it so; I must make my will real. Will must have an existence, for by this my will first becomes recognizable by others. The thing must be *res nullius*, otherwise a will would already be in it. With respect to the occupation of something, one can distinguish between the form and the matter. A question arises whether, if I give form to a thing, I can also take the matter into possession. It was said that the form is mine, not the matter. [But this is a mistake.] The *matter* by itself is certainly not for-itself; against my freedom, it is nothing for itself. If I will [to possess] a thing, I also will [to possess] the matter. And the form then signifies my will. What I grasp with my hand, what I lie on, I possess. But this is always only temporary. This taking into possession gains scope through tools – for example, the sea is taken into possession where the ship touches it; also, the sea is the property of the country whose coast touches it. Possession also extends to other things insofar as they can be [juristically] connected to mine because they are [physically] attached to mine (*principale – accidens*). To this context belongs what is found in positive law as *accessio*. Here belong, for example, alluvion as well as game that is on [24] my land. But wounding [the animal] is already the beginning of possession.

It is a matter for the understanding [to determine] what belongs to whom. Rocks and metals can be considered accidents, but also not. So too treasure. To find the right balance [of considerations] is a matter for the understanding; [pros and cons] must be weighed. Here belongs as well the law pertaining to [things found on] beaches, which law has rightly been recognized as unjust.⁹¹ Also relevant to these accessions is *cura*.⁹² As well, *accessio artificialis* (paintings on another's canvas) is distinguished from *accessio naturalis* [e.g., alluvion]. By possessing something, the main thing [*principale*] is mine and [as an add-on] the accident. The converse [view] is that really the product [accession] is

---

90 UN75: It lies in the nature of the matter that priority must here give the advantage.
91 UN75: Things that have washed up on the beach are not, in the nature of the thing, precluded from being my [i.e., the finder's] property [as the law would have it]. [Translator: The law to which Hegel refers gave a beach resident ownership of things washed up on the beach by right of natural accession. His point is that there is nothing in the nature of the thing that favours the beach resident's claim over that of the finder, and so the issue should be settled by the understanding's weighing of advantages and disadvantages. See *Outlines*, para. 55.]
92 Translator: In Roman law, *cura* was a guardianship of a minor past puberty, to which role was attached a duty to manage the minor's wealth.

claimed, but that the producing thing [*principale*] is claimed along with it. [On this view,] what is taken into possession is only the product (for example, the wild animal and fish, etc.). But the meaning [of extending possession from the accident to the principal thing] is: he at the same time takes into possession the enduring thing, the universal.[93] (One wants the exclusive right). Here belong more detailed determinations having to do with the will to possess the universal (for example, when one restrains one's manner of enjoyment so that one can always enjoy).

A second [UN75: ideal, higher] way of taking into possession is forming.[94] I thereby give the entity [*Ding*] the predicate of thing [*Sache*] [into which I put] an objective, lasting form. Now my presence is not needed.[95] There are a great many ways and means of forming according to the difference in objects (for example, taming animals, cultivating land, feeding animals, pulling trees). The third way of [taking into possession][96] is designating that something should be mine. Here is this [sign] whereby I make a *thing* mine. I do not give my form to it – I merely symbolize its being mine. Physical grasping is also a sign – also there for others, but it is not only a sign. By contrast, the sign [that is intended as a sign] is only for the imagination of others.[97] A sign is an existent that is supposed to harbour a meaning different from its own (e.g., the colours of a cockade). For example, newly discovered lands were marked by the first possessor with a cross.

[B. Use of the Thing]

[25] The second [determination of ownership] is that [the thing] is *mine*.[98] Inasmuch as it is, I no longer leave it as it is but rather annul it, negate it. Thus, essentially connected with this [determination] is the ideality of the thing; this is the dimension of use, of utilization in general. Here use means to consume more or less. What I use I partly wear out. In this use lies the reality of my possession. It follows from this

---

93 UN75: Because those who take possession are assumed to be rational, the universal, the enduring possibility, is taken along with the product.
94 Translator: The first was physical occupation.
95 Translator: Here Hegel seems to forget that physical grasping also confers a right to possess even after the thing is put down.
96 Translator: Ringier wrote "of forming," but this must be a mistake, since Hegel treats signing as a way of taking into possession distinct from forming.
97 UN75: Marking expresses the idea that I merely signify the mine in the thing. There thus arises a relationship to another.
98 Translator: "mine" in the sense of being subordinate to my ends.

[that] if I have the complete use of the thing, then the thing belongs to me; it is my property. It's just a different side of me. The entire use is the way in which my will is manifested in the thing. Whoever has the entire use is the owner. If use and ownership are distinguished, then the usufruct, the use, cannot exhaust the concept [of use]. If a distinction is present, this can only mean that the use is partial or temporary. If I cede use to another [while maintaining ownership], then merely temporary or partial use is understood.

A distinction is made between *usufructus* and property – here belong *dominus utilis* and *dominus directus*. In the result, an empty lordship [in the non-user] is created; for example, a feudal relationship is usually such an empty lordship.[99] [Where] the masters have beaten their dominion into money, the true meaning of these dominions is that they are [by virtue of the rents collected by the lord],[100] essentially *dominium utile*. There are, [however,] many relationships where the *dominium utile* and the *dominium directum* are separated. In this relationship, [the lord's] mastery consists, not in relating to this thing as such; rather he has an existence solely in relation to my [the vassal's] will.[101] That would be an empty lordship. The particular relationships that partly belong here include, e.g., [a] the use of the *superficies*. The *superficiar* has use of the surface towards his salary; [b] the emphyteutic contract, that is, the right to plant and use the ground [on condition that the user improve the land for the owner]. Such a relationship [26] cannot be dissolved.[102] If I have something for my use in its entirety [with no time limitation], I am the owner.

Furthermore, the thing is a singularity: I own as this [individual], and the thing [I own] is a particular this. But another distinction must be made [between the singular thing and] the inner universality of the thing; this is the thing abstracted from its practical qualities [making it useful for my particular needs]. Its universal quality is its ability to

---

99 Translator: Hegel's point in this paragraph is that, while the distinction between *usufructus* and property is unproblematic as long as the tenant's right to use is temporary, it becomes a conceptual monstrosity if the tenant's right is of indefinite duration, since there are then two separate owners of the same land. The feudal relation between the *dominus utilis* and the *dominus directus* was such a monstrosity. It left the owner with an "empty lordship," for he was lord over something he had no right to possess, use, or alienate.

100 Translator: See *Outlines*, para. 62.

101 Translator: This would be the case if the tenant had use of the land indefinitely in return for fealty to the lord.

102 Translator: It is the indissolubility of these relationships that puts them into the category of empty lordship.

satisfy need [in general or as such]. We call [a thing's] general capacity to satisfy need its value, and in that respect, it can be compared; it can be sold. This is where money is relevant; it expresses the general value of the thing. According to the concept of ownership of a thing, it belongs to me as a singular thing, but it is not only a singular thing; rather, it is also something general, and this is value, and insofar [as I am the owner of the singular] I am the owner of its value.

However, with a feudal contract, this does not occur. Only the use is bound to my person; I have no claim to the value. But if [as in an entailed estate] the use is mine indefinitely [in the sense] that it remains with my family, then I am to be regarded as an individual within the family; therefore, I am not the owner of the value. If an individual is enfeoffed with a fief, one can say that it stood within his power to accept it or not. But this is not the case; it was given to the entirety [of the lineal heirs]; I am only one of these. For that reason, the possessor of an [entailed] fief may not give it away. Such a relationship may well exist, but when the family dies out, the asset reverts to the [heirs of the] feudal lord. The feudal lord has to that extent a kind of property. But his type of use is completely contingent [on the vassal having no heirs]. However, the other [kind of fief – the fee simple –] is quite in accordance with the nature of the fee. What I as an individual own, I own in accordance with the concept [of ownership – that is, I own its] value.

These determinations [possession, use, ownership of value] make up full property, and the honours [attached to the entailed estate] imply nothing other than that for me [the possessor] there is still an intractable knot. To that extent my property is unfree. The human being feels free when the matter is rational, when it accords with its concept. As the moment of mere [empty] lordship [27] falls away, [the fief] becomes the common property [of lord and vassal];[103] the moment of lordship is then simply the right of property. Only in modern times has the concept of free ownership been properly developed. The Christian religion prohibited slavery; there must be no slaves in Europe. However, the freedom of ownership has arisen only recently. By considering the right of mere lordship as something concrete [through the rents the lord receives], we have a [genuine] owner of the thing.

It can be that community [of property] in respect of things prevails even if it is a matter of choice whether they are owned in common. One may question whether community of goods is something

---

103 Translator: The lord shares the use through the rents and tributes he receives; see *Outlines*, para. 62.

rational. One could also say that community of goods ought to exist. [But this would be a mistake.] It is different in marriage, where neither one stands to the other as an [abstract] person. But where the one against the other is a person, matters stand differently. What is certain is that strictly private property must exist.[104] What pertains to the subject of brotherhood does not come into consideration here; rather we are concerned with the Other. Right is higher than disposition – that is, Right is serious; I can't make demands on [another's] disposition. We have seen that I exist as a person. As a person, however, I am a singularity;[105] if I am [a singularity], then property should be mine as a singularity. I as a singularity should be free in my concrete existence. Plato lacked something here: with him, particularities do not come to their right. Further reasons [for private property] do not belong here: for example, to promote industry, or to have pleasure in material things and in the display of one's wealth and energy. All this has to do with extraneous circumstances. The human being as such is not satisfied [with these explanations]. What in modern times has been said of the dissolution of servitudes is based on this principle [of individual personality].[106]

Insofar as the moment of lordship ceases to exist, all the determinations [of communal property] reduce themselves to joint ownership. Insofar as [the arrangement] is one of joint ownership, then this implies that the commonality is dissolvable. This does not preclude one from entering into a location contract [permitting another to use one's land in return for services] but [28] this location contract must be time-restricted, for otherwise I would have surrendered my individual personality.[107] A [time-unrestricted] share is not possible, even if one says that it could be based on a contract. We distinguish [between what people choose to do and] what is appropriate to the concept [of ownership].

---

104 UN77: One can ask whether community of goods is inherently rational. This question must be answered in the negative, because the presentation of free personality is inconsistent therewith.
105 Translator: not a member of a brotherhood.
106 Translator: By "servitudes" Hegel must mean the personal services to the lord that typically went with feudal land tenure as well as encumbrances on property for the personal benefit of a lord such as his hunting and judicial privileges. What we today call servitudes – encumbrances on property for the benefit of other land (a right of way, for example) – do not contradict the principle of free personality; they reconcile the use rights of neighbouring persons.
107 Translator: UN77 wrote *Sozietätsverträge* (partnership agreements) rather than *locatio-Vertrag*.

By virtue of my having private property, the use of the property is in my power.

It has been remarked with regard to the feudal relation that it [gives the lord joint] ownership of the matter. The tithe is also such a relationship. The tithe lord receives a definite tenth [of the yield] that proceeds from a certain technique of agriculture.[108] Often it is actually forbidden [for the tenant] unilaterally to change the [technique], where the tithe lord could lose. If I increase the yield of the land, I [may] have to give the lord more than I owe, because my costs for this land development are very high. In England, attempts were made to take the tithe away from the clergy. But tenants resisted, because they agreed with the clergy that they should give less [than a tenth], i.e., some fixed [amount], so that they could improve yields in the field without having to give more than usual. It is remarkable to a rational mind to fix such a thing [as agricultural technique] for all time. We regarded it as social progress that much of this sort of thing was done away with. The Roman agrarian laws evinced just this struggle between common and private property. However unjust the expropriation [of the patricians] may have been, the higher interest that there be private property asserted itself.[109] There is one more thing to consider.

Use is the external manifestation of ownership. Therewith ownership steps into time. Use is the sign of my ownership. It appears in time. In general, the objective reality [of ownership] in time is what continues through time. It follows that ownership is valid [only] as a continuance [in time]. Without this, my will has no existence in this thing; it doesn't show itself. Thus, for others the thing becomes ownerless. This is the reason for prescription.[110] It has this thought determination for [29] its basis: I must show that the thing is mine. This sign [of ownership] is not confined to use.

---

108 Translator: Ringier wrote *Ort der Kultur*, but UN (77) heard *Kulturart*, which makes more sense.
109 UN77: With tithing, it is common for the tithe payer to be under a duty to obtain the tithe lord's approval for a change in agricultural technique. Clearly, this provision is likewise [like the entailed estate] very restrictive and incompatible with the freedom of property and industry. Wanting to determine for all time some [rule] for external and sensible things already runs against current thinking. We see this also in the progress of society; as thought develops, we no longer find repose in settled ways of doing things. The Roman agrarian laws evinced just this struggle between common and private property. So unjust were the first acquisitions of the patricians that the higher interest of private property asserted itself.
110 Translator: lapse of ownership through disuse.

[C. Alienation of Property]

The third moment [of ownership] is that I can alienate my property. Possession is negation.[111] I can alienate the property. The matter is mine only because I can alienate it. The *glebae adscriptus* cannot do this.[112] [However,] I can alienate the thing only insofar as the thing is by nature external to me.

A capability, activity, or skill are also in my possession. [These too can be alienated. However,] there are kinds of things that are inalienable [UN78: such that, if they are factually alienated, my right to them never lapses.]. Such are those that belong essentially to our personhood: our ethics, religion, conscience, etc. cannot be alienated. The mind is first a mind when it is a mind of one's own. Insofar as the mind remains at the stage [where it has not been taken up into the self], it is an external, natural mind, because it is only a potential; its inner being is abstract externality. Insofar as [the mind remains in that condition], one can sell one's freedom. Such an alienation, however, contradicts the idea of mind; the mind ought to be self-consciously [*für sich*] what it is. If a human being is made a slave through a contract, the contract is null and void. The same is true of one's ethics; this too can be alienated [in an empirical sense], but the guilt does not go away. Such a contract is inherently and actually null and void. The same is true of religion. I can make myself into a passive being who accepts what another determines – that I must believe this or that. Insofar as I will to think for myself, I have the absolute divine right immediately to do so. These rights are imprescriptible.[113]

I can alienate something from both my mental and physical skills. I can commit [30] to work for someone. If we want to call it power [instead of skill], then the expression is different, but then the externalization is not distinguished from [that of my] power [in general]. To the extent that [I alienate] the entire compass of my activity by committing to work for someone for my entire life, I have done what I may not do: I have alienated something inward. If I were to alienate the totality of my product, then nothing would remain for me. Therefore, I can alienate [my productivity] only temporarily – only by a [limited] quantity. If I

---

111 UN78: Use appeared as the negation of the thing. I can now further detach myself from the property and alienate it from me.
112 Translator: A *glebae adscriptus* was a serf so tied to the land that when the land was transferred, so was he.
113 Translator: They cannot lapse through disuse.

alienate all the particulars, then I alienate the universal. A slave or serf or domestic servant must do the same thing, but the [slave and serf] are distinguished [from the servant] by just this [UN79: that the former are bound to work for another for life]. Accordingly, this makes for a fundamental distinction.

Here belongs the question concerning book publishers.[114] In acquiring a property in a writing,[115] I can alienate it, and it then becomes the property of another. One can think that the other who [now] owns it can also make copies of it. [This is not so.] When I produce a thing, I give it form. The form is always mine. If what I produce is something mechanical [like a list of names], then it is not something peculiar to me; anyone could have made it. [So, anyone who buys it can also copy it.] Mechanical work is something quite generic. Now, a book is also [in one respect] something external [and mechanical – rows of words on paper]; everyone can copy and reprint it. But nevertheless, [the author's] property remains.[116] With a true work of art [a painting or sculpture], this is not the case [not everyone can copy it]. A special talent [re]produced it. Only the fame in the imagination [of others] remains with [the original artist]. With an [original] artwork, it is understood that another person could not have produced it; he could only have reproduced it. But if [the copier] adds something of his own, then it is his own artwork. And the copy always leaves the original far behind. Reprinting [by contrast] is something quite mechanical, and so the thing [the reprint] does remain [the author's] property and indeed does so qua the thing. The thoughts, [however,] have become public ideas for all. By communicating them, they cease to be mine. Another will say he also thought of this, and he will present [the idea] again.

If they are not his thoughts, however, we call this plagiarism, scholarly theft. Plagiarism is more a matter of honour than of theft.[117] With books, it is primarily [31] plagiarism that makes books expensive. Books on geometry, etc. come out every six months. The tenth book is made from the previous nine [making them superfluous]. Positive laws [seek to] remedy the mischief, but they will be effective only to a minor extent as long as honour is not forthcoming, because one book makes the other

---

114 UN79: Here belongs the question concerning intellectual property [*geistiges Eigentum*].
115 Translator: Ringier wrote *Indem ich etwas Geistiges geworden*, but I follow UN, who wrote (79) *an einer Schrift erworbenen Eigentum*.
116 Translator: because the form of the matter is his.
117 Translator: because there is no property in ideas.

redundant. With regard to literary work, when a copy is sold, everyone who has a copy is capable of duplicating it. Whoever reads a book has acquired only the product, not the production process,[118] and to that extent the ways and means belong to the author. So too with other inventions. The inventor often remains the owner [of the ways and means by which his idea was executed]. The one who invents [something] is, as it were, the first possessor; and in that sense [the ways and means] are his property. In communicating what he owns, he also parts with the single product. But the possibility to communicate it further is his. If something has already been extant for a long time, then prescription becomes applicable. As long as the author lives, he still has the right – he can improve [the work]. But after death, the right is discontinued, and that it should forever be the property of the family is remarkable.[119]

A major consideration [with respect to the duration of copyright] is the public interest. Everyone who externalizes something must direct himself to what concerns everyone. If a book is too expensive [because copyright keeps the price high], the public has the right to complain, because its need thereby comes weightily into consideration. But national monuments belong to the people – it is the Mind [of a people] through which they remain the property of the people. Thus, it is said: we dragged antiquities, [e.g.,] an anthemion,[120] out of Greece. But because this Mind no longer lives, these things became alienable.

One can also speak of the alienation of life. Do I have a right to take my life? The main point of view [from which to deal with this question] is the moral one [concerning what is and what is not courage]. With regard to justice, one could say that the whole of my life, of my external being, is not external to me, so that I cannot consider life as alienable. All justice is an existential realization of the freedom of all. Insofar as I alienate my life, I alienate [32] my [freedom and therefore my capacity for] rights [UN80: and this I have no right to alienate]. On the other hand, by sublating [cancelling qua natural but recovering qua rational] my life [in the State], I sublate [abolish as one-sided but preserve as

---

118 Translator: not the mind that went into the product.
119 UN79: Through the sale of a book, the single copy is alienated, not the possibility of duplicating it. The particular form of the book is the subjective element to which the author is entitled. The particular connection of thoughts that makes up the content of a book is, as it were, first taken into possession by the author and is therefore his property. Use [by others] enters here as a kind of prescription, so that an invention, a book, becomes with time, the property of all.
120 Translator: An anthemion is a pattern of painted or sculptured lotus flowers and palm leaves used to decorate ancient Greek pottery and architecture.

realized] the Idea's side. But this sublation is itself an existential realization [of freedom]; this negation is at the same time an existent for others [UN80: whereby I demonstrate my freedom]. [However,] this is only a possibility.[121]

Courage is just that which can abstract from [life]. But courage is formal when this abstraction is mere abstraction.[122] [Whether courage is true or not] depends on the content [for which one risks one's life]. The positive content must be an idea,[123] the content that completes the first formal moment [of risking life and without which] the alienation of life indicates nothing but this merely formal daring. The content [side] is injured if the formal [side] constitutes [courage] on its own. The universal right to sacrifice life can be spoken of only in ethical life. That the human being has a duty to give his life for the Idea of ethical life is certain. But doing it by your own hand [is another matter]. This is an absolute contradiction, for one enquires here about [a right to do] something whereby all right is cancelled. We see [suicide] as a misfortune that is contrary to what is right. In being motivated by an Ethical Idea to sacrifice his life, a man exposes his life to danger, and the cancellation of life comes from outside him. As an immediate person, I am an expression of the Ethical Idea, and so I must offer my life for this Idea. But the force must come not from myself, but from an external source.

---

121 Translator: "this is only a possibility" can mean that I risk my life for the Idea but do not kill myself; or it can mean that not all risks of life are risks of life for the Idea.
122 Translator: "when this abstraction is mere abstraction," i.e., when this abstraction is merely for the sake of showing indifference to life.
123 UN80: the Idea.

[Second Section]

[Contract]

The transition [to contract] consists in this: I am essentially an owner, [my freedom] has existence, but I alter the existent in use. I consume the *thing*, but I must posit myself in the thing alienated from me.[124] I must posit the thing also as external. To alienate the property and, in the alienation, to remain owner – [that is the problem]. I must put the thing of which I am an owner outside me [without ceasing to be its owner]. The alienation of property is the mediation of the [contradiction] that I am the owner [of what I cease to own], and this suffices for the abstract concept of contract.[125]

The [33] process by which I am – remain – an owner in ceasing to be one and because of that become an owner [in an objective sense] – that is the transition to contract. That I am an owner is the enduring moment. The generality of this determination [of ownership] presents itself as a general Will, not the will of a plurality. This can also be understood from the [other] side: in [unilaterally acquired] property I have given my [freedom] an existence; but because I have this [property] only in my individual opinion, this moment is mere externality [without objective confirmation].[126] The genuine reality of positive freedom [requires] that I look at the existence of my freedom in [another] will. By

---

124 Translator: in order that my ownership be valid objectively.
125 UN81: The unity of alienating and maintaining ownership is the abstract concept of contract.
126 UN81: The existence of my freedom [in unilateral possession and use] must be considered as inadequate to its concept, because I have only the opinion that the external thing is mine. The reality [of my freedom] consists in this, that I behold the existence of my freedom in the will of another.

virtue of that, this [other will] is identical with my being: [this unity of wills] is the positive identity in which I view myself [as an owner]. This is therefore the ground and element for my will's existence.

The further thing, then, is that I have property, but mediated through the will of another. This mediation requires closer consideration. It is no longer the same relationship [as possession and use]; it is rather that I have property through the will of another. Thus, contract is a rational moment [in the development of property]. I seek the other's agreement, wherewith it[127] is my property. [Empirically speaking,] contract depends on the need from which I proceed. We take something into possession for the sake of this interest [in the satisfaction of need], but reason demands this. And here too [in contract], it is a necessity of reason that I have property through another. People enter into contracts from need, but [when] they exchange with one another, donate, etc., this is the fulfilment of reason. I divest myself of property and indeed in such a way that it becomes the property of another – here too [on the other side] free will is involved. There is here a doubled will. In exchange, [the will] is both augmented and doubled, [Angehrn, Bondeli, Seelmann: in contrast to] donative purpose.[128]

A contract can be made, and the real [empirical] doings can be distinguished from what is going on in the ideal world. Persons are independent. The contract proceeds from their free choice [*Willkür*]; it is for a particular will that they enter into a contract. There are only two [self-interested] persons who contract – even if they are also moral persons. They have particularistic objects. The [34] specific particularities are always only two. The contract proceeds from free choice. [UN81: An ethical relationship has not yet come about here.] [But] what proceeds from the free choice [of each] is a common will. What comes about is always a common will, which has its cause in the [particular] will. [A common will] is a general will posited only by [the parties]. [UN82: An equality of particulars as persons is already an ethical relationship.] Also, the contract concerns only matters of particular [interest to the parties]. As [they are] particular, independent persons, it is their free

---

127 Translator: What is the "it"? It cannot be the material thing I possess, because this is what I alienate. Nor can it be the matter promised in return, for I cannot *remain* the owner of something I never owned. It must be the value of the thing that I alienate.

128 UN81: In so-called real contract, in exchange, this doubled will is double on both sides. [Translator: "on both sides," i.e., for both parties, whereas in gift, the donee has property through the will of the donor, but the donor does not have property through the will of the donee.]

choice that makes the contract, and for that reason, the subject matter [of the contract] is only a particular [interest].

A few applications can be considered here. Marriage is erroneously viewed as a contract. So too the state, but this is false. The latter has been the general opinion [of the state]. As far as marriage is concerned, marriage contracts can certainly occur. Marriage, to be sure, proceeds from the individual. But marriage is an ethical relation; the persons cease to be [separate] persons. Accordingly, marriage is no contract. Kant viewed it as a contract by which each person was supposed to possess the other with a view to the sexual connection. This is a shameful view; any ingenuous person would shudder at it. Likewise, the State is the independently existing universal Will, originating not in the free choice of the individual, but in the obligation and necessity of [the human being's] universal rational nature. And the will of the State is a universal Will. It is a higher necessity, which can be viewed as a power [UN82: of Reason]. Frequently, the power has been physical. Rousseau famously started from this idea.[129] Here [on the contractarian view of the state], individuals are considered as self-sufficient persons. Precisely these atoms make up the general [Will], the foundation of the state. The object of the contract must [then] also be something external [to the individual]. The State is emphatically not external; it is rather the independently existing universal necessity. But [on the contractarian view,] if the state needs men [to risk death for its defence], the individual is nowhere to be seen.[130] What is in and for itself rational is here only the accidental.

A vow is also not a contract; it is a matter of conscience. It's different if I have physically donated [a thing; then ownership is transferred]. [But] what is a matter for conscience I can take back. It is absolutely [35] my own. It's up to me whether I want to fulfil [the vow]. If I have lived in accordance with a vow, I have the absolute right to retract it.

Contract is formal according to its abstract concept when the two sides have different purposes [one to give, the other to receive]. Contract involves two wills. If I agree to alienate something and another agrees to accept it, this is a formal contract. This is gift. A real contract occurs when something else is added, namely, when I [the alienator] will also to be an owner or to remain an owner. I cease to be an owner and yet remain one, and by virtue of that become one [objectively]. This

---

129 Translator: "Man is born free, and everywhere he is in chains."
130 Translator: "The individual is nowhere to be seen" because if the state is viewed as being instrumental to life, then its right to demand life will be denied.

CONTRACT 41

is the rational side of contract, the universal and enduring [element in the transaction]. This universal and enduring [element] is value. This value remains with me; only the quality, the character of the possession, changes hands. That I remain an owner of value is really the point of contract.[131] [Thus,] if one does not receive the same value, it is a *laesio*, which is also legally defined. The law assumes a *laesio ultra dimidium* [*vel enormis*] (e.g., where gold is exchanged for copper).[132] It lies in the nature of a contract that the qualitative thing [I receive] have the same value as the thing I give for it. My will must still be preserved in the thing [alienated]. Possession is not objectively confirmed [as property] and is distinct from property.

Contract is a common will; the other side is that this common will gains existence, [and] this is the performance. Both can be separated. Performance, i.e., the realization, is to be distinguished [from the contract]. Making a contract as such is called stipulating. The stipulation counts as a *contractus unilateralis*.[133] The stipulation is one of the forms of drawing up [a contract]. The content of the contract's subject matter can be very extensive. These particular items become particular fixed arrangements. This is called stipulating. Whether or not the particular aspects are related to the essence of the contract, they belong to its content. The stipulation by itself fixes the contract. A question arises as to whether the contract is complete on its own [with the stipulation] and whether I am bound by it to perform [or whether each party's performance is essential to the other's being bound]. It seems that in the Roman concept of contract, immediate performance is necessary [for the other to be bound] (real contract). Under [36] this [category] are reckoned the *mutuum, commodatum, pignus,* and *depositum*.[134] But [even in these cases,] the contract is complete before I put the thing into [the other party's] hands. The contract can be complete before the performance. With a bailment, this is self-evident. When, as is here [in

---

131 *Dies, daß ich Eigentümer des Wertes bleibe, dies ist überhaupt Bestimmung des Vertrags.*
132 Translator: *Laesio ultra dimidium vel enormis*: the injury suffered by a party to a contract who has received less than one half of the value of what he sold. Under Roman law, the seller could rescind such a contract.
133 Translator: A *stipulatio* was unilateral in that one party asked whether the other promises and the other responded, "I promise." The promisor was then unilaterally bound to the promisee.
134 Translator: *Mutuum*: a loan of a fungible thing, repayable by a substitute. *Commodatum*: a loan of a non-fungible thing, repayable by returning the very thing loaned. *Pignus*: something pawned as security for a debt. *Depositum*: A gratuitous bailment (e.g., depositing one's coat in a cloakroom free of charge).

bailment] the case, I give something with the intention of storing it, the contract is already formed beforehand. The stipulations were accompanied by gestures: they shook hands. With the Romans there was a tradition of making symbols – a sign.

The stipulation by itself is the substantial thing, and the performance is merely a sequel. Fichte maintained that my obligation begins only with [the other's] performance.[135] It is only then that the [other's] will is in earnest. It is easy to regard this thought as shallow. If neither [party] begins [to perform], then [obligation is put off] to infinity; in addition, [obligation] would depend on how much the other had accomplished [towards full performance]. Inasmuch as [full] performance is something intellectual, the mean [point at which part performance creates obligation] would be quite indeterminate. As far as the matter itself is concerned, a contract entails the full obligation to perform by virtue of the stipulation. The contract is an act of the will. By stipulating, the other has expressed his will and has also finally declared it. The externalization of the will is in speech or in some other sign – this is the form through which he gives the will existence, whereby he becomes intelligible. The agreement as a matter of the will is therefore the substantial element; the performance is merely an accident over against the substance – it is nothing in itself. In the stipulation, the substantial thing has already occurred. The will already exhibited a sign in which it has its existence.

Contract is different from promise. If I promise something, I also externalize my will, but this has more the sense of a subjective will. [In contract,] the main thing is that I have now alienated the thing. In promise, something is to become the property of another in the future. Accordingly, [in contract,] the substantial side has already occurred with the stipulation. I cannot unilaterally change my will, because the thing has already become the property of the other; if I don't want to perform, then I infringe his property.[136] The essential thing is to distinguish the externalization of the will [from the performance]. [In contract], the substantial thing is already contained in [the stipulation]. The performance is merely the external sequel.

---

135 Angehrn, Bondeli, Seelmann: Johann Gottlieb Fichte, *Beitrag zur Berechtigung der Urteile des Publikums über die französische Revolution*, in Johann Gottlieb Fichte, *Sämmtliche Werke*, ed. I.H. Fichte (Berlin: von Veit & Comp., 1845–6), 6:108–16.

136 Translator: Hegel's expressed view on what is transferred at contract formation is at odds with the view his philosophy of property seems to require (the implicit view). The expressed view is that the thing is transferred; the implicit view is that the

CONTRACT 43

[37] We can also bring up the classification of contracts. We can state this [now] because the determinations in accordance with which contracts divide themselves already lie in the foregoing determinations.[137] The conventional divisions of contract are the real, consensual, nominate, etc.[138] However, these are inessential distinctions. In the state based on the rule of law, the typical treatise on contracts is stuck in a rut [where inessential categories are thoughtlessly repeated]. Having [the nature of] contracts in view, the [true] determinations are the formal and the real (formal contract is gift); that is, the concept [of contract] contains both kinds.[139] Indeed, the main distinction is between formal and real contract. Further distinctions have been derived from [the distinction between] ownership and use. Thus, the first [species of formal contract] is a gift contract, and, more specifically, an outright gift of a thing, that is, a gift properly so called. The second [species of formal contract] is then the loan of a thing; this is also a gift, but a gift limited to a certain portion [of use]. In this connection appear [more] particular distinctions, such as loans where the borrower must return the specific thing loaned, indeed the individual thing or a thing of the same kind. (The species of the thing is really individual, but I [the lender] view it as generic). [Thirdly],[140] I can donate a service (the use of my powers). Such a service is then also a *depositum* (I provide him with a service while reserving [my powers]). A will might also be considered a gift,

---

thing or its equivalent is, because what the transferee ends up owning is the value of what he alienated. The expressed view makes breach of contract indistinguishable from a tortious withholding of another's property; the implicit view preserves the distinction between breach of contract and tort.

137 Translator: "already lie in the foregoing determinations," i.e., they already lie in the nature of contract considered as a simultaneous alienation and validation of ownership by means of a stipulation alone.

138 Translator: For real contract, see the following note. In Roman law, a consensual contract denoted one that was enforceable by virtue of the agreement alone; no performance was necessary. A nominate contract was one having a specific name – for example, a contract of purchase and sale or a contract of loan.

139 Translator: The real contract belonging to Hegel's classification is different from the real contract of Roman law that he mentioned earlier. Hegel's real contract is an exchange where (in contrast to the formal contract of gift) each party both gives and receives, and it is enforceable by virtue of the agreement alone. Roman real contract is one where (in contrast to consensual contract) obligation on one side depends on performance on the other.

140 Translator: Ringier wrote "secondly," but this seems mistaken. The first species of formal contract is outright gift; the second is the gratuitous loan of a thing; the third is the gratuitous loan of services.

but in application it has still other connections; here enter family and social relationships.[141]

The second [main division of contracts besides gift] is an exchange contract. [Within this category belong, first,] a simple exchange, indeed, an exchange of one thing [for another]. A thing is, on the one hand, a specific thing, on the other, a universal, a thought – value. This thought made into a thing is money. Money can be metal (seashells, paper), but the concept of money is nothing other than the pure value of a thing. Money represents all other things; it encompasses all things. One can obtain everything with it. [The first subdivision of exchange is] exchange of a specific thing or commodity for another or [the exchange of] money for a commodity.

The second [subdivision of exchange] is letting. [This is] when I give the use [of something] and obtain something else for it, a rent. This is also [38] an exchange. The [time-limited] use of a thing is a distinction within the concept [of ownership]. I can repeatedly let a specific thing ([for] interest and the like). Thus, the latter remains my property, or the matter can be a universal thing, for example, money. If I lend out money, then this is a universal thing, [and] I am the owner of the value [of the money].

The third [subdivision of exchange] is the wage contract, *locatio operae* – that is, I render my service. The manner of its alienation – that it be restricted to a definite time or also a definite service – is crucial. These are the three kinds of exchange contract. A *mandat* [is a contract of service] where the service is of an intellectual nature, [one whose exchange value] is indeterminable, where no commensurability enters. The remuneration for that service is called an honorarium.

There is yet a [fourth][142] thing to add, [namely], the completion [through guaranteed compensation for breach] of a contract: *cautio*.[143] The general [category] is the pledge relationship. By giving someone use (with or without interest), I am the owner of the thing. He has only the [temporary] enjoyment of the thing. By giving it over it to him, I see him in possession of the thing itself, but I am still and always the owner. The relation [of pledge] enters in order that [in leaving use of the thing to another] I might remain in real [not just intellectual] possession.

---

141 UN83: Wills do not really lie directly within contract. That such a transfer of property exists does not lie in the nature of the thing [because a will does not effect a present transfer].
142 Translator: Ringier wrote "third."
143 Translator: A security.

[However,] I cannot remain in possession of the actual property, because I have left it to him; I can remain in possession only of the value. This occurs through the pledge. Through it, I remain the possessor of the value [of the thing possessed by another]. The value of the pledge is mine. It is itself only a specific thing and, as such, it is my property. The mortgage and surety are particular techniques [for remaining in real possession of the value of the thing while giving up possession of the thing itself]. It is nothing other than a completion of contract.[144]

---

144 Translator: The pledge is the completion of contract in the sense that, not only is intellectual ownership of the promised value established with the agreement, but actual possession of that value is as well. Thus, the future is entirely absorbed into a conceptual present.

[Third Section]

[Wrong]

This constitutes the third Section of the first Part. Performance [of a contract] is a particular doing, a concern of the particular will. That it ought to be done is something necessary; whether I do it depends on my choice. [39] This separation [between ought and is] is that in virtue of which wrong gets posited. That I have, for example, something in my possession is the side of the particular will. This particular will has [so far] been a consideration external [to the main matter].[145] [Nevertheless,] this particular will is an essential moment [in the realization of freedom]. I am the realizer of the Concept. The particular will as such must come forward not only as [something] necessarily posited along with Right, but also as an essential moment [inwardly] connected with Right.[146]

There are here [in contract] two immediate persons who relate themselves to each other. The particular will can concur with what is Right, but it can also be a particular will for itself. It can just as well *not* perform [its contractual obligation]. So far, the self-renunciation of the particular will has not occurred. Accordingly, the standpoint here [in abstract Right] is just the particularity of the will, which is still immediate in its concept (Right as Concept [still without existence]). As regards the existence of Right, this involves the particular will. It falls to the particular will to realize the Right.[147]

---

145 UN83: We saw with property that it is essential that my freedom have an existence; and with contract it is essential that I externalize. The particular [will] is [thus] present everywhere, but it has still been left to the side [Translator: because the foundation of abstract Right is the free will abstracted from realization].
146 Translator: This is what distinguishes the stage of morality.
147 Translator: Hegel is using the term "particular will" in two senses. In one sense (the sense meant in the first paragraph of this Section) it is essential to the realization of

I relate myself to [my] particular will. The particular will expresses an oppositional relationship to the [general] Will as it exists in itself. The Right in and for itself is not a matter for the particular will [to lay down]. In being laid down [by the particular will], Right is laid down as pretence, and Right as pretence is precisely what wrong is.[148]

There is here a threefold pretence [each a different kind of wrong]. The first is that my particular will wills what is objectively Right, but, while willing it in itself, it is in the wrong with respect to the subsumption of the case under the Concept of Right. But the Right in itself is the [abstract] Concept. Right is in essence something that must exist [through cases being subsumed to it]. [Here] the negation [of Right] occurs in the subsumption.[149] This is the civil lawsuit. (The three stages [of wrong] can be compared to the judgment. In the simply negative judgment, I say that a thing is something other than [x], for example, the flower is not yellow. [Here] I grant that it has a colour; I negate only the particular. So, too, in the first pretence [of the particular will to determine the Right]).[150]

---

the general Will and so is both contained in and differentiated from the general ("I am the realizer of the Concept"). In another sense (the sense relevant to the standpoint of abstract Right and wrong), the particular will is undifferentiated from the generic will; it is the generic will of each particular person with its particularistic ends. This is the will in its immediacy – the will abstracted from realization.

148 Translator: Wrong in general occurs when an action inconsistent with the mutual respect of persons makes a pretence of being permissible. Without the pretence of permissibility, the action does not contradict the Right as mutual respect, and only what contradicts the Right is wrong. There are three ways in which an action inconsistent with mutual respect might make a pretence of being permissible:
(1) the actor might be unconscious of the pretence, sincerely but mistakenly believing that his trespassory action did not constitute a trespass; this is innocent wrong;
(2) the actor might consciously dissemble an action he knows to be inconsistent with mutual respect as one consistent therewith; this is fraud; (3) dropping the dissimulation, the actor might, by intentionally coercing another, explicitly deny that mutual respect frames permissible actions, and this is crime. The criminal too is unconscious of his pretence, not because he honestly believes that his action was consistent with mutual respect, but because he honestly believes he has a permission to act in ways inconsistent with mutual respect.

149 Translator: The innocent wrongdoer's wrong consists in his making an honest mistake regarding the subsumption of his case under the Concept of Right. He thinks his action was right according to the Concept. It wasn't. For example, he mistakenly thinks that the thing he took from another was his own property.

150 Translator: I grant that you have property rights; I simply deny that this is your property.

The second pretence is that the particular will does not will to do what is objectively Right, [but] wills only the appearance of Right; this is the wrong of fraud. (As in the [corresponding] judgment, here the universal is negated [but not the particular]; it is the infinite judgment in [40] its positive form – the judgment of identity that says: the singular is the singular.)[151]

The third [pretence] is crime (the negative infinite judgment or the nonsensical judgment – for example, if I say: The ellipse is no candle).[152] In crime, the singular individual's [right] is violated and also the universal, the Right as such. The third [form of the particular will's pretending to determine the Right] also negates the façade.

[A. Innocent Wrong][153]

The first [kind of pretence] is civil wrong, innocent wrong. Here wrong is present, but it is only a wrong in the subsumption [of the particular to

---

151 Translator: The fraudster truthfully says, "This particular cow, Betsy, is the cow you agreed to buy (the singular is the singular, Betsy is Betsy)," but he knows that it is defective in some way and so knowingly receives an unpaid-for value behind a façade of selling the very thing the buyer agreed to buy for the price the buyer agreed to pay. So, he denies property rights in general but affirms this individual's right inasmuch as he obtains an unpaid-for value by persuasion and consent rather than by force. This is the inverse of the innocent wrongdoer's simply negative judgment, which infringed the particular but not the universal.

152 Translator: See G.W.F. Hegel, *Science of Logic*, trans. and ed. George di Giovanni (Cambridge: Cambridge University Press, 2010), 567–8. How is the criminal's judgment like "The ellipse is no candle?" If the subject and predicate of a proposition are such that there is no encompassing universal allowing a particular judged as not belonging to one species of that universal to be subsumed to another (as in Socrates is not a god but a human), then judgment is impossible, and so purported judgments will involve the contradiction of making a judgment while removing the possibility of judgment. Similarly, the criminal denies the category of rights, thus making judgments of right impossible, yet nonsensically judges that he has a right to his action.

153 Translator: *Unbefangenes Unrecht*. The wrong is innocent in the sense that it is ingenuous or guileless. Here, the wrong's pretending to be right is ingenuous in that the wrongdoer is unconscious of the pretence; he sincerely believes that his action accords with Right. This contrasts to the disingenuousness of the fraudster, who disguises an action he knows to be wrongful as according with Right, and to the culpable guilelessness (called shamelessness) of the criminal, who openly claims a permission to flout a form of Right regarded as merely conventional. Knox and Nisbet translate *unbefangenes Unrecht* as "non-malicious wrong" and "unintentional wrong," respectively. However, malice is a particular motive, and since Abstract Right takes no notice of the fraudster's or the criminal's motive for wrongdoing,

the universal]. The Right in itself is demanded [by the wrongdoer]; he merely denies that the particular case falls outside universal Right. The determinations of objective Right, the legal grounds, make up the middle term [between Right and the particular case].[154] But the determinations of Right are several; various collisions can arise, where the result in accordance with this legal principle can vary from the one in accordance with that. [Each party] makes a claim based on a legal ground. They do not will injustice. There exists a pretence [of the particular will to determine the Right in itself] that must then be removed, but here [where there is no court yet, the particular will] has absolute power [to determine the Right]. The state of nature is the state of injustice.[155] For Right to exist, there is needed a judge who decides right and wrong. The Right in itself has not realized itself [in a judge-less condition]. Both parties demand justice. They are in the wrong only with respect to subsumption. The general Will that is not at the same time a particular will is not present here.

[B. Fraud]

The second [kind of] wrong is the second [kind of] pretence. [Here] the particular will does not choose the [Right] in itself but rather only the appearance of Right, only the external detail [of the transaction]. Certainly, the matter [bought or sold] is not only singular but also universal – it has also a value. One doesn't want the singular thing [by itself]; rather, one wants the universal[156] along with it, [but] the universal is not intended by the fraudster.[157]

    Knox's translation mischaracterizes civil wrong's difference from fraud and crime. Nisbet's translation is better but too far from the German.
154 UN84: In civil litigation, the Right in itself is not violated but rather demanded. That such a legal dispute can arise owes to the fact that Right is not an abstract universal but rather also a concrete [totality] of manifold determinations. The legal principles make up the middle term whereby the particular is subsumed under the universal.
155 Translator: Observe that Hegel says "injustice," not "non-justice," as Hobbes and Kant would have it. The particular will's claiming a right to determine the Right is wrong (a pretence of right) because there is already a social validation of property in the institution of contractual exchange, one whose normativity the unilateral will contradicts.
156 Translator: the value.
157 Translator: The fraudster gives the victim the particular thing he wanted for the price the victim agreed to, but he knows that he is not giving the victim equal value for what he (the fraudster) received.

[C. Force and Crime][158]

[41] The third pretence [and] the third wrong is the violation of the Right in itself as the [wilful] violation of an individual's right.[159] [This is] wrong on both sides.[160] We have here to consider the definition of force. This is a violation, which [idea first] enters here.[161] The concept [of force] is this: it is a wrong that violates the object [the Right] in general, both on its external side and on its conceptual [*an und für sich seienden*] side. The first thing is that [the Right] is violated as an immediate existent.[162] A rightful[ly] [held] object is violated on its immediate, existing side; I can be violated because I have property, because my will is outwardly [embodied], has existence. By [means of] this external side, I can be seized. This matter can suffer violence, and since my will is placed in this external existent, it too is thereby seized. This is how I can suffer force.

I can not only be coerced [on isolated occasions] but also subjugated. My bodily personality can be brought under [someone's] power. But on the other hand, I can just as well not be coerced, because I can abstract from everything. I can abstract from all the external existents by which I can be seized. Whoever wants to grab me, then, will get only an empty shell. I can be coerced, but only if I choose [attachment to the thing by which I am coerced].[163]

The wrongfulness of force consists in this, that [to say] that a free being may be forced is a contradiction. The meaning of force is that the

---

158 Translator: Hegel uses the term *Zwang* in three senses: direct seizure, coercion through threats of seizure, and force, a generic term embracing both seizure and coercion.
159 Translator: The pretence here is that the criminal implicitly (by virtue of his wilful act of force) claims a right to do what is, so far conventionally, wrong; so wrong makes a pretence of being permissible.
160 Translator: Innocent wrong infringes an individual's right but not the Right as such. Fraud violates the Right as such but not the individual right, because the individual's free will was respected (no force or coercion was applied). Crime violates both the individual right and the Right as such.
161 Translator: Neither innocent wrong nor fraud is a violation of freedom because in both the right to freedom is respected.
162 Translator: "as an immediate existent," i.e., as the right in one's body or in an item of property.
163 Translator: But in *Outlines* (para. 92) and in the previous paragraph, Hegel says that because the body and property are necessary for the existence of freedom, we can be coerced through them. We can detach ourselves from them, but the law cannot expect us to.

contradiction is the will's self-contradiction. Its self-destruction means nothing other than that force is annulled and, indeed, again through force. It lies in the concept of [a right of] force that [the right of] force is annulled by force.

The rightfulness of force is that it is a secondary force that cancels the first; the secondary force is in general just.[164] What will later be specified as punishment is force, and indeed, a secondary [force] that cancels a first. The breach of [positive] duties, [42] for example, duties towards the state, does not [at first blush] seem to be [a case of] force. But if I breach a contract, that is definitely a [case of] force.[165] And so too is it with the former.[166] My being enjoined from breaching contracts and [other] duties is just the secondary force. Force is especially so called when that which is violated appears with a reality [e.g., an item of property] of its own. [But failing in a positive duty is also an exercise of force. Thus,] if the natural will remains in a condition of savagery, it exerts force [against its nature]; it fails to do something [leave the condition] that lies in the Idea. If the Right is violated in its existence [e.g., in property], then this is [clearly a case of] force. Force in its negative specification is exerted against something that already exists; [but] the other side is persistence in a natural condition that is not suitable to the Idea [of realized freedom]. Such a state of nature does not concern us. We are at a higher standpoint. In such circumstances heroes arise who take charge of the Idea and stop us from doing things that are culpable before the Idea. That [stateless] condition is a wrong against the Idea.[167]

Objectively speaking, force is generally essential as a second force. Abstract Right is a right of force. It is also usually defined in that way.[168]

---

164 UN85: The right of freedom with respect to force is that [the second force] be [nothing but] the self-contradiction [of the first], that it be the self-destruction [of the first]. The [worldly] manifestation [of this self-contradiction] is that force is annulled through force. This is the right of freedom in force. The rightfulness of force is that it is a second force that cancels the first.
165 Translator: Here again Hegel assumes that the breaching party withholds something that already belongs to another, that the other's contractual property is in the thing rather than in the value of the thing. Counterfactually, this makes breach of contract a tort and a knowing breach a crime.
166 Translator: If someone cheats on his taxes, he withholds something that belongs to the state.
167 UN85: Persistence in a state of nature contradicts the Idea. If someone rises up and forcibly pulls those living in a state of nature into an ethical relationship, then this, to be sure, appears to be a [case of] force, only not in the aforementioned sense.
168 Translator: We think of legal (as distinct from social or political) justice as the justice of a coercive response to wrong.

It is a right of force because wrong is violence against the existence [of freedom]. Thus, an injury to the existence of our [freedom] is an external deed, an external violence, and this then is also a [case of] force. The first force, as a violation of an embodiment [of freedom], is the real wrong; mere damage pertains only to externals. This is crime in general – the [negative] infinite judgment we saw earlier.[169] Here [in contrast to innocent wrong,] we have no difference between the action and the will; rather we have both in their identity.[170] We have a violation that occurs through a willing; the external deed and the will are regarded as being quite identical. Nowadays, [it is said,] there are no longer as many evil people as before because people are more educated. To the contrary, [educated people] know how to form inwardly all sorts of [justifying] ends and purposes, and they hold to be good much that is criminal, evil; instead [of being better], they are dissemblers, that is, [people] who know how to make evil appear good. [43] This makes up the sphere of penal justice in general.

Crime is a violation; it violates the sphere of [a person's] freedom, an existence [of freedom]. Because the sphere of [freedom] is an outward existence and crime the negation thereof, the negation also has an outward existence. As an external action, crime is not only a simple thought determination; it must have an external side. This [external aspect] varies in extent, as a consequence of which crimes are necessarily differentiated. For example, theft, murder, compelling religion, etc. are, to be sure, crimes, but since existence is qualitative, crime must be regarded as diverse. Quality, difference come into play with regard to theft and robbery. Both [crimes] violate the personal presence of the will. [But] theft with a break-in is certainly a worse crime than mere theft. It attacked my protective means, my defences (my castles). Crimes are therefore by nature varied because they are external [actions]. These differences must be fixed here at the outset. The greater or lesser danger to public security constitutes yet a [further] distinction.[171]

---

169 See this translation, 48.
170 Translator: The innocent wrongdoer does not will his action's inconsistency with Right; the criminal does.
171 Translator: The qualitative differences between crimes must be fixed "here at the outset" – that is, prior to civil society, because they derive from the nature of crime as an external action that violates an existence of freedom. The greater or lesser danger to public security constitutes a further distinction that enters with civil society.

The inevitable consequences [of a criminal act] are already contained in the nature of the crime and in the manifestation of its nature. Dangerousness is [salient] from a further standpoint, which, however, does not deserve to be overly elevated. It is the danger of an inherently serious violation [of Right]. This violation qua violation of Right ought not to be; and the justice that befalls [the criminal] is just this, that the inner nature [of the act as a self-contradiction] should be manifested. The [inner] nature is a violation of freedom and therefore a nullity; and this must be [actually] annulled. The crime should be annulled because it is inherently a nullity making a mere show [of validity]. Through civil satisfaction, only the damage is cancelled; but it is not only damage that has occurred but [also] a violation [of Right], which must be annulled. The annulment cannot yet take the form of punishment;[172] rather, the form of annulment manifests itself first as revenge. The violation of freedom must be cancelled.

[44] Where does the violation exist? First of all, the Will in itself, the Right in itself, cannot be injured; the Idea [of Right] purely as Idea is not an existent; it is elevated above all images of injuring. The Idea is the invulnerable life. Neither [once victims are compensated] does the violation have its existence in the one who was injured, nor in the others who were injured by the crime. The criminal [wilfully] violated a right; this implies something negative.[173] Accordingly, this violation is a negation with the form of externality.[174] The external side [the injury to the victim] cannot be made good.[175] The positive existence of the crime lies only in the criminal's will, and it is therefore [a matter of] laying hold of the criminal's positive will. However, his will exists as his external [body], and so he is apprehended in that. It all turns on where the negative has its seat. Its seat is not the Right in itself because it lies in the nature of Right to abide. Nor does the will of the injured harbour the negative; on the contrary, he rejects it, for the positive existence lies only in the will of the criminal.[176] It is his will that has committed the

---

172 UN86: The form of punishment is here still inapt because this comes to the fore only in the state.
173 Translator: "something negative," i.e., that there are no rights.
174 Translator: "with the form of externality," i.e., the criminal did not merely negate rights in thought or speech.
175 Translator: because time cannot run backwards.
176 Translator: The victim rejects the non-existence of his right because the non-existence of rights is just something that the criminal (practically) claims. Thus, the only place where the negation of rights has a semblance of reality is in the criminal's will.

crime. His particular will, which has opposed itself to the general Will, constitutes particularity as such. It is here that [juridical] nihilism has its positive existence. What is to be cancelled is the will of the criminal. Compensating the injured party does not restore the Right.[177] By contrast, the negation of the previous negation does [restore the Right]. This is the essential concept [of retribution].

Legal scholars have thought a lot about this matter [of punishment], but one must say that their efforts have led them astray, [and their errors] have even passed into legislation. The main point is that they saw punishment merely as an evil [UN86: that, instead of cancelling the first, stands beside it]. A second evil is superfluous considering that the first was already one too many. The second evil is added, and it is thought of as the second, the subsequent. However, one should think of it [instead] as the evil of evil.[178] Because they thought of [punishment] as a merely external [additional] evil, they said that one must look for something positive in the evil [to justify it]. This they called a goal [of punishment]. [For us,] the positive thing consists in this, that the negation of the negation is an affirmation. Since they could not find [the positive thing] in this [45] concept [of retribution], they had to look for a positive goal. They said that [abstract] Right has the positive view that positive [goals for punishment] are forbidden.[179] The positive thing was supposed to be the reform of the criminal; others say deterrence. But of course, deterrence [and reform] are positive sides [of something that also has a negative side]. Quite different is the oneness of the concept [of crime and retribution] itself. As [external] sides, [deterrence and reform] can be absent or not.[180] The shallow idea is this: such-and-such follows from crime; therefore, it must stop. But in that way the human being who is punished is made into a means; he is not treated as a free being. The reasonable must be present, and only then is he regarded as free.

Many can take this path [of viewing punishment as a means to an end]. But in the first place, this [kind of punishment] is not a moral

---

177 Translator: Compensation alone does not restore the right because the criminal denied rights as such, not just the victim's right.
178 UN86: The main point in false views of punishment theory is that crime and punishment are seen only as successive evils, not as [standing in a relation such that] one cancels the other.
179 Translator: In reality, abstract Right merely views the pursuit of goals as being properly constrained by retributive justice.
180 Translator: they may or may not work.

action.[181] Naturally, one can allow oneself to be deterred or not; but this has to do precisely with bad [empirical] psychology; only the reasonable is effective. The more one wants to make punishment a deterrent, the more the mind rebels. But punishments carry the idea and implication that the mind is preserved therein. Deterrent punishments have only made men all the more bitter. Montesquieu says of the Japanese that punishments were made very hideous, but the crimes that were committed became all the more grisly.[182]

Threat theory is just as deficient.[183] It has come from the Kantian philosophy. It wants to repress the sensuous motivating forces [of behaviour]. It is said that the threat represses sensuous drives, but one can then say that the worse the crime, the stronger the threat must be. But one can also say the opposite [for the following reason]. The state threatens in order to deter, but people can allow themselves to be deterred or not. [If not,] the state is tasked with carrying out the threat, and people are also given their due. However, if the threat is [justified as] the means [of preventing crime], then one must remain with the [unexecuted] threat.[184] But [one might object,] does not the right to execute the threat lie in the threat itself [because unexecuted threats are not threats]? But [goes the reply] least of all may the state threaten something that is not just.[185] What [the state] threatens must be intrinsically just, because it is the state that is threatening it. Are we going to say that justice [46] consists in this, that the criminal knew that the threat would be carried out? [Are we going to say that] threats generally give [the threatener] the right to do what was threatened [if the victim knew the threat would be executed]? As for the improvement of the criminal, this is indeed an

---

181 Translator: It is technological manipulation rather than punishment, and, even if the person is deterred or reformed, this results from a calculation of advantage, not from moral education.
182 Baron de Montesquieu, *The Spirit of the Laws*, trans. Thomas Nugent (New York: Hafner, 1949), bk. 6, chap. 13, 85–7.
183 UN87: Threat theory has found its chief advocate in [Paul Johann Anselm] Feuerbach [1775–1833]. At its bottom lies the Kantian view of freedom's struggle against sensuous drives. [Translator: For Feuerbach's threat theory of punishment, see his *Revision der Grundsätze und Grundbegriffe des positiven peinlichen Rechts, Erster Theil* (Erfurt, 1799), 49ff.]
184 Translator: One must remain with the unexecuted threat, because once the threat fails to deter, its justification as a means to prevention is spent.
185 UN87: But at the very least, the state may not threaten something that is not inherently just, and so nothing in this pretentious expression goes towards grounding

essential side [of punishment].[186] But the crime as such must be cancelled in external existence. Improvement is also something ambiguous.

The nexus between punishment and crime is just only as their identity within the concept [of crime as a self-destructive denial of rights]. The mind can make un-happen what has happened. The will is not the absolute determinateness of mind [it also has a universal side]. That is why crime can be made innocuous. The state can view the crime as an event [of no normative significance]. It can pardon, but this no longer belongs to the sphere of justice. However, if a court includes considerations of mercy, it ceases to be just. The general nature of the reversal is this: crime turns back against criminality itself (one hears this often in spiritual stories). What is first of all to be considered regarding crime is the justice in crime in and for itself.[187] The other moment is that the crime is also directed against the criminal qua criminal. This is the reasonable in and for itself. In religious terms, it is essential to convince the criminal of his crime, so that he doesn't believe that he is being beaten to death like an animal, like a mere animal.

The will of the criminal is also determined as [something] particular. [His] particularity must receive its due. The repayment of crime is united with the rational meaning of crime [as a denial of rights]. But the particularity of [the criminal's] will is also included in this reversal. The criminal, in committing the act, does this as a particular individual. He did it; his personal opinion is precisely that he did it. But since, as a particular [individual], he is also a universal [agent], he has done something of universal [significance] in his particular determination. This is just [a consequence of] the rational side of his nature. His particular action has a meaning partly peculiar to him, but [partly] it also set up a law – a law under which he subsumes himself. [47] He has violated [someone], so it is permissible to violate him as well. That the same thing that he did befalls him is implied in the deed. Others do not recognize [his law as valid] in and for itself, but he recognized it,

---

the right to punish. [Translator: The right to execute the threat cannot come from the bare concept of a threat, for if it did, every unlawful threatener would have a right to make good his threat.]

186 Translator: The rational agent in the convict's shoes would see the nullity of his principle and accept the normative authority of the general Will. But the justice of punishment does not depend on the criminal's actually being improved. Hegel will later say that actual improvement is for the criminal himself.

187 Translator: What is the justice in crime? Hegel cannot mean the retributive justice because that is "the other moment" mentioned in the next sentence. Perhaps he means that the category of crime has a place in ethics as the radicalization of the particular will needed to show its nullity and in that way to prove the normativity of the general Will (which so far is merely something posited by the particular will in contract).

[so] it may be applied against him. This is the second side directly connected to the first. Notably, Beccaria grasped this [connection] and said that one may not punish with life.[188] The answer lies in what has been said.[189]

Against the right of the state to impose the death penalty, the presumptive will has been adduced.[190] The rational must be presumed. [However,] the state is not [based on a] contract such that someone would have to perchance consent to laws; it is everyone's duty to enter into a state. [The true idea about consent is this.] The will brings forward an action in which another is violated. That is a simple action. At the same time, his action expresses a law. Therewith I externalize my universal side. When I say "I," I say all; I have thereby externalized myself as a universal, because formally I am a rational being. Accordingly, through such an action I have set up a law that, however, comes back only at me. That is the formal side. There can be no talk of a presumptive will to allow [or not allow] oneself to be killed. In this respect, the criminal is honoured in punishment, because the [penal] action is then in accordance with the law he has set up. In punishment, he receives his own law. Precisely this is the honour that befalls him. All other views [of punishment] fail to preserve the honour of the criminal – he is treated as a means.[191]

In being brought under his law, the individual [criminal] is violated, and this is what we call discipline [*Züchtigung*]. Discipline is different

---

188 See n. 190.
189 UN87: Crime by its nature turns back against itself. Against a criminal, punishment simply makes count what lies in his own inherent and actual will. The will of the criminal is essentially determined as a particular will. Particularity also has its right. In the first instance, the criminal who commits the action does something in particular, and his deed is a violation of another's freedom. That *he* has done such a thing is his particular will; at the same time, however, he has done something of universal significance or has set up a law. The animal as such does only particular things. Do what he will, however, the human being therein simultaneously does something universal.
190 Translator: By Cesare Beccaria (1738–94) in *Of Crimes and Punishments*, trans. Jane Grigson (New York: Marsilio, 1996), chaps. 2, 16. His argument is that since self-interested individuals will give up the smallest portion of their liberty consistent with public order, they cannot have consented to give up the entirety, and so the death penalty is illegitimate force.
191 UN87: In a deed that constitutes a crime, there is also the [matter of] consent [to punishment] to consider. The express consent of the individual is not required in order to treat him as a criminal [he impliedly consents by virtue of the wilfulness of his crime]. Further, crime is avenged in punishment insofar as [punishment] is considered rationally and thus insofar as it is treated in accordance with the idea that it flows from crime itself. In punishment, the criminal's own law is visited upon him.

from improvement [which connotes an inward change]. In discipline, his will is [UN88: violated] in his existence. Mind you, discipline can serve improvement. He comes thereby to feel the nullity of his particularistic will [because] in discipline it is posited as negative. He becomes conscious of the fact that his particular will is justified only if it accords with the Concept [of Right], otherwise not. In morality this is expressed so: do unto others what you would have them do unto you.[192] Still, this presupposes that I should will the Will that is in and for itself. Discipline cannot be made the purpose [of violating the criminal's will]. It is more the purpose with children, but still not entirely. With reform, [48] the inward state of the will is made the purpose. That is absolutely an act for [the individual] himself. Reform is essentially a matter for my own will, and this cannot be the direct purpose of another.

The specific form [UN88: in which this turnaround of crime can be demanded] is called retaliation: *jus talionis*. This is a violation of the violator; the term *retaliation* implies both. We said earlier that a crime is specified qualitatively and quantitatively. The cancellation of the violation is [likewise] specified in both respects. This identity [between the crime and its cancellation] is more precisely what is called retaliation. This is therefore the true [UN88: view of the nature of punishment], and it is the ancient view. The general rule is that the criminal should have done to him the same as he did. But the same, not in an external sense, but rather in an inward [conceptual] sense.[193] Just as in exchange I remain an owner of the thing while receiving different things, so here. One has to take an [equal] value.[194] The injustice must be repaid to me according to its value. With murder, payback is qualitative; his blood must likewise be spilled.[195] But with other [crimes], payback consists in an [equal]

---

192 UN88: This expression is indeterminate inasmuch as it is merely formal. It must always be determined beforehand what objectively I should do to people and what they should do to me.
193 UN88: The same thing that was mentioned with respect to exchange enters here as well. In any case, the matter goes on within the sphere of the will [not externally]. This ideal sphere, which stands altogether above the qualitative, all the more allows commensurability between one and the other.
194 Translator: Here Hegel implies that the thing of which I remain the owner in exchange is not the thing promised to me but the value of the thing alienated.
195 UN89: With [the crime] qualitatively determined as murder, the only true retribution is the death penalty, according to the expression: whoever sheds [human] blood, [by man] shall his blood be shed [Gen. 9:6]. [Translator: With murder, which is the absolute extinguishment of personality, the only equality is qualitative sameness: the death penalty. With other crimes, which impair freedom qualitatively more or less, equality must mean equivalence.]

value, imprisonment etc. When one says an eye for an eye, a tooth for a tooth, this is formal. And people have sought to refute this [principle] with absurdities [suppose the victim has only one eye]. Just as one renounces qualitative sameness in exchange, so one must not remain with the [qualitatively identical] violation of the criminal. Every action in its immediate existence is also something inherently general.[196] How the value is to be determined depends on custom as well as on the social status of the person.[197] There must be nothing cruel in the infringement. Equalization is a matter for the imagination; the imagination of a people [decides] whether this is worth that.[198] In this sense, therefore, the most important point of view is retribution [not qualitative sameness]. But it is not the individual who [finally] exacts retribution.

At our standpoint, we do not yet have a court; rather we have the concept of the unilateral will. This being only the particular will, it is left to it to execute the Right. But then the cancellation of crime is to that extent only revenge. However, the form of revenge is not essential [to retribution], but rather only one form [thereof], one that must be transcended. Revenge can be justified. In the [49] so-called state of nature, revenge is justice. The execution of justice through revenge is altogether accidental because it is the action of a subjective will. The subjective will can inject its idiosyncrasy into the execution of justice. Through this modification, justice can become unjust. Since the subjective will is wounded [by the crime], his entire personality is invested. He proceeds quite unjustly.[199] This retribution is thus something contingent. However, it should be not contingent but necessary; otherwise, it is revenge. Because it is the particular will [that exacts retribution], two particular wills oppose each other. The first violation has its cause in the particular will, against which the reversal of crime [in retribution]

---

196 Translator: All specific criminal injuries to the person and property are more or less injurious violations of the right to freedom punishable by a violation of the right to freedom of an equivalent injuriousness.
197 But see n. 540.
198 UN89: A more precise yardstick is nowhere to be found.
199 UN89: Revenge can be perfectly just in its content. In a so-called state of nature there can be heroes, adventurous knights, who make the administration of justice the object of their particular wills. This substantial will can now inject its particular sensibility into the administration of justice, and thus the administration of justice can exceed the proportionate and become unjust. The subjective will can invest its infinite worth and zeal into every insult. Furthermore, by the individual's stepping forward in his particularity, revenge makes the particular will malicious; there are two particulars that confront each other.

has something necessary about it. [Yet] the particular will that steps forward to repay [the wrong] injects its particularity [opining]. [Now] the other [the wrongdoer] stands on the same footing [as the wronged], and therein lies the injustice.

The duel is this unseemly[200] relationship wherein the injured party appears with the same right[201] [as the wrongdoer]. [The duel] is customary in the right-less condition; it is a vestige of barbarism that, if it still exists, is still barbaric. Only in the military is it allowed for other reasons. I have committed a wrong, yet confront [the aggrieved] on the same footing [as the one I have wronged]. The realization of justice is something merely accidental. It is the particular will [of the injured party] that opposes the other, and this it must not be. [Retribution] becomes a contingent action – a new violation instead of the erasure of a wrong. This gives rise to a cycle to infinity. This is still the case with many peoples. Enmity is inherited. Revenge is pursued for years, and if it is satisfied, it starts anew. In statutes, many offences, even robbery and theft, are not viewed as public crimes. This is also the case in England.[202]

The fact that a particular will executes justice is a contradiction, because [justice] is a necessity [not something dependent on choice or relative power]. We have not yet arrived at the elevation of the immediate will to the general Will. [Yet] a transition has been made, [and] this transition is implied in [the person's] becoming reconciled to crime.[203] Through the nemesis [of crime in retribution and of vengeful retribution in crime,] the [50] immediate, particularistic will gets transcended in punishment. [UN91: Justice as such asserts itself against the merely immediate, particularistic will.] Justice becomes dignified for me through its necessity. In [its vengeful] realization, justice is something immediate. Mediation is a sublation of immediacy.[204] The structures [e.g., property, contract] we have considered are nothing other than presentations of the abstract will. In general, the moral standpoint involves this: the particular will is at the same time general. Thus [the will] is not general [immediately]; it becomes general only through this mediation [of crime and revenge]. The will is not immediately a moral will. The moral will is the will that goes into itself. This constitutes the moral standpoint.

---

200 UN89: repugnant
201 Translator: "with the same right," i.e., with no better right than the wrongdoer.
202 UN90: It follows from what has been said that there is a demand for an objective Will, that is, in this case for a court of law.
203 Translator: "becoming reconciled to crime" as something necessary to the confirmation of the general Will's normative force – to the realization of Right.
204 Translator: Mediation is a sublation of immediacy, where the particular will is cancelled qua immediate but preserved qua constituent element of Right's realization.

[SECOND PART]

[Morality]

[51] The first thing we had was freedom in its immediacy. Now we have the will no longer as a person but as a subject. Only at the beginning is [freedom's] existence immediate, [UN91: a natural existence]. The Idea [of freedom] must no longer have existence immediately [in ends given by nature]; rather it must have the [embodiments of the] will itself for its existential reality. The moral standpoint hinges essentially on this: I have accomplished the Good with my particular knowledge and will. The person is the [abstract] idea [of the will], and [in contrast] the [moral subject's] will is [both] general and particular.[205] I am no longer an [abstract] person, but rather am inwardly differentiated by a purpose. I have an aim in me; this is particularity. The general [Will] comes to my own awareness. The [individual's carrying out the] general Will is what we will later call the Good.[206] The other side is the subjective side, particularity for itself. To this [side] belongs partly inwardness, [partly] scope for a particular existence – [for my individual] welfare. It is the moral will that we are considering.

Like the will [in abstract Right], morality [*das Moralische*] must have existence. *Moral* is meant here in a quite general sense.[207] Someone who acts in a way suited to the Good is *moralisch*. I am *moral* when, as a particular will, what I do is imbued with my knowledge and will.[208] We are speaking about purpose, responsibility; to say that something is attributable to me is to say that it was my purpose.[209] Contained in this

---

205 UN91: [At the moral standpoint,] the particular will as such constitutes the existential reality of the general Will.
206 See this translation, 75ff.
207 UN91: ...not [simply] as that which is opposed to the immoral.
208 Translator: "what I do," i.e., what counts as my action.
209 Translator: This will later be modified; see this translation, 67.

aspect [of freedom is the requirement] that my particular will be present in what I do.[210] The relation to the Good belongs to this standpoint. The right of the subjective will in general is what we have to consider. The human being has the right to demand [as a condition for deserving blame] that he have known that what he was doing was contrary to duty.[211] What follows is detail.

First, [the attribution of an action to me requires] the immediate identity of my will with what I do, that an action have been intentional.[212] So, the first thing is [52] this formal identity.[213] The second thing is the particularity of the action – this particular action (here the concept of action enters for the first time).[214] This particular side has [two aspects:] on the one hand, the determination of purpose, on the other hand, the determination of welfare. [Regarding the first aspect,] I am the determiner. Into the determination [of formal choice] I put what is mine [my concrete purpose]. The content of the action, insofar as it is mine, corresponds with my purpose. The second aspect is the particular [concrete purpose] as such. This [concrete purpose] has the right to be in the action.[215] Here belongs [the idea] that my welfare must be [aligned] with my purpose.[216] The third thing to consider is me acting in a relationship to the Good, me as a conscience.

The moral standpoint is the standpoint of finitude. At the moral standpoint, the difference between the will as it inherently is [and ought to be] and the particular will enters. This difference is fundamental [to this standpoint]. The immediate singularity is cancelled; the will is reflected into itself. [But] there is something [still] there from which [the

---

210 UN91: Here it is essentially demanded that what I do [i.e., what counts as my action] occurs through my particular knowledge and will.
211 Translator: Later, this becomes "that he have known or ought to have known …"
212 Translator: The next sentence shows that "intentional" is meant here in the formal sense of having been chosen by the agent.
213 Translator: The identity is formal in the sense that an action, for example, killing a patient with morphine, can be chosen without being desired or aimed at. The purpose is just to alleviate the pain.
214 Translator: "Here the concept of action enters for the first time." In abstract Right, there are deeds (willed movements of the body resulting in x), but no actions because actions are individuated by purposes or by what one subjectively knew about the situation. For example, raising an arm is signalling a wish to speak or assaulting someone depending on one's purpose, and purposes first become salient at the moral standpoint. Assaulting someone who is in fact a policeman is assaulting a policeman or a common assault depending on whether one knew the victim was a policeman, and subjective knowledge too becomes relevant only at the moral standpoint.
215 Translator: I have a right to act in accordance with my self-determined ends, to pursue my welfare as I see it.
216 Translator: This is against paternalism. My welfare consists in the satisfaction of my purposes. No one can impose on me a conception of welfare external to my own.

will] has exited. In its abstract meaning, [particularity] itself implies a two, a particular against a particular. This standpoint is the relationship of ought, whereas the true return is to simplicity.[217] The particular will should conform to the general Will, but here this is only an ought. Philosophies that remain at this standpoint conclude with the mere ought. The moral standpoint opposes reality.

At the moral standpoint, the will is [directed] to a content [consisting of] a purpose; in Right there is also a content, but it is indifferent [to purposes]. The purpose [in the sphere of abstract Right] is my abstract freedom; the side of particularity [of my concrete ends] is a matter of indifference. Right is the standpoint of abstract freedom. The moral standpoint is the standpoint of concrete freedom. The purpose is to know that I am free.[218] At the juristic standpoint, no actions occur, [whereas] at the moral standpoint, they surely do.[219] [To be sure], a crime is an action,[220] [but] the inward side [of crime – purpose] is first considered here [at the moral standpoint].[221] In Right, there are no positive commandments, only prohibitions [whereas in morality, there are both].

Through the diversity in my actions, I give myself a content-rich existence. The more precise details are the three aforementioned points of view. (1) The right of the particular will [qua formally intentional]. (2) The right of the particular will with a content [a specific purpose]. [3] The third is the right of the particular will, but such that the particular purpose raises itself to a universal purpose. This is the right of conscience – [which turns into] evil. These [the universal and the particular] must be synthesized [53] and with that we make the transition to ethical life. The moral standpoint [UN93: is the entry point to][222] the Will that is actually and self-consciously there.

---

217 UN92: The moral standpoint is not yet the ethical standpoint, where there is no longer an ought [fixedly opposed to an is].
218 Translator: The purpose is to become free and self-consciously so.
219 Translator: At the juristic standpoint, no actions occur because actions are individuated by purposes, yet purposes are not cognizable at the juristic standpoint because they are identified with natural ends externally given to the free will. At the moral standpoint, purposes become salient as self-determined purposes, hence as belonging to freedom.
220 Translator: For example, theft is a taking individuated by the intent to take something belonging to another.
221 Translator: The motive for a crime first becomes cognizable at the moral standpoint, which thus excuses crimes committed under duress or necessity. However, crime at the juristic standpoint was distinguished from innocent wrong by the formal intentionality of the wrong, and this was already an inward element.
222 Translator: Ringier wrote: "The moral standpoint can only enter if the Will is actually and self-consciously there." It is doubtful that Hegel said this. UN wrote [93]: "The moral standpoint is the entry point to ethical life."

[First Section]

[Intention and Responsibility][223]

Germane to the right of the subjective will in general is the concept of responsibility, which we now consider. When I do something, I produce a change in existence. As a consequence, the thing [produced] has the predicate of mine. That is responsibility in general. In a [loose] sense, we say that [what causes] something to happen to someone is responsible. Thus, for example, you blame the stone that has struck you. If one wants to explain an empirical event, one says that this or that is responsible for the change. All the circumstances that are contained in the event are responsible. [Thus,] one finds that Louis XVI, the court, and philosophy were responsible for the French Revolution. [Here,] responsibility means nothing other than that the moment can be found in [the event]. This is a case where the mine [my causality] is effective in a more or less remote manner. [Another such case is this:] I am an owner, and by being one, my property is an external thing. For example, animals are my property. I have to answer for whatever happens through such property. It is mine, and therefore it is my fault.[224]

---

223 UN93: Action and Intention [*Vorsatz*]. [Translator: Knox, Houlgate, and Nisbet translate *Vorsatz* as "purpose" and *Absicht* as "intention" (*Outlines*, 115, 118; and G.W.F. Hegel, *Elements of the Philosophy of Right*, ed. Allen W. Wood, trans. H.B. Nisbet [Cambridge: Cambridge University Press, 1991], 143, 147). However, Hegel tells us at UN98 that what he means by these terms is just the opposite. As used by Hegel, *Vorsatz* means intention in a broad sense that includes both purpose/desire and knowledge that an outcome will result from one's act. In either case, one wills (chooses) the outcome and is therefore responsible for it. He uses *Absicht* to mean intention specifically as purpose/desire. It would be eccentric to limit responsibility to such a narrow conception of intention, and Hegel doesn't.]

224 UN93: A deed is in general something concrete that contains a multitude of conditions. Responsibility is first something quite formal. The most varied circumstances are often cited as being responsible for great world events. I am more or less responsible for a result depending on whether the mine penetrates it more or less.

However, real responsibility begins more specifically where I am responsible for the deed, in fact to blame for it, insofar as it lay in my intention, insofar as I willed [chose] it. I produce a deed insofar as I willed it, insofar as it was my intention. It is no longer merely my deed; it is my action. And I acknowledge as my action only what I willed, what I [intentionally] did. According to this [modern] perspective, one acts against [the background of] a situation; the situation is something external. One can be mistaken about what one is dealing with. The circumstances within which I act determine the [objective] nature of a deed.[225] But I acknowledge as included in the action only those circumstances that I knew about.[226] So, it is with the story of Oedipus.[227] His deed was a patricide, but the action was a mere fight, as was customary in those days. But he took the [54] whole thing upon himself; he considered himself a patricide. However, this was because the difference [between a deed and an action] was not in his consciousness as it is in ours. According to the concept of that epoch, the entire [range of circumstances] lay or should have lain in the totality of his consciousness. If someone suffers innocently, something non-rational impinges on him. [Oedipus] had the high knowledge to solve the riddle of the Sphinx, and [yet] this [that responsibility for deeds is circumscribed by one's knowledge of the circumstances] he did not know. The tragedy is precisely that he suffers innocently; it is a higher revenge for [the hubris of] wanting to know everything.[228] [As a finite being,] I hold myself accountable only for what I knew.[229]

Furthermore, the action also has consequences. Here one can again ask: To what extent, if any, are they attributable [to the actor]? Is an action to be judged according to its consequences or not? The action is an external concrete existent that has manifold ramifications. These are precisely the consequences. On the one hand, this externality [can be] the development of the action itself.[230] The action, the soul of the

---

225 Translator: For example, the circumstance that the man whom A assaulted is a policeman determines the objective nature of the *deed* as an assault of a policeman.
226 Translator: So that if A didn't know his victim was a policeman, his *action* was only a common assault.
227 Translator: As Hegel explains, the story of Oedipus exhibits a contrary perspective from which one is responsible for one's deeds. No distinction between deeds and actions is recognized.
228 UN93: Herein lies the heroic: the human being expects itself to encompass the entire range of phenomena that lie before him.
229 Translator: Later this is modified to "for what I knew or ought as a thinking being to have known."
230 UN94: They are nothing but the manifestation of the nature of the action. [Translator: For example, the destruction of the building lies within the action of setting a match to it.]

entirety, the whole action, is the action along with its [inevitable] consequences. These are the necessary consequences. [If by consequences we mean just these consequences, then] the action can and must be judged by its consequences. To that extent, it is right to charge people with consequences.[231] [Some] consequences make explicit the nature of the action. One must distinguish [cases] where one acts from nothing but a sinister side.

At the same time, consequences have another aspect to them. Because an action is both mine and an external existent, actions undergo change.[232] An action can waltz away into remote consequences that no longer belong to me. That alone belongs to me which lies in [the action], which is posited by me. We can say that one should attend to consequences and one can just as well say that one must attend only to the action [it depends on what one means by consequences]. But consequences often reveal what kind of action it was. The action carries the essential consequence in itself; to that extent, [the consequence] can already be discerned in the action. If something terrible springs from an action, one must be attentive, doubly attentive, to what the action really is for itself. One must learn from nature how to discern whether actions are right or wrong.

The following collision arises. In general, whenever I act, I entrust what belongs to me to externality [chance, other wills]. Others can [55] make of [my action] whatever they please, but nevertheless I am the one who set it forth.[233] It thus happens that when the action of a criminal has no important consequences, he is not charged [with the same crime] as one whose [action] developed fully. Where the fire did not break out, the arsonist is not punished as severely as when the fire destroyed buildings. And that is not unjust.[234]

---

231 UN94: According to this aspect [of consequences], the action must certainly be judged by its consequences, and it is right for people to be attentive to the consequences of their actions. I can be charged with consequences if they are nothing but the development of the action itself.
232 UN94: Inasmuch as the action is an external existent, many things attach to it from outside.
233 UN94: However, here, as at the standpoint of morality as a whole, there arises a collision. In acting, I expose what is mine [in the action] to alien forces that can make of what is mine something much different than I intended.
234 Translator: The missing steps in this argument can be supplied as follows. A consequence (e.g., a razed building) implicit in an action (of setting fire to the building) belongs to the action. Therefore, I cannot say that I'm responsible only for my effort – that the outcome belongs to chance. I'm responsible for the whole action – burning down the building. But then someone who intended the same outcome

INTENTION AND RESPONSIBILITY 67

However, this [difference between action and consequence] is more precisely summed up in the difference between general and particular consequences. The isolated existent [I produced] stands in an imperfect [contingent] connection [with further results]. I did only the singular thing [lit a piece of straw], not the alteration in existence [the burned-down building] the singular act further caused. [But there is one whole action here; I burned down the building.][235] Otherwise, the homicidal arsonist could say: I touched only [a piece of] straw or a single point. But the single point is connected to others, and in the singular, he injured the general. The individual is charged [with the result] because he is a thinking being who knows what he is doing, who knows the connection between what he did [and the result]. Just for that reason the actions of children and imbeciles are not attributed to them. This [that one is responsible for outcomes a thinking being would expect would follow from his action] is the claim of objectivity. To this right of objectivity the right of subjectivity stands opposed.[236] Here arises a collision [between the objective and the subjective] that can become terrible.[237] There are circumstances [apart from childhood and mental incapacity] that excuse – [bad] upbringing, etc. But against these stands the claim of objectivity. It is a collision that is perennial and that cannot be eliminated. Here [only] an approximation [to the ideal knowledge of the thinking being] is possible; [knowledge of] the whole [action] is only an ought. [So much for] the moment of self-consciousness having regard to intention.

    I intended and who tried just as hard as I did to produce that outcome is less culpable than I am if by chance he failed. So, attempts are punished less severely than completed crimes, and that is not unjust.
235 UN95: Action is first of all a universal.
236 UN95: If the subject asserts the right [to be held responsible only for what lay in] his particular knowledge, so, on the contrary, does the objective have its right, and the particular consciousness, insofar as it acts [must be fixed] with the knowledge of what it is doing.
237 UN95: Here the Ought and the Is oppose each other.

[*Second Section*]

[Purpose and Welfare]

The second moment is that self-consciousness have itself in its action not only in a general sense [as choice] but, secondly, in accordance with its particular content [its purpose]. The subject is a particular [individual]. Its particularity should be in its action. Its action should not be a merely general thing. The subject [56] has the right to satisfy itself in its action. The human being who is merely used [for] an end is not satisfied in its action. The subject who is a particular [individual] also has a particular content. This is what purpose means in the context of action.

To begin with, we have for the specification of purpose no more precise content than that of the particular subject itself. This particularity is the natural [will], for the natural will is a particular will.[238] In that the free will realizes itself, its individuated existence is the particular will itself. The individuated terrain of freedom is the particular will as such. In that the particularity of willing is an essential moment, the particular will here has its right. The natural will can be [the particular will], but it does not appear [in the moral sphere] as the particular will.[239] The natural will is inclination. However, in [thoughtful] consciousness, [inclination] gains a direct connection to [the individual's] general [well-being]; so connected, the natural will counts [morally] as the particular will. [The satisfaction of] whatever is generally needed, when reflectively related to the whole, constitutes welfare. But the universal

---

238 UN95–6 This particularity is a feature of the natural will. In [abstract] Right, we abstracted from this.

239 UN96: The natural will enters here, but not as an immediately natural will, but rather as that whose ends are known and desired from the standpoint of reflective consciousness and therewith enter into the element of the general. In that way, as the particular [inclination] deliberatively [integrated into] general [well-being], it is *welfare* in general and not an isolated, particular inclination.

does not yet penetrate the particular completely [there is still a natural, given content]; rather the universal can only *appear* in the particular, and that is its welfare. The individual has the right to make its welfare its purpose, but only as reflected into the entirety [*Ganzen*].[240] To begin with, this particularity makes up the content [of the will]. Thus, the individual has the right to insist on his welfare. He has the right to be self-interested in his action. This is a right that lies in particularity, something which, abstractly considered, should not be looked upon as something inherently bad. [Whether acting from self-interest is bad] depends only on whether it comes at the expense of general well-being.

Taken generally, subjective satisfaction is willed by subjective self-consciousness. The fact that the subject finds its satisfaction in its action does not make the action bad, [a truth] that must also be adhered to in judging history. Great individuals have done great things. If one says, however, that [these actions] reflect no merit on individuals because they acted from a [57] desire for glory, then this is just the temptation to make action oriented to individual [self-interest] into something bad. This [dichotomy between self-interested action and meritorious action] is in general a false dichotomy; it is an abstract judgment of the mere understanding. This historical judgment then engenders the generalized possibility of belittling all great men, since only one side [of the matter] is considered. A people cannot act; an individual must do this, but action is not something bad just because particularity lay in the [doing of the] universal. In the development of the One,[241] every moment must attain its right; [each] must give itself an independent formation. The universal Will by itself is an abstraction. Concrete particularity is the particular will, and this is an essential moment [in action]. Crucially, my particularity has a right [to seek satisfaction], and when I act, my particularity as such has acted. Only the particular [individual] as such can act. Thus, particularity has its right. This particularity assumes various forms. When I do something, I must have an interest in it.[242] I have [my interest] in different ways when, through the action, my insight [into the value of the action for me] crystallizes. This is subjective freedom as such. It is essential to subjective freedom that my insight be engaged in the doing.

---

240 UN96: On the other hand, he does not have the right to satisfy this or that inclination or passion just because it is his; rather he is entitled only [to the satisfaction] reflected into the entirety [of his welfare].
241 UN97: In the development of the Idea ...
242 UN97: The right of my subjective freedom in general is that I find myself as a particular [individual] in what I do.

In religion, something counts as true on divine authority [UN97: just as in states, especially in ancient states]. One imagines [the truth] solely as something given; I have to lay aside my insight. As in a legal process,[243] it claims to be valid without consideration for my insight. Whether or not it seems [right] to the parties, the verdict stands. [Nevertheless,] subjective freedom should try to find itself [in the decision] – should find its own reasons [for it]. Or if [the decision is based on] reasons that are not mine, I should at least have confidence in [the decision-maker]. Having confidence means that I so trust the insight of the other that it is as if it were my insight. In trust I see myself [in the other].

Immediate acceptance [on authority] is also found in the theoretical [sphere] – for example, [if we assume] that things are externally given to us. Jacobi says that we believe [in a thing itself], that we don't know it based on reasons.[244] However, even *belief* would be too much [for the realist], because this too presupposes reflection.[245] The right of particularity is the right [to hold important] this difference [between reflection and acceptance on authority]; everything must be mediated through my insight. Even if my insight cannot [58] confirm it, it can happen that I can say '*yes*' to it for reasons of honour. Thus, another form of [assent, besides insight] is our [participatory] activity. That is to say, when we contribute to [what we have to accept], our activity lies nearer to our interest. This is because doing is the translation of the subjective into the objective, and we call the outcome, or at least a part of it, ours. Notably, this appears in the [popular] way of thinking: everyone wants to be where the action is.[246] In Thucydides, this [idea] occurs frequently; everyone believes that where he is not, things are not going well.[247]

If the interest evinces a [specific] content, then it is called purpose [*Absicht*]. *Purpose* is precisely the more specific content that one puts

---

243 UN97: As with a judge's holding ...
244 "Dear Mendelssohn, we are all born in faith and must remain in faith, just as we are all born in society and must remain in society ... How could we strive after certainty if certainty were not known to us in advance; and how can it be known to us otherwise than through something that we already know with certainty? This leads to the concept of an immediate certainty, which needs no reasons, but which absolutely excludes all reasons, and which is itself the one and only representation that corresponds to the presented thing." F.H. Jacobi, *Über die Lehre des Spinoza in Briefen an Herrn Moses Mendelssohn* (Breslau, 1789), 215, https://archive.org/details/ueber-dielehrede00mendgoog/page/214/mode/2up?q=ueber+die+Lehre+des+Spinoza.
245 UN97: ... because belief already appears as something limited, bounded.
246 Translator: *Jeder will auch dabei gewesen sein*.
247 UN97: In Thucydides, it occurs several times that in the Peloponnesian Wars, everyone thinks that if he isn't there, the event didn't take place. [Translator: Dieter Henrich suggests (UN316) that Hegel is referring here to the story of Alcmaeon,

into the external form of the deed. The purpose counts for me as what is really the essential thing [in my action]. My knowledge that [an action will produce] something [or] my desiring it, is called general intention [*Vorsatz*].[248] The content must be my content. Against the purpose, the action now becomes a means [of realizing that purpose], and the other content [the means chosen] is [also] considered my own. Here belong the deviations [from pure purposes] that moralistic judgments have in view.[249] We are speaking here about the *particularistic purpose*. Purpose in general and more precisely the purpose of welfare simply expresses the contrast with [abstract] Right in general [where purposes and welfare are excluded from consideration]. The particularism [of purpose] is therefore essential; I have a perfect right to the more precise content of [my] welfare. The fact that my welfare is also my purpose makes welfare the concrete compass [*Umfang*] of particularity. Here the following contrasts at once appear. The principle of particularism [that I have a right to act in my self-interest as I see it] is precisely the great principle of modernity in contrast to antiquity.[250] It stands out everywhere. The art [of the ancients] is plastic, that is, objective. Against the plastic we set the Romantic – the particularism of chivalry, adventurousness. The ardour of love is given a much higher right than in antiquity. This particularism is thus now the emergent [principle].

We have to consider the State as a totality in which the principle of particularism can develop, yet only in connection with the whole. In judgment, it is common to look for secret motives, that is, anecdotes concerning idiosyncrasies. In this judgment, the excellent is removed;

---

whom an oracle told would have no release from guilt for the murder of his mother until he found a place on earth that had not been seen by the sun or existed as land at the time of the murder; Thucydides, *The Peloponnesian Wars*, bk. 2, chap. 8.]

248 UN98: With crime it is enough if it is proved that someone had the intent [*Vorsatz*] for a certain action. [Translator: As Hegel understands it, the difference between *Absicht* and *Vorsatz* seems to be this: *Absicht* means intention specifically as desire or purpose; *Vorsatz* includes within intention both desire/purpose and knowledge that an outcome will result from one's act whether or not the outcome was desired or was the purpose of the act. The latter is the sense of intention employed in criminal law.]

249 UN98: In this opposition between purpose, considered as the particular content of an action [e.g., Napoleon's desire for fame], and the [action's] objective nature [e.g., Napoleon's spreading the ideas of the French Revolution] fall moralistic judgments in general. Here we are not yet speaking of the Good. That thought forms the third moment of this sphere [of morality].

250 UN98: The principle of particularity is the general principle of modernity and is a principle of a higher quality than that of antiquity. This holds true of all aspects of life – of science, the state, and religion. The principle of antiquity is plastic in thought and action; the principle of modernity is romantic.

[it is said] that, when a great man accomplishes a great thing, [59] his particularity is simultaneously active. He comes to fame and honour through these actions; he is the one who did this. In historical judgment, this is often viewed in the following way. Caesar acted from a desire to dominate; he had a hunger for honour, and [so what he did] was not done morally. The people [who make these judgments] want a general to triumph, but not that he be a victor, [UN98: to do great deeds but not become famous]. Monkish virtues are not the virtues of the real world; in them particularity does not enter. Wherever you go in the world, particularity is [involved] in actions. This [moralistic judgment] is the way to make all great men small. One clings to particularity, which is also in the action, and one makes this [necessary] particularity into a mere particularity. For valets there are no heroes, but not because the latter are not heroes but because the former are valets. There are also psychological valets who accept no heroes just because they are valets. This is the envy that cannot bear greatness, but envy wears the cloak of morality.[251] One holds fast to the particular [in action]. Great men have accomplished what they desired.[252] It is said that virtue should be selfless and not seek satisfaction in action, but this is tantamount to saying that one should not act.

We misunderstand particularity [when we] make the great appear contemptible [on its account]. Yet we also say that the state should care for the welfare of its subjects – that is, it should satisfy the individual's particularity. Some want [the state] to teach the people religion; others want [it] to judge and mend them, but here it is recognized that it is indeed right [for the state] to satisfy particularity. The individual believes he has suffered a wrong if his particularity is not satisfied. Purveyors of anecdotes believe they have performed a miracle when they tie great deeds and stories to small, low reasons. [Their thought is that] if [a building] is thoroughly rotten and a light gust of wind [60] or a small stone comes along, the building will collapse. [They think that] nothing great can ever arise from lowly causes.[253] [But contrary to this way of thinking], the truth about a person's actions is the entirety of his

---

251 UN99: This is the envy that also manifested itself with the Athenian people, namely, with the banishment of Aristides. In our civilized times, this envy knows how to give itself the form of morality.
252 UN99: Great men have fulfilled their wills in great deeds and therewith found their satisfaction.
253 UN99: Great events always have great causes; it is therefore empty chatter to say that small events were the cause of great ones.

actions, and his idiosyncrasies are beside the point. It is then said that one must search the secret folds of the heart, and then everything will be filled in for us. That's also the way it goes with authors. One believes that one first gets to know authors when one hears them in common conversation, but that is precisely the insignificant side. The man who has brought forth fruit is entitled to demand that he be judged by these fruits. It is impossible for a hypocrite to be something, to accomplish anything great.

Particularity is not the root of the substantial, but I am something substantial only through willing [and accomplishing] this or that [end]. Particularity falls on the side of existence, reality. Reality has a great deal of influence over the ways and means of bringing forth [particular ends]. Substantial work is the measure [of a human being]. Particularity has its right. This applies generally to the relationship of particularity to substantial universality. In its content, the particular can be thought of as welfare; what welfare is cannot be specified further. Right and welfare thus stand against each other. Both can [coincidentally] agree, but they can also come into collision.

Which must yield to the other? Because it concerns the real existence of the person, Right in general is the fundamental [principle]. The particular first has substantiality in conforming with freedom. To forward welfare at the cost of freedom is most certainly wrong. The further elaboration [of the priority of freedom over welfare considered as particular end-satisfaction] is the concern of morality. [However,] a higher collision can occur [between Right and] particularity as a whole [life]. Welfare is an abstract expression; welfare in reality is now [the satisfaction of] this [purpose], now [the satisfaction of] that. These determinate ways [of pursuing welfare] are somewhat sporadic, but welfare in its real determinateness is [an individual's] life as a whole. This side of particularity has here a higher right against the side of abstract Right.

What [is needed to] gain life is [the subject of] what is called the law of necessity. Life appeals, not to an equity, [but] to a right of necessity, and this right to life as a whole must indeed be viewed as a right of necessity against the other right.[254] For example, [in a collision between] life on [61] one side and property on the other [life must prevail]. If

---

254 Translator: This is against Kant, for whom necessity is an equity against strict right; see I. Kant, *The Metaphysics of Morals*, trans. Mary Gregor (Cambridge: Cambridge University Press, 1991), 60 1 [6:235–6].

life is lost, then rightlessness is therewith posited.[255] What stands on the other side [of life] is doubtless a right, but it is the [right to] a mere isolated existence [of freedom], and [so infringing it] is not violating the capacity for rights in general. This [right] to the particular must thus give way to the right in the universal. So, if life can be saved only through the infringement of another's property, then [life] takes precedence.[256] The right of necessity comes to the fore not only in extreme cases [where it is an exception to law]; it is rather itself a legal principle [embodied in other laws].[257] That a debtor should have a *beneficium competentiae*[258] and that a [debtor] craftsman should be left with the tools of his trade are [legal] determinations that have their basis in a right of necessity.

Thus, particularity has its right. Insofar as it comes into collision with abstract Right, it must yield; but in the law of necessity, personality [existent in a life] takes priority.

---

255 Translator: If a life is subordinated to a particular piece of property, then the existence of personality is subordinated to a thing, and so rightlessness is posited as a principle.
256 UN100: A right of necessity can be invoked only when the totality of right-bearing capacity is endangered.
257 UN100: One finds the right of necessity sanctioned also in civil law codes. [Translator: This seems to be directed against the view that "necessity knows no law."]
258 Translator: This is a Roman law doctrine permitting a debtor to reserve his means of subsistence from a creditor.

[Third Section]

[The Good and Conscience]

The third [moment of morality] is the stage that constitutes the moral sphere in its strict sense. In necessity, there appears the opposition between the particular will [of the individual whose life is in danger] and the abstract will [of the property owner]. Both are equally essential moments [of freedom]. Particularity constitutes the essential existence of the abstract will. The Concept [of freedom] is complemented by particularity and turned into the Idea. In their opposition, both [abstract Right and welfare] are cancelled [qua absolute]; on its own and isolated, each is an abstraction, something animal-like. In [the realization of] Right, particularity is an essential moment. The truth of both [abstract Right and welfare] is their unity[259] [wherein] the Will's universality obtains existence through particularity and, reciprocally, the particular [will] gains substantial reality through the universal. The truth of both is the Good in general, which is just as much the Right, with which the particular will accords and is equally carried out, but in agreement with each other. When we say that the Good in general is the purpose of the world, we [62] picture therewith [the idea] that abstract freedom is executed through the particular will. We picture [the idea] that [freedom] is not a mere thought, [not] something [merely] intended, but rather something executed. It is therefore implied therein that the objectively existing Will is actualized in such a way that the particular will accords with the universal and the welfare of the individual is attained. Particularity can realize itself only in connection with the universal; it must be in itself objective. Otherwise, it comes to nothing.

Now this sphere of the Good contains various determinations. The Idea of the Good is also the Idea of Truth, [for] here too there is an

---

259 UN101: the concrete universal.

interpenetration of the subjective and objective Will. The Will's particular side gathers reality into itself.[260] Whether one calls it subjective or objective is a matter of indifference. As willing what has Being both inherently and actually, the will is good. [But the good will] is just because of that thoughtful. In Being in and for itself, there is also the true. The truth in itself is as much the side of thought [as that of action]. This Good has more precise determinations. The Good is first of all what one calls the Idea – that is, an abstract thought. [Second,] the Good ought to be done, ought to be accomplished. The Good is not contained immediately in the particular will. The Good is first of all a thought; it obtains its reality through the particular will.

What is left to consider is the Good in connection to the will. Objectively considered, welfare is realized freedom. As such, the Good is the Idea, but it is also abstract; [it is] the subjective Idea.[261] For that reason it is also the Idea [of the Good] in self-contradiction. Subjectivity, abstract subjectivity, is the opposite of the Good. [It is] the will as pure form.[262] The Good is supposed to be the identity [of subject and object], but [as an abstract Idea of the Good] it is also the opposite, [the Bad]. It is thus the Idea without determination; determination falls outside it [in the opinion of the moral actor]. The pure determination [turns out to be] just the subjective [will]. Qua [merely] for itself, the Good is just the thought of the Good in general; it merely *ought* to be.[263] If the Good is, on one side, the Substantial, then particularity should also belong to it. [Individual] welfare should be just as much [in harmony with] universal [welfare]. The Good is in that respect the last end – the last thought. [63] If one remains with the [Idea of the] Good, only the void comes forward – abstract talk. The purpose of this [talk] is to inspire, to edify. Real teaching is not about inspiration and edification. [The satisfaction one gets from the latter] is like the satisfaction one gets from a lot of declamations and fine speeches about the Good; one remains unsatisfied.

The next question is: what is good? Such determinateness is not present in the Good as such, but it is necessary thereto, and [the Good]

---

260 Translator: There is no in-itself outside freedom outwardly realized as a world through the particular will of the individual.
261 Translator: This could mean that the Good is here one-sided in relation to reality or that the Good is here filled out by individual subjectivity. UN101: The Good is first still the abstract Idea tainted by subjectivity.
262 UN101: ... as pure discretion and [arbitrary] decision.
263 UN101: The Good is here thoroughly tainted by an *ought-to-be*.

must pass over to this determinateness, [for] it is the concrete identity of freedom and welfare. The form [of the Good] must contain substance. These determinations are thus the particular[s]. The Good must particularize itself; in considering action, I must have regard to the particular in asking [myself] what to do. Whoever wants to act must will something specific. [UN102: Goethe rightly says,] whoever wants to do great things must be able to limit himself. Whoever remains only with the Good as such is a formal man.[264] Purity is then the abstraction from the real. Such men are vain. They scarcely want to take on any form that they believe will defile them with the outside world, [an attitude] that, to be sure, has something beautiful about it.[265] But these people pass over into unreality. They are extinguished in this longing. Their will must remain a longing, but they are able to keep this longing pure. In recent times, this has also appeared in the Fichtean philosophy. The Good must determine itself. Insofar as the Good lies in acting, the determination has the following more precise form.

The particular good's more precise definition is that it means duties [and] virtues. These express the particular good. The virtues are nothing other than [determinations of] the Good as it exists in the [individual] personality.[266] The [term] natural is appropriate to virtue because virtue is the Good reflected in individuality. Duties can be demanded because they are universal[ly binding], something that should be the substantial reality for everyone. However, virtues cannot be demanded [because] they make up the particular nature [of the individual]. Because it is the moral [not natural] will that decides for the Good, it has [64] duties, not virtues. Conversely, what is a natural matter is not a matter for the self-determining will. For example, bravery is [both] a virtue and a duty, not just a virtue. Alexander and Caesar had the virtue of bravery – they possessed a peculiar quality [of character].[267] Likewise, rectitude is a duty, [UN102: but it appears also as a virtue]. Where it appears as a virtue, it is always in the form of particularity [UN102: as, for example, with Aristides, the virtue of such a plastic will]. Morality is what can be expected of everyone [regardless of his natural character]. Virtue is a matter of individuality.

---

264 UN102: Whoever merely remains with thoughts of the Good is an empty, unworthy man.
265 UN102: One speaks in this sense of beautiful souls. They think they defile themselves in contact with the particular and real.
266 Translator: Here the word *Persönlichkeit* is used in the concrete sense of individuality.
267 UN102: The bravery of an Alexander and a Caesar cannot be demanded, [for] it belonged to the peculiar genius of these men.

The other side [of the determinate Good is duty]. The form that the particular good has is duty; nevertheless, duties and the Good are distinguished from one other. When we speak of duties, we say that a human being should do his duties and satisfy himself therein. From what follows from [doing his] duty he should abstract. Duty constitutes the completely universal side without regard to particularity. [Yet] in the Good, the moment of particularity is also contained. We demand that, with the fulfilment of duty, the particular will also [be involved]. Joined [to the Good] is the side of particular subjectivity. Because the Good determines itself and in its determinacy ought to be a determining ground of the will, the will has to adhere to what is contained in the concept [of the free will] as such. (So, having regard to what particularity is, this will makes up the particular). Duty is thus the substantial Will insofar as [the substantial Will] is the object of the particular will and insofar as this will counts as something substantial. One uses the expression reasonable. Reasonableness is nothing other than the concept [of the general Will].[268] The substantial *Will* is [the will that adheres to] duty. [The will that adheres to] duty can also be called the good will. This will is essentially the thoughtful will. Duty is [the particular will's thoughtful relation to] the substantial. The Good is the True. If someone says that human beings cannot know the truth, then he also takes the Good away from them. The emptiest of all talk is saying that no thought is involved in the good will.

The determination of duties makes up morality in general – ethics. By ethics, however, is understood more the doctrine of virtue, a natural history of virtue, insofar as virtue is something general.[269] [65] [Nevertheless,] it is also [a doctrine] of obligation. In a certain sense, ethics [is a] doctrine of duties. The word *ethics* has been considered a more noble word than *morality* (it is Greek). Moral discourse, insofar as it remains with [the] generality [of reasonableness], becomes utterly tedious and facile talk. It is for that reason that moral discourse has come into disrepute.

What are the duties? One demands of morality that it specify these duties. Duties should be nothing but the particularization of the Will that is in and for itself. It is important that these duties be set before people. A scientific treatment of duties consists in showing their

---

268 UN103: The reasonable is this, that the general Will has its reality in my will.
269 UN103: Actually, there can be only a natural history of virtues.

necessity. The determinations that make up the content of duties are nothing but the essential relationships that come forth from the Will.[270] The determinations are relations, relationships of the will insofar as it is universal. These relationships are substantial relationships. They constitute the Objective, and duty has the more precise meaning that one ought to conduct oneself, behave, in accordance with this relationship. You think of this bond and you say: this is a relationship, and you ask, what must I do in this relationship? The essential thing is that they are relationships [evincing] the Truth; this relationship is my duty (e.g., if I am a father). If I have the concept of this relationship, then I have the concept of the duty belonging to it. A duty is not an isolated thing but the particularization of the subjective will,[271] not [something] alongside another as in the imagination, but a moment of a whole, [belonging to] relationships considered as universal moments of the objective Will.[272] By conducting himself within this objective Will, the actor [assumes] the reciprocal duties involved in particular relationships. A doctrine of duties is therefore nothing but the development [from the objective Will] of these substantial [relationships]. Individuals are aware of the duties inhering in relationships merely as an appendage of themselves. [However], it is in this form [as essential relationships] that duties should exist for the individual, that [duties] are his substantial reality.[273] For the individual, [essential relationships] are the duties.

[66] These duties cannot be developed from the moral standpoint. It would be shallow [to do so].[274] If an ethics becomes established as a requirement at all, it does so only when the ethical Spirit is considered. [From the standpoint of the ethical Spirit, once the relationship is

---

270 Translator: The essential relationships that come forward in Hegel's ethics are proprietary, contractual, spousal, parental, the relationship to law, collegial, and political.
271 Translator: "subjective" is likely a mistake made by Ringier. From what precedes and follows this sentence, it is clear that Hegel regards duties as determinations of the objective Will.
272 UN104: Duties make up a system; a duty is not an isolated thing.
273 Marginal note: A particular consciousness [of the Substantial] means: To see this substantial relationship as your own: this is your substance; this is who you are; you know yourself therein, this is where your true willing and acting should be.
274 Translator: It would be shallow because from the moral standpoint, the relationships of which Hegel is speaking appear as merely given, belonging to custom rather than to rational thought. They would be the subject matter of a natural anthropology, not of an a priori doctrine of duties.

presented, it would be] superfluous to say that this or that is a duty; it would also be superfluous here to deduce duties. For the moral standpoint, duties have no reality [independent of the inwardness of the moral will], because the moral will is the will as [subjective] consciousness, so that what it knows is only something ideal, only something posited within itself. Since the will is enclosed within itself, it is only the simple essence; it can make distinctions, but the distinctions are merely ideal. In duties, [however,] even according to our [pre-philosophical] conception [of them], there lies [the idea that] they are first of all absolutely binding and intuitive.[275] They are untouchable by the individual, but at the same time they are his essential nature. The distinctions [known to] the moral will, [by contrast,] are in the moral will as such [not in reality]. They are merely posited, not anything independent for themselves. [True,] the moral will recognizes duty – that my particular will exists as particular but includes the general Will. [However,] in its self-relation, this general Will is [abstract] thought; the knowing will implies this [self-enclosed] relation. Its self is merely this simple generality. [The general Will] is its concept, its essence. [For the moral standpoint,] whatever is a duty has but the form of this general relation [of the particular will to the Will as such]. The moral will comes to no [specific] duties. For a genuine duty to exist, one has to let go of the subjective will. A system of duties cannot exist for the moral standpoint.[276]

[The inability of the moral standpoint to generate a system of duties] comes nearer to the forefront in the form [that standpoint] takes in the Kantian philosophy, which includes [a doctrine concerning] the duty and conduct of consciousness. The reasonable will, which is reasonable because it does not relate itself to another, is free and infinite. In making this, its essential nature, its purpose, [the reasonable will] performs duties. So, what then should count as a duty? When we say duties, we think of them this way – that the duty has a content. The question arises: where in practical reason is there a determination whereby a content could be recognized as a duty? There is nothing in this will but the [67] identical relation to itself. The further thing is that the will should be identical to itself in its content and that the content of the will not be self-contradictory. This is what the Kantian philosophy

---

275 UN104: In duties there lies first of all this, that they are absolutely other, exalted above our particular will.
276 UN104: The moral will recognizes duty in general, but remains with this generality. For a real duty to exist for the particular will, it is precisely necessary that it [the will] not be particular but rather have immersed itself in the [objective] matter.

specified as a criterion [for what counts as a duty]. The moral consciousness has no criterion other than its self-identity. In exhibiting this character, the content exhibits itself as just. If I want to [know if I may] do something, I should ask myself whether, when I think of this course of action as universal, it can hold up. If I give someone a deposit and he keeps it, this would be a contradiction; theft is also such a contradiction. If everyone made [taking property] a maxim [of action], this would likewise be a contradiction.

It is a logical observation, [however,] that the proposition of identity is purely vacuous.[277] With that criterion [of non-contradiction], everything depends on the position I start from. If I appropriate something that is not my property, there is no contradiction [unless I presuppose property]. The same is true of theft with the Spartans; if one assumes that they merely possessed [things in common], then nothing was stolen. Measured against this simple consideration [of self-identity], one finds absolutely no contradiction.[278] I can imagine every absurdity as not contradicting itself. This [test] is entirely formal. Through the idea that everything derived [from the universalizability test] is justified, one can justify everything, for example, the desertion of an entire army [which contains no contradiction]. Nothing [by which to specify duties] is available but this [empty] principle. It is absolutely essential [for the moral standpoint] that consciousness stay within itself. But this is now only a quite general attitude of mind, which is precisely why no action comes from it.

When we give up this abstraction, the next relation is that the substantial is [grasped], not merely as the abstract substantial [the duty to which is indifferent to welfare], but as the general Will [united with the welfare] of the particular individual;[279] in that way the essential is fulfilled [through individual self-fulfilment]. This unity [of duty and welfare] is, first, the Good, but in connection with the will. The Good is how the goal of the will determines itself; it contains the Idea [the concrete unity of the universal and the particular] in general. In thinking that the Good merely ought to be, [however,] the opposition [between

---

277 UN105: ... is an empty form of the understanding, from which one cannot proceed one step further. So, in setting up that formal principle, nothing at all is made out in the matter itself.
278 Translator: One finds no contradiction unless one presupposes the very institution whose validity the test is supposed to establish.
279 UN105: The abstraction having been given up, the next determination is that the will be determined as the unity of duty and particularity – that is, particularity in general, welfare.

the ideal and the real again] presents itself. The Will that [objectively] is must be realized throughout the entire world. Because this Idea [of the Good actualized] is itself [held] in an abstract form, it is again something unexecuted; it is only a subjective Idea. At the standpoint of this reflection [into thought], [Kant's] so-called postulates come forward. That the Good be executed, that the [68] course of the world be proportionate to the goal of freedom, that the particular will be conformable to the universal, [all] this comes forward as a postulate at the moral standpoint considered as a standpoint of reflection into self. The difference [between the Good and its actualization] shows up in the [abstract] Idea [itself].[280] For that reason, the Kantian philosophy arrived only at the postulate [of the Good actualized].

The active consciousness cannot remain with this [abstraction]. In acting [for its particular ends] it simultaneously brings forth the Good. The active consciousness does not see the opposition [between the subjective and the objective] as a perennial one. It is itself [through objectifying its purpose] the refutation of this opposition. The active consciousness appears first as a singular consciousness, and the Idea [of the Good] is supposed to be the universal. If the singular acting will is able to cancel this opposition [between the subjective and the objective], how much more must this opposition be untrue for the Will that is in and for itself?

[First,] the right of the moral consciousness is [UN106: that what I have to acknowledge as the end of my action must be determined as in general good].[281] Action should be [regarded as] good – that is, it should [be regarded as] issuing from a will that, qua free, has the character of universality and so is in general good. What [should count as what] he does should be his own [intended action] and should [reflect] his essential [self-determination]. [That is why, secondly,] a [wrongful] action cannot be attributed to me if I do not know that it is an offence.[282] The action as it exists must first have been an intention.[283]

---

280 UN105: We arrive here only at an ought, because the moral standpoint is in general the subjective distinguished from the objective.
281 Translator: Ringier wrote, "The right of the moral consciousness is that which should only be an end."
282 Translator: This must mean "if I do not know that my particular action comes within the definition of an offence," for example, if I mistake the thing I take from you as mine or as ownerless. It cannot mean "if I do not know the general action [e.g., theft] is an offence."
283 Translator: The action as it exists (for example, the taking of what in fact belongs to another) must first have been an intention (I must have known it belonged to another).

Furthermore, it must also be stated that [the action] has consequences, that, thirdly, the universality [of my free will] should be [reflected] in my will's external existence and be perceived by me as good. In that respect, children are incapable of responsibility. They lack [self-]consciousness.[284] Just as little can the inward connection between the action and [self-]consciousness be present in the insane and the mentally defective. In this regard, however, other collisions [with normal responsibility] enter, namely, in [cases of] momentary passion, [where] the lack of consciousness of the reasonable is assumed. However, this [anger] cannot count as a justification [for the wrongful action].[285] If the action is looked at as an outburst of the moment [rather than as an expression of the will], then the actor is not accorded the honour of rationality.[286] He must be rational, and it must be presumed that he is rational; he should [69] avoid such states [where passion overwhelms reason]. Anger etc. cannot be included [among the conditions] owing to which responsibility ceases. Since the action should have been known by me with the determination of whether it is good or evil, [responsibility is present].

The Good is what is valid in and for itself. This validity has all sorts of determinations. First, [it has] the determination of being the lawful, [UN106: that which is legally permitted or forbidden]. This is a validity [whereby] the Will's objectivity [above subjective opinion] is expressed. But the Good has a still more concrete form. Knowing whether something is good or not is knowing this from reasons. In that case, we say that we are convinced about the matter. I know it based on reasons. At a higher level, I know this determination [that something is good] from the Concept [of the Good].[287] Since [at the moral standpoint] I have a right to determine whether an action is good or not, I can demand that

---

284 UN106: Children are incapable of responsibility because, first, they are aware only of the immediacy of their act and, secondly, an awareness of the inner value of the action escapes them.
285 UN106: This consideration can hardly count as a mitigating factor, still less as a justification.
286 UN106: Insofar as the human being is considered [merely] as a passionate being, he is not accorded the honour due a rational being.
287 UN106: I can know what is legal, and my knowledge of that is merely the knowledge that [this prohibition] has general force. The further knowledge, however, is that I know the law, not merely in this immediate way, but from reasons. In that

some [law] be binding for *me*, or [in other words] I can demand to be convinced by reasons.[288]

It all comes down to how far the moral consciousness is justified in making such demands. If I act, then I change an existing state of affairs, but not only externally, [for] an action has a relation to the will. By acting in this [expressive] sense, I posit a change in existence. I put something [a claim or maxim] into the element of objective reality, [which] element is the valid [objective] Will. This valid Will is expressed in an ethos [*Gesinnung*].[289] If I act, I posit an existent that is legally determined [as legal or illegal]. If I act against the law, I bring forward something [a principle] antithetical to [law].[290] For my action to be an action at all, it has to bring something forward [in existence]. The [element within which] my action has an enduring existence is just that objectivity which the Will expressed [in law] is. It is up to me to know if [my action] is lawful. But I can demand more of myself; I can well understand that in order to produce something of lasting significance, [my action] should be in accordance with law. But it can be that I do not inwardly hold myself morally bound [to conform to the existing ethos]. [At the moral standpoint], it is left to me [to decide] whether I am satisfied with this [ethos] or if I want to go beyond it. But then a case can arise where, because I am not satisfied with what is legal, my particular [conviction] is at variance with what is generally lawful. And so, I can claim that I do not have to act without conviction; still less do I have to act against conviction. [70] I can go further and say that my conviction, my will, as such is the Good and that a good purpose justifies my action [UN108: not only before God but also before the law].

The form of conviction is my affair. The authority of law stands over against my conviction; I must at least have the humility to credit [the law] with as much authority as I claim for myself. From me only legality is demanded; whether or not I do it out of conviction is my business. But when I refuse to act against my conviction, I make a demand that [legality] not be required of me (this is against *conscience* – Quakers). My conviction, my conscience, is my particular [way of] thinking, [and ways of thinking] can differ. Where positive obligations must

---

case we call the knowledge conviction. A higher [knowledge] is that I understand the [law's] purpose in light of the Concept [of the Good).

288 UN106: As a consequence of my moral right, I can claim that something is valid for me not simply as having the generic form of being the law or as resting on specific reasons, but as demonstrably rational in light of its concept.

289 UN106: This element is the valid Will in general, and this is expressed in positive law.

290 UN106: If I act against the law, I do the opposite of an action; I bring forward something negative, nugatory.

be fulfilled, the duty falls into the sphere of particularity.[291] In law, no questions can be asked about my conviction. It is out of toleration [not duty] that the state accommodates Quakers. The state [UN107: insofar as it is inwardly strong] might well tolerate such private persons, but taken objectively, one should be not only a bourgeois but also a citizen. If someone wants to enjoy the benefits of the State – that is, the positive benefit of having his entire being in the State – he should also fulfil the duties [of citizenship]. Because Quakers don't want to wage war, they have been employed in transportation or have been required to pay money [for the war]. So, in this way they do contribute. With regard to those duties that are left up to me, I can proceed according to my conscience; but with objective duties one cannot give in to conscience. The third [determination of the right of the moral will – the right to specify the Good in accordance with one's conscience][292] is also inapplicable in the case where I do something from conviction that is legally proscribed. It is said [in defence of one who breaks the law from benevolent intentions] that God sees the heart; but for that very reason, because the judge is not God, he must look at the objective action and not the heart.

The ultimate purpose and the action stand under what, according to [the moralist's] knowledge and will, is good. What is determined by me as the Good is supposed to count as universally valid. [However,] the subjectivity of knowledge and conviction stand opposed to what is Right in and for itself. According to [the moral] standpoint, it is necessary that [the Good] be derived from me, and [my conviction that such-and-such is good]is supposed to be the final justification. It is [71] said that a moral purpose that shows that I willed a universal should justify an unlawful action. This is what holiness means for many – for example, Crispin. The holy Crispin stole in order to gift.[293] In such an action, there is, first of all, something particular that they do and secondly, something that only they do. Such a well-meaning act stands opposed to the lawful. The first requirement [of action] is that the action must accord with the concept [UN108: of the will]; the first duty is lawfulness. The [satisfaction of] particularity can only follow this. [Particularity] has no support if it does not have this stronghold [in the rule of law]. But [the moralist] means to say: in general, a good purpose justifies the action, no matter the kinds of collision [with the law] the action evinces.

---

291 Translator: "The duty falls into the sphere of particularity," i.e., what counts as fulfilling the positive duty is left to individual discretion.
292 See this translation, 62.
293 Translator: Legend has it that St. Crispin, the Christian patron saint of cobblers, stole leather to make shoes for the poor. UN108: Men would often rather be noble and magnanimous than law-abiding.

The question thus arises: what does the Good have by way of determination? Here the Good has absolutely no further determination; it is quite general, and also ought not to have anything further.[294] The Good as the contentless generality means nothing more than whatever can be a positive purpose of the will. For example, the purpose to do good for the poor, to hate the bad, to eradicate evil – these are all moments connected to my particular well-being. But from this it follows that everything is a positive because everything is a moment of the developed human will.[295] In this sense it has been said that there is no such thing as evil; the criminal does not will evil for evil's sake; there is always something positive [in his will]. In hate and revenge there is only a desire not to be violated. Whoever ruins himself in self-indulgence wants the vitality of self-feeling. From this it follows that one can find a good reason for everything, [UN109: for every wickedness and shamefulness] because there is something positive in it – that is, one can point to something positive. An action has manifold sides. Someone who conducts himself badly in a difficult situation [can say] that he thereby fulfilled essential duties. All the corruption wrought in the world had reasons. [UN109: Men and governments have invoked good reasons for everything.] Notwithstanding those reasons, governments, etc. have brought the community to ruin. In everything good there is something bad and in everything bad there is something good. Everything is in some sense positive.[296]

[72] This is the ultimate, innermost, and gravest point [to which the claim to absolute autonomy leads], one which constitutes human deception. In desiring the Good, they desire something formal. This is something subjective, an intended good; but the merely particularistic good is the bad. Precisely this good will, insofar as it wills only the Good [in general], remaining with the abstract Good, is equally and at once evil. [In its realization,] the universal concept of the will is thereby the opposite of the [universal] will. Likewise, the desire for the Good, [mere] good intention, is at once evil. The Good is [here] the one, the universal, the simple, that which does not yet have any differentiation because difference originates [only] in [me], and I am the subject who wills the Good.[297] The heart believes that it is the most concrete thing

---

294 UN108: ... and it also ought not to have anything further, for an action, a purpose, is supposed to justify itself just through [the conviction that it is for] the Good.
295 UN108: It turns out that everything can be taken as a positive and shown to be a good thing.
296 UN109: ... and with that all opposition between good and evil is cancelled.
297 UN109: It has already been observed that the simple Concept of the Will, which is not yet dialectically mediated, is also *not* the Concept, but rather the immediate, the *negative* of the Concept.

when it is precisely the most abstract thing. So, willing the Good is also called vitality; underlying this vitality is just feeling – ardour, heat.[298] If feeling wants the Good, then [the Good] is subordinated to caprice. This abstract Good is taken for the truth, whereas, precisely because it is abstract, it is the untrue. In this connection, it is said that one can know only the finite. That the determination of duty is my subjective will, that knowledge is merely subjective, that the truth is likewise subjective – this is the decadence of the philosophy of our time. What then is the Good? The answer one then receives is: whatever I take it to be according to my mere conviction. Therewith is expressed something subjective, but this is precisely evil, which is thus something intended.[299] By expressing this, I express the abstract.[300]

The expression that the end justifies the means deserves attention simply because it was once celebrated. This expression is quite without sense and empty; if the end is just, the means are also just;[301] means have a higher purpose only in something other.[302] But the question is only whether, if other [illegal] means exist, it is right to use these other means. If the ends are holy, they certainly sanctify the means. However, the expression [that the end justifies the means goes further]. It says that if the ends are good (and all are good), it follows that I should commit a crime [if a crime will bring about the end]. A crime is a violation of a duty that [73] is also good. [So, the expression] means nothing else than this: in order to do good, I am justified in injuring a good; the

---

298 UN109: This abstraction is also called vitality, just as, in general, the emptiest and most impoverished stuff is praised as liveliness.
299 UN110: By making my bare feeling the criterion for the content of my deeds, I have turned caprice into a law.
300 UN110: In such times, consciousness retreats into itself. Socrates was executed by the Athenians because he reduced duty and religiosity to mere inward knowledge.
301 Translator: This must mean that if the end is just, the means, assuming they're legal, are also just.
302 UN110: It is self-evident that the end and means must correspond, and if the end is just, the means are just. In general, one can indeed say that sacred purposes sanctify the means. But that expression is not understood in the way just explained. What supposedly follows from an end's being good is that it justifies me in committing what is in itself a crime. That expression means only that I am justified in injuring a good in order to do good. The decision as to what is good always falls to my subjectivity. It is said, however, that if a purpose is truly good, it is still always my subjective opinion that I pursue in it [because] if a purpose is wide-ranging [e.g., to promote the Good], it is believed that one has more of a right to enforce it [than if the purpose is narrow and controversial]. Here occurs the idea that one good can be subordinated to another. This is, to be sure, the case, as will later be shown, and this subordination is necessary if there is to be a system of duties. However, if I declare that my intention and insight determine what is subordinated, then objectivity is here again lacking.

higher authority of the ego is always in play. Therewith other ideas also apply. If the end is truly good, a comprehensive good [e.g., the welfare of humankind], then I put it forward as justifying [my action] regardless of whether I intended [that purpose]. From the fact that a purpose is comprehensive one believes that it is [incontrovertibly] good, but it is just such a purpose that least of all requires a bad means.

Accordingly, if a crime is an injury to something good, then one cannot say that one may injure the good in order to do good. [This is because] crime is not merely [an injury to] something also good; rather, it is an injury to something objective, and to this one cannot oppose a good intention. For having [a good intention] does not entail having a determination [of the Good]. [Good intention] by itself cannot count as Right. If [I believe] it is necessary that what appears to others as Right be subordinated to what is also Right, then it is I who subordinates here. The subjective imagination can believe that it has a right [so to subordinate other ends] if its purpose is comprehensive. As comprehensive, it is higher than other [ends]. For example, we can posit as a comprehensive end the freedom and welfare of a people, so it is the purpose not of an individual but of an equally comprehensive substantial reality. [However,] it belongs to the people – it is its business – to act comprehensively; [the comprehensive good] should be posited, carried out, precisely by the entirety.

Goethe says that the murder of Caesar by Brutus and Cassius was the stupidest deed that was ever done.[303] This affair, this act of will, was supposed to make a difference [to the world. Yet it did not]. [UN111: The form of the Roman world was in no way altered by the death of a single individual, Caesar.] What happened to the world through [this act] was done by a few individuals. It remained a mere isolated, naked act, a crime, and therefore a merely common crime precisely because it had no [world-historical] consequences. What was contained in the Will of [the Roman] world could also only be fulfilled by that world. People [who think that good intention justifies] believe that [Caesar and Cassius] erred only with regard to particulars.[304] It is easy [UN111: and the most forgivable thing] to err; [the important thing is that] the [74] Good was desired. In that way, [the crime] is minimized. One can [indeed] err about many things whether or not an iota of change occurs. But when the mistake is made by a

---

303 Angehrn, Bondeli, Seelmann: J.W. Goethe, *Materialen zur Geschichte der Farbenlehre*, 2. Abteilung, Römer, in *Goethes Werke*, ed. E. Trunz (Munich, 1982), 14:45.
304 UN111: ... [only] with regard to what is good.

conspiracy, that is something different; precisely the mistake ad hominem is the greatest offence. Whoever [UN111: acts not in accordance with objective Right but in accordance with Right as he knows it] makes his fancy the highest principle of action. He thereby says that he wants to know [what right and duty are] from himself against the whole world, and here error is no matter of indifference. Before [he acts] he says that knowledge as I know it is the deciding factor, and afterward he says that error is possible here. This is a contradiction.[305] Here is just the innermost and deepest point where good and evil touch – the point where evil originates, the innermost heart of evil. This point is the highest abstraction, the speculative pinnacle.[306] Evil should not be conceived as arising in an accidental way but rather as occurring and originating eternally.

Evil lies in the nature of mind. It is [the mind's] destiny to withdraw from its naturalness – as ego, as will and knowledge. Here he is evil. In that he wills his lusts, he is evil; he has only to choose this position. By virtue of his inner diremption, he knows that he is in his desire. It is through reflection that the mind first raises itself out of nature and thereby first becomes sinful.[307] He is not evil by virtue of the immediate desire to which he surrenders; it is rather that, because the Good is his subject, he is evil on principle and for reasons. He inserts into the Good a content of his arbitrary choice, of his desire. The standpoint of mind's separation [from nature] is therefore a necessary standpoint. It is also necessary that [mind take] the standpoint of desiring the Good. But that he wills what is particular to him or that he remains at the standpoint [of subjectivity], that he wills only the abstract [Good] and places only his peculiarity into it – that is his doing and his guilt. The human being must desire the universal Good, but his remaining there, his inserting any preferred content into this Good, or his obeying his natural will – this [is attributable to] his particularity. Remaining in particularity is the fault of the individual.

So evil comes forward in mind as a phase, but as a phase that must be overcome. Still, as a moment, it also appears in the Good.

---

305 Translator: Before he acts, he says that truth as I know it counts as truth. Afterwards, he says that it does not.
306 UN111: We stand here at the highest point of inwardness, at certainty. It is said that this is something holy, but it can just as well be called evil. Because the extremes here immediately pass over into each other, this [certainty] is the speculative pinnacle where good and evil can be grasped only in the transition of each to the other.
307 UN112: It is rightly said [Rom. 4:15] that the Law, that is, this reflection on the universal, first institutes sin.

A human being who wants to act must [sometimes] be "evil" (that is, a bad man), someone [75] who sacrifices much, who bends and hurts.[308] He must have the character capable of injuring what one could otherwise very well let count [as worthwhile] (a [military] general, for example). Accordingly, at this standpoint we see the will that is self-consciously an abstract will, that knows itself as the power of abstracting, as a power that can renounce all content, that knows itself as capable of doing this; and good and evil are here utterly indistinguishable.[309]

The standpoint of conscience – the will's self-knowledge as the universal, infinite power that supposedly transcends all content – is first expressed in what [Friedrich] Jacobi has said: that the human being is inwardly [innocent] insofar as he does [what his conscience regards] as true, that for him all commandments can be valid or invalid [as his conscience decides]. He says that robbery, theft, fraud, lying – all this the human being may do. There is a saying: the righteous man has no law. The Stoics said: the sage can do anything. He can rob, murder, steal. In these [expressions] lies [the idea] that in the power of self-consciousness, everything fixed is unfixed. If the righteous man does [something], it is lawful. Relevant here is an [oft-] quoted passage from Jacobi: I am the atheist who will murder, deceive, etc., as Desdemona lied.[310] I will lie and deceive like Pylades is portrayed as doing for Orestes, will murder like Timoleon (fratricide), commit suicide like Otho (the Roman emperor who provided his own death date in order to end a war), commit temple robbery like David,[311] pluck out [as Jesus' disciples did] ears of corn on the Sabbath merely because I'm hungry, because the law is

---

308 UN112: A man who lives a concrete and full life must also know how to be bad. In the pursuit of an essential purpose, many purposes that could otherwise very well be worthwhile are bent [to the dominant purpose].

309 Translator: Hegel's point is that, at its most self-consistent position, the moral conscience evinces the general nature of original evil. Evil originates in the mind's irruption from nature such that it freely wills under the aspect of the Good a particularistic content given by desire. But that is exactly what the moral conscience does.

310 Translator: Jacobi's reference is to Desdemona's response (*Othello*, act 5, scene 2) to Emilia's asking her who did this deed. "Nobody. I myself."

311 Translator: Jacobi's reference is probably to David's persuading a priest of the Tabernacle to hand over for David's followers consecrated bread that only priests were permitted to eat (1 Sam. 21:1–6). In Mark 2:23–8, Jesus adduces this episode to justify the breach of Sabbath law in plucking the corn. But it is strange that this is spoken of as temple robbery.

made for the sake of human beings, not human beings for the sake of the law.[312]

The human being as such is the conduit for the law's realization; he is the actuator through which the law becomes real. The law is without being, has no existence without human beings. The practical law [UN113: of the Kantian and Fichtean philosophy, against which Jacobi speaks,] is by itself something merely formal, contentless, the law for the [reflexive] understanding. It enjoins nothing definite; nor does it come to any duties. Jacobi calls the universal [76] law in human beings the magisterial right of thought.[313] Herein lies, to be sure, the magisterial right. With that [phrase] is doubtless expressed the self-determining self-consciousness, but it is assumed that this is the [arbiter of the] just. To say that this content is the just is once again [to leave the just] indeterminate. This ideality is the concept of subjectivity that has not yet come to substantiality.

Accordingly, the second form [of the Good] is the form of conscience.[314] It is the holy, that which decides concerning actions and duties. Conscientious is he who turns Right and duty into a law for himself. In conscience, [however,] what the Right and obligatory are is not determined. Insofar as conscience is a formalism, it is one-sided, and the content [of duty] comes down to whatever I've done. Conscience has no content.

A third formal *Gestalt* [of morality] is one that has in modern times come forward in the form of irony. Irony stems from Socrates. With him it was, to be sure, a kind of pretence in that he allowed validity to [UN113: one-sided] propositions asserted by his students, but then led them forward in order, by developing their statements, [UN113: to demonstrate their invalidity]. In that way, they were led to the opposite

---

312 Translator: This is a paraphrase of Mark 2:27. The foregoing passage, taken from Jacobi's open letter to Fichte (1779), actually reads: "Yea, I am the atheist and the godless one, who, against the will that wills nothing, will tell lies, just as Desdemona did when she lay dying; will lie and deceive as Pylades is portrayed as doing for Orestes; will murder like Timoleon, will violate law and oath like Epaminondas, like Johann de Witt; commit suicide like Otho, rob a temple like David – yea, pluck out ears of corn on the Sabbath merely because I'm hungry, and the law is made for the sake of human beings, not human beings for the sake of the law." Friedrich Heinrich Jacobi, *Jacobi an Fichte* (Hamburg: Friedrich Perthes, 1799), 32–3, https://archive.org/details/jacobianfichte00jacogoog (my translation).
313 Jacobi, *Jacobi an Fichte*, 33.
314 Translator: The first was the Good abstracted from the particular will, exemplified in Kantian morality; the second is the Good determined through the particular will, exemplified by Jacobi. The third is irony, exemplified by Friedrich von Schlegel.

[of their proposition]. Accordingly, it is this dialectic that validates itself in an unbiased way.[315] The boundedness [of the propositions] gives them their firmness.[316] It was especially [Friedrich von] Schlegel who took irony as [UN113: a moment of] the Divine. In irony there lies a profound revenge [UN113: of the rational], but it is something ambiguous. In general, irony is the coming forth of ideality, the transcendence of fixity.[317] But [irony is] transcendence conscious of itself as transcendence [so that there is also consciousness of fixity]. Transcendence certainly has something beautiful about it. The gods in Homer appear with this irony.[318] In their figuration there appears at once the scent of their finitude and their transcendence of [finitude]. That [the Greeks] sacrificed to the gods can also be called irony. They burned the bad part and ate the good part themselves. A barbaric irony is the transition to opposites – [e.g.,] when a man is all contrite in the morning, declaring the nothingness of all self-feeling, and then in the afternoon rolls around in every lust. In irony lies the presentation of opposites.

The most beautiful form of irony is the [77] serenity of the Greek gods: to be in the thing [to have material shape] but at the same time also to be with oneself; serenity and being with oneself [in the other].[319] [Serene] self-forgetfulness manifests itself in the mother, who knows herself in her child, beholds it, and overflows with joy. This aspect of joy is the most beautiful side of irony. Italian music finds precisely in the deepest sorrow the most blissful self-feeling. If the feeling of the negative [that is self-consciousness] presents itself, then [irony] is no longer serenity. Then self-consciousness is at the same time [a consciousness of the] vanity [of things]. Here what is missing is that the will does not give up its subjectivity; instead, self-consciousness keeps objective reality [*die Sache*] away from itself [and then declares its instability]. Irony is the [form of] consciousness that merely plays with everything, that wants to be master of the noble and excellent, [UN114: so that it is

---

315 Translator: unbiased because the inversion of the proposition into its opposite comes from the mouth of the advocate for the proposition.
316 Translator: The proposition put forward as absolute falls to the ground but stands firm insofar as it is limited.
317 UN114: ... the transcendence of fixity, hence also of seriousness.
318 UN114: In Homer, the Olympian gods appear with this irony (irrepressible laughter at Hephaestos [the lame god of fire: *Iliad*, bk. 1, line 595], Aphrodite a stroke to the cheek [actually, to the chest, delivered by Athena: *Iliad*, bk. 21, line 423], [the fearsome] Mars [Ares] shrieks like 10,000 [when speared by Athena: *Iliad*, bk. 5, line 860].
319 UN114: Serenity and self-forgetfulness can be viewed as temperaments of the highest virtue.

only choice that condescends to busy oneself with it]. What is positive in this irony is [the judgment of the] vanity [of finite things]; vanity in everything I do – I am vanity. This irony is precisely the pinnacle [from] which one can go this way or that,[320] the form of emptiness. In modern times it has doubtless again come to the fore.

More closely related [than this emptiness to irony considered as a presentation of opposites] is an older idea. Formerly, there was much talk about hypocrisy. A hypocrite is someone who does evil behind a pretence of [doing] good, someone who is therefore aware of the evil. Inasmuch as the pretence is condemned as hypocrisy, it is assumed that there are actions that are inherently vicious and that are also known [by the actor] to be evil, and that the good reason [offered for the action] is merely a pretext. What's more, because the hypocrite wills the vice, he uses the Good as a means to evil.

This idea of hypocrisy gets lost at the moral standpoint. [Here] what is right and good lies in the inward determination [of the Good] and in the value of action generally; [so] the assumption that something can be objectively a crime no longer holds. According to this position, there is always something good in what is desired. In recent presentations [of this position], we have seen [a thesis] that has been elaborated with great eloquence: insofar as the human being acts in accordance with his instincts, he does well.[321] By stating [the position] so, one grants to the heart a right against the law. [78] It was this goodness of intention ranged against what stands on the other side as vice that the earlier point of view named hypocrisy, because that view assumed that there are objective crimes. [Hypocrisy] consisted in this, that what was done was held out as good and that the individual was himself this inner contradiction [because] what he desired was not the Good. [However,] in the position [now under consideration], where consciousness can determine anything as good, hypocrisy really falls away. To the [earlier point of view], presenting a collision [between good and evil] as a collision between good and good would appear as mere hypocrisy, [because] on its assumption [a collision between one good and another] is the lowest of collisions, a mere collision within a subject. If we see theft at the theatre such that the fact of the matter is known [to the audience], good intention is not something that is truly serious.

---

320 Translator: into despair or into the Substantial.
321 UN115: Recent presentations have deployed great eloquence to show that what people do in accordance with their instincts is good, since these instincts were placed in them by God.

Also falling away is the earlier view of the judgment of vice and sin. This view assumes that there are ways of acting that are forbidden by God.[322] In the habitually evil way of life there is a contradiction within the reality of this way of life, an inner violence that the evil will does to conscience. However, if good intention – the pure will – is what constitutes the worth of an action, then that demerit [of an intrinsically evil act] drops out. In this good intention, there is no opposition between evil and good. Because I am and [because] my heart impels me, I will the Good. If the wicked man lives shamelessly in sin, he can feel no pang of conscience. In this way, the belief in vice disappears entirely.

These are the [thought] forms that immediately come forth at this stage of consciousness. A determinate content [of the Good] is not to be found here.[323] The content is contingent on who inserts it. Most importantly, goodness can be predicated of such a content, but for that reason – because one wills the abstract Good – everything can count as good. The content appears at once contingent and arbitrary. It does not appear so, nor does the content decay, because it is not external to the universal [Will]. [It is because] the predicate "good" is not external [to the individual] but is rather in himself.

There is one more aspect to touch on. The will that is ironic or hypocritical is aware that it [79] can play with every content. At this standpoint, the contingency and arbitrariness of the content [of the Good] is reality; this is what [the subject] is and what it wills.[324] However, the will that [unlike the ironic will] does not regard the content as a matter of indifference becomes embarrassed about the content [it gives itself].[325] The will that is aware that it depends on this content falls into collisions [between one duty and another]. One content is presented to him, but at the same time another. He is now driven to settle the collision for himself. So, it is essential that such an individual come to a resolution; morality must make this decision. Multiple contents [duties] present themselves, and then there is a contradiction.

This stage of reflection takes many particular forms. It can [produce] a kind of fear of acting, a distrust of reality, [because] it is possible that

---

322 UN115: In that vice is spoken of, it is assumed that there are ways of acting that inherently contradict human and divine law.
323 UN115: A determinate content of the Good is not to be found at this standpoint. Only arbitrary will and preference, subjectivity as such, decide.
324 UN116: The subject knows itself as that which stands above everything.
325 UN116: The will that … does not take the content as a matter of indifference, becomes embarrassed with his content [because] he has no criterion of decision.

a good may contain something else that contradicts it. If the soul generally takes such a direction, it becomes scrupulous [to a fault]. This indecision is afraid to tackle anything. This [kind of] rumination makes action difficult. The tendency is to have reservations about everything. Still, this reflection is [from one point of view] correct. When duties are performed, many individuals come into contact with each other. The terms of these various relationships must again be perfectly honoured. There is always something that one can wish would not be injured [by a moral choice]. The more cultivated the soul, the more of these sides [of a situation] there are, and how many of them are to be left unsatisfied or injured?[326]

On the other hand, this reflection makes it easier [to act], especially if the reflection is directed towards a presupposed general purpose. [This is so because], once formed, this purpose again contains many particular [components]. For example, if a man makes it his purpose to make good use of his life, to train everything [UN116: after the fashion of the Niemeyer pedagogy][327] – benevolence, compassion, the ear – [then] if he does so, he can now exercise benevolence, [compassion] etc. If he achieves what he wanted, he will have developed [many capacities]. Then everything will have been made easier. This conscientiousness has choice to the full. The reason is precisely that the purpose is so general. A man becomes educated by virtue of giving himself over to objective matters; in that way he grinds down his subjectivity. He can educate [80] himself only if he forgets himself, only if he wills to make objective matters his own [matters]. In making objective matters his own, he has an objective interest, not a subjective one.

This is what should be spoken about first. When it comes to the substantial, all other ancillary considerations [that might bewilder and paralyse the individualistic moralist] fall away. When the individual, [faced] with these choices, gets engaged on so many fronts and sees that he must give up something, this strikes him as a sacrifice. One can always find plenty of such sacrificed [values], which, considered singly, can also be goals. When it comes to the matter-in-itself, [however, the educated man] forgets the sacrifice and the importance of his subjectivity. When the [objective] matter is held fast, the many qualms fall away. The man of experience and education can, to be sure, consider

---

326 UN116: With action, there is always something that one can wish would not be neglected. The more cultivated the soul, the more possibilities of disturbing other relationships arise.
327 August Hermann Niemeyer (1754–1828).

other things beside the main object. The judge can spare many while still proceeding with the main matter for a judge.[328] But if he thinks only of sparing, he forgets his judicial office. For a while there was much talk about the importance that little things have for the mind. It has been said that in morality there are no matters of indifference – [that] it is precisely part of moral action to have regard for a host of trifling considerations. [UN117: This is to be understood in the sense explained above.]

Accordingly, over-scrupulousness falls away [if the substance of the matter is grasped]. If a subject has a true purpose, he holds fast to it. Many collisions thereby fall away. In the case of collisions within the nature of things, the resolution of the collision is already determined by the objective subordination [of one duty to another]. Only a few collisions remain for the individual – collisions that pertain only to his individuality.

In the ancient tragedies, we see great conflicts. In *Antigone*, we see, on one side, [family] piety, and on the other, we see that other ethical substance, the state. We see these two great relationships in conflict with each other. They exist in conflict inasmuch as they are mutually free and, as sculptured individuals, [Antigone and Creon stand for] these simple, great sculptured shapes [of family and state]. We see, as it were, gods in battle. Likewise, in [Aeschylus'] *Oresteia* we see a great conflict. We see the idea that [81] murder [a crime against human law] will be avenged, and we also see the piety a son [owes] a mother – hence the punishment for this crime [of matricide]. We see the conflict emerge because these two relationships [to the state and to the family] are, so to speak, coordinate with each other. That is why the crime does not have to be punished; instead, only the form of punishment is present.[329] The one who has the duty of revenge is also the criminal, the son. This was the time of heroes, when it fell to individuals as such to enforce ethical moments. That is why we see princely individuals act in tragedies. The modern bourgeois tragedies have something insignificant about them because [the characters] are already enclosed within [structures belonging to] the substantial Idea, and conflicts can enter only rarely.[330] And

---

328 UN117: (A judge who acts strictly according to law but in doing so proceeds gently in all other matters).
329 Translator: In the play, the jury splits evenly on the question of guilt, and Athena breaks the tie in favour of Orestes. The Furies are then placated with a ritual recognizing their divinity.
330 UN118: ... because there are burghers here who are enclosed within an objective organization [e.g., a corporation] and for whose decision little remains.

in these conflicts the unethical is already posited.[331] No doubt, there remain many collisions for the individual, and it is for conscience to resolve them.

One expects that a [science of] morality will highlight these cases of conflict. It thereby becomes a casuistry that considers particular cases [of conflict]. Subjects expect such a science to submit finished solutions [UN118: to all cases, off the shelf, as it were]. For example, one such case supposes that two shipwrecked men are on a beam [that will hold only one]. There is a lot of talk about this. [UN118: One has children, the other none; one has many, the other few]; the children [of one] can have a mother, the other's not. One can be a physician, the other a jurist, etc. Here there is a lot to calculate. It is immediately apparent that it is pointless to expect [UN118: a decisive moral answer] if such features are combined. There is a need of the moment. The cases are infinitely varied. If you want to decide these cases, you sink into an infinite multiplicity [of features]; you are never finished. You are in a field of contradiction. Here a decision must be made in this utterly particular case, in this one case, at this instant. This is the place where arbitrariness rules. Here the particular is the crux, not the universal. Therefore, it is also impossible to make a generally applicable decision.[332] The individual [case], specified in its unique way, is precisely the singular, not the universal.

In other cases, you might [82] remain with an abstract principle and accept it as fixed. For example, if someone bursts [into a room] in a rage to murder someone [who has hidden himself and asks me where he is], should I tell him where he is or not? It is soon said that one should tell the truth. But there would be many things to consider. Such truthfulness is precisely of a kind that has nothing behind it. Telling the truth with respect to transitory things – for the most part there is nothing in it. Every minute kills a thousand truths. The outward should correspond to the inward, but in saying that [the hunter's quarry] is in this or that closet, speech is an action. If I say it, I kill [the man in the closet], and I leave nothing to God. It is as if I gave [the murderer] the dagger. Giving him the immediate possibility [of murder] is an action. What I do is help him. It would be nothing more than hypocrisy, a supercilious steadfastness [to think] one had nothing to be sorry for.[333]

---

331 Translator: Because only the unethical can conflict with the ethical.
332 UN118: In such particular cases, the particular must also decide, that is, the individual, and no objective decision can be expected here.
333 UN118: There is a way of deciding where one remains with an abstract principle and holds fast to it as the decisive thing. In his moral [philosophy], Fichte presents

Such cases of collision [of duties] can be easily decided, but the real decision falls completely in the case. It is the particular individual who must decide. This decisive particularity is what we call character.[334] So, you can't look to moral [casuistry] for [the answers to] such cases. If at first it seems that there are so many moral conflicts, one must ask [when confronted by such] great conflicts, what relationships come into conflict. The hesitancy, the indecisiveness of men is the origin of many conflicts. [It is] the beginning of softness. Dignified, substantial action requires self-forgetfulness, wherein [one's] idiosyncrasy vanishes. By contrast, ruminations that always want to know if one is doing something excellent have this softness [about them].[335]

Accordingly, the moral standpoint is this: Freedom is [the basis of] Right.[336] [In abstract Right,] freedom has its existence only in a thing. [At the moral standpoint, freedom has its existence in the particular will.] Freedom in the particular will is the ground of the Concept.[337] This [the Concept] is what gives the particular will its right. This right of the particular will is a moment of the Idea. Its right is [1] to be [reflected] in what it does, that [what is understood as its action] be its own, that its action have been intended, [2] that welfare also have a

---

the case where an enraged man with a dagger bursts into a room and wants to murder someone who has hidden himself. The question is whether another who is in the room and knows the whereabouts of the hidden person is absolutely required to tell the truth. In general, it is hard to tell the [empirical] truth and few do. Thousands of ordinary, common truths disappear every minute. In general, a man should undoubtedly be at one with himself and thus exhibit the Idea. However, in the case mentioned, speech is not only speech but [also] an action, and indeed, one by which it is as if I handed a dagger to another who wants to murder someone but has no dagger. This self-identity that I have achieved by telling the truth would be nothing but a supercilious, ridiculous loyalty to truth; I would have only posited myself as self-concordant [while aiding murder]. [Translator: Hegel's argument doesn't address Fichte's point that the man questioned can try to dissuade the intruder and thus neither lie nor aid a murder. But suppose the hunted person is someone to whom the man questioned owes a duty of rescue – for example, a spouse or child. This is now a moral conflict of a kind Hegel argues the moral standpoint cannot resolve according to principle, hence must leave to arbitrary discretion. At the ethical standpoint, by contrast, there is no conflict; lying about a fleeting truth is justified when necessary to fulfil a familial duty.]

334 UN119: A man can act only insofar as he is a particular individual. The demand for a casuistry of this sort implies that one wants to be relieved of the trouble of having character. A man can be relieved of this trouble by having a conscience advisor, a confessor (who receives sugar and coffee); and such a conscience advisor knows how to provide good and pious grounds for everything.
335 UN119: The reflection that always wants to know if one has here or there acted admirably leads to softness and self-conceit.
336 UN119: In general, therefore, the moral standpoint is freedom in the particular will.
337 UN119: The particular will, subjectivity, is the true ground of freedom.

THE GOOD AND CONSCIENCE 99

place, and [3] third, that he know [his action] as good or not good.[338] But at the same time, the moral will is only this formalism, so that when [the moralist] wants to determine something from this standpoint, the determining factor is the arbitrary will.

Knowledge [that something is good] and willing what one knows [to be good] is [still] something [83] subjective. It is [a subject's] calling to give himself an objective reality, not [merely] to have objective reality in his thought in the same way that he is a subject [in his thought]. It is only the abstract universal that [the moralist] knows, the abstract Good.[339] One can have many good reasons and purposes, but this standpoint begins from a presupposition. The moral consciousness is not a philosophic consciousness. Philosophic consciousness is rational consciousness and for that reason it ceases to be a formal consciousness. So, when good intentions are asserted at the moral standpoint, all these [intentions] are forms of immediacy.[340] The moral standpoint is honest. In that it is not a philosophic consciousness, the moral consciousness is the standpoint of reflection [away from something presupposed]. The moral consciousness does not claim to be a philosophic consciousness. In all its forms it readily admits that it is not rational.[341] Thus, when it says that one cannot know the truth and so must surrender to feeling, it has therewith renounced all rational knowledge. Rational consciousness does not draw from feeling. Subjective knowledge, because it is subjective, can have no objective content [of duty]. It can only remain within itself, with its conviction.[342] This content is an immediate one. Rational knowledge is not immediate knowledge.

The moral standpoint, if it wants to stand alone, is a one-sided standpoint.[343] Generally, the moral consciousness emerges in a time of decay, because the publicly recognized law no longer holds with full force. There is here a rupture [between the inward and the outward].[344]

---

338 UN119: ... and that what he does have the determination of goodness and be known by him as such. [Translator: (1) is a right against penal liability for unintended deeds as well as against legal liability or moral blame for the unforeseeable consequences of actions; (2) is a right to the free pursuit of one's personal interests and to others' reasonable care for one's welfare; (3) is a right against paternalism.]
339 UN120: But [the moral standpoint] produces from itself no immanent content.
340 UN120: So, no matter how well-meant the ends pursued at the moral standpoint are, whether they come from emotion or enthusiasm, they always carry the defect of immediacy.
341 UN120: ... that it is merely subjective.
342 UN120: The content it gives itself – belief, enthusiasm, epiphany – is always an immediate one.
343 UN120: Morality is always only a moment of a whole.
344 UN120: We have already recalled Socrates [UN110, n. 300]; in that time, a rupture appeared between the inner and the outer.

The discovery of the self is precisely what constitutes the dissolution. Accordingly, this standpoint is as one-sided as the standpoint of [abstract] Right.[345] Taken by itself, this standpoint [of morality] collapses in on itself; the comparison [between what morality claims to be and what it is leads to] a third thing outside this principle. This inadequacy is its own [a self-inadequacy]. It is a self-contradiction [of the moral standpoint] that what counts for it is only the universal Good [and yet determination of the Good then falls to individual caprice].[346] Conscience [84] (the sheer inner self-certainty [of one's goodness]) is just this [inner contradiction]. The Good is the empty and indeterminate, just as I, in knowing [the Good] from myself, am the indeterminate. The straightforward consummation [of the moral standpoint] is just this fading away[347] of the mind, whose reality merges with the self.

These are nothing but the consequences of the Kantian philosophy. [Kant's successors] did not adhere to his starting point in its speculative rigour.[348] To adhere to the Kantian philosophy is to express the truth as a postulate, a beyond of this world. Whether the Good is realized [in this world] is a contingent matter. The beyond is just the harmony [of the universal and the particular will such that] the particular will is also good, that a moral world order exists, that this order conforms to the universal Good. This moral world order is the Good, that which ought to be. [However,] it persists as a beyond. But the finite [one-sided] is not the true, not the Absolute; rather subjectivity is just the untrue, an internal contradiction. The Good is supposed to remain merely an abstract universal [over against the natural subject]. [For Kant, the Good and the natural subject] should each keep to itself, and [yet] both should harmonize. That is a contradiction, so not the truth. That neither the [postulated] Good nor the subjective [conscience] is the truth, that [the true is] rather the universal Will in identity with the form of subjectivity – this constitutes the transition [to the next sphere]. This is the truth. It [the truth] fulfils [the individual's] subjectivity, its pure regard for self, but at the same time [it has] within itself a determinate and differentiated [content of duty].

---

345 UN120: The truth is but the truth of the standpoints of morality and abstract Right.
346 UN120: Duty and purpose require determination, yet only the form of the universal counts for it.
347 UN120: atrophy
348 UN120: As this standpoint was developed further in the Kantian philosophy and as it was adhered to as the ultimate one, its self-contradictoriness became more and more apparent.

[THIRD PART]

[Ethical Life]

[85] Abstract Right is the existence of abstract freedom. The moral standpoint first [brings to salience] the subjective [intentions, purposes, insight, welfare]. Their unity is the truth; this is what is called the *ethical*. Only the *ethical* is the truth and, as such, it is the necessary, the first. It is on this ground that abstract [Right] and subjective [morality] must first develop. They cannot exist by themselves; they must have a foundation of this kind. There can be neither a condition of abstract Right nor a condition of the *moral standpoint*. The ethical condition is always their underlying ground. If either one or the other standpoint dominates, then one of them is overweight on the foundation.

The *family* is older than the state. In general, it is an ethically strong nature, a dignified and substantial living together. In science, the abstract [isolated] moments must be considered first [in order to prove the truth of their underlying ground – the third entity].[349] This third entity, which is alone the truth, is *ethical life*. It is the Good integrated with subjectivity. It is the universal in the subjective – each integrated with the other. It is this unity that we have to consider. The conceit of the subject has disappeared, as has the abstract [universal], and the concrete [universal] is the truth of both.

Accordingly, *ethical life* is first of all the Idea of freedom, but of a freedom that is alive. The Good is not an otherworldly beyond.[350] The truth is not always something that merely ought to be. What is real is the living Good – the Good or the freedom that [individual] self-consciousness has for its existence. [Individual] self-consciousness has the Substance

---

349 UN121: In science, the abstract moments must be considered first, because the truth can be grasped only through them.
350 UN122: Here the Good is not displaced to a beyond, to a moral world order; rather it is real and present.

for its ground; it knows [the Substance] as its own will's essential nature, not as a yoke. *Ethical life* is therefore both the in-itself, the objective, and the for-itself or subjective. It is known by the subject as the objective reality, but as the subject's own [essential nature], wherein it lives (fish in water, lungs and air).[351] The [subjective] moment must be preserved in the objectivity of ethical life.

This ethical life is, accordingly, not the abstract universal in itself; it is rather a system of determinations of the Will, because it is posited as [86] united with subjectivity, [which] has put aside its obstinacy. The subject must give up its isolated subjectivity, so that the Good can have the infinite form [of subjectivity] within itself. [The Good] is therewith the inwardly differentiated, and what [contains] the difference is the Concept, the pure form [of the Good] itself. This pure form is the authoritative, the Good. These differences [of objective Good and subjective endorsement of the Good] are therein essential differences, essential moments. Because the objective Good has the [subjective] form within it, its determinations are posited through the form itself; hence they are rational [not given immediately]. This content is then for the first time something true; therefore, it is fixed over against subjective consciousness precisely because these determinations are rational. These determinations of the Will are what we earlier called duties; they are the essential content [of duty].[352] The Good is then for the first time the real universal Good, the truly objective [Good].[353] The abstract is the [isolated] subjective [consciousness]. The abstract is a mass and weak, just as the rule [over a mass] is strong in contrast to the weak, but for that reason, it is itself weak. The same is true of religion. Qua [exclusive] particular, it has its opposite only in another [external foe]. Only insofar as religion has internal sects does it constitute itself firmly. Only insofar as [social] estates have opposition within themselves do they have power and reality. For the most part, practice demonstrates this. Applied to Protestantism, [internal division] has been considered a shortcoming. But only so is it something rational.

This rationality [of content] is, then, independent [of the subject] and actual [in the subject]. It is Law, institutions. That it be expressed in [written] words is not a requirement. It is in and for itself. That is why the ancients called the rational in and for itself the Divine.[354] It has no

---

351 UN122: The subject is in the object [as in] its habitat, its element.
352 See this translation, 78–9.
353 UN122: The Good is for the first time a self-unfolding and self-determining.
354 UN123: Its [divinity] consists in this, that it is exalted above the arbitrary will of the individual.

beginning; it is not posited in time. Positive laws are but the external manifestations. It is said that it is divine. It has been revealed; an oracle declared it. The other against which the eternal Being in and for itself stands is the subjective consciousness. The Divine is [this consciousness's] will, its spiritual, true, essential nature [*Wesen*]. The relation [of subjective consciousness] thereto consists in constituting [the Divine's] reality, so that the eternal, inherently objective Being becomes something willed, something real. It [the eternal Being] has its performing will in [the particular consciousness]. [We see a similar thing in nature.] Without realization [by the individual], the animal genus would be the merely [87] abstract, the merely inward. Accordingly, this existence [in the subjective consciousness] is the realization of the inherently objective Being. The interest [of the subjective consciousness] is to be the rational[ly necessary side of itself]. Individuals must bring forth [the Divine]. They are the accidents by which [the inherently objective Being] comes into experience.[355] It is the essential nature that works in them and that thereby externalizes itself through them. It has been said that everything one does is to the honour of God. [Individuals] are the actuators of the universal. However, they are not in the universal as immediate [instinctual] beings, as is the case with animals that do not have the genus for their [conscious] object.

By contrast [to the animal], self-consciousness is precisely this, that it knows that it is a purpose for itself.[356] By having [their essential nature] as purpose, individuals themselves bring it to presence. By their having it for their object, the essential thing is this relationship [between the essential nature and subjective consciousness, which is] the unity of the Idea.

Belonging to the [general] form of knowledge is the form of belief, of trust. The human being knows the law, not as something foreign, but rather as its own. It is not even a relationship of faith, because [faith] already assumes a kind of reflex thinking.[357] It is rather that individuals have their self-feeling [in the law], know themselves therein. Thereby we have worth because it is we who bring [the law] to realization. This can be called the witness that the mind bears to the laws. If the mind gave no witness, then there would be an opposition [of law to the

---

355 UN123: Individuals are accidents of the universal Substance. This universal Substance first appears to peoples as something given.
356 *Daß man sich Zweck ist, von sich weiß.* UN123: The concern of self-consciousness is to know its essential nature and to have it as a purpose and to realize it.
357 Translator: a reflex thinking whereby faith opposes itself to a knowledge equated with finite understanding.

individual]. In an ethical relationship, this separation is non-existent. The subject knows [the law] as its essential nature.

The development of this knowledge can go further. [After immediate trust], the law can be understood from reasons. Understanding from [historical or instrumental] reasons is finite understanding. This finite understanding always has presuppositions that then hold as a foundation. The ethical consciousness can certainly reason [from purposes]; if the purposes that comprise the reasons are themselves contained in the truth, then this movement [of thought] is reflection of the right kind. But if consciousness makes itself the ground of such reasoning, then the [true] foundation has been destroyed.[358] [Knowledge in general] can take the forms of the relationship of consciousness [to an objectively given law]. It may be trust or [speculative] reflection, in which case [the opposition of law to the subject] does not appear. Only if evil, self-conceit, [88] interferes is there a separation [between law and the subject]. If one seeks the ground of existence, then that [ground] is the truth. But [the truth] gets along by itself without [the seeking]. To know [the law] truly is to know it through the Concept. An ethical relationship is the identity of Being in itself and Being for itself.[359] [To be ethical] is to have a sense of the substantial. Knowledge [of the substantial] can take various forms [trust, speculative reflection].

By being in an ethical union, individuals gain their genuine right. The right of the Substance is to exist. It has its existence in the knowledge and volition of individuals. On their side, individuals instantly gain their right therein. It is their essential nature – that which they receive through [the Substance]. They thereby fulfil their destiny, because the ethical union is that [destiny]. The unity of Being in itself and Being for itself, of Substance and self-consciousness, is the essential nature. The ethical individual is the representative of the Substance. In that the ethical is real in individuals, it is the general soul, the general manner of their doing things. On the one hand, it can be expressed as law, but law is [here] the way of reality; it is second nature, not first nature. It is thus their soul, their nature – freedom that has become necessity. The Mind that is really there appears. It appears inasmuch as its existence is the multiplicity of individuals [who bring it to life]. Just as much is it a profusion of relationships, a continuous flux. This infinite variegation of life is the appearance of the essential nature; therein appears Mind

---

358 UN124: But if consciousness makes its particularity and especially its conceit the foundation, then ethical consciousness is destroyed.
359 UN124: The ethical relationship is thus the identity of the particular will with the universal.

itself. Every individual in whom the species is present is the universal, which manifests itself in the particular. Only as so [realized]is Mind genuinely Spirit. Self-consciously accomplished, the living law is the ethical Substance, Mind realized [UN124: in a family, in a people].

We said that in this realization of Mind, self-consciousness is the representative of the universal. [This must be qualified so.] As a natural being, the individual does not immediately accord with the universal. The transition [from first to second nature] is made possible by the fact that an ethical world surrounds the individual. The individual human being confronts a world that, however, is an ethical world. He educates himself to [that world].

[89] For us, things [sun, moon, stars] are immediately there; because they are there, we hardly mention them. So it is with the customary ethos.[360] Because it exists [independently of us], it is valid. [People] comport themselves towards it in such a way as to grant its validity. Individuals who have the same will have seen that [UN124: at the moral standpoint] it is a contingent matter whether consciousness knows if something is good or not. [At the standpoint of immediate ethical life,] this contingency falls away.[361] The individual's conformity to [custom] now consists in his having it before him as something [he treats as] authoritative. [Custom] is, and is authoritative immediately, without reflection, and for that reason it has a general validity as well as a validity for the individual.

Insofar as [the individual] is a merely natural consciousness, he has to slough this off. And this sloughing off falls, on the one hand, to discipline, cultivation, education; [UN125: on the other hand, he has the universal, the authoritative, always before him.] The negative [that he must shed] concerns only the [instinctual] form of his relationships. He need not shed anything positive; rather what he has to shed is, as it were, the bark, the surface. His education consists in conforming himself to the world, but in such a way as to grasp it with his inner self. One becomes accustomed to this and that, only receiving [not evaluating]. Therewith, his remoulding to custom is no constriction of his individuality; it is his deliverance [from immediate nature]. There would be a constriction only if I wanted something else. Here, in this relationship, I am what I [veritably] am. I am not another [self] opposed to the one I [really] relate to; rather, by being in an essential relationship, by conducting myself in accordance with that relationship, I am in [accord with] my own

---

360 UN124: The customary ethos, qua immediately there, has the same authority as Being in general (sun, moon, stars).
361 Translator: The contingency of knowledge of the good is unimportant here because insight is not required for the validity of custom.

concept, one which at the same time has an outward presence. In what I do in accordance [with an essential relationship], I obtain a view of myself as I really am. The human being finds itself cramped and repressed only insofar as it has an idiosyncratic "should" [UN125: and "may"] in itself. This is then a subjectivity that objectivity does not engage with.[362] Repression falls away when his particular will directs itself [to the objective reality]. The ethical living together of human beings is not a constriction. One's vision of oneself, one's positive freedom, is present by virtue of [one's] being [with others] as a person. The individual who lives in accordance with the customary ethos can be called righteous or [90] virtuous. He gets his purpose from the ready-to-hand customs to which he himself belongs, on which he himself depends.

There is an old question someone once asked regarding how he should raise his son to be ethical. The answer was: make him a citizen.[363] Then is he righteous; he accomplishes the Right [and] continually brings forth [ethical] relationships. Rectitude is thus the first thing to be demanded of ethical people. The virtue of the ancients belongs to a time [before laws] when [ethical action depended on] individuals' having a special natural gift [for doing the right thing]. Now is the age of rectitude.[364] Virtue is thought of as belonging pre-eminently to Hercules, because he appeared as a hero, clearing away this or that monster. That was his peculiar heroism [at a time when] the only thing present was the discretion of individuals. The virtue of outstanding men was superbly described

---

362 UN125: What oppresses him is his own subjectivity. By conducting himself ethically, he frees himself. The ethical living together of human beings is their liberation; they come therein to a vision of their [true] selves.

363 UN125: There is an old story about a father who asked how best to raise his son to be an ethical man and about how Socrates answered him: educate him to be a citizen of a rational state. [Translator: In *Outlines* (para. 153), the reply is attributed to a Pythagorean, following Diogenes Laertius, *Lives of Eminent Philosophers*, 8.1.16. Here Hegel is perhaps paraphrasing Xenophon, *Memorabilia*, 1.3.1.]

364 Translator: In *Outlines*, para. 207, Hegel defines rectitude (*Rechtschaffenheit*) as "the disposition to make oneself a member of one of the moments of civil society by one's own act, through one's energy, industry, and skill, to maintain oneself in this position, and to provide for oneself only through this process of mediating oneself with the universal, while in this way gaining recognition both in one's own eyes and in the eyes of others." See also this translation, 149. UN125: The age of virtue in the strict sense was antiquity; our age is more an age of rectitude. Hercules was especially famous in antiquity for his virtue, because he did the right and rational thing at a time when they were not yet present as a public reality. In a democracy, there is not the consolidation of the whole around a focal point that is required for [collective] action. Since the individual did not emanate [as an office-holder would] directly from the constitution of the state, the state was tied to the will of particular individuals.

by the Greeks and Romans. It was part of their constitutions to leave more of what was generally a matter for the state to the discretion [of great men]. The Greek and Roman constitutions were not like those of the present; there, everything depended on the one right person. [Everyone] depended on an individual figure to do this or that necessary thing. For just that reason, [these men] did not act as righteous [*rechtschaffene*] men; rather, they acted more according to their peculiar manners.

Because virtue precisely involves the individual side, it is indefinite. The universal can be determined. By contrast, the particular is incapable of a more specific determination. Aristotle calls the virtues a mean between two extremes;[365] they fall into the quantitative. The absolute is the universal.[366] *How* the duty is performed falls to the immediate habit of the individual. Virtues also depend on variable circumstances – for example, the virtue of generosity. [The requirements of this virtue] vary with one's station, as does [the virtue of] frugality. Since virtue is relative to particular circumstances, only general things can be said about it, so that it remains indeterminate. [For example,] bravery [*Tapferkeit*] must have the [91] prudence of fearfulness and the daring [*Mut*] of recklessness; but [what the right balance is] cannot be determined.

The ethical is at the same time self-consciousness, reality, activity. It is in that respect a Mind – the appearing Mind, the Mind [or form] of reality. The Mind of a family [or] of a people is a real existent. By Mind we understand inward form. The real Mind is in essence something inner; [but] its reality involves a multiplicity of particular interests.[367] [Mind] is the universal that allows these interests free play, and at the same time, it is the universal Substance of this external appearance.

If Mind is raised up [from its entanglement with finitude], it is the object of religion.[368] And, since realized Mind is conditioned by space and time, it is necessary that its self-consciousness mainly engage the finite. The real Mind is to that extent sunk in the ways of finitude. As self-realized, universal self-consciousness takes the form of [concrete] Mind. [However,] self-consciousness must picture its concrete being as a Mind [separated from finitude]. [Thus,] the state is named Athens and

---

365 Aristotle, *Nicomachean Ethics* 2.1106a ff.
366 UN126: The absolute [qualitative] measure [implicit in the quantitative mean] is the duty. It then itself falls further into the quantitative [because what counts as fulfilling the duty depends on circumstances, such as one's wealth].
367 UN126: [Ethical life] is the universal to which all interests, all particular activities, return.
368 UN126: It is necessary that real Mind, which manifests itself in individuals and their activity, also be represented as a universal. The moment of religiosity is thus something inward. Athena is at once the goddess and the real Mind of the Athenian people.

the goddess is named Athena. [Athena] is Mind, the universal Mind [purified of the physicality of Athens]. They don't say the goddess Athens. [Similarly,] the ancients separated the sun and the god. The sea, the sun, was a god for them [but the god was Poseidon or Helios, not the physical sea or sun]. Likewise, Athena was for them not the goddess Athens, the city. The Divine is the immediate, [inner] reality of the whole, differentiated [from Athens] only as to form, not as to substance. Religion relates itself to the representation of what the ethical reality is, but in universal form. Because the Good is the universal, it contains no particular determination. In the same way, [the object for] religion is the ideal in which all particularity is [UN126: dissolved]. [But it is a mistake to accentuate the universal at the expense of the particular.] If one says that the spirit enlivens [while] the letter kills, this can mean that, in executing only the spirit, one misses the particular.[369] Mind is in the state not only as inward form but [also] as Mind realized [in a concrete state]. If one adheres to the [universal form] of Mind, specific duties are therewith nullified. If one takes religion as the basis of the ethical, one is, on the one hand, right, but this can also be twisted so that specific [duties] are allowed to wither away, which then wrecks everything.[370]

In ethical life lie duty and right. The ethical [community] has an absolute right vis-à-vis the individual. In contrast to it, the subject is only an [92] accident. [To be part of an ethical community] is thus a duty for the individual. Together with his duty, [however,] the individual has his right. The reality is that [in the ethical community], the individual attains his true existence. Therefore, duty and right coalesce. In abstract Right, the relationship is that my freedom has an existence in something; [there] duty and right are divided between two persons [my right is your duty]. In the moral sphere, I had duties towards the Good, but I bind myself to these duties. My right in the moral sphere [to attribution in accordance with intention, to pursue my welfare as I see it, etc.] is quite formal. Both [duty and right] ought to be one, but it merely ought to be [one] precisely because at the moral standpoint I am a subjective consciousness and a subjective will [over against a world whose laws might or might not recognize rights of self-determination]. That [right of the subjective will] should also make up the concrete existence of my freedom [in a

---

369 UN126: If one wants to observe laws and duties only according to their spirit, it can happen that one nullifies the particular determination thereof.
370 UN126: If one makes religion the basis of ethical relationships, one is right insofar as the substantial and essential are discerned in the particular; on the other hand, endowing religion with authority can lead to the destruction of all form, to fanaticism.

state]. In ethical life, law and freedom are one. If I am ethical, I fulfil my duty, and this duty is also my right.[371] The ethical community is therefore [the ground of] my real existence. Inherently and self-consciously, the ethical community is the ultimate [association], the unmoved.[372] It has a right to me [to my civic action], because I am its existence. But this is not a right against me; rather it is my [own] essential nature.

Human beings have the utmost feeling for the ethical. The human being recognizes duties only insofar as he has rights. The slave has no duties because he has no rights. The absolute right is to have *rights*, to gain freedom as a present reality. Therefore, if human beings are not accorded rights, they will not recognize duties.[373] But this proposition should not be taken in a formal sense. Someone who feels aggrieved with respect to a single matter does not believe that he now has no duties to fulfil.[374] Formally speaking, freedom as such is involved in a single right, but the rest of his freedom's existence is not imperilled [if that single right is infringed]. His freedom can remain otherwise intact.

We now go into more detail. The ethical is rational, and rationality is concrete, only insofar as it posits the determinations of its Concept.[375] The abstract Will and the particular will are the two moments of ethical life. Taken in isolation, they have only a formal truth. The differentiation of the ethical into the moments of the Concept is not a differentiation into abstract [isolated] moments; rather, [ethical life] is now the True, and the [formerly] abstract moments now come [93] forward only as ideal moments of ethical life. The ethical posits itself in forms of itself; it thereby posits particular spheres, [of] which it is therefore the foundation. It determines itself [and] thereby limits itself. But this means that it gives itself [determinate] shape and so makes itself a totality [comprising the spheres]. We'll now tarry with these abstract – with these ideal – [types of ethical life]. As a moment of the totality, the limitation

---

371 Translator: The duty is also my right because the ethical community requires my free devotion to duty and so respects my freedom as a right.
372 UN127: The ethical community has no duties; [it] is not once again obligated to something other than itself; it is the unmoved mover. [Translator: This must mean that the ethical community as a whole (comprising public and private sides) has no duties. Hegel has just said that in the ethical community the individual has the rights developed in the moral sphere, rights that the public side of the ethical community has a duty to recognize for the sake of its existence.]
373 UN127: Human beings have the feeling that if their rights are not acknowledged, they are not obliged to recognize their duties either.
374 UN127: The difference between the quantitative and the qualitative must be kept in sight here.
375 UN127: The ethical is rational only insofar as it differentiates itself within itself, only insofar as it lays out its Concept.

is not a defect [an external limit] but rather the [particular] shape [of the ethical]. When we posit different [forms] of the ethical, they become determinations of which the ethical is the underlying ground.[376] It is just a mistake to think of the determinate only with the form of the finite. It is true that a man does not attain his destiny if he is only a father of a family, [UN128: only a member of civil society], etc. [But] the truth is not without these differences [of spheres]. If one stops [at a single sphere], then it would be a barrier. We see this in people too. Whoever habitually considers himself the smartest shows in front of all that he is mainly bad. But people always go beyond that, and for that reason they are beyond it.[377] It is infinitely more difficult to grasp the positive than to express only the negative. The man who wants all [without wanting anything in particular] wants nothing at all.[378]

The first form [of ethical life] is the immediate form. This immediacy in ethical life is the *family*, the first ethical substance. The second [form] is always the stage of difference – of the splitting up of ethical unity. The second [form] is to be the other of yourself;[379] this second [form] is therefore the loss of your unity, your bifurcation; [it is] the standpoint of relativity.[380] This [second form] is thus one in which the particular [individual] is posited, in which the particular [individual] steps out for itself, [and] in which particular families stand over against each other, but independently. [Families and individuals are] essentially related but in such a way that they relate to each other externally. The legal constitution has its place here. The universal is an external order – a civil society – where everyone is at once self-interested and linked with others. The abstract universal constitutes Law. The third [form of ethical life] is then the return of the ethical Substance to itself. Through this return, [the Substance] first becomes a spiritual one, it having thereby incorporated the moments of the second [form]. Here, therefore, [ethical life] is self-conscious; it is the daylight of ethical life. [94] The third [form] constitutes the State, the ethical State. The third [form] has the whole for its conscious purpose and is active for this purpose.

---

376 UN127: In the rational, the boundary is no external barrier.
377 Translator: This odd example does not appear in UN's notes and may be Ringier's addition.
378 UN128: Abstract reflection is surprised at how much there is to do when it demonstrates the limits of something; but with that it is beyond the matter and has not grasped it. It is infinitely difficult to understand this position [that superseded spheres are preserved as moments] and to justify it.
379 Translator: Here your essential nature is external to you and repressive.
380 Translator: It is the standpoint of relativity, where your essential nature is abstraction away from, so conditioned by, something given.

[First Section]

[The Family]

The first stage [of ethical life] is therefore the *family*, the immediate ethical substance. [UN128: The knowledge of this substance is] an immediate knowledge – feeling, sentiment. The feeling of ethical substance is *love*. The substance has for the elements of its existence singular self-consciousness[es]. It is a relationship of individuals who know themselves as members of the whole, who know themselves no longer as self-seeking individuals but rather as [being] in a union. Accordingly, entailed by [this union] is the surrender of particularism; the individual gives up his [separate] personality as such and has it only in this unity. The family is thus a Mind – a whole in which individuals find themselves. By losing particularity, they win their essential being. The individual does not constrain himself in love. By giving up his [separate] personality, he gives up his fences or exists as Idea.

The family is thus divine, holy. In antiquity, this Mind manifested itself in sensuous intuition; the family housed the Penates. Abstract Right includes no Penates, nor does morality, wherein I am particularity reflected into myself. Conscience is something divine and sacred, not as an abstract self-certainty, but only as an ethical conscience. As such, it has given up its abstract ideality[381]. In the family, therefore, there are no rights, for the [separate] personality has disappeared. Here Right means not to be a right-bearer, not to be an abstract person.[382] Formal right comes to the fore in the family only when the family dissolves. Only then can the individuals litigate against each other. The right to be a family

---

381 UN129: identity
382 UN129: The higher Right of ethical life [demands] precisely that one not be an abstract person.

member is thus merely an abstract right.[383] A break-up, a contradiction [of the family] occurs when someone, for example, dies or if someone feels himself offended; [95] this is what first gives rise to the legal form. The first [stage of the family] is the family in its immediate concept; this is marriage. The second [stage] is the family in its external existence [family property]. The third is the education of children, [which is,] on the one hand, [the union's] return to immediacy in the child and, on the other hand, the disintegration of that union – dissolution.

To have itself for its purpose has been called the Mind of the family. The form of the relationship has been specified more precisely as unity in feeling. This is the relation of love, of trust, and indeed in such a way that, not only does one love another, but the mutuality [of love] is itself known by them. One has its self-consciousness [in the other]. But it is not only that one knows and beholds oneself in the other; it is rather that one knows that the other is for itself only by relating itself to the first.[384] I know the harmony and also feel the other's knowing it. Each knows that the other knows itself in the first. Here one sees at once the surrender of the other's personality and the preservation thereof. As Shakespeare has Juliet say: "The more I give [to thee], the more I have."[385] That's it exactly. A more particular form of love is trust, which has to do more with particular purposes. In love there is also trust, for here my particular purposes are also the other's; in taking care of its [interests], the other also takes care of mine. I therefore trust the others because I know that [my interests] are as close to their hearts [as their own]. That is the character of this substantial unity. As love, this substantial unity takes the form of sentiment; it is not yet reflected upon. It is not a universal in the strict sense. The third [stage] is the dissolution of the family – the exit from this unity.

[A. Marriage]

Marriage is in general a substantial relationship. As this substantial relationship, it is concrete, and for that reason it is rich in moments, none of which by itself constitutes the [96] point or purpose of marriage. Sexual

---

383 Translator: The right to be a family member is an abstract Right in the sense that it is entailed by the family Mind's right to exist; it is not a right original to the individual person as such.

384 UN129: Each is conscious of itself through the other (Goethe). However, not only does each know *himself* in the other; rather, each also knows that the other knows itself only insofar as it knows itself in the other.

385 *Romeo and Juliet*, act 2, scene 2.

satisfaction can be viewed as one moment of marriage, as can sexual reproduction. *Mutuum adjutorium* [mutual assistance] is certainly also an element. Marriage has its benefits. Such benefits are, [however,] only particular sides [of marriage]. If one turns them into basic drives [for marriage], one gets a one-sided [view]; this is just as erroneous as considering magnetism a factor sufficient for gathering.

The concept of marriage is substantiality, ethical life. [UN130: It is the immediate ethical substance. As such, marriage has a natural moment; this is the relationship to one another of natural sexes.] In concept, the status of the relationship between the sexes is such that, first, the animal qua inward organism is not independently for-itself, nor, secondly, is [the animal related] to external inorganic nature, but rather, third, [the individual animal] is related to itself [in the other].[386] [The connection is] the organism in its totality. Both moments are united therein. There is here also a relationship [of each] to itself. What is, indeed, still present [carried over from purely animal mating to human intercourse] is that, for one thing, [the sexual relationship] is the genus and, for another, it is the [concrete] existence of the genus. In the [purely] animal organism, the genus is not realized qua genus;[387] the universal does not exist as a universal, as it does with Mind. In nature, the genus exists only [as sunk] in immediate particularity, in a singular organism. The genus then appears only as [an external] power, only when one [organism] gives up its singularity and puts itself into another.[388] [In nature,] the being of the genus collapses into the particulars. Hence it appears only as the transition [from one generation to the next]. Mating is the genus process whereby [the genus] that [UN131: formerly expressed itself] immediately [in the sexual connection] is brought forth [in the offspring] as something produced. In the product alone does their unity come to sight for the producers, but again only in the form of singularity. [Mating] is thus the natural moment [of marriage].

In the mental sphere, the relationship [between the sexes] acquires a different form. In Mind as self-consciousness, the genus is [not the natural genus but] the known unity [in love of the parties].[389] [The union

---

386 UN130: ... but rather that [the individual animal] is related to itself [in the other], so that the connection is at the same time in the organic individual. [Translator: That is, in the sexual connection, both individuals form one organism.]
387 Translator: ... because the genus is not a purpose for the animal organism.
388 UN130: The individual gives up its singularity, and the genus is thereby brought forth. But it comes forth only as a shining through.
389 UN131: ... the genus is here not merely biological but known union, known substantiality.

is] known and desired as an essential relationship. As such a [known and desired] relationship, it is the relationship of spiritual love; this is what makes the relationship ethical. It is just this, that the individual renounces its [separate] personality, the certainty of self, its being-for-self, and love [97] grows from the negation of [separate] personality. In this way, the natural [drive] is a moment [of the relationship], but only a moment. It is not the natural genus [that primarily appears in the relationship]; it is rather the known genus and, as such, it is the substantial unity that is desired, of which the natural is only a moment. Accordingly, that is the basis and definition of this relationship. It is one-sided, unethical, and incorrect to make the sex drive the most important thing [in marriage].[390] The relationship consists in this, that what materializes is the genus; the genus does not remain unconscious, but rather it is the [known] ethical universality. The natural relationship is thus transfigured into a spiritual one, without its disappearing. [Marriage is] the spiritual union as felt and, at the same time, as immediate.

The sexual relationship must be spoken about with embarrassment (a virgin's wrath).[391] Shame discloses the entire [nature of the marital] relationship. One must not say that [sex] is something natural and therefore can be spoken of like other [natural things]. In the field of medicine, this is what goes on because it is necessary. Nevertheless, one must not speak about it, but rather it is essential to hold fast to

---

390 UN131: ... as Kant did in his [doctrine of] natural Right [*Metaphysics of Morals*, 6:278].

391 UN131: When marriage is spoken of, [the sexual side] should, on the one hand, be spoken of with embarrassment; embarrassment is the virgin's wrath at the merely natural and therefore improper and unethical. [Translator: "Virgin's wrath" is perhaps a reference to Pliny the Younger's description of a vestal virgin's wrongful execution for unchastity: "Cornelia invoked in turns the aid of Vesta and of the rest of the deities, and amid her many cries this was repeated most frequently: 'How can Caesar think me guilty of incest, when he has conquered and triumphed after my hands have performed the sacred rites?' It is not known whether her purpose was to soften Caesar's heart or to deride him, whether she spoke the words to show her confidence in herself or her contempt of the emperor. Yet she continued to utter them until she was led to the place of execution, and whether she was innocent or not, she certainly appeared to be so. Nay, even when she was being let down into the dreadful pit and her dress caught as she was being lowered, she turned and readjusted it, and when the executioner offered her his hand, she declined it and drew back, as though she put away from her with horror the idea of having her chaste and pure body defiled by his loathsome touch. Thus, she preserved her sanctity to the last and displayed all the tokens of a chaste woman ..." *The Letters of the Younger Pliny*, trans. J.B. Firth (London: Walter Scott, 1900), bk. 4, letter 11, http://www.attalus.org/old/pliny4.html.]

the ethical moment and not to emphasize the merely natural. On the other hand, the natural side should not be considered as something sinful, degrading, as a blemish. It is crude to understand the [marital] relationship from its merely natural side; on the other hand, it is a false delicacy to view [the natural side] as merely degrading and wrong.[392] These are the two extremes. The first is the unspiritual side, and it is one-sided of human beings to give themselves over to this drive merely because it is natural without raising it to ethical life. The other, sanctimonious, view is just as misguided. Erroneously, this has been called Platonic love. [Plato, to be sure,] spoke of a disembodied love – the love of the true, of the beautiful.[393] But this has been [mis]understood as the soul's merely abstract love [for another human being]. If one remains at the merely spiritual, this has been called an ideal love. Thus fixed, it is one-sided. Platonic love goes further [than love between human beings] towards a complete understanding of love. The sanctimonious view is that the mind should be far from sexual love and cultivate only Platonic love. The relationship is [then] pure. Wieland[394] wanted to ridicule this [love] in all [his] novels; the transition is [then] conceived as a fall into [98] the sensuous.[395] But [the sensuous side] should not be understood so, should not be understood as a contradiction of the ethical. It is in no way in itself something unethical and degrading.

The one is in the other. The external manifestation of the magnet is the line – that is, the magnet presents the nature of the Concept in a simple way. In a naive way, one can show someone that the Concept is realized in nature, that it has presented itself in the magnet. This is what Schelling considered the first natural potency.[396] The poles are not independent; they do not have a sensible reality but rather a polar reality. Neither can be separated [from the other]. So, that is the sort of thing that characterizes the sensible. The [poles of the] magnet do not exist indifferently beside each other. As is the case with light, magnetism has no [separate] parts. [The poles] have an ideal reality. The one exists only insofar as the other also exists. This is precisely the speculative

---

392 UN131: ... as a blemish to which we are subjected merely because of the imperfection of human nature.
393 Plato, *Symposium* 210c–211e.
394 Christoph Martin Wieland (1733–1813).
395 UN131: All of his novels begin with a so-called Platonic love and then present it as descending to the obscene.
396 F.W.J. Schelling, *Ideas for a Philosophy of Nature*, trans. Errol E. Harris and Peter Heath (Cambridge: Cambridge University Press, 1988), 115, 118.

[Concept], the unity of opposites. In the individual point there is also the combination of both. [Similarly, in the sexual connection] the nature of the Concept is presented in a quite sensuous manner if we see [in that connection] only animal lust. [Abstracted from love,] this [animal] side appears as an instinct, on its own a hostile drive. However, it has only been made into something hostile [by failing to integrate it with love]. If the spiritual side is explicit, if it raises itself to being, then the relationship is on the right footing. It is when one behaves as a natural species that [sex] becomes a dead self-indulgence.[397]

The relationship [structure of marital sex] is entirely the same as the one in [abstract] Right. Freedom is the ground. Existence is only the sequel thereof. The content of a determination of contract law is the essential nature [the Concept, mutual recognition]. The natural side [satisfying some material want] is the enclosure, as it were, of an intellectual unity. The ultimate forsaking of mediation is precisely [the intellectual union's] passing over into a natural union. The ethical union is devoid of lust.[398] Lust gains strength with satisfaction. When the spirit behaves so as to become a natural union, this means nothing other than that the immediate still figures as a moment. That moment is, on the one hand, required, but at the same time, it must be only a moment. The same is true in Right. The natural side has value only in being taken up into an ethical union. The abstractly natural union is [99] not worthy of the human being. The [purely] spiritual union is likewise something one-sided. [It is like] a contract without performance. The destiny of human beings is therefore to be a member of a family [UN132: and to sanctify the sensuous relationship by lowering it to an ethical moment].

In general, the marital relationship makes marriage the sacred and religious [institution] it has been taken to be. When one thinks of marriage, one thinks only of the ethical moment; the sensuous moment is pushed into the background. This religious side constitutes something mystical: the union of whole personalities.[399] This union is Spirit,

---

397 UN132: The natural becomes ethical in that it is understood as a moment of the unity of both sexes. The spiritual is always the essential and substantial. The spiritual unity contains [the natural element], so that it immerses the form of the immediate naturalness of the self-interested person in unity and the unity is made into genus.
398 UN132: ... devoid of lust in that [the ethical union] has taken up the natural union into itself. [Translator: By "lust" Hegel seems to mean sexual desire made hostile (*feindselig*) by abstraction from ethical love.]
399 UN133: This union of whole personalities gives marriage a mystical or religious character.

the holy, in and for itself holier than [individualistic] conscience, the merely abstract certainty. Accordingly, from time immemorial, marriage has been seen as something for the Church.[400] Marriage has the aspect of a civil contract, but that is only a subordinate aspect. The essential thing is the religious aspect. In marriage, abstract personality is surrendered. But the personality is surrendered only to the substantial union [in which it is preserved].[401] Because the person is placed in that substantial union, marriage is something that stands above my pleasure, whim, etc.; I have renounced all these things. From this it follows that marriage is inherently indissoluble. The indissolubility of marriage [might] spring from the ardour of a party, from the ends of the particular will. But it is just the particular will that must be bound. I have given all this up. That is also what God says. What God has joined together, let no man put asunder.[402] Insofar as one has embarked on marriage, one has therewith renounced contingency. The union has the highest right against you; what God has joined together, let no man put asunder.[403]

It is possible that higher purposes [that excuse divorce] exist, for example, for monarchs. It might be a duty for them to divorce [in particular circumstances]. [But] if divorce is allowed for ordinary people, this can only be for the sake of inward hardness of heart. Marriage in Roman law is most unethical.[404] [Because marriage is a substantial relation], the clergy must be involved in divorce. Hard-heartedness is the reason why divorce is permitted. It is odd that one can acquire higher powers because of [stubbornness].[405] It is education that makes divorce frequent.[406] The difference between the estates [100] also comes in here,

---

400 UN133: ... as something that needs a Church blessing.
401 UN133: The surrender of personality in marriage is different from the one in slavery, because the emergent substantial unity is mine.
402 Matt. 19:6.
403 UN133: The Divine in marriage is the obligatory that has an absolute right against particular likes and dislikes. Christ says further that divorce was permitted by Moses merely for the sake of hardness of heart, but from the beginning, that is, according to the Idea, this was not so. [Translator: But see this translation, 125–6.]
404 UN133: Only with the Christian religion did marriage become instated with its true right. [Translator: In Roman law, a marriage could be ended by the unilateral decision of either party for any reason.]
405 Translator: Ringier wrote *Selbständigkeit*, but *Starrköpfigkeit* makes more sense.
406 UN133: In times of education, divorces are demanded more frequently [because] reflection increases the difficulty people have in maintaining a substantial relationship.

appearing outwardly [in attitudes towards marriage and divorce]. In the simple [peasant] estate, which has not arrived at this reflection, at this brittleness, [UN133: and at the determined pursuit of particularistic purposes], marriage has been kept intact. There, idiosyncrasy is more easily overcome. In the higher estates, divorce is more frequently demanded because of education [and the development of the] understanding. It must also be granted more.[407] Law can make divorces difficult, so that particularistic purposes [not relevant to the ethicality of the union] meet obstacles. We give up the execution of this or that purpose and we maintain the ethical relationship more if we know that it is not easily broken.

Marriage must be entered into in accordance with the will of both [parties].[408] The same is true of exit. It used to be the custom for [parents] to arrange a husband and a wife for their children. They saw to a righteous husband and a righteous wife. The [financial] precondition [of the marriage] was necessarily the concern of the parents. The two who were appointed for each other then came to love each other just because they were obliged to marry. The other beginning is the more modern one, the beginning from inclination.[409] If there are several [possibilities], their will must certainly be the main thing. According to this other [modern] beginning, the individuals start from their inclination just because they are individuals. The girl says that her husband must be so and so. Equally, the fellow can conceive an ideal [wife]. The more reflection develops, the more can idiosyncrasy be cultivated. One can say that the relationship's first starting point, where the parents look after their children, that is, where the parents are more ethically minded [than the children], can be regarded as the more ethical one. The second starting point is a beginning from idiosyncratic choice. It is more ethical when a fellow says that he wants to have a wife for the sake of having a wife, and the same is true of a girl.

---

407 UN133: ... more [reasons for divorce] will have to be admitted here so that it can happen.
408 UN134: It is the will in general, the concrete will as the inclination of individuals on which marriage is founded. Marriage cannot be forced. With regard to the starting point [of marriage], the will can now possess a more idiosyncratic form. Higher education leads to greater demands [for individual satisfaction].
409 UN134: In an ethical relationship, there is both the consent of the parents and that of the [couple], both equally desirable.

Passionate love is not marital love.[410] In modern times, passion persists, taking itself to be something higher – divine. It is right about that.[411] But not as excluding [everything else] such that what one wants one wants only for the other and what the other [101] does it consciously does only for the other. [In romantic love,] everything surrounding [the relationship] relates to the emotion. To be sure, this passion must be named beautiful, and in a beautiful nature, love takes on this [UN135: character]. You are aware of no higher purpose; you wish to live like this forever. You believe you're completely happy in life, and you are [once again] youthful because you put aside the personal. But on the other hand, it is at the same time passion, because this immersion in another is equally a confinement. We've seen that love is ethical, divine, Spirit. As a mind, the human being has other purposes. Marital love becomes passionless. You are in this element. Passion is gone because parting is not a possibility.[412] [Romantic] love fills the soul completely because it is confined, and that is why it is passion.[413] The lover is completely self-satisfied in [the other]. There is in her [besides the union] at the same time the form of difference. The union is not completely settled, and for that reason not only is union present but also difference, from which arises the voltage.[414]

In marital love, by contrast, these hindrances have fallen away. Those who live in it live without hindrance because the harmony is fulfilled; hence there awakens the need for detachment in pursuit of other purposes. In marital love, a drive towards action is generated. From

---

410 Translator: In the following discussion of romantic love, Hegel no doubt has in mind Friedrich von Schlegel's celebration of it in *Lucinde*, published in 1799; see *Outlines*, para. 164.
411 UN134: In many narratives, love appears as passion, as the exclusive, divine [love] that is demoted in marriage. Love in general sees itself as exalted, divine, [and] it is completely right about that. As stated, it is that whose nature is in general the surrender of personality, so that one's own personality is rediscovered in the beloved object. In a noble nature, love takes on this high character. But, further, being overcome with emotion is to find oneself fulfilled in this state, to know no further purpose. Love is thus a passion because this boundlessness, this immersion in the other, is equally something bounded; [it] appears bound to a particular form. As a mind, the human being has still further purposes for the state, science, and the universal as such.
412 UN135: Passion is no longer present because the obstacles that formerly stood in the way have disappeared.
413 UN135: Qua confined, love is passion.
414 UN135: Passionate love still has the moment of difference in it. It is precisely because it is unsatisfied that the love is passionate.

marital love, in which the harmony exists, activity for further purposes originates. The man's purposes lie primarily outside [the marriage]. He is no longer a mere solitary individual; rather, in marriage he has won a [substantial] ground for his particularity. His particularity is, so to speak, a truly legitimate one, because it proceeds from a whole [for whose welfare he works]. The right of the [solitary] individual as such is formal right; his welfare is a particularistic welfare. [Concern for] the welfare of one's family is no longer selfish; it is rather [concern for] the welfare of an ethical whole. Accordingly, marital love is the perfect consciousness of identity [with the other]. The fact that [the husband] is [102] not an abstract singularity in his activity means that in his activity he has a substantial purpose [*Beruf*].[415] [Thus,] a man is first grounded as an individual insofar as he lives in marriage. This limitation [on the self-seeking will] also accounts for the image of satisfaction [associated with] this state.

To the extent that passionate love awakens our interest, it makes for a passion opposed to the presentation of love in its ancient form. It is especially in modern times that the interest in the passion of love has arisen. In antiquity, this did not occur.[416] This constitutes the distinction between the ancients and the Romantics. In modernity (for example, with Shakespeare), love is identified with the energy of particularity. In antiquity, when loves appears, it is marital love (Hector and Andromache). In our tragedy, the passion of love is placed in opposition to duties, etc. But in [passionate love] there is always [only] a particular interest [at stake];[417] if it is lost, nothing of inherently important Being [is lost]. If obstacles stand in the way of the passion of love, the obstacles affect [only] a particular interest. With the violation of Right in general, the universal is violated, but here only the particular [is affected].[418] It is through an arbitrary choice, an accident, that he finds his happiness only in this individual. In all novels and tragedies, this frostiness

---

415 UN135: In marital love, therefore, there is the consciousness of perfect identity, out of which the individual can determine purposes [the welfare of his family] for himself of a higher substantiality [than his particular welfare].
416 UN136: With the ancients, passionate love first emerges with Euripides. In the Romantics, the principle of subjectivity emerges with strength; in the ancient world, by contrast, subjectivity is only the form of a universal content. [Translator: Dieter Henrich suggests "Hyppolytus" as Hegel's reference to Euripides (UN320).]
417 UN136: To be sure, love has its right; but insofar as it appears as passion, particularity gets mixed in with it.
418 UN136: A universal [principle] would be violated if an individual were forced to live in an unmarried condition.

always mixes [with heat]. The subject is a heroine and a hero. If they hadn't wanted just this [individual], there would have been no need for so many declamations. In the *Antigone*, it is ethical [powers] as such that strike and grate against each other. When the passion of love occurs in the *Antigone* (in this most sublime work of art), it is subordinate.[419]

The persons who enter into marriage are of different sexes; it is a natural distinction. They are therefore distinguished from each other.[420] [Marriage] is the ethical substance in which there is a real distinction as much on the natural side as on the mental side. Because it is the substantial Mind that differentiates itself within itself, [the difference] is an essential distinction. We are speaking of the intellectual and ethical meaning of the natural and mental difference [between the sexes]. The difference is the differentiation of the Concept. One sex is masculine, the other feminine. [103] One is the tearing away, the separating, but also the power to preserve itself in this rupture. To one sex belongs the power of [independent] being-for-self and its abstract energy. It is the man who can rarely be satisfied with one-sidedness.[421] Objectivity in general belongs to the universal.[422] The condition of the man is that he battles. He must accept struggle, enmity, hatred – acquisition as well. Likewise, objectivity [in its] universal form – for example, of the state, art, science; this is what befits the man as such.

The other side is that of the woman. Her character is to preserve spiritual and ethical harmony. One must not think here of the splitting of the mind according to ordinary psychology;[423] for when spoken of in this way, one can mean that the woman is denied [UN137: certain mental powers of] the other side – as if the powers of Mind could exist in isolation. One must not think of such a thing at all.[424] The ethical Mind

---

419 Translator: This is the love between Haemon and Antigone.
420 UN136: The persons who enter into marriage are not different generally; rather their difference is a real and specific one: man and woman.
421 UN137: The man can be satisfied grappling with abstractions, theoretical matters. [Translator: This apparent contradiction between UN's notes and Ringier's (see also n. 425) can perhaps be resolved in the following way. The masculine is the side of abstract universality, but it cannot be satisfied with one-sidedness, and so it is also the urge to realize the universal objectively.]
422 UN137: On the other hand, the universal, objectivity in general, belong to the man.
423 UN137: By the way, one should not think here of ordinary psychology, according to which the particular powers of the soul are conceived as lying indifferently beside each other.
424 UN137: The difference can concern only the manner in which [one Mind] expresses itself. One sex presents the spiritual form in its simple purity, while the other sex presents opposition, the separation from unity.

must be foundational for the woman [too]. Mind is not severed into some such thing as powers; rather, Mind has all the powers [within it, so that each side has the other within it]. In one form [of the division] harmony prevails; the other roams about in the extremes. The man stands on the side of opposition; he therefore expresses power.

Accordingly, these particulars – tension, activity, struggle – belong to the man [on one side]; on the other side, abstract universality, rupture in general [are his].[425] He is understanding as such; theoretical sciences are more a matter for the man, [as is] bitter labour. Study with regard as much to theoretical as to practical knowledge, knowledge purely for the sake of having it, purely for the sake of knowledge, without using it, comprehensiveness for the sake of comprehensiveness – all this is a matter for the man.[426] Women are not content with this – so it is with the French, who have more of the feminine in them [UN138: than Germans]. Thus, the sciences of the understanding – [e.g.,] jurisprudence – are a matter for the man. Women are also capable of doing this, but we must thank God that they don't get involved with these things. Genius in art and science [104] is a property of the man; the state is peculiarly for the man. The state is a whole; it is the element of the man. Everything great that has come forth in the world, that has made epochs, in all these things, the individuals who stand at the peak were necessarily men.[427]

Here, in fact, is where the universal must be self-consciously and firmly grasped. But with this is connected precisely the greatest rupture. Particularity must be mastered. A great character consists just in this, that he has endured a great struggle.[428] It is false to say that the most intelligent men are most likely to achieve [great] works. All great works [UN138: of science, art, and history] presuppose a rupture – a rupture identical to a separation from oneself. [This is] a separation that does not occur in the uncomplicated, harmonious character of a woman.[429] Struggle occurs through the power of opposing and through

---

425 UN137: To the man belong struggle, tension with organic nature and with the world in general. Also belonging to him more is abstract universality. The man can in general be more one-sided than the woman.
426 UN137: We Germans are especially great at [assembling] complete collections.
427 UN138: On the whole, no woman can be said to have made an epoch. But inherent in such great works is that tremendous power to hold oneself in opposition.
428 UN138: The great character is he who has overcome in himself a great struggle, a great agony, an infinite tearing apart. With mere naturalness, great works of art will not be accomplished.
429 UN138: To be sure, the excellent then offers again a vision of harmony, but not an immediate one, rather one that has been produced.

the power of overcoming opposition. With this is also connected, as regards the state, a focus on purposes, setting plans, creating designs that relate to reality. Ruling involves precisely this concentration of character [UN138: that holds fast to a purpose and has no regard for anything that stands opposed to it]. The feminine character is like a flower – a quiet blossoming without struggle. To the man, the woman is just this vision of [his potential] self, the [potential] harmony of his spirit.[430] To the extent that the man attains this harmony, it is for him a restoration. The man begins with opposition. The young man thinks that nothing was missing [from the world] until he can do something. And after he has sown his wild oats, he comes back [to the humdrum].[431]

The sense of the whole is greater in the woman, the sense of what is fitting and proper, etc.[432] Her element is ethical life in the form of love. For this reason, the woman has [the qualities of] patience, nurturing, resignation. Reflection stands opposed to patience. Men are much more sullen than women, [UN139: who remain in the beauty of the ethical Mind]. Women better endure sorrow. In [*The Song of*] *the Cid*, the major female [character, Elvira] is [105] remarkable: her heart was so shattered [by rape] that at the end, God did not really know if she was deserving of punishment. In general, women are more alike than men, who are so many individuals. With the Germans, originality is precisely the angel of Satan, who beats us with his fists.

The [UN139: peculiar] circle of the woman is the family.[433] The man's life [is lived] in two spheres: the public and the domestic. Not only domestic life but, more so, the public life is the man's. The woman's sphere is the home. In her [way of] thinking this too is evident: her mind's [orientation is to] the present, to knowledge of particulars. When women engage in arts that require reflection, it is easy for this present-oriented [turn of] mind[434] to suffer as a result. Women are often accused of vanity. This is not, however, conceit or selfishness. The

---

430 UN138: The man needs the vision of this harmony in order to rediscover it himself.
431 UN138: The man begins with an opposition, sets an ideal before himself, goes on an adventure. At the beginning, the youth thinks that when he comes into the world, it must become completely different, that until now it has been completely lacking, and then he often falls back into the completely ordinary, even vulgar.
432 UN139: With the woman, the sense of the whole, the fitting, the durable predominates, and herein is also a warm concern for the particular. The woman is more concrete than the man; in her is presented substantial ethical life.
433 UN139: ... and private life; the woman is enthroned in the family. Domestic life and public life are the two spheres over which ethical life ranges.
434 UN139: ... this being awake to what is there at every moment with which women are adorned ...

woman seeks her own [good], just as the man does. [It is rather that] the woman's satisfaction [UN139: takes her in the direction] of vanity. [She thinks that] what should count is not her particular purpose but her personality. Men are more at home with selfishness and conceit, without being aware of either.[435]

Because women are so directed towards particulars, when they have influence on matters of state, they are inclined to pursue, not the universal, but the personal. In this regard, intrigue [and] consideration of persons are often on display. If a woman or a youth comes to rule a state, the former wills the particular, the latter the shapeless, the imaginary. Insofar as the woman has within her the lofty, the true, the substantial, it comes to her exquisitely in the form of religion. Women are more religious than men. The realization of strength, conquest, are the man's; the beautiful ethical wholeness, the calmness, are the preserve of women. The man needs virtues; he throws himself into life.[436] One virtue is enough for women – the fact that she appears.[437] These are the main points of difference between these subjects. Barbarians held women as slaves; in over-cultivated [106] countries women are on top. Here too the truth falls in the middle.[438]

National institutions regarding the quantity [of spouses] vary: monogamy, polygamy, polyandry. Much has been deduced [about the nature of marriage] from [its different forms] and indeed from the number of husbands and wives. The number is equal [in monogamy];[439] where polyandry prevails, there are more husbands, and [where polygyny prevails,] the converse. But this concerns only the natural [sexual] relationship, and from this absolutely nothing follows for the nature of marriage. In consideration of the ethical, and this is the essential [aspect], marriage must be monogamy, because it is the relationship in

---

435 UN139: Men are more often accused of a self-conceit that pursues some particular [interest] and wants to represent it as something universal.
436 Translator: This sentence and the following one are lines from *The Virtue of Women* (1795), a poem by Friedrich Schiller (see *Schillers Werke: Nationalausgabe*, vol. 1, *Gedichte in der Reihenfolge ihres Erscheinens 1776–1799*, ed. Julius Petersen and Friedrich Beissner [Weimar: Hermann Böhlaus Nachfolger, 1943], 286).
437 UN139: Schiller observes that the [mere] being there, the appearance of women is in general their virtue, while men have to go into battle, into conflict, breaking the peace with themselves and the world in order to regain it.
438 UN140: Women have been treated differently in different times by different peoples; between both extremes lies treatment with dignity.
439 Translator: It is difficult to believe that Hegel said "equal" (*gleich*), as if the parties' each having the same number of spouses could count as monogamy. This sentence is not in UN's notes.

which the person renounces its [separate] personality, surrenders and wins back the whole person, when the other does likewise. From this concept it follows directly that marriage must be monogamy, because [otherwise] one would be wronged.[440] There would therefore be an injustice. The inner meaning of this relationship is felt substantiality. It can emerge only through complete devotion.

The second moment[441] concerns the marriage of blood relatives. The marriage of close blood relatives has been permitted by [some] peoples. Among Christian peoples it is absolutely forbidden. This has been explained in terms of a natural inhibition. This suggests a feeling, something dark. It is [indeed] a feeling, but not a merely vague one. It must also have the form of thought. Marriage is this: persons of two different sexes surrender their persons to each other, and the erasure of personality must take place through a free devotion.[442] Marriage between close blood relatives is incompatible with that [idea].[443] Those alone should come together who were previously separated. Blood relatives are those whom nature unites. They are already naturally one. Those who enter on marriage must not already be in this identity. That is the basis for the [feeling of] inhibition. A marriage must be first established by them [by their free wills]. The rational, the Concept, contains just this [idea]: the different should become one. The magnet exhibits this [idea]: what should unite must originally be separate. These [rational] determinations [of marriage – monogamy, the prohibition of consanguineous marriages –] incorporate what manifests itself as instinct, what can [by virtue of their being rational] be expressed in the form of duties, hence in the form of justice and also in the form of virtue. It is superfluous to repeat them [in terms of] these forms.[444]

[107] That marriage can be dissolved has already been spoken about. It is a relationship [based on] sentiment. It is a possibility of [the partners'] will, their feeling, their inclination that the ethical relation might

---

440 UN140: ... when marriage is not monogamous, one party would be essentially violated, because he would not gain himself back [in his surrender] in a complete way. The inner meaning of the relationship can emerge only from the unreserved [and] reciprocal devotion of personality.
441 Translator: The first was whether marriage must be monogamous.
442 UN140: Therefore, the marital bond must be a matter for the free will.
443 Translator: The idea seems to be that the rational free choice of the other is compromised by the natural affinity.
444 UN141: The aforementioned determinations of marriage could now be expressed in another way, and this could be noted in each chapter. Those determinations could be considered from the viewpoint of justice and virtue. But it would be superfluous to repeat these forms. [Translator: See this translation, 80.]

weaken in them. Marriage without sentiment is an empty externality, something it should not be. The true ethical life [involves], on one side, the indissolubility of marriage. The [partners] are individuals who realize the [family] community. As individuals, [however,] they can be changeable, uncertain; they can be so or otherwise. On its own, the individual is unreliable. It is in ethical life that the individual first has its substantial ground. This is therefore something grounded, secure. Conscience is the pinnacle to which the individual drives its [abstract] subjectivity. In marriage, the individual is rooted in something that has ethical breadth, so to speak. Through marriage, the dark interior [of the solitary conscience] becomes something objective and fixed. Therefore, the universal [State] has an interest in the individual's having, not only a certainty [of its value as a conscience], but also [a knowledge] of the truth [of its value in the family].[445] Marriage should therefore be honoured and protected by the public authority.[446] In ancient histories, revolutions originated in an offence against marriage (Trojan War, expulsion of the Tarquins).[447] When the inward [substantiality] is violated, it rises up and stands firm against the power that violated it.

[B. The Family's Wealth]

Because the marital union is a moral person, it must have property. Like the person itself, the family must have property. Because the family is not a merely abstract, accidental person, there enters into [UN142:

---

445 UN141: In general, marriage constitutes the substantial basis of the State as it relates to individuals. The State can really rely on individuals only insofar as they stand in such a relationship of ethical union as the family. As isolated individuals, they are unstable and unreliable. The inwardness of personality appears as something stable through marriage. In the family, the self-certainty of pure individuality is no longer the unsteadiness and abstractness [of conscience]. Through marriage, the sensibility side [of individuals] becomes something objective, stable, and ethical. The State therefore has an interest that its organs not be as changeable and capricious as unmarried individuals.

446 UN141: There must be an ethical authority that maintains the right of marriage against the caprice and opinion of individuals. This authority has to distinguish between mere caprice and changeability, [on the one hand,] and the total estrangement of souls, [on the other]. In the latter case, a separation must certainly be possible.

447 Translator: In Homer's *Iliad*, the Trojan War was the consequence of the Trojan prince Paris's abduction of (or elopement with) Helen, wife of King Menelaus of Sparta. According to Livy (*History of Rome*, bk. 1, chaps. 57–60) the expulsion of the Tarquin kings of Rome and the beginning of the republic resulted from the rape of Lucretia, wife of a Roman nobleman, by Sextus, son of the Tarquin king, Lucius.

property the determination] that it should be a lasting property. Here, the need is not merely an abstract need [of an isolated individual]; much more is this an ethical whole that must be cared for. The care for it is now a common care, no longer a selfish one, and for that reason it possesses an ethical character. In the history of states, we see these two moments [UN142: that marriage was introduced and with marriage a secure property] emphasized: marriages were endowed. The Greek heroes are credited with founding marriages with secure property. The isolated person [108] was not respected even in the [popular] imagination, but that a family be cared for as a family – this was an ethical requirement.

Wealth can be of two kinds: land ownership (secure wealth) and the ability to satisfy the needs of others. The management and disposition of the family wealth are relevant here. [UN142: That the man is mainly responsible for the management of family wealth follows from what was said before.] No member of the family really has a private property against another; rather they have a right in a common property. Both [that family property is common and that the father is the manager] can come into collision. The father of the family might be a wastrel; it is then essential in states that a law take away the management of [family] wealth from a profligate father. Because no member of the family really has a private property, what is laid down in many statutes – that each [person] of the couple holds private assets – drops out. Such a relationship is thoroughly unethical for several reasons. The first is the bond created by the new [nuclear] family and not by earlier [extended] relationships. [Secondly,] to have regard [as the Romans did] for the facticity of a *gens* [or] *stirps* is the furthest thing from marriage. The new marriage is an independent family. [A situation where] daughters can have no share of the family [wealth] should not be allowed.[448]

---

448 UN142: In Roman law, the dominant position was that the wealth of the married couple remained separate. Not only did the wealth of the deceased wife not fall to the surviving husband; it did not even fall to the children. It reverted to the family of the wife. It is a thoroughly unethical relationship for the wife to retain a private wealth. Making family property secure and lasting has a political meaning that will be considered later. The natural consequence of securing a [family's] wealth [through primogeniture] is that daughters are either excluded from the inheritance or receive only a small part. This is a contingent choice that the state need not guarantee. [The state] is concerned, not with this or that family, but with the family in general. With the endeavour to give [family] wealth an external stability, the individual's own activity and energy were sacrificed; the family members became, in a certain sense, *glebae adscripti* [serfs tied to the land]. The [family's] immunity from liability [for the individual's debts] that seems advantageous in one respect turns out to be quite disadvantageous in another.

[C. The Education of Children and the Dissolution of the Family]

The third moment is the dissolution of the family in general and the education of children. The children are members of the family; in the children, the parents' ethical life becomes visible to them. In the children, the unity that exists within them emerges.[449] The individuals who arrange marriages are ungrounded presuppositions, immediate persons. Their purpose is that there be generations. In the sphere of nature, the Concept, which returns to itself, which is a circle, turns into a line.[450] Children receive sustenance and education [from the parents]; parents receive obedience and [family] service from the children.[451] However, [parents as individuals] have no [109] right to them as servants, still less as slaves. Parents have a right to the obedience of children. Children are children – that is, the deciding will is not in them; this belongs to the family. Parents have a right against the arbitrary will of children, but not an unlimited one, rather [only] insofar as its purpose is rearing. Nor, with children, do punishments have regard to justice. Children must deserve punishment, but they must be educated by it.[452] [The punishment] raises a "no" against their impulsive will. Punishments essentially have the purpose of rearing. The punishment should [respond to] the negativity [unruliness], the capriciousness [rather than to the single act].

The purpose of education is that [the children] become independent persons. They are already free, but only potentially. The purpose of education is that they become free [actually]. On the one hand, they live in the family and have therein their positive home, [UN144: but on the other hand, they also have, against this, a negative vector in that they are destined for independence]. The positive side is that they live in the element of love and trust, that the ethical union is brought forth in them

---

449 UN143: In the children, the ethical union of the parents becomes real for them.
450 Translator: The family is the Concept's return to unity from the separation of the universal and the particular will in morality; but because the family is an ethical substance enmeshed in nature, the restored unity is embodied outwardly in natural offspring that beget further offspring, etc. Thus, the circle, instead of closing, becomes a line of generations.
451 UN143: The children are members of the family, and they thus have a right to be nourished and educated. Their parents can demand obedience from them and also service, but only in a way that is consistent with the family relationship [in which every member both serves and is served]. Parents have no right to consider their children as slaves, as was the case in Roman law.
452 UN143: Punishment is here essentially of a subjective, moral nature.

and becomes fixed as a feeling of grounded-ness.[453] It is a misfortune for a human being if he is torn from the circle of the family early and has to replace it with his own energy. One can ask whether, if a child has bad parents, it would be better to pull him out of the [family's] education. What would be won on one side would be lost on the other, [for the child] would no longer live in that feeling of grounded-ness. A child who loses his father early loses much, but if he loses his mother early, he has lost much more. A child must have lived in the element of ethical love.

[UN144: The negative side is that the child must go forth from this merely immediate form of ethical life, that it become for itself.] The point of education is the other side, which involves the dissolution of the family. The child has a dual feeling within itself. On the one hand, [it has] this trust, this love. On the other hand, it has an urge to grow up. It suffers the revenge of a higher sphere – dissatisfaction. The child himself has the longing to grow up. Therefore, one must not think that this state [of family bliss] is the happiest. It was a pedagogical mistake [to think] that one must not disturb the happiness of children. It is the feeling of dissatisfaction that draws children to grow up. The [110] pedagogy of play made this [mistake]. [It taught that] one must tell children that they are nothing on their own.[454] The pedagogy of play, which wants to remove [self-dissatisfaction], invalidates children's own urge impelling them to go further. [UN144: The consequence is that the children, through such treatment, lose interest in something higher, substantial.] This conceit thus becomes satisfied with the condition they are in. Here we have two sides: on the one hand, ethical love to enjoy; on the other, [the drive] to exit from this sphere (the negative side). The new families that the children found then become their substantial destiny.

The ethical dissolution of the family consists in this, that the children themselves become persons. For the Romans, children were non-persons. [UN145: In Roman law, even adult sons were incapable of owning property [[while the father was alive, unless he released them]]; only a *peculium castrense*[455] was allowed them.] This is one of the unethical provisions of Roman family law. It was followed through

---

453 UN144: It is essential that one first know ethical life as unreflective love and trust.
454 UN144: Adults who always behave childishly with children become contemptible to them.
455 Translator: booty taken in war.

consistently (the triple sale, etc.).[456] It is a bitter chore to have to continue paying attention to this rubbish.

The transition [from the family to its dissolution] results in inheritance, a change by the death of [the parents].[457] The family wealth is inherently common property, [though] the father has the right of disposition. [It follows that] when he dies, the children do not inherit a new property. The death has merely brought about [the circumstance] that the deceased no longer has a share of the wealth. Fichte and a few others have sought to explain inheritance in another way. They said that after death, the estate is ownerless;[458] anyone may take it into possession. Because the relatives are [generally] first at the deceased's side, they grab it first, and this has now, in a contingent way, become the rule.[459] This [explanation] is refuted by the above.[460] If the family has split up, very often a dying person will find himself without relatives, [so Fichte's explanation is unconvincing]. As we saw, however, [inheritance by family members] is no accident. [The explanation for inheritance given above] is the universal ground [of inheritance], but it is only the universal ground.[461] In civil society, where the standpoint[462] of the particular person is the essential purpose, the siblings soon disperse [becoming heads of their own families]. Of course, the love remains, but each enters independently into

---

456 Translator: According to the Law of the Twelve Tables, table 4, 2, a child, even an adult child, could become freed from the *patria potestas* (which included the right to kill his children) before the father's death only if the father released the child by ceremonially selling the child into the slavery of another, who would then immediately free his slave. With sons, the ceremony had to be repeated three times.
457 UN145: The death of the parents brings about a natural dissolution of the family.
458 J.G. Fichte, *Grundlage des Naturrechts*, in *Fichtes Werke*, ed. Immanuel Hermann Fichte (Berlin: de Gruyter, 1971), 3:367; and Fichte, *Foundations of Natural Right*, ed. Frederick Neuhouser, trans. Michael Baur (Cambridge: Cambridge University Press, 2000), 318.
459 UN145: They said that the property of the deceased becomes really ownerless, and it was positive law that raised to a rule the usual contingency that the relatives take possession of the deceased's estate. This is a merely external account.
460 Translator: "by the above," i.e., by the fact that family wealth is common property, hence survives the death of the father.
461 Translator: Family property is the natural ground of inheritance, but it is altered at the individualistic standpoint of civil society, where the father's testamentary will is respected.
462 UN145: independence.

a status of its own. The spiritual bond weakens; each family member exists for himself with his [own] interests. At more distant degrees, there can even be uncertainty as to whether someone belongs to our family.

With the moment of independence, the arbitrary will enters. It enters in a specific sense with regard to [111] wealth. [UN145: With individual independence, there enters the free choice to shift wealth around according to merely subjective ends.] Where patriarchal organization dissolves, this other moment enters relationships all the more. The consequence of this freedom of choice is that the arbitrary will is recognized to the extent that even stipulations made in the event of death are valid [after death]. It is said, therefore, that one can make a will. This will derogates from the first state [where the common family wealth does not pass on the father's death but merely continues without his sharing in it]. Free choice is recognized therein. Nevertheless, it must be limited by the first rule [to protect the family members]. Disinheritance is only partially allowed the parents; the child is guaranteed a mandatory portion. With siblings, free choice enters [without restriction].

One can actually view this [testamentary] power in the following way. An individual creates a spiritual family, a circle of friends and acquaintances, a family that is not a family in the real sense. Testamentary disposition is nothing other than [the testator's declaring, in effect]: this is my family [that, after my death, should] enter into possession of the wealth that was really already communal in the sense of [belonging to] a friendship.[463] Strictly speaking, that I can dispose of my wealth on death makes no sense. If the will is violated, no wrong has occurred at all. One can regard [respect for the testator's will] only as piety. The rightful aspect is just this: if I have a circle of friends, then this was my family, which then has a claim to my wealth. The free choice [to dispose of family property as I please in contemplation of death] has nothing ethical in it at all. There is nothing ethical in my leaving my wealth to someone in order to show my affection – wealth that I, in any event, do not possess. The greatest expansion of the power to make a will would violate the ethical relationship [of the family]. The result would be ignominious subservience [and] legacy hunting. One can learn enough about this

---

463 UN146: Only as so understood does the testamentary power acquire a rational sense [since the testator's will no longer exists].

from Lucian.[464] On the other side, [those hopeful of an inheritance] are kept in a state of dependence. Often treachery also intrudes. The main thing is that [the wide latitude granted] caprice is the cause of all this. This permitted arbitrariness is the opportunity for much wickedness.[465] Frequently, this creeps in as well in pious foundations. In general, inheriting is one of the most sordid aspects of human life. Even more so is bequeathing.[466]

We see that families dissolve in a natural way into a multiplicity of individuals.[467] The next relationship [arises from] the *outward dispersal of the family*. A nation[468] [112] means just this, that it was naturally born of a tribe, which was born of a family. In a nation, there are many independent families; they can unite either through imperial conquest or free will. Such a multitude of families constitutes civil society, but this must be distinguished from the State; [civil society] is merely the state as the understanding conceives it, the state based on need. Everything depends on whether the substantial is the purpose [of political union].

---

464 Translator: This is Lucian of Samosata (c. 125–180). Perhaps Hegel is thinking of Lucian's monologue *The Disinherited*, in which a physician pleads his case to a jury after being capriciously disinherited by his father, then reinstated when he cures his father of madness, then disinherited again when he is unable to cure his stepmother. Cf. the following speech by Plutus, the Greek god of wealth, from Lucian's *Timon the Misanthrope*: "Pluto and Plutus are not unconnected, you see. When I am to flit from one house to another, they lay me on parchment, seal me up carefully, make a parcel of me and take me round. The dead man lies in some dark corner, shrouded from the knees upwards in an old sheet, with the cats fighting for possession of him, while those who have expectations wait for me in the public place, gaping as wide as young swallows that scream for their mother's return. Then the seal is taken off, the string cut, the parchment opened, and my new owner's name made known. It is a relation, or a parasite, or perhaps a domestic minion, whose value lay in his vices and his smooth cheeks; he has continued to supply his master with all sorts of unnatural pleasures beyond the years which might excuse such service, and now the fine fellow is richly rewarded. But whoever it is, he snatches me up, parchment included, and is off with me in a flash, ... leaving the disappointed ones staring at each other in very genuine mourning over the fine fish which has jumped out of the landing-net after swallowing their good bait." *Timon the Misanthrope*, in *The Works of Lucian of Samosata*, trans. H.W. Fowler and F.G. Fowler (Oxford: Clarendon Press, 1905), 1:39.

465 UN146: [Consider] the bequest of a merchant, according to which the inheritor would have to visit the London Stock Exchange every day. This condition was so burdensome for the inheritor that he gave up the huge fortune he fell victim to.

466 UN146: The wide latitude that this power to bequeath has in Roman law must therefore be called pernicious.

467 UN146: ... into a multiplicity of families. These families comport themselves to each other as independent persons. The next thing, accordingly, is that we consider the relationship of such persons to one another. Many families may stem from a common root, or alien families may enter into commerce. Such a plurality of families makes up what is called civil society.

468 Translator: The word here is *Nation*, not *Volk*.

[Second Section]

[Civil Society]

Families arise and disappear. This makes for the transition to civil society. One transition is the transition of the Concept, which is something [the inner side] other [than the empirical side].[469] The family is the substantial unity that does not yet have any opposition [within itself]. The wholeness of ethical life, which is the unity of the Will, is contained in the family in an undivided, substantial way. But the further [development] is this. The Concept realizes its moments, steps into opposition, so that ethical life is lost.[470] The concrete person is for himself. Over against it stands the generality, the connection between [persons]. What was united in the family is here torn apart.

The end of civil society is the person. Therewith is asserted the principle of self-interest. Everyone is for himself. [But] the second [principle of civil society] is that these different individuals are inherently identical [as self-consciousnesses]. They are not aware of their inherent identity; instead, each is for himself. Their identity is an inward, hidden one. So [qua identical], they stand in a relationship to each other, but [because they are unconscious of their relation,] this is a relationship, not of freedom, but of necessity. They are at once unconsciously identical [and consciously unrelated].[471] Freedom [by contrast] is being related to oneself in the other. Their particular interests inherently link

---

469 UN147: The inner transition of families to civil society is the transition of the Concept [to bifurcation].
470 Translator: The Concept (the family's simple unity-in-difference of the collective and the particular member) realizes its moments (such that the collective is a genuine universal made up of many families and the particular individual a truly differentiated individual person), steps into opposition (between the general and the individual) so that ethical life is lost.
471 UN147: They are interrelated against their knowledge and against their will.

them because by nature they are not self-sufficient. [But because they are unconscious of it,] this nexus is merely an external one.

This manifests itself in the following way. My end as a particular individual is to look after my interests [and] needs. In doing so, I encounter other I's [and] can satisfy [my interests] only by means of others. This relation to others is for [me] a relation of necessity, because it is not a relation of freedom.[472] That I as a particular individual relate to others is a matter of necessity that [113] I must eventually submit to; I am thus in [a state of] dependency. This is the sphere of need. The others are again [loci of] particular interests, etc. independent of me. Further, the basis of this [state of] dependency is the inherent identity of those who are thus related to each other. In general, they are the same. When all these particulars [who take themselves for] absolutes interfere with each other, they behave like animals.

Furthermore, the existent universal enters inasmuch as my satisfaction is mediated through the satisfaction of others. I must be what others want if I want to satisfy my needs.[473] I must therefore not be eccentric around others; rather, I must present myself in an agreeable way. In that way, I must generally give myself the form of universality. I have to make something of myself in the eyes of others. Precisely because this [process] is mutual, idiosyncrasy in *contrast* with one another gets blunted, and there appears the form of universality whereby I am something for the other, count [for the other], am recognized. The situation is therefore not as it is in the family, where I count as I immediately am. What binds the family is the bond of love. The parents love the children and vice versa even when they are very bad. [By contrast,] in this sphere of particular interests, the element of universality enters [from outside]. Here the universal realizes itself [behind the back of individuals]. [Here] the form of universality is given to the material. The universal appears in the form of the [human] understanding.[474] This is the stage at which the natural is worked off, the stage of cultivation, [UN148: which consists in the particular's transformation into the

---

472 Translator: This unhelpful explanation is not in UN's notes. It is a relation of necessity because I am dependent on others whose ends are foreign to mine. UN147: The others are for me inscrutable. This relation to the other is a relation of necessity. I must knuckle under because I cannot satisfy my needs without the help of others, and I am therefore dependent on alien others.
473 UN148: In that I can satisfy my needs only through the will of others, I am for the others [and] must be what they want and must comply with their expectations.
474 UN148: However, this universality is still only formal, and it is the understanding that asserts itself here.

universal]. To that extent, what we consider here is the glimmering of Reason, often [in the case of law] of reasonableness itself. This glimmering of Reason is the understanding.

In the mediation [of interests] there are two moments. [First,] I care for my welfare through mediation with others, who are also self-interested wills, [also] inherently particularistic. I comport myself towards a completely independent stranger [and he to me], but [secondly,] the stripping away of idiosyncrasy that shows itself here is the emergence of reasonableness.[475] The mediation has [reasonableness] for its middle [term between our respective subjectivities]. In that way, I return to my end-status [Selbstzweck]; I become a universal [end-in-itself] for the other, and the other becomes a universal [end-in-itself] for me. [The parties] thereby break free of each other's idiosyncrasy [114] and are thus independent. This constitutes the moment of return [to self from the other], which is the moment of reconciliation [of dependence and freedom].

[Civil society] is the sphere of contingent benevolence, malevolence, of evil, of chance, and therewith [it is] the sphere of necessity.[476] All arbitrariness of will, all fortune and misfortune mingle here in the general blight. Here everything has free play – need, misery, depravity. In this sphere of external necessity [and] contingency, which is the grimmest thing, the reconciling factor for freedom is the glimmering of reasonableness. [Civil society] is the sphere of hard labour, the sphere where one works off idiosyncrasy. It is also the sphere of good-heartedness, etc. But from this contingency results the form of universality. This is the sphere of estranged ethical life, of necessity. This is the [condition] to which a state of nature of ethicality and felicity has been counterposed.[477] When one sees the frightful depravity in large cities, one must certainly deplore the fact that such a thing could come to pass. Such a thing could absolutely never emerge in a patriarchal relationship. The principle of bifurcation [of state and individual] was precisely the reason why the ancient patriarchal states collapsed. As *Luxus* (which is

---

475 UN148: ... at the same time the moment of universality also enters as the glimmering of reasonableness.
476 UN149: On the side of particularity, [civil society] is in general the sphere of arbitrary will and chance, of ethical, moral, as well as of external contingency. Hence it is also the sphere of necessity, in that every individual is dependent on [external and indifferent] others.
477 UN149: Indeed, noble and great minds, such as Rousseau, have been moved to lament civil society by the sight of the manifold miseries to which civil society can give rise.

just what they called this condition)[478] appeared, those states fell. It is in precisely such cases of [the individual's] isolation that bifurcation, separation [of the universal and the particular] manifests itself. And since those states were based on trust, they could not withstand this bifurcation. Because the higher form [of State] in which [union and bifurcation] are bound together was missing, they had to perish.

That[479] is what forms the basis of the Platonic state. [Plato] understood this. He knew his time.[480] Because he also saw the principle of the negative but grasped it only as a negative, only as an enemy, he did not know how to help himself other than by splitting it off. For that reason, he tolerated no private property in his state. Nor, for the same reason, did he establish families, precisely because they are small [particularistic] units. In respect of this aspect [of his state], Plato is one-sided. To that extent, his state is only an ideal, since it has no reality.[481] The same principle [the simple Concept] that [115] is in the family is the principle of [Plato's] state. It is in the Christian religion that the principle of the universal worth of [individual] personality was first announced and the ground therewith laid for a deeper understanding of freedom [...][482]

[A. The System of Needs]

[A. 1. The Nature of Need and Its Satisfaction]

[...] The second moment,[483] then, is the differentiation of need, and this then leads to attentiveness to these differences. Along with needs, the

---

478 Translator: The German word for "luxury" is identical to the Latin *luxus*, meaning "excess."
479 Translator: "That," i.e., the insight into the incompatibility of individualism with the Concept's unity.
480 UN149: Plato understood the essence of the state, but only under the form of his time. Thus, he sought to banish the principle of individual personality from the state entirely. The Platonic state ... does not have the reality whereby the principle of infinite personality can unite with the substantial unity of the whole. This substantial unity is in general the basis of the State. Plato understood correctly the principle of the Greek world; he knew the further progress of this principle only as corruption, and this he sought to excise.
481 Translator: "since it has no reality," i.e., since it has excluded what belongs to reality.
482 Translator: The editors of the Ringier manuscript tell us that, from this point, two pages of the manuscript are blank. See appendix 2 for a translation of the corresponding pages of UN's manuscript from the Henrich edition (150–3).
483 Translator: The first moment (see appendix 2) is the satisfaction of animal need.

means [of satisfying them] also multiply. The human being can make everything in nature into a means, and with these relationships, reflection arises to judge the relation between means and end. These means become once again needs; [satisfaction] splits into a chain of satisfactions. It is a characteristic of refinement to divide [need] up in this way and to find the right means for each need.

Also part of [human] needs are the so-called comforts of life, whatever serves to shorten [the time to do] something or to get rid of unpleasantness. This [process of refinement] drifts hither and thither in indefinite ways. [UN153: There are here no immanent bounds.] It is, however, very inapt to inveigh against the comforts of life [in praise of a simpler life]. Take, for example, the watch. This can also reach the level of luxury, but it is of endless service for human beings, for example, where businesses, [especially] cooperative businesses, need to be carried on. The watch alone removes what would [otherwise] incur much wasted time and embarrassment. Many human needs spring from [the need] to become independent of the seasons. [Here belong] clothing and shelter. The human being is [physically] less protected against nature than the animal, and this is not a drawback. The mind must create protection; it must interfere [in merely physical adaptation for the sake of mental adaptation].[484] That is why the human being does not [116] sleep on the ground like the animal; he makes himself a bedstead. The human being must also cook. He who is mentally very active cannot make do with food that uses up [in digestion] a great deal of the organism's energy; rather, the food must already be assimilated, already partially digested.[485] So, [these specifically human needs] should not be lightly dismissed; such needs spring from a higher culture. Such needs are based, not only on [UN154: personal] comfort, but on a universal [humanistic] ground.

There has been a great deal of declamation about tea- and coffee-drinking, [UN154: which doctors, financiers, and clergymen have opposed in manifold ways]. Many, especially in the Campean stories, believe we can save a lot [UN154: by giving them up, (as, for example, a certain class of people in England has now abstained from beer and

---

484 UN154: This is not a drawback; rather, because the human being is directed towards the mental, everything that comes into relation with him must have the character of being produced by him.
485 UN154: People accustomed to a ruder way of life can also be satisfied with raw food. Those who are directed to a mental life must pursue physical culture to a certain degree.

the like)].[486] Everyone can believe what they want about this. People have thought that [over-consumption] can be remedied if all other individuals came to the same conviction, and so they have wanted to persuade them [to give up certain wants]. But all individuals are the collective. If one looks at this matter from the standpoint of the individual, one implies that [what one consumes] is a matter of individual choice. If one thinks that [all should give up coffee, beer, etc.], then one regards this as a necessity. [But this is a false necessity, as events have shown.] [UN154: At one time in Germany,] adversity led to less consumption of sugar, coffee, etc. because of their cost. People sought aid in substitutes, and we saw many acts of courtesy. [But] they found that [UN155: coffee has many mental benefits and that, relative to these benefits,] there is no cheaper drink for the common folk. With bread, coffee makes for a full meal and also causes a slight stimulation.

Needs relate to individuals as such; [actions to satisfy them] are completely self-interested.[487] Soon, however, the thought intrudes that one [individual's needs] are the same as another's, and so they become inherently social; [UN155: straightaway, the general appears here]. This sociality of needs is what brings forth fashion. This is to put oneself on an equal plane with others. As much as one can also speak against fashion, it is nevertheless not something to be underestimated. With a lot of needs, there is no determining ground [for choosing this or that means] other than to do as others do. With regard to ways and means, [the decision] is undetermined. And it's not worth the trouble to utter a single word about this; one must leave it to another – the tailor – to make [the suit] this way or that.[488] In this way, the human being acquires a lot of needs that have opinion as one element. As a consequence, the human being is no longer dependent on natural necessity, [UN155: but rather has a relation to a self-made necessity, and herein lies progress towards freedom].

[117] Taken together, this multiplication of needs is what we call luxury. It encompasses this entire side [UN155: of external conduct]. This

---

486 Translator: This is a reference to Joachim Heinrich Campe (1746–1818), a linguist and a writer of travelogues and books for children. Angehrn, Bondeli, and Seelmann write this about him (p. 233): "In the Theophron [1783], there are remarks in several places about the harmful physical and psychological effects produced by the desire to drink, especially by the drinking of strong and heated drinks, wine and coffee."
487 UN155: ... everyone eats and drinks for himself.
488 UN155: Precisely by doing what others do in such matters, one shows one's indifference to them.

is a side where contingency, caprice, opinion, etc. play a part and gad about. On the one hand, luxury is part of cultivation; its significance is that we relate not to natural necessity but to mental needs. [On the other hand], the increase in comfort entails an increase of need, of dependence. If one grows, so does the other.

[A. 2. *The Nature of Labour*]

To satisfy needs is to give oneself [an external] reality.[489] The individual comports himself through his needs to an external world. The more particularized his needs are, the more particularized must his means be. This particularization requires [UN156: a particularization of] labour. The means are also the property of others and can be acquired only through exchange. In this way, the human being relates himself to a human [product]. The means are a product of a labour process. What [we] consume is human labour. These labour-mediated things now spin out very extensively. In what one consumes, one consumes nothing but the direct labour of many human beings, and they too have used the labour of many. This labour has for its precondition the labour of others. Whoever makes clothes must have a dwelling, food, tools, fabric, etc. In short, these labours are intertwined. What has the most value is human labour. [UN156: The immediate material is a minor thing by comparison.]

Work is in general a necessity, a dependency. Need teaches the necessity of work. It tears the human being out of himself and forces him to deal with the external world. Need is at first something subjective. At first, need is just this inward contradiction [between what I want and what I have].[490] But the negative is this: the inward contradiction becomes an outward one, an opposition to an external thing that I require in order to satisfy my needs. Need is the avenue through which the human being steps out [into the world]. Need is [UN156: at first a blind] force for self-externalization, for coming out. I must make this contradiction my own [problem]; I must interest myself in [resolving] it. I must turn my mind to this opposition – to the satisfaction of [118] need. In order to acquire objects, I must also engage theoretically, [judging] how I should comport myself to the other. It is therefore need that

---

489 UN156: The individual must make the external world conform to his need.
490 UN156: Need is first merely something subjective, the inner contradiction that I do not have and possess in existence what is inherently in me [that I at once have it and do not have it].

tears us into this contradiction [between having the thing in want and not having it in reality]. We consider [this contradiction] as something that should not be. The contradiction must be overcome, or one must overcome need [as such]. So the imagination tells us, but need is necessary, and the more natural a man is in this respect, the closer he is to the animal.[491]

The ways and means of satisfying needs must be thoughtfully considered; and so thinking enters in the form of an [instrumental] understanding, [UN157: which thinks the relation between the means and the specific end]. This is the next aspect of the [process of] cultivation that labour has already started: attention to differences, concretizing general ideas. The human being, by virtue of having particular, outwardly directed purposes, steps into [outward] existence. To decide is precisely to seize on a specific purpose. It is through determination that we first step into reality. What emerges therewith is the cultivation [of the mind]; through this [process, the human being] acquires mental agility.[492] [To appreciate how the differentiation of needs and means educates,] one need only consider the people who live with few needs. In the mountain valleys, there are only a few ideas that circulate; they would be easy to count. When one converses with such a person, [UN157: the ideas echo, so to speak,] for a long time. They are almost incapable of moving from one idea to another.[493] Compare them to a businessman [or] a landlord. They flit every moment from one subject to another and, in the other, immediately forget the first. The main reason for their *homesickness* is that these people, who were thrown out of their simple country [life] into the hustle and bustle [of the city], could not endure it physically or mentally. In general, cultivation through labour arises from the urge to be active. Savages are lazy; the ancient Germans spent the entire day [lying] on bearskins. It all comes down to the habit of being occupied. There is more mental activity in one day of [the life of] an educated man than in the entire life of a savage.

---

491 UN156: We call it need and think of it as something that should not be, and we are quite right about that, because the contradiction should be overcome. But the ordinary, unreflective imagination understands by this that need in general should not be. Need, however, is not only an external necessity; it is an inward one. Through need and needs the human being is torn out of the dull absence of contradiction.
492 UN157: Immediately connected with [determination] is [the ability to] survey this multiplicity of differences [among potential means]. The human being learns to grasp and survey intricate and manifold differences.
493 UN157: Sensuous ideas predominate here, few combinations that express the unity of multiple relationships.

CIVIL SOCIETY 141

More specifically, the individual, in relating itself to natural objects, must [119] engage with everyone.[494] It must [therefore] tame its arbitrary will; it must adapt to all kinds of ideas. Natural crudeness (indefiniteness of thought and action) gets sloughed off. The uneducated man is not powerful, either in his body or his mind. This is the discipline of the human race, to which it must submit [UN158: through labour]. To human nature, [this discipline] comes across as bitter. [But] through the power that it exerts against [its immediate nature], the mind wins its freedom. The contradiction one overcomes is the contradiction to freedom. What one acquires on [the positive] side are the habits and skills [UN158: that count universally and] through which one becomes master of oneself.

Concerning the more precise modes of labour: As work itself becomes more and more specialized, it becomes more and more abstract and simple. Concrete needs split into a multitude of [more particularized needs]. [Correspondingly,] labour becomes more and more [socially] divided and therewith more and more abstract. Because it is the thinking human being who works, he himself brings forth [this abstractness]. Because labour becomes simpler, productivity increases. The [worker] doesn't have to think, doesn't have to go from one task to another. Through this division [of labour], time and effort are endlessly saved. This was Adam Smith's point in his *Wealth of Nations*. It is not only utility that rules here but also thought.[495] This is what drives [Smith's] example of the pins. One individual alone can barely produce 20 [in a day]. This job requires 18[496] operations. A factory of 10 persons [each confined to one operation] produces 12 lb. a day or together 48,000 pins; [thus,] each makes 4,800 [a day].

However, in this sphere [of the Ethical Idea's glimmering], much is also lost.[497] The labourer becomes more dependent, more apathetic. All variation ends and becomes a repetition of the same thing, resulting in mental stupor. Also, the human being becomes more dependent. In many cases, he finds himself abandoned [to chance], no matter how hard-working he tries to be.[498] Because production has become so

---

494 UN158: … it must make its particularity count [for others].
495 UN159: It is thought that rules in this [divided] mode of labour, although it appears at first that need brings it about.
496 UN159: 10.
497 UN159: But in this sphere of glimmering, what is gained on one side gets lost on the other.
498 UN159: If the article of the industry to which the worker belongs falters, the worker finds himself in distress.

simple, no concrete mind is necessary, and the human being can leave his work to the machine. Thus, the culminating point of extreme mechanization involves an inversion: the human being [120] can walk away from it.[499] The machine has become so far removed from the tool that the active mind no longer directs [the work]; rather, everything is left to natural powers. Yet the human being has reason to be proud of the tool.[500] It is the middle term [between human agency and nature]. In tools, the human being mediates [its self-activity] with external work. Here too [in tool-making] there is a cunning of Reason: he reveals the other as being for him. For that reason, human beings were always proud of their tools – for example, of the plough. We no longer know who the inventor was; only the objective thing is preserved [UN160: through all generations].

[A. 3. Capital]

The purpose of labour is the satisfaction of needs. In that respect, labour appears [at first sight merely] as a means. Labour is the intermediary between [the labourer's needs] and the objective reality of need-satisfaction. However, labour has a higher purpose – [UN160: education]. Whether it satisfies the [immediate] purpose is not our concern. [In reading *The Iliad*] we do not care whether Troy is destroyed; [UN160: the interest lies in] the preceding labour, the struggle. Accordingly, the labour is the point. [This point has two sides: the particularistic and the general.] Possession is self-interested; each is only for himself. But at the same time, the opposite straightaway enters. While each has himself for his end, the satisfaction of his needs turns around completely into the satisfaction of the needs of all others. The means that the human being procures directly for himself are produced only for their [exchange] value; he seldom enjoys them himself. Through this mediation and intertwining of needs, it happens that everything is interconnected, that through the satisfaction of my needs, the needs of others are also satisfied.

---

499 Translator: The inversion is that the tool that was once a means for human agency becomes a machine that subordinates and finally replaces human agency. UN159: The machine and the tool are different; with the machine, the principle of motion is sought in a dynamic natural power and not in the active mind. By contrast, the tool is merely a means that the human being, which is the active one, uses.

500 UN159: ... because Reason is expressed therein. The tool forms the middle term mediating between human activity and external nature. This is the spirit of Reason: the human being preserves itself by turning an external other [to its purpose] and allowing [the thing's immediate naturalness] to rub off.

This is in every respect very important; this changes our former views [about poverty, luxury, and charity].[501] One use of wealth [above necessities] is [to provide] food and drink [to the idle poor]. The other use is luxury. The real effect [of the modern approval of luxury] is to require us to be active [in order to have our needs satisfied].[502] One can declare along with the rich man that if he ought to let [his excess] flow to the poor, this is [exactly] what he does now [by selling it to those who work].[503] Accordingly, there is a far more ethical way of [distributing] wealth than the mere giving away of excess [to the idle]. The [exchange of superfluity] makes for a certain level of expenditure on the part of the different estates; and this depends on their income.[504] One expects the individual to make an effort. The more he improves himself, the more he does for others.

[121] What directly follows from this condition [of social labour] is that skill produces works [UN161: that are needed by others]. The work is exchanged with other works. There is a mutual need for individuals to provide labour. This creates the possibility for all to have a capital [UN161: in the general ability to satisfy needs], one that each can share. The immediate and first [form of] capital is land. The second capital asset is then the specialization of labour. By virtue of being in civil society, the human being has [a share of the human] capital, of the cashbox, so to speak, but on condition that he train himself [hence contribute to the capital]. As a consequence, the human being enters into a new form of capital. No longer mere nature [land, livestock], capital is rather human productivity. The possibility [UN161: of sharing in the general capital] depends on other circumstances.

The exercise of skill involves a capital. [UN161: The acquisition of] this skill depends on [UN161: various favourable] conditions. These have to do with the particularity of individuals. How the individual wants to partake of the [social] treasury is his affair. Inasmuch as the

---

501 UN160: In ancient times, a wealthy man supported others directly. He fed the poor, gave them drink, and clothed the naked.
502 UN160: This use [of wealth] has the higher effect that others obtain the satisfaction of their needs only on the condition that they be active.
503 UN160: One can rebuke the rich man on moral grounds for using a great deal for himself and his enjoyment, saying that he should let his excess benefit the poor; [yet] this he does too, but in a mediated, rational way [involving mutual action]. That said, there is also a luxury that is barbaric and absolutely to be condemned.
504 UN161: ... and on the individual's status in civil society. From one point of view, complaints about luxury appear as empty, merely moral declamations.

manner and extent [of his partaking] depends on the individual's particular endowments, the natural dimension has its direct and rightful relevance.[505] Here, natural equipment is important. What matters here are the circumstances of one's birth – fatherland, parents, estate, the virtue of parents, etc. This is the place for the inequality of individuals in respect of their character, their talent (this is the natural element). The inequality of individuals necessarily enters here, an inequality with respect to their particularity. Particularity as such is an essential element; it is precisely the exercise of this particularity that primarily [UN161: makes for the reality of] freedom. Inequality is [thus] sanctioned here. [Particularity] also combines [individuals] into general groups (estates).

The more precise relationships and necessary connections [in the system of needs] are a matter for national economics. [UN162: There are needs that have to be satisfied, and there are means for satisfying them.] These two sides yield the general [UN162: poles of consumption and production]. Consumption should not remain something negative; it is also a means for [further] production. National economics considers the hustle and bustle of individuals in accordance with this [production] side [of the economy]. [122] The value of these means of satisfaction is [UN162: determined in the following way]. The [value of the] works that are created must together amount to the value of what was consumed [in producing them].[506] On the one hand, the individual should only acquire them and consume them. [However,] consumption is not the last thing, not where the process stops. [It is a means for sustaining labour.] One must work in one day as much as is necessary for subsistence. This [amount] varies with each people. The value of things depends, not on gold and silver, etc., but on the general fact that I have to make my product as dear as is necessary for me to subsist. Extracting gold and silver is not profitable in itself; rather it is labour that makes value.[507]

---

505 UN161: Here, particularity and inequality have completely free play; that in respect of which I do not distinguish individuals is their general [capacity for] rationality ...

506 UN162: Handicraft in general, daily wages, these are the ultimate elements of the price of things relative to each other. This now also establishes a mean value of what an individual needs [to reproduce his labour].

507 UN162: Extracting gold and silver is not work different from other work, nor do the mines of Peru and Chile yield more than what any other worker can earn by hard work.

Consumption and production stand in tension in the following way.[508] The greatest consumer is the state. It consumes many things without producing anything of the kind.[509] For example, gunpowder is fired; this is a final consumption, as are many others [by the state]. Justice, security, etc. are a producing and a consuming.[510] This consumption must be covered primarily by taxes. [UN162: The effect of taxes on the price of things is another important object of national economics.] The value of money relative to qualitatively determined products constitutes another important relation. By exacting taxes [to pay] for its consumption, the state brings about an increase in [the price] of things. [UN163: Free choice is itself a factor that must be taken into account when calculating national-economic relations.] Erroneous calculations [of state revenue] are often made because of the unpredictable choices of people.[511]

In [the midst of] this randomness, necessary relationships arise.[512] From another perspective, this colourful hurly-burly [of the economy] organizes itself into general groups that objectively form quite cohesive structures. These systems, [each of] which constitutes a generality, are what are called estates. Calling the wish to make them the same an absurdity would be an understatement.[513] Their differences rest on the fact that the kind of needs [they have], and therewith the manner of their work and education, are specified in opposition to each other. The first estate is the substantial estate;[514] the second is the formal or reflecting estate – the estate of particularity. The third is the universal estate, which also has the substantial for its end [UN163: but no longer in an immediate way. To the universal estate chiefly falls the work of the state.]

---

508 Translator: They stand in tension because the value of products is inherently measured by what the producer on average expends during the labour process and needs to replenish his power; yet in society, the producer may not be able to sell his product for that amount because price is determined by the factors extrinsic to production that Hegel mentions next – opinion, caprice, money supply, taxes, etc.
509 UN162: The higher state institutions are all of a kind that do not directly intervene further in the circle of production.
510 Translator: This may mean that whereas in the private sector, one produces for another to consume, in the public sector, producer and consumer are identical.
511 UN163: Doubling a tax does not necessarily double its yield. The free will of people engenders significant changes in many abstractly correct calculations.
512 Translator: Ringier placed this sentence before the previous one, but I believe it fits better here.
513 UN163: We have already spoken of the shallowness of the demand for a universal sameness among human beings [see this translation, 27].
514 UN163: The first estate is the immediate one, the estate of substantial life.

We see these differences in reality. In every state there is agriculture, and then there are towns. [123] The estates divide into individuals. [On the one hand,] individuals [join an estate] in accordance with their [UN163: goals,] consciousness, and free choice. On the other hand, however, this assignment also depends on external circumstances. Whether an individual is suited [to an estate] depends on his resources, on the merit of his parents. [Perhaps] by chance he saw [an occupation] in his youth, acquainted himself with it, and developed a passion for it.[515] [Thus,] the preceding idea [that assignment to an estate is a matter of free choice] is a vague generality.[516] The human being finds a relationship to be harshest when his reflective understanding shows that he is forced to do this or that.[517] One is reminded of the caste spirit of the [UN164: ancient Egyptians] and Indians. One need know only this [about these peoples] in order to [be able to] assert that they cannot have gone far [UN164: in free development]. Of course, there are also spheres [in Europe] that one enters by birth. But this is not relevant here.[518] In any case, free choice must be involved in order to give the form [of freedom to assignment by accidental circumstances].

The first estate is the agricultural one. This estate deals only with nature. The farmer has an asset (not a capital), something fixed and secure, a soil, where the form [given to the material] is the least [important element].[519] Trees and livestock must be cared for, but forming constitutes the smallest part. The main element is what nature gives. The first of their ways concerns their needs. These are located in the ground – natural products. Planting, seeding are aspects that involve the understanding, [but they are subordinate to what nature provides].[520] To be

---

515 UN163: Nowhere is there an absolutely insurmountable natural necessity. The determining grounds for adopting one or the other estate can only be very fortuitous.
516 UN164: It is in general only the form of freedom that shows itself in the choice of estate.
517 UN164: ... when he is destined to an estate by mere birth.
518 UN164: We will see later ... that birth is also a necessary moment in the State. In India, everyone has to keep a large number of servants, because each has his own sphere of employment from which he cannot depart.
519 UN164: One can say that the farmer does not so much have capital as the substantial family has an asset. [Translator: This modifies Hegel's earlier statement that the immediate form of capital is land.]
520 UN164: One's own reflection is in general the subordinate thing in this production; the means are received in the way that the organic life of nature puts them in one's hand.

sure, [agriculture] can now also be pursued in a man-made way. Still, [even] with this enlargement of the artificial element, the whole business bears, in general, an unsophisticated aspect.[521]

There are ways [of receiving satisfactions from nature] besides those of the farmer. There are hunting peoples, fishing peoples. Agriculture, however, is the quintessential [*wesentliche*] way [for the following reasons]. The hunter leads a wandering life, has no fixed property, at one time [has] superfluity, at another bitter shortage. The same is true of nomadic peoples, whose way [of life] is also uncertain. With agriculture, need-satisfaction first becomes secure, and the need for property arises.[522] Land is a universal resource. It contains mere possibility. As something fixed [in space] and higher [than hunting and fishing in respect of formability], it is ascertainable and distinguishable. Property is specified definitely [as this field and not that] and can also [124] be formed. It is here that private property is established, and that is why agriculture constitutes rational property. Peoples have therefore justifiably viewed the invention of agriculture as a divine endowment. Creuzer in particular has emphasized this [UN165: mythic side].[523] Agriculture is ordered to the periods of nature and so also to provision for the periods that lie ahead. This involves one's own reflection, which is less determined by [natural changes than are pre-agricultural modes of subsistence].

[The distinguishing characteristic of the agricultural estate] is the simple attitude that one must direct oneself in accordance with what is. This attitude is therefore also a substantial attitude – [one of] family feeling, love, trust. If this understanding ventures out into thinking, it becomes something clumsy, useless cunning, mistrust. The fact that this understanding stays within the substantial attitude must be taken into consideration [in law and education]. For example, the fully developed

---

521 UN164: This culture can now also be pursued in a more man-made way, so that agriculture is carried on more like a factory business. Nevertheless, the business always remains of a simple kind.
522 UN165: With agriculture the human being first gains repose, and true property first arises. Nomadic people give no form to the land; its belonging to them does not become an objective reality. With agriculture, the full character of property [possession, forming] is present. Farming constitutes the rational, complete way in which the concept of property is realized.
523 Georg Friedrich Creuzer (1771–1858), *Symbolik und Mythologie der alten Völker, Fünfter Theil: Geschichte des Nordischen Heidenthums* (Leipzig: Carl Wilhelm Leske, 1822), 408, https://archive.org/details/symbolikundmyth07monegoog/page/n408/mode/2up.

ways of private law have no application here. So, too, in respect of religious instruction, etc.[524]

The next estate is the estate of reflection. In this sphere, the driving force is not the [direct] connection with natural products but rather the [human] forming of natural products. This is the business estate. This estate needs for its [own consumption] very little of what it produces. This is the stage of ideation. The work [of this estate] is therefore not something substantial.[525] The business estate relies more on its own skill. The capital from which this estate draws its sustenance is its skill and the entire network of civil society. This is the "land" from which this estate draws its capital.[526] Its understanding is instructed in a higher [grade of] education. Its education must have a different form [than that of the agricultural estate]. [The businessman] himself is what must be cultivated. [The individual raises himself to] self-reflection, self-knowledge, knowledge of his purposes. Consciousness of rights becomes a stronger element. The first estate forgets a wrong sooner; it handles an offence against personality more easily. [In the business estate,] an insult is felt more keenly [because] more weight is given to [social] distinctions. [This estate is divided into three grades.] The first [125] grade is real handicraft.[527] The second, more abstract, [grade] is industry.[528] The third grade is then the brokering of exchange, the mercantile estate. Thus, money [UN166: the universal means of exchange] necessarily enters here as well. For the first [agricultural] estate, the only thing to do is to live and to

---

524 UN165: [This estate's] basic attitude is this: It is so, and one must direct oneself in one's occupation in accordance with [what is], which presents itself as an external necessity without [need of] the will. The attitude is thus a substantial one: love, trust, faith make up the predominant character type. With respect to what must be done, this estate takes its stand primarily within a relationship of trust and obedience ... A finely developed private law is not for this estate; it needs a simpler system of justice, one based more on faith and trust. With regard to religious education, this estate can argue that a broad erudition should not be laid before it.

525 UN166: ... is less concrete, and it relies more on its own will, industriousness, and hard work.

526 UN166: In general, this estate [operates] in the field of mobility. This gives the business estate's attitude and way of life a form different from the one we observed in the first estate. The individual comes to self-reflection; on the one hand, he is dependent on externality, but on the other hand, he makes himself independent. Consciousness of freedom enters here decisively.

527 UN166: The [craftsman] is still occupied in a concrete manner. He works for the needs of other [specific] individuals.

528 UN166: The work [of the industrialist] is more abstract; he works not for [specific] individuals [but for the aggregate].

have. The second [business] estate wants to get rich; this [ambition] has no bounds, either objectively or subjectively.

The third estate is the universal estate. [This is the estate that devotes itself] to the interests of society insofar as these interests are general. [This is] the estate that devotes itself to the commonwealth [*Gemeinwesen*]. However, because [UN166–7: this estate must be above work to satisfy needs directly,] it must either have private wealth or be indemnified by the state. [The civil servant] must find [in the state] the satisfaction of the interests he has as a particular individual.

Accordingly, these are the [social] relationships that are found in the nature of things.[529] Because these differences[530] are present in the Concept, they must also be present in reality.[531] Individuals are not the main thing; rather the divisions of the Concept are. Individuals assign themselves to [these divisions].[532] The ethical disposition of these individuals is rectitude – doing what one ought to do in the [occupational] position one is in.[533]

The second moment [the first is the position and its duties] is professional honour.[534] One is not a member [of an estate] by nature; rather, one must make oneself a member. As labour becomes divided, the divisions acquire the form of universality. So, too, must the individual raise his particularity to the universality [of a profession]. The human being [must become] a somebody – that is, he must belong to a certain position in civil society. The human being can be a somebody only by being recognized by others. In this system, each is only what he is in the recognition of others. That is the necessary moment of professional honour; through this moment he first gains his objective existence and attains his goal. Status carries honour; it holds validity in the imagination. Everyone is a member of the whole and by virtue of that, he is something real.[535] Freedom in this sphere is at the same time dependence, but through education, [dependence] is once again freedom.

---

529 UN167: These are the modes of employment that spontaneously present themselves and that lie in the nature of things.
530 Translator: "these differences," i.e., unreflective unity, reflection into self, reflective unity.
531 UN167: The [estate] distinctions present here should be seen neither as a misfortune nor as a pretension that some have claimed at the expense of others.
532 UN167: We don't want everyone doing everything.
533 UN167: ... doing what the position into which fate and your own choice has placed you brings with it.
534 UN167: ... that consists in fulfilling [the duties] that pertain to the estate of each.
535 UN167: The honour of the individual is to belong to an estate and to be recognized therein.

[B. The Administration of Justice]

[126] The second sphere [of civil society] is the administration of justice. [UN167: In the system of needs, freedom merely glimmers. Freedom is mixed up with raw materiality.] The reflective self-consciousness of freedom is the free being's positing [UN167: and willing] itself as free. Freedom, insofar as it has existence not as a glimmering but as free self-relation, is the stage of justice. As distinct from a glimmering freedom, the next truth is self-conscious freedom. The substantial basis of the entire [process of] mediation whereby individuals satisfy their needs [through exchange] is property. The system of needs cannot exist at all without rights. The greatest boost to freedom[536] is a strict, impartial administration of justice; without that, everything is weak. The basis for security is that property in its full reality holds good. In places where slavery exists, industry invariably lags behind. This is because the basis for everything, namely, that I as a particular individual can realize myself, is missing. The right of property constitutes the foundation of the second stage.

However, we are concerned here not merely with justice as such but with the realization of justice in the specific location of the judicial system. Justice in itself is now filled out with the concept of existence. Ethical life contains that moment: freedom as such and its realization. Its realization consists more precisely in the education of the particular will [to the general Will], to which the individual raises himself.[537] For justice to be realized, the system [of needs][538] must be such that it is receptive to justice and, secondly, that it wills justice. But this is nothing other than the particular will's [becoming educated by the system of needs to the general Will], whereby justice comes to its reality. The [system of] needs is therefore both the [sphere of] the particular will and the soil of justice.[539] In the system of needs, justice is inchoately present as a need. Family life awakens concern for the future; directly involved therein is [the thought] that what I have should remain mine.

---

536 UN168: to industry.
537 UN168: This entire second sphere of ethical life is the splitting apart of ethical life. Individuals raise themselves through work to universality. For justice to be realized, the ground must be smoothed by individuals' being receptive to it. This occurs only through the [education] of the particular will that is presented in the system of needs.
538 Translator: Ringier wrote "the system of reality."
539 UN168: The system of needs is thus an essential condition for the emergence of the rule of Law.

In its strict sense, the administration of justice first emerges at a certain level of schooling in community [UN168: as history shows]. Property also exists in a [127] patriarchal condition; but [there] people do not litigate with each other so much as fear each other. The same is true of Oriental [UN168: despotism]. In that substantial unity, the rule of Law is subordinate [to the despot's will]; property is merely permitted to the individual. As a consequence, human beings must become indignant if justice is to grow in this damaged soil.

It is what we saw in the Concept [of Right]: I am here as a person.[540] Education makes it possible for the individual to be understood as a person. It is only by arriving at an understanding of the general that it becomes possible for the individual consciousness to become conceptualized [as a person], hence to count for another. In the immediate empirical view (in the sphere of love, etc.), the [individual] is not thought of as a person.[541] Individuals have to know themselves as persons. It is a hugely important step for human beings to arrive at this understanding of themselves. It was [UN169: on the one hand] right to inveigh against cosmopolitanism. Certainly, if one remains at this superficial [position], there is something lacking. But one must not go to the other extreme. It is a tremendous step in education to think of someone as a human being, as a person. This was not so among the Greeks and Romans.[542] It is a great progressive step to have raised to a pinnacle [the idea] that [this particular individual] is a human being.

The form of education [that teaches how] to grasp the general Will is a necessary result of the particular will's being able to make its right to be a person count. The knowledge and will of the particular will are the real existence of the general Will. The foundation of the administration of justice is that justice is willed by the particular will. Naturally, the spectacle of injustice arises in cases of collision [where each side equates his opinion of justice with objective justice. As against this conflict of

---

540 Translator: So, persons are equal before the law. But beside this principle, Hegel's earlier statement that the measure of punishment is partly determined by the person's social status (see this translation, 59) cannot stand.
541 UN169: This first occurs through thinking.
542 UN169: With the Greeks and Romans, it was not the case that the human being was considered deserving of recognition simply as a human being. Later, distinction was again improperly emphasized, and the question was more whether a [being] was a Jew or a Christian, an Englishman or a Frenchman, than whether it was a human being.

opinion,] the administration of justice entails that [objective] justice has power, hence reality, and that it is known that such a real power exists. This knowledge that justice has validity is likewise determinative of its being valid. [Justice] is this power only through the particular will.

[B. 1. Justice as Law]

[128] The first moment [of the administration of justice] is that what is just becomes publicly known and pronounced. This is to say that what is objectively just becomes posited. What is objectively just should therefore become positive law; it should become real. The first form of reality is that [justice be an object of] consciousness.[543] The laws must be set down; they must be made known. General laws are necessary. To make laws means to bring to consciousness through thinking what is objectively just. Precisely in that way does justice receive the form [adequate to its] universality; through that [process of legislation] alone does [justice] become capable of attaining its true determinacy. This is the necessity of law or of the legal. A distinction is drawn [within positive law] between customary law [and written law]. Customary law is not like animal instinct; it [too] must become known. If it remains what is called customary law, then it is not a written law and [so] not an internally consistent, developed system. The universality of thought thus remains cloudy. Customary law can also be written; it can be found in books [UN170: and is distinguished from truly written law only in being an incoherent collection].

In justice's becoming known lies its objectively true determinateness. If [justice] is merely something inwardly felt, it is [tainted by] subjective particularity – natural will, inclination, heart. Only in being thought out is it freed from the merely arbitrary.[544] Customary laws are not instinctual; they are also known through thought.[545] In and for itself, the universal is the universal [apprehended by] thought. Even if many do not consider it so, [customary law] still belongs [to thought]. In its content, customary law is also something known; as customary law, however, it is something cloudily known. Knowing it that way, as the ancients did,

---

543 UN170: What is objectively just should be present as law, as an object of consciousness.
544 UN170: That justice be determined through thought, that it be made objective and an object of knowledge, is a right of mind in general.
545 UN170: However, the customary has the character not so much of the pre-written as of something practised by all.

is an imperfect mode of its existence.[546] Nevertheless, what is called customary law can also be collected – *loix coutumières, Landrecht.* Its difference [from a law code] is that it is a somewhat shapeless collection, where principles are expressed and embedded in concrete cases, and it is thus often incomplete.[547] From this method, a great deal of confusion arises in respect of lawgiving. [129] In Rome, a Caesar [made justice publicly known] ingeniously. In England, there is a kind of customary law that, though called unwritten law, is nevertheless written. It is [contained] in the decisions of various law courts, etc.[548] No court is really bound by the authority of previously decided cases; [rather,] it must speak in accordance with the [unwritten] principles. The court is [thus] a sovereign as well. Cognoscenti [UN171: of English jurisprudence] cannot describe this confusion enough. This is the most woeful condition in which a legal and juridical constitution can find itself.

If a nation does not have a law code, it should make one. One must not think that completely new laws [need to be] invented; rather, the present law must be organized in an intelligible way. Such a law code need not [include] new things. The greatest insult that can be levelled at a nation is to deny its capacity to make a law code. The right of consciousness to know the law is a right to a law code. If the language is foreign or the tomes too thick, [UN172: or if a lot of glossators and legal scholars have to be looked up], then we have a situation like the one with Dionysius, who hung the tablets so high that no one could read them.[549]

Everywhere, a prince who, like Justinian and Frederick the Great, gives his people a law code will be considered a great benefactor. If the law is in the hands only of scholars, they are the masters of the others who do not know. The university is [then] nothing but the means by which others can acquire an instrument of domination. The Napoleonic

---

546 UN170: The form of customary law emerges from an uneducated era, when one took the universal only as something [empirically] done by all, not yet as something present in and for itself. With a merely customary law many inconsistencies arise because of the contingency of knowledge [of the law].
547 UN171: The difference is then that it is something of a shapeless collection, shapeless especially because the universal is not lifted out and the particulars are not set out in their subordination thereto and under each other ... The Twelve Tables, the [decisions of the Roman] Senate consuls, the *responsa juris consultorum* make up a colourful jumble that has become much worse in Germany. It has thus come about that one can cite now this, now that great commentator [to support whatever proposition].
548 UN171: Blackstone says that one needs at least twenty years to study it.
549 Dionysius I (430–367 BC), tyrant of Syracuse.

Code, although it appears to be the great word of a [single] individual, was a boon.[550] And they burned the book![551] One will always find something to criticize in it. It must be reviewed. Reviewing means nothing else than [showing that one] is smarter than others. And to show this, the reviewer wears himself out. [UN172: It is in general the bad habit of Germans never to be capable of finishing.][552] There comes to mind the wife's reply that bad weather is always better than no weather at all. The burning of the Napoleonic Code was an adolescent mistake (the donkey and the dead lion).[553] It would have taken a kind of bravery [for Romans] to burn the *Corpus Juris* [but not for Germans to burn a French code]. With the Napoleonic Code, all [130] serfdom was abolished, and from that one can surmise why there was so much clamour against it.[554]

Accordingly, justice must be posited. What has obligatory force as justice, has [such force] insofar as it is the law. Therefore, if one asks, What is justice, the answer is: what the law says. It can happen, [however,] that [UN173: particularity exerts its influence and that consequently] the law is at variance with what is inherently just. Justice as the legal in general is positive justice. In positive justice, justice is that which accords with law. Positive jurisprudence has to keep to the task of getting to know this law historically. It takes authority in a generic

---

550 UN172: Where it has been introduced, the Napoleonic Code is becoming ever more recognized as a boon. At the very least, the fact that this law code was finished is Napoleon's doing, even if the material content is not his. The completion of a law code is a ruler's [achievement]; left alone, the jurists would never finish.
551 Translator: at the Wartburg Festival, 18 October 1817. This was a nationalist rally organized by university student fraternities (*Burschenschaften*) and timed to coincide with the three hundredth anniversary of Luther's ninety-five theses. At its conclusion, books were burned, including those (like the Napoleonic Code) symbolizing French domination. The organizers invoked Luther's burning of the papal bull excommunicating him, but Hegel mocks this association because Luther's act took courage, whereas that of the students, occurring after Napoleon's defeat, was a case of "the donkey kicking a dead lion."
552 *Outlines*, para. 216: "It is misunderstanding which has given rise alike to the demand – one that is chiefly a German sickness – that a legal code should be something absolutely complete ... and also to the argument that because a code is incapable of such completion, therefore we ought not to ... produce a code at all."
553 UN172: The fact that the Napoleonic Code was burned at a solemn occasion can be considered a sad manifestation of our youth. When Luther burned the Roman Bull, it was still valid in Germany, and that is why it was a brave act. The fable of the donkey who kicked the dead lion may come to mind.
554 UN172: A large segment of those who wrote and railed against the Napoleonic Code knew well what was dangerous to them. The Napoleonic Code contains the great principle of the freedom of property and the eradication of everything that stems from the feudal period.

sense as its principle [without distinguishing between just and unjust authority].[555] One can indeed still keep busy [with such an enquiry]. One can try to lift the general out of the concrete as well as to deduce the particular [from the general], and one can try to show exhaustively the still further particularizations of the particular.

To know the content of positive justice is to understand, to know, what the lawful is. Many factors influence the way justice becomes actual in a people as well as the condition [of its legislation].[556] The people may originally have had bad institutions (the Romans). The constitution is the most powerful basis on which [the specific realization of justice] depends.

The Concept of justice remains in its universality; the application requires a honing [of the Concept] to the utmost determinateness. For example, for a [specific] punishment to be announced, manifold other determinations are required. The particular [punishment] does not lie within the conceptual determinations [of punishment].[557] In its application, the law should be determinate with respect to time and space. Positive justice must express [itself down to] the last point of decision; [yet] the last decision does not lie within [the Concept of justice]. Take, for example, the age of majority. No concept can specify this as twenty-five years; this belongs to positive law. For one individual, this will be too early, for another, too late. The law requires a definite decision. A terminus must be fixed; we can't get embroiled in examining [every individual to determine how mature he is]. With royal houses, [the age of majority] is lowered considerably. The same [indeterminacy exists with respect to] the term of a punishment. Positive law must add this.[558]

[B. 2. The Existence of Law]

[UN174: Because the law is a universal that must be applied to particular cases,] there is [131] here a duality [of terms] in relationship: the generality of the law and the particularity of the law. Laws should be

---

555 UN173: In philosophy, we have to develop what is just out of the concept of freedom; positive jurisprudence, however, has authority for its principle and has to keep to what is historically present.
556 UN173: The condition of education is especially important here.
557 UN173: The qualitative and quantitative determinations belonging to particulars are of no concern to the Concept.
558 UN173: For example, setting a twenty-year prison term for such-and-such crime is a determination that cannot be immediately derived from the Concept [of a just punishment].

simple [UN174: so that they can be easily known], and they are simple only if they are general. [Yet] the subject matter of law is the particularity of the finite. The content of the finite in civil society are the relationships [of interdependency we have discussed]. This finite material multiplies itself more and more [UN174: as we have already seen with the multiplication of needs]. This is therefore also true of legal relationships. No bounds [to this process] can be drawn; therefore, [the law] cannot be simple. There is a contradiction here: by its nature, the finite cannot be adequate to the universal. The finite is inexhaustible. [This means that], for the sake of [the extensibility of] its material content, a law code can never be absolutely complete.[559] There is an incommensurability here [between the law's endless determination as it is applied to circumstances and the completeness and simplicity of the law itself]. The law must be adapted to the relationships [of civil society]. Therefore, the law code must be adapted to the requirements and level of cultivation [of civil society].[560] But it cannot be absolutely complete. This is a field [where only an] approximation [to completeness is possible]. To be sure, the more the law is specified, the more complete it becomes from the point of view [of determinateness]; but from another point of view, specification is a bad thing. If the understanding wants to subsume [particulars to universals], then the more differentiated the aspects [of a social relationship], the more applicable legal grounds there are [for supporting] one side and the other.[561]

Most importantly, with [the application of law] comes the distinction between the letter and the spirit. There are [determinations of law] that can be used in accordance with their letter [but] against the essential thing in the case.[562] The law must become written. Therefore, the letter can be used in a way contrary to justice. Each party brings forward legal grounds. The judge's task is to invalidate those opposed to the essential aspects of the case.[563] It is rightly thought that the spirit of the law is more excellent than the letter. [Still,] the essential determinations

---

559 UN174: To speak of an absolutely complete law code that encompasses all particular cases is an empty ideal.
560 UN174: [Notwithstanding that a law code can never be complete,] it remains valid that a law code suitable to the needs of a people should exist. With a people whose trade relations are simple, the laws of trade can also be simple. To demand that a law code be finished in the sense [of encompassing all cases] is to postpone the matter ad infinitum.
561 UN174: ... the more legal grounds there are that can be used for chicanery.
562 UN175: ... against substantial justice.
563 UN175: The task for the judge is to distinguish the particular and subordinate aspects from the essential ones.

[of the law] must be present not as spirit but as expressed. Otherwise, every whim of the court would be given the greatest of all devices.[564] Montesquieu wrote a book called *The Spirit of the Laws*. With [that term] he grasped the universal. But he also had to delineate it.[565] The law's having a letter is the guarantee of freedom. It is irrational to speak ill of the letter. On the other hand, the law can degenerate into an empty formalism, as is the case in England. In many [132] cases, injustices have arisen from this (cf. cases: B. Thomson instead of Bartholomew Thomson or bynight instead of by night).[566]

We have seen [in abstract Right] that property is the side of [freedom's] existence. Therein my will has an existence for others.[567] Others should respect this matter because they see my will in it. In civil society, the existence [of freedom] is the [public] recognition and legal force [of property]. The ways [in abstract Right] by which I will that [a thing] be mine recede in civil society.[568] In [abstract Right],[569] recognition in general is required from others, [hence] a sign, not a particular form of sign. But the form that I mean to give [to the thing] by labour is the same form that others give. [In civil society,] however, this indeterminacy disappears. In civil society, the demand arises for acquisitions of property to take a form [e.g., registration in a public registry] that relates to recognition by the public authority.[570] These forms are formalities, the point of which is [to ensure] that my property will be recognizable as mine by others.[571] Recognition that something is mine is [now] based

---

564 UN175: ... otherwise every decision would fall to individual insight and to the subjectivity of the judge.
565 UN175: By the spirit of the laws, Montesquieu understood nothing other than the universal principles on which the particular laws of peoples were based. In that way he also determined the spirit as letter.
566 UN175: A Bartholomew Thomson was acquitted after his crime was otherwise fully proved because "B. Thomson" was written in the indictment. The English have pushed empty formalism to an extreme. [Translator: The "bynight" example is not further elaborated.]
567 UN175: The predicate "mine" that I give to a thing must at the same time be something objective.
568 UN176: Property in civil society is based mainly on contract; direct acquisitions are less significant.
569 Translator: reading abstract Right instead of civil society.
570 UN176: In civil society, the means by which I bring to recognition that something is mine are extended. Inasmuch as the public authority recognizes something as mine (a plot of land registered in the mortgage book), the indeterminacy of forming is cancelled.
571 UN176: The formalities are by no means superfluous; rather they are the rational means by which a thing's being mine has an [objective] existence.

on a definite general recognition. These formalities are the proofs [required for] recognition. Because the formalities are external, they can be annulled and altered, spun out to infinity.

By virtue of this determination [whereby property gains objective reality in civil society through public formalities, recognition, and enforcement] the form of crime and its annulment takes on a particular meaning. Crime is not only an offence against the individual. Through crime, the validity of existent [UN176: freedom] is also violated; the *validity* [UN176: of law] is violated.[572] Whoever commits a crime thereby says that, as a general matter, [UN176: laws] do not count for him.[573] Crime therefore becomes more serious [UN176: because not only inherent but also realized [[freedom]][574] is violated]. Therein is contained [the kernel of truth in] what the viewpoint of dangerousness expresses.[575] There lies [in crime in civil society] a further, real possibility [of the subversion of a lawful condition]. The nature of crime does not change [in civil society]; the side of existent [freedom is still] what is violated. But a larger existence is violated.[576] In crime, all are violated.[577] In that sense, crime concerns the universal [condition of rights]. In caste states it is believed that if a crime befalls an individual [belonging to one caste], the others are not affected. In the ancient tragedies, we see crimes piled on crimes, [yet] the chorus of citizens takes itself to be [133] uninvolved in it.[578]

In civil society, the general recognition [of rights] is established by the will of all. If a violation were not punished, it would be posited as something permitted. [Nevertheless,] when civil society is [UN177: firmly] established, a power exists such that this violation sinks into

---

572 UN176: Crime injures the recognized existence of freedom in general, the validity of law.
573 UN176: I scoff at the general recognition.
574 Translator: UN wrote "infinity."
575 UN177: Therein lies what is understood as the dangerousness of crime. One says: if [crime] is valid, there is no longer any security.
576 Translator: because rights are now generally recognized and valid.
577 UN177: It is not only my individual will that is violated by crime, but [also] the general Will.
578 UN177: Where civil society in this specific sense has not yet emerged, the rest do not regard it as an offence against them if a crime is committed against someone. Where the estates of society are estranged, the members of one estate do not grieve in the least over a violation of a member of another (Indian castes; murdered Jews). Similarly, with the Greeks, we see how in their tragedies, the chorus sees crimes committed by persons belonging to royal families as something that does not concern it.

CIVIL SOCIETY 159

insignificance.[579] [By contrast,] we see [weak] conditions of civil society where a simple theft is punished with death. In France, death was meted out for a theft of five sous. In England, for forty shillings.[580] Inherently, the existence of Right is something eternal; [nevertheless] society is justified in meting out the harshest penalties for small guilts if that is necessary [for the maintenance of order]. In a well-ordered civil life, punishments are mild. After a long war, punishments (especially for theft) must become more severe.[581]

The third moment [of the administration of justice] to consider is the *realization of justice – the courts*.

[B. 3. The Court]

Law is generally enforced justice, and as such, it stands over against particular opining and willing and has to make itself count against them. Justice is [objectively] justice insofar as it has real existence and is asserted [against wrong]. The court is inherently necessary [for this], something active [in the realization of justice]. Individual will and individual consciousness must will the just as such. Private revenge can be justified [where there is no public authority], but in its [private] form, it is the work not of the general but of the particular will. [The execution of justice] should not, however, be at the mere pleasure of the [aggrieved] individual, as is the case in a world of chivalry and quixotic carryings-on. The courts can have emerged historically in whatever way – from patriarchal relations or from [feudal] lordship, [UN178: under which it was viewed as a private right to judge and appoint judges]. Herr von Haller, [UN178: who wrote a large work on the restoration of political science,][582] sees the [administration of] justice, not as

---

579 UN177: One might think from the foregoing [i.e., that in civil society crime violates not only the person but also the validity of law] that the penalties for crimes must be much more severe in civil society than in earlier conditions. Yet just the opposite is shown. If civil society is violated, there is something so firmly established against [the crime] that the violation sinks into insignificance.
580 UN178: In general, penalties must always be adapted to the condition of civil society.
581 UN178: It used to be that, after wars of many years, when the armies were dismissed, crime greatly increased. In such circumstances, a sharpening of lawful punishments is entirely fitting ... There is a tremendous difference between the punishments of earlier times and contemporary ones.
582 Carl Ludwig von Haller (1768–1854), *Restauration der Staatswissenschaft*, 6 vols. (Winterthur: Steinerische Buchhandlung, 1816–34). See Hegel's withering critique of von Haller's book in *Outlines*, para. 258.

something rationally necessary, but as a mere favour that princes, etc. granted out of grace. During the era of the law of the jungle, the dominant view [UN178: was that everyone had to obtain justice for himself.] The power of a court was viewed then as an improper suppression of freedom.[583]

[134] As it steps forward, the court has the duty to pronounce what is just. It is the insight of the court [UN179: not that of the parties] that must decide [UN179: what is right]. The court is the organ of the law. It appears [UN179: both in mere civil litigation and] also with crime. [Where crime is concerned,] it is not the injured party who appears [against the accused] but the court.[584] Through punishment, the law becomes truly reconciled [UN179: with itself] again. It re-establishes itself and therein manifests itself as having dignity and power. Just as much does the law become, through punishment, something to which the [criminal] can become subjectively reconciled. It is not an alien fate that overpowers the one who is punished; rather in [the trial and in his punishment] he is considered a free being.

Everyone must have the right to stand before a court (*jus standi in judicio*), but also the duty to appear before a court. If I cannot stand before a court, then my objective right is not recognized, nor is it acknowledged that I am competent to appear before a court. One is therefore under a wardship. It was that way in Rome with the representation of [plebeian] clients [by patrician patrons].[585] [Today,] however, lawyers are retained by the parties, and that is not the same thing. Here too belongs the other side [of the right of standing]: that every [aggrieved party who wishes to vindicate his right] must stand before a court, that he must not take revenge himself, that it is the court that pronounces justice. Likewise, everyone has the duty to stand [before a court] if justice is sought against him. In the era of the law of the jungle, [disputes]

---

583 UN179: The development of the administration of justice is an important side of history; [before, there was only] private revenge on the one hand, and, on the other, a relationship where everyone thought he didn't have to be dragged before a court but, rather, it was for the injured party and his family to make things right with him. It is the insight of a court, not of the parties, that must decide what is just, as much in a merely civil dispute as in a crime. Therewith [the process] loses the form of direct revenge; it is in civil society that punishment first enters.
584 Translator: Here Hegel assumes the inquisitorial system rather than the adversarial one, in which an impartial court umpires between the state and the accused.
585 UN179: Similarly, in earlier times in Germany, serfs and bondsmen were not entitled to appear before a court to protect their right.

were resolved with one's own fist, and because of that, this [era] has been extolled as a golden age.[586] This is now the idea behind the duel.

[In court,] the parties have to demonstrate their right; they have to prove it. Before a court, I have no right that I cannot prove. This can be very painful [if I feel that I'm right but can't prove it], but this cannot be otherwise. The further development is the legal process [of appeal]. It is essential that this process be made legally definite. This entire process, however, falls into the [realm of the] finite [where each step is *a* step, so cannot be inherently final]. More or less can be achieved, so that it is indeed often considered fortunate if one hasn't attained one's right.[587] [UN180: There must be procedures available whereby it is left to] the parties to decide whether they want to see the matter through.

One can ask the court of justice for equity; there must be procedures whereby [equity] can also be executed. These are then arbitration boards and courts of equity. It is a laudable [135] procedure if one may not commence formal proceedings before the matter has been put before an arbitration board that looks to equity. The English have such courts of equity, where circumstances decide [the case].[588] Ordinary legacies, etc. come before such tribunals. So, for example, if a formal will is drawn, but after death a codicil is found that hasn't been completely written out, [in a court of equity] this will be considered. [In dispensing justice,] one has two dimensions to consider: the uniqueness of the case and *l'intérêt de la loi*. One can say: if formalities are absent, great uncertainty will result. But, as has been said, [to be intransigent about formalities] one must have convinced oneself that this lack [of certainty] holds true notwithstanding [the certainty in] the matter at hand. It is a big mistake to move from a single case to such possibilities, saying [even if there is no uncertainty about the testator's intention in this case]: doing this will result in uncertainty [in subsequent cases]. From such excessive wisdom great injustices are often perpetrated.[589]

---

586 UN179: In the era of the right of the jungle, everyone sought his right through his own fist, and whoever committed a wrong thought that he had the same right as the injured party, that objective [justice] and the power of the objective had no right over him, so that justice had to be personally sought against him.

587 UN180: The court process can become so complicated that the parties become discouraged from pursuing their right. The legal process of the Empire was so slow that it was viewed as a blessing if a territory obtained the *jus de non appellando* [the right of a territorial prince to prohibit his subjects from appealing to the Imperial Court].

588 UN180: ... where the judge decides according to the overall situational context, for which pre-written formalities may or may not provide.

589 UN181: Formalism is thereby established, and it is a false wisdom that pleases itself in the enumeration of general possibilities.

We saw that laws should be so well publicized and comprehensible that everyone can know and understand them. The legal process [whereby] I realize my right must also be knowable for me, and for that reason it should not be long drawn-out and complicated. Otherwise, it becomes a mystery [UN181: to which the parties must blindly submit]. In what concerns my affairs, I have the right of self-consciousness [to the possibility of insight].[590] It is in my interest as well as the interest of others [UN181: that the legal process be transparent]. There is a dual interest [involved here]: the interest that the Right in itself be done and the interest that it be known as done. [One might think that] countries where trust in the court still exists can be indifferent to [transparency] considered as a requirement of justice. But it is necessary [for realized justice] that people know that justice is being expressed, not only that they believe it. [UN181: One cannot exactly say that justice is better administered through transparency.][591] If one says that adjudication expresses justice better if it is transparent, then one can fall into the other extreme [justice can be done better in camera than openly]. No, the Concept [of justice itself] demands that it be *known* as having been done.[592]

Adjudication has to subsume a particular case under a general law. [UN182: There are two sides to this.] In the first place, one must analyse the particular [event in terms of a legal concept]. For example, whether a contract exists, whether performance occurred. Crime has the same external side: what are the [136] ambient circumstances of the act? Was the victim robbed? Where [e.g., in his home or outside the home]? Then, the external reality must be qualified – for example, whether the death is manslaughter or murder.[593] This qualification is not yet a judgment, at least not yet a judgment with regard to justice.[594] The other side is that the case is subsumed under a law. These two functions come forward in the judicial decision. The application of the

---

590 See this translation, 70.
591 Translator: It is not that transparency is more likely to produce just outcomes.
592 UN181: That justice in itself be done is the first part of civil freedom. With the higher education of civil society, however, there arises the further demand that justice be known to be done through the transparency of the administration of justice. One can adduce many [instrumental] reasons for the one [right] and for the other; but it is never the essence of the matter that is thereby made to count.
593 UN182: With such an action as a crime, not only the external reality but also the inwardness of the action must be qualified, whether [the action] is a murder or a manslaughter.
594 Translator: The accused might be the wrong person, or he might disagree with the prosecutor's legal characterization of his action, or there might be excusing factors.

law is the activity of the law through the judges. They are the organs of the law, but they are not machines.[595] In the Roman court system, this distinction [between the legal characterization of an action and the subsumption of the case under law] appeared [institutionally]. The praetor [who applied the law to the facts] named and briefed a judex [to ascertain and characterize the facts], whom he instructed on the distinction. With crime, the first and most important thing is to characterize the crime. In a public [as opposed to a civil] proceeding, it is more or less up to the will of the prosecutor whether he wants to propose a serious or a not-so-serious qualification [of the crime]. If the judge finds that the serious qualification does not apply, the [accused] is acquitted. And he cannot be charged again for the same action. This is certainly a great imperfection in the judicial process.[596]

The judge initiates the entire proceeding. In that way, the right of the parties is secured, and it lies directly within the function of the judge to relate the criminal to the law and punish him. With regard to the first point, the [characterization] of the particular action, one must ascertain all the circumstances. This is not a judicial function; any educated person can discover this. Anyone can also make legal determinations, for example, that the corpus delicti has been made out [as well as determinations regarding] witnesses and instruments. These determinations always leave the fact of the matter [*die Sache*] still uncertain. The ways and means [of proof] cannot [bring us] closer to certainty. If there are two witnesses, then a kind of universality comes to pass. However, not all circumstances can be specified, nor can the nature of the circumstances [be absolutely known].[597] That would be a completely universal

---

595 UN182: ... because it is for them to discover the essential side of an action and therefore to know under what law to subsume the action.
596 Translator: Ringier's version makes it sound as if Hegel is against the double jeopardy rule. But UN's version is quite different. It shows Hegel objecting only to the mutual exclusiveness of criminal indictments in England at the time. UN182: In England, it is more or less up to the prosecutor whether he will attach the most serious character to the legal action or a milder one. If the prosecutor chooses the more serious qualification and the judge finds that the crime is not supported [by the evidence], then neither the judge nor the prosecutor can step down to the lighter qualification. This is a great imperfection in the judicial process. [Translator: In *Outlines*, this becomes a complaint that the judge cannot correct an indictment mistakenly charged by the prosecutor (para. 225).]
597 UN183: With all these things uncertainty always remains; and no matter how many details one ascertains, and no matter that something should be taken as proved, still, the fact will not be known thereby in its universality. Because the fact to be established is so external, it falls to be determined by the common understanding.

knowledge, [which is unattainable here]. The judge qua judge can make no claim [of expertise] about such matters.

Ascertainment of circumstances is not the only thing [required]; there is also the side of [the defendant's] perception and intention. The individual must have known and willed what he [137] did. Here, too, general considerations and rules can be given, but the conclusion can only be determined in the particular case.[598] In that sense, the ultimate [decider] is the conscience of the one who judges. Knowledge of external things, of external circumstances, is a subjective knowledge[599]. [UN183: So too is knowledge about an individual's perception and will a merely subjective certainty.] It rests on testimony, assurances, and [degrees of] confidence. For assistance, the court must ultimately have recourse to the oath. [Swearing an oath] is a requirement that counts as a religious conversion, but it nevertheless indicates only a subjective [belief in the truth of one's statements].[600] One invokes in aid [of objective truth-telling] the idea of God: "So help me God." Before this idea all particular interests disappear. The power of this idea – that it drives away all untruths – makes [swearing an oath] a solemn act. The other thing is that, [given the penalty for perjury,] the accused ties his welfare to [the truth as he perceives it of] his testimony, and over this [the correspondence of his testimony to the truth as he perceives it] he has power. The main thing is the awesome idea of God.[601] It is something inward, a matter of conscience, but also, with this idea [of conscience], one can be inscrutable [it ends all enquiry].[602]

Accordingly, [adjudication] has two aspects: the first is fact-finding, and this knowledge is that of any educated person. [The second is declaring the law.] The finding of fact is ultimately a subjective decision, *animi sententia*.[603] The law declaration aspect is expressed by the judge. The right of self-consciousness [to insight] is vindicated with respect to this [declaratory] aspect by the fact that the law is accessible, so

---

598 UN183: ... but here too the final decision falls to subjective conviction [and] conscience.
599 UN183: certainty
600 UN183: This too is nothing other than a subjective estimation, an assurance; the sincerity of the oath is guaranteed by the conscience of the one who takes it.
601 UN184: The main thing is the idea that the absolute truth, the substantial, must be brought forth.
602 UN184: In all this, the subjectivity [of conscience] can solidify all that the oath contains and form a hard, inscrutable point over against it.
603 Translator: T.M. Knox informs us (*Outlines*, p. 353) that these words were part of the oath of the Roman judex ("I swear to the best of my belief").

that one can know the reasons for the judgment.⁶⁰⁴ The other aspect, however, is the decision in the instant case. With respect to this particular aspect, too, self-consciousness has a right to be satisfied that the judgment was properly rendered. That judgment, however, is subjective. For me to know that [my case] was rightly decided, I must have confidence in the people who give the verdict. I will have confidence if those who give the verdict are from my estate, my sphere [of society]. I can have confidence [in the decision] if the decision-makers are related to me [by similar experience].⁶⁰⁵ This is the principal reason for the institution of the jury trial, for being judged by one's peers (equals).⁶⁰⁶ Because these two functions [fact-finding and law declaration] are completely different, it is necessary that they be performed by two different [organs].⁶⁰⁷ The [138] right of self-consciousness that everyone know that he was given his due must be protected. And this knowledge is to be taken from [the defendant's] confidence in those who judge him. With respect to the subjective side [of the judgment], confidence relates to the subjectivity, [not to the expertise,] of the people who have to judge. The fact that this side is chiefly a matter of confidence [in like subjectivity] underlies the institution requiring this part of the judgment to be pronounced by men from the same estate [as the defendant]. One must have experienced the [defendant's] particular circumstances.

This [need for] confidence with respect to the aspect of [fact-finding] has been satisfied in many countries by the jury trial. In England, to name one, the jury trial is viewed as a palladium of freedom. [The judge cannot satisfy this need.] The court stands over against me [as the universal to my particularity], though it is [also] on my side. The direction

---

604 UN184: ... and by the fact that the dispensing of justice takes place in public.
605 UN184: This is because we are concerned here with particularity, with all the particular relationships the person encompasses. This particularity does not admit of objective definition; rather, one must have lived therein oneself in order to make it one's own. One can, it is true, have a general idea of the [defendant's] particularity, but one cannot appreciate its significance [unless one has experienced it].
606 UN184: This is chiefly what makes the jury trial such an important political institution. It has already been mentioned that subjectivity is an important aspect of proof in a judicial proceeding. The certainty that justice was rendered to me relates to the subjectivity of those who decide the matter. Thus, one must speak here primarily of confidence. In this part of the judicial process, men who do not stand over me as a judge but who are rather on a level with me must speak.
607 UN184: It is in general necessary that [functions] differentiated in concept should also be executed by different individuals, should be allocated to different officials.

of the judge's education must be only towards the universal. I trust judges [of fact] who are closer to me much more than I do others.[608] This is the right of self-consciousness [with respect to the judgment of fact]. Inasmuch as [this right] is the essential thing here, we can pass over other reasons [for the jury] – reasons having to do with utility and consequences. The nature of a thing must be drawn from a relationship [here to justice]. Justice is better secured through jury trials; that cannot be said of other kinds of trial.

[UN185: Reasons of a singular kind cannot decide the matter.] Publicity will have no influence on an honest, upright judge, [and] one can adduce examples of false verdicts by juries. [However,] this possibility exists as much for [judges without juries] as for juries. One can also [respond] that, because of their publicity, wrongful verdicts [by juries] are more easily known; one does not know much about the others. [UN186: For that reason, juries cannot be compared with ordinary courts.] We do have several examples of injustices from English jury trials. With such examples, [however,] one must distinguish between time periods.[609] Perhaps a hundred years ago a jury often misspoke. But one must compare this, not with [verdicts by judges] nowadays, but with [those of] ordinary courts of that time.[610] Indeed, in those days, torture was applied in the ordinary courts. The ordinary courts were satisfied with confessions extracted by torture, but with jury trials, there would have been less likelihood that a witch would be burned.

Accordingly, the main thing is that it be possible for Right and laws to be known. So, too, must the [legal] process be transparent. A central feature of [139] laws is their comprehensibility; otherwise access to these laws is difficult. Legal rules are then something alien, and burghers are serfs of the estate [of lawyers]. To be sure, burghers could stand before the court, but [if laws were incomprehensible,] they would have only

---

608 UN185: To the judicial office belongs a way of looking at things that makes objectivity, the law, its object. For that reason, we trust judges with law, not with … the verdict.
609 UN186: When adducing examples, one must not take them out of their temporal context, the customs of which differ essentially from ours.
610 UN186: … the judgments of the other courts [without juries] were at that time also often barbaric. In the Middle Ages hundreds, indeed thousands were condemned to death for witchcraft by German courts, which followed Rome's laws and Rome's procedures. It can be assumed that there would have been fewer atrocities of this kind before juries, or at least that they would not have lasted for so long.

ears to hear and understand nothing. The legal process would behave towards them as an alien fate.[611]

[C. The Police and the Corporation]

The second part [of civil society] dealt with justice, but only as something abstract.[612] Over against it stood the particularistic welfare [of individuals]. The third [part] is then the higher ground, which unites both [in the idea of the well-being of all]. This would be the stage of the Idea – the union of the particular and the universal Will. The [institution] that places both in balance and allows particularity as such its right can in general be called the Police, [which is] the state relative to civil society. Its task is to bring the welfare of the individual into harmony with justice.

[In the system of needs,] the contingency [of welfare] remains. We saw earlier[613] that one has a capital in one's labour. However, one can become incapable of work; one can have mishaps. [Moreover,] whether this [or that] branch [of industry] thrives depends on a larger context.[614] This contingency also exists in the administration of justice. [In a civil case,] it cannot fully make up for the damage that has occurred. Likewise, it is often unable to bring the criminal before a court. It is for the third part [the Police] to remove the contingencies that occur here. With regard to this [part], there are several determinations to consider. First, the cancelling of contingencies can occur in a contingent way, [UN187: namely, through the particular wills of individuals]. Secondly, [because] this manner has nothing universal or necessary about it, [UN187: the cancellation of contingency occurs by a universal method,

---

611 UN186: There must, first of all, be understandable, public, and accessible law books by which the laws can be known. Further, the legal process must be knowable; to that end a transparent administration of justice is required. And it is further to be wished that the administration of justice be apportioned between judge and jury. If laws are incomplete and the legal process secret, then burghers stand in a kind of wardship; and if the administration of justice is in the hands of a particular class, then that class executes a master's law against burghers, who are in a sense their serfs.
612 UN187: The first [part] in this sphere [of civil society] was the maintenance of particularity as such; the second was that this particularity was raised to substantiality – the freedom of the particular individual. However, this is merely abstract Right.
613 See this translation, 143.
614 UN187: The branch of industry to which [the labourer] has applied himself can, because of public circumstances, decline, with the result that a large number of individuals can fall into distress.

which at first is an external power]. Thirdly, this clearing away [of contingency] occurs in a manner truly internal [to society]. The first means is the morality of the individual; the second is the Police; and the third is the concern of the corporation for its members.

[C. 1. The Police]

[The administration of justice actualizes the rights of abstract persons, but does not concern itself with the particular individual.][615] [140] On the side of his particularity, the individual has the possibility [of partaking of the wealth of civil society], but it remains a matter of chance. This contingency can be removed by the particular will itself. That is the moral sphere. The well-being of others is the end of morality.[616] People help each other in need. There remains a lot for the individual to do [even assuming that the state carries out this function].

However, this removal of contingency [in the satisfaction of need by individual morality] is itself contingent; it is a mere ought to be. [The moral discretion] wherein this ought lies is something accidental. From the thought of what ought to be we must advance to what is necessary and real. [Morality says that] people should love one another. This is left, [however,] to their particular wills. The philosophy of merely reflexive thinking has to do only with the ought, with approximation [to a goal]. One can imagine that if we educated people, they would help each other reciprocally. But this is precisely just imagining; one says "if" such-and-such would be, but this is exactly a mere "if." People often think that it is a learned way of speaking to bring in a lot of "ifs," so [to appear to say] something subtle. It is often the people who talk the most about the spirit who are the least spiritual. If one wants to speak [loosely] about spirit, friendship, soul, then one speaks precisely without spirit.[617] The rational should not be a matter of mere disposition; rather, disposition must take concrete form, must be present objectively, must be objectively institutionalized.[618] [Talk about] a spirit without institutions, without objectivity, rings hollow [UN189: because without

---

615 UN187: Particularity is not realized through the administration of justice ... At this stage [of the Police] the individual is considered as much in his particularity as in his personhood.
616 UN188: The end of the moral individual is his own well-being and the well-being of others.
617 UN188: To let the rational depend on disposition, spirit, friendship, and the like, is precisely spiritless.
618 UN188: Spirit is just this, that the merely inward becomes objective.

true institutions and laws there is no genuine spirit]. What the individual can contingently do on his own is infinitely small compared to the effectiveness of the state. [UN188: Though the contingency of disposition may have value in isolated cases,] we must not remain with this.

The next higher [stage] is care for the general [well-being]. Everything that is by nature common or general must by nature be treated as such.[619] These things are a matter for general care. The specific nature of this stage is [that it is directed to] a goal. [The goal is] that the particular occur in a general way, [i.e.,] that the well-being of the particular individual be promoted in a general way.[620] Care unites the general and the particular [interest]: the [well-being of the] particular individual is laid down as a [general] end.

The union [of the general and the particular] is at first only an external connection [over against the system of needs]. There are, first of all, purposes [of the individual] that themselves impinge on the external world. The general interest is not yet posited within the particular will; it shines in [from above]. [141] The power that effectuates it is therefore merely an external power.

The more precise objects of care are considered in the special sciences. Among them is the concern of the Police that the criminal come before the court and also that crimes be prevented. [Also] necessary are [regulatory] arrangements whose restrictions involve otherwise lawful actions. I was [just] going about my business; in this respect, the action can be lawful. But because the action [UN189: steps out into the external world], it can harm others or wrong them. Its not harming others is also a mere possibility. It is also an object of regulatory care to remove this aspect of contingency from permitted activities. Therein also lies the reason for regulatory penalties. Owing to the possibility that actions, although [otherwise] rightful, will impinge on others, it is a matter of chance whether I harm the other or not. [Regulatory prohibitions seek to remove this contingency.][621] The aspect of injustice consisting in my failure to observe the prohibition is the basis of regulatory penal law. A limit [to risky activity] cannot be set down [a priori]; one can count up all the benefits and harms.[622] Taking account of everything can therefore

---

619 UN189: In the entanglements of civil society, there are many common needs whose satisfaction must therefore be provided for in a common or general way.
620 UN189: ... that the well-being of all individuals should come to its fulfilment.
621 UN190: The Police must therefore ensure that I take thought for the possibility of injuring others.
622 UN190: With all [activity] one can point to a harm that can result.

stretch into infinity. Here [UN190: custom], fairness, and the threat of the moment make for determinations in fleshing out [due care].

As for the rest [of Police functions], these concern the satisfaction of needs themselves. Among these needs are found common interests that, if they were to be dealt with individually, would involve a great deal of work. This work is left to a few [in government]. For example, if every individual had to take the trouble to investigate whether imported merchandise is good, or whether medicines really have the specified ingredients, etc., etc., [these tasks would consume too much time because] they require work and skill. These functions are taken over by a few. There are also many common utilities and needs that must likewise be provided for in a communal manner – for example, roads, bridges, etc. The relief [afforded individuals] on this score is immeasurable, and the mere communality of such arrangements makes it possible for a higher life and education to develop and flourish.

[UN190: Under Police is also understood the administrative authorities in general.] This order is an external one [vis-à-vis the system of needs] and if the state is understood [solely] in this sense, then it becomes a police state [*Polizeistaat*], a need-state. So [it is with] Fichte. His state looks like a giant galley. In his state, for example, everyone must [142] always carry a passport with his likeness.[623] The Police must know what every burgher is doing at every hour. [UN191: If the universal vindicates itself against individuals in so external a manner, it is easily experienced as being harsh.]

Because this order is an external one, there is much indeterminacy in [its execution]. Inasmuch as the execution [of general laws] relates to particular [situations], it is custom [UN191: and the state of culture] that [supplementally] forbid many things. The state, insofar as it must have a police [power], is imperilled by this dimension. Supervision must not go too far, and if it interferes in the family's internal affairs, then it appears to attack the inward person. The soulless fall victim to Romans.[624] With them, familial bondage held sway, and over against these [relationships] stood the censors. But it is an equally great evil to intervene thus in what is internal. Only general matters [should be] regulated such that all can benefit; and these general institutions can then be used by everyone. They belong to the large [social] capital that everyone can utilize.

---

623 Fichte, *Grundlage des Naturrechts*, 295–6; and Fichte, *Foundations*, 257 (see n. 458).
624 UN191: The soullessness of the Romans shows itself ... in the efficacy of the censors, whose activity extended deeply into internal family relations. The grim evil of family bondage was supposedly mitigated by a second evil.

Crucially, [however,] there remains this aspect – that the individual has only the possibility [not the assurance] of acquiring the means of his subsistence. [UN191: The question arises here whether the individual can rightly demand of civil society that it care for his particularity.] If the individual has an entitlement vis-à-vis civil society, then the latter has a duty to care for the particular individual. If the individual has a right, then [civil society] has a duty, so that its care does not remain discretionary. The individual has a right to the administration of justice, etc., but it [UN191: also] has this right [to care for his welfare, but] only conditionally – namely, on condition that he acquire a skill. This is his right, and it is conditional on his [having a] skill. In the family, it is not so; one does not demand skill as a condition for caring for the child. But does civil society have such duties towards the individual?

This relationship [of duty is derived, or], this question is answered, in the following way. The individual has entered into a relationship with a whole; he has been torn out of the family [economy], and civil society has taken its place.[625] The individual is a particularity. [In civil society,] individuals become alien to each other. Here, therefore, the family bond gets another form, not the one that it has in its substantiality. The family has a paternal land as the basis of its subsistence. [In civil society,] the [143] relation [between the individual and the whole] changes. Because civil society [now] constitutes [the individual's] capital, it has a duty [to ensure] the possibility of [the individual's] always having work. That [compared to the family] is the higher care of a higher Police. The whole must therefore take care that occupations are available. If there are a lot of unemployed, they have the right to demand that the possibility [of work] be restored. However, [developing] the ability to work is the condition [of having the right to civil society's care]. But civil society has an unconditional duty of concern for the individual's acquiring a skill; and if he can't [acquire one], he must be otherwise provided for. It is not this or that idiosyncratic need that must be capable of being satisfied in civil society; rather civil society is itself the totality, [UN192: the essential basis and ground on which the individual rests the side of its particularity].

Inasmuch as civil society constitutes the Substance of [UN192: the spheres of] particularity, the individual stands in a relationship to [it as] to the universal Substance. [In civil society,] the individual has the universal purpose of its substantial being and formative education.

---

625 UN191–2: In a patriarchal relationship, the family remains continuously that which encompasses all the individual members.

Therefore, civil society is, for this [particularistic] side [of the human being], its essential nature, and [so] the individual relates himself to this nature, not only ad hoc, but essentially. The particular individual stands in a relationship with a multitude of other particular individuals.[626] For example, the individual buys something; if the relationship is correct, they're square. One can picture the relationship to civil society in the same [transactional] way. The relationship to civil society is then conceived only as a relation of individual to individual. [But that is an incorrect view.] [UN192: The relationship is one between the particular individual and the universal essential nature.] Whatever particular needs I may have, I have the right to satisfy them in civil society. If I am incapable of acquiring [the conditions of satisfying them on my own], then I have the right to find these conditions in my essential nature. Therefore, the individual has a right against civil society, and the latter has a duty towards the former. Civil society has to concern itself not only with the general [Will]. If it concerned itself with the individual only in its general aspect, this would be something abstract.[627] Individuals, however, are singulars, and they must be cared for as singulars.

[144] It follows that individuals must acquire the requisite skill and, further, that institutions must exist to provide for this. However, the Police has the right [to demand] that this [duty to train oneself] be adhered to, for example, that parents [ensure] that the child obtains a skill. The child is a son of the family, but it is also a son of civil society. If the child has lost the care of parents (for example, by becoming an orphan), civil society must step into the role of parents. [The Police] also has the right to restrain those who, by their profligacy, are nearing the point where subsistence would be impossible.[628] A father of a household has the right to petition the [state] to educate his children if he cannot. But at the same time, the Police has the right to demand that the father manage his resources properly. Above all, civil society has a duty to sustain the public wealth (commerce). But it also has the right to prevent

---

626 UN192: ... but this relationship is always a merely isolated and transitory one.
627 UN192: If civil society concerned itself only with the general Will, its usefulness [to the individual] would be only a possibility [contingent on his owning property].
628 UN193: Profligates who make themselves incapable of maintaining themselves and their family must be restrained by civil society and disciplined. [Translator: This looks intrusive, but child welfare laws protect children against parental neglect, while insolvency and receivership laws allow individuals to evade the devastating consequences of their imprudence.]

CIVIL SOCIETY 173

the emergence of a rabble. That is the worm in civil society. I say this because poverty is a universal effect of civil society as such.[629] Acquiring the necessary capabilities requires a capital – health. Qua natural, the circumstances [conditioning capability] are accidental. The lack [of health] makes it impossible to acquire the necessary capabilities.

I exist in civil society as a moment. There enters here, however, a disproportion and an element of chance. It can happen that I cannot partake of the [public] wealth, that I cannot meet the conditions of [receiving] a share. Besides that, it is a product of civil society itself that in one location there are riches without measure and in another location, poverty and misery. As wealth increases on the one hand, so misery on the other. [The cause of this relation is this.] As products become more generic, they are produced with greater ease. They become more widely used. The circle of my business expands and therewith the circle of my profits. The concrete product (handiwork) has a very limited circle [of purchasers]. The more generic this [product] becomes, the more the circle [of buyers] expands, and this [mass production] is [145] aided in the end by the machine. Concrete occupations [handicrafts] are brought to ruin by factories. This is how wealth accumulates. The supplier in wartime accumulates great wealth. So too the manufacturer. The merchant's circle also becomes larger. Capital accumulates and because of that he can expand his business. If he has less capital, he does not gain as much as when he has a lot.[630] The English, who have an extensive world trade, have a large capital. There, wealth is amassed.

With this accumulation arises the other extreme – poverty and misery. The concrete workers lose their jobs, and small capitalists are ruined by big ones. In England, machines make more than one hundred thousand people redundant. The English also have external relations – trade. This is the field of possibility, of uncertainty, and hence the inevitability of [exposure to the international market].[631] So, others lose [their jobs] – for example, weavers in Germany because of [imported] English machines. In addition, the fragmentation of work [into minute tasks] makes workers more dependent [on factory and machine owners]. And they are compelled to make do with the least [required for

---

629 UN193: The emergence of a rabble is generally a consequence of civil society, and, on the whole, it arises inevitably from it.
630 UN194: The owners of greater capital can be satisfied with less profit than those whose capital is smaller [hence their business expands]. This is the main reason for the great wealth of the English.
631 UN194: As a country's industrial products extend far abroad, so does the prosperity of particular branches of industry become exposed to many contingencies.

survival], and often cannot even have that. So, the extremes [of wealth and poverty] arise. [UN194: Poverty is thus a condition of civil society, one that is unhappy and forsaken on every side.]

The poor have a claim that civil society remedy poverty. It is not just about a depression in their [material] comfort; rather, with that comes about a moral degradation. They lack the consolation of religion [because] they don't have clothes [UN194: for church or because they have to work Sundays too]. If you set up weekday religious services for them, they miss work. It is also the case that in the city, teachers of religion preach to an educated public, and [so] the poor are not taught the gospel. The university has the task of turning [UN194: clergymen][632] into scholars, but something entirely different is needed [for the poor]. [University teachers of religion] do not speak to the hearts of the poor; the inner voice does not speak to them. So too with regard to the justice [system]. Even if these institutions are very knowledgeable, [the poor] cannot have access to them and would rather let themselves be wronged. The poor are also abandoned with respect to their health. All enjoyment [of life] is denied them. Nor is it possible to [UN195: refer][633] them to the city's art treasures.[634]

[146] Not only is there an external distress [UN194: that weighs on the poor], but a quite different conflict arises: the conflict between the soul and society. The poor feel themselves scorned.[635] All around them, there is satisfaction, and they have nothing; they must go hungry. Here, the [civic] consciousness that civil society is precisely supposed to raise gets smothered. This is not a natural distress; it is not nature that is hostile to [the poor]; [poverty] is not a misfortune that nature inflicts on them. Were that the case, they could say, "It is so – it is fate." But here the enemy is a will – in general terms, a [socially] mediated reality. [The poor] feel themselves dependent, not on a sensible reality, but on a will, an arbitrary will, a [UN195: human] conventionality. And this is what puts them into this conflict [with society]. We have seen that in the ethical union of the universal and the particular, duties exist only if rights exist. Where rights have no existence, the individual's existence

---

632 Translator: taking UN's *Geistlichen* over Ringier's *Gottesgelehrten*.
633 Translator: taking UN's *verweisen* over Ringier's *verwenden*.
634 UN195: If you want to refer the poor to the enjoyment of artistic creations, they likewise lack the means for such enjoyment and would have to regard such a referral as mockery.
635 UN195: ... and excluded, and there inevitably arises an inner indignation. He is conscious of himself as an infinite and free being, and with that arises the demand that external existence correspond to that consciousness.

is [dependent on] arbitrary will; he stands right-less. Therefore, he also has no duties [to civil society]. This condition [UN195: of inner indignation] is inevitable [given poverty]; the consciousness and sentiment of duty disappears in the poor.[636] Emergent from this feeling is the [moral] decay, the shamelessness that is summed up in the name "rabble." The rabble thus arises especially in a developed civil society, for it is this that splits into extremes [of wealth and poverty].

Where individuals have not arrived at the self-consciousness of their rights, they remain in [a state of] natural poverty. At worst, they become accustomed to unemployment – to idleness. [However,] as self-esteem dies [from idleness], the [inward] consequences [of poverty] emerge. Odysseus himself says that the beggar must be insolent with envy [and that] hate then joins in as well.[637] In general, it is not just the [external] side of poverty that must be eliminated, but also the [internal] side of moral decay. In this connection, Goethe says: "Who ne'er his bread with sorrow ate … he knows you not, ye heavenly powers … You let the poor become culpable, then lead them away to their torment."[638] […][639]

[147] The means by which civil society [tries] to remedy poverty is to seek new land – to set up colonies – once again to acquire territory. The [poverty-stricken] class acquires new property and [the motherland] acquires a new market. Thus, people still migrate to New England. That [America][640] made itself independent [of England] was at first considered a loss. But it is much more an enormous benefit, [because] England has gained there a huge market. England has had tremendous sales there recently. But where is land to be found? That is an empirical question. What is certain is that it is across the sea.

---

636 UN195: Because the freedom of the individual has no existence, the recognition of universal freedom disappears.
637 Translator: The source for this reference is uncertain. Hegel may be alluding to the incident in *The Odyssey*, bk. 18, lines 16–18, where, from the kind of envy that begrudges someone a good, Irus the beggar insolently orders Odysseus off a doorstep he (Irus) is occupying. Subsequently, Irus's insolence turns to hatred as he comes to blows with Odysseus. I am indebted for this suggestion to Professor Ed Sanders of the University of London, who translates the relevant Homeric passage in *Envy and Jealousy in Classical Athens: A Socio-psychological Approach* (Oxford: Oxford University Press, 2014), 37. In bringing together in one sentence "insolence," "envy," and "hate," Hegel may be thinking of Aristotle's analysis of these concepts in *Rhetoric* 2.2.1378b; 2.4.1382a; 2.10.1387b–1388a.
638 Johann Goethe, *The Apprenticeship of Wilhelm Meister*, bk. 2, chap. 13.
639 Translator: Here Ringier breaks off, and we fill in the gap from the Henrich edition of UN's notes (pp. 196–8) in appendix 3.
640 Translator: Ringier wrote "Nordamerika."

The sea is the element of mobility and the last of society's quests. Civil society is, on the one hand, too poor, on the other, too rich.[641] Poverty means that too much is produced; [in that sense society is] too rich. The workers are too poor [to buy what] they nevertheless produce. There is too much capital – that is, [too much] productivity [relative to purchasing power].[642] That is why it is politically prudent for a nation to expand its trade. This already occurs through [establishing] colonies. In that way, the poor return to work; they must therefore seek the expansion of trade. Thus, [civil society] strives [for something] beyond itself. At the bottom of this [self-surpassing] is, on the one hand, the interest in profit. The higher interest, however, is that workers now have the means of subsistence.[643]

Barbarous [peoples] are at first in hostile relations with each other. They are [merely] for themselves.[644] However, trade is a lawful connection between peoples. [Traders] have to recognize each other as right-bearing persons, as property owners, who [can] give away something of their own only from their free will. Through this connection, human beings arrive at a universal recognition. Empirically, they emerge from their mental dullness.[645] With this outlook arises the thought that

---

641 UN199: Civil society is, on the one hand, too poor to maintain its poor. On the other hand, this has the meaning that civil society is too rich. The poverty of workers precisely entails that there is no buyer for what they produce. There is thus too much capital, and more is produced than the nation can consume.
642 Translator: Cf. T.R. Malthus, letter to David Ricardo, 7 July 1821, in J.M. Keynes, *Essays in Biography* (New York: Norton, 1963), 118–19: "We see in almost every part of the world vast powers of production which are not put into action, and I explain this phenomenon by saying that from the want of a proper distribution of the actual produce adequate motives are not furnished to continued production. I don't at all wish to deny that some persons or others are entitled to consume all that is produced; but the grand question is whether it is distributed in such a manner between the different parties concerned as to occasion the most effective demand for future produce ... If it be true that an attempt to accumulate very rapidly will occasion such a division between labour and profits as almost to destroy both the motive and the power of future accumulation and consequently the power of employing an increasing population, must it not be acknowledged that such an attempt to accumulate, or that saving too much, may be really prejudicial to a country?"
643 UN199: The higher [interest] is that trade is the path, the lawful way in which nations come into connection with each other.
644 UN199: ... and thus form a point that excludes the other from itself.
645 UN199: Nations' coming to know each other is one of the most important aspects of the development of the modern world. Through it, human beings come out of their narrow-minded ideas.

someone can be a human being without doing as we do, or without having the colour we do. That is why travel is so educational. The natural element of travel is the sea – this broad street. Rivers and oceans are the greatest binders. Mountains divide, rivers [148] unite.[646] Accordingly, it is always two shore dwellers who are most closely connected with each other. For a long time, Norway was connected, not with Sweden, but with Denmark, etc.[647]

Initially, therefore, the sea is the means of communication towards which a people should work.[648] A people that remains locked up within itself cannot attain a free culture. In ancient times, we see this in the Egyptians and in the Indians. These peoples did not want to be seafaring. [They] developed themselves to a high degree, but they were nevertheless mentally dull. Both worshipped cattle. They honoured these animals more than human beings. During famines, they fed animal life first and let people starve. The other side is that they completed immense works – artistic works – but the people employed for this purpose were used merely as hands.[649]

The sea is to trade what land is to agriculture.[650] The sea is, as it were, the poetry of trade and industry; [UN200: there arises here a bravery to which trade inherently progresses]. Sailing the sea is the result of civil society itself. From it arises the idea of the universal community of human beings as human beings.[651] The universality of thought is implicit therein. It is unbearable for humans to think there is still something [unknown] yonder. Impelled thereby, they venture outward.[652] Mastery of the sea earned [humans] the simple observation that wood has a smaller specific weight than water. The earlier Europeans came to other peoples with a low opinion [of them], the Portuguese and

---

646 UN199: For a long time, especially with the French, the superficial thought that rivers were natural boundaries prevailed.
647 UN199: Land and mountains separate much more [than seas]. Denmark and Norway were connected, Livonia [roughly Estonia and Latvia] and Sweden, England and France, Greece and Asia Minor.
648 UN200: Every people that has a attained a certain stage of development must inevitably push to the sea.
649 UN200: These peoples produced immense works of art, but not as free productions, rather as works of despotism.
650 UN200: [The sea] enlarges the breast, and in the quest for profit, he who pursues it also renounces a selfish purpose.
651 UN200: ... the particularity of nations, their customs, their culture, etc. disappear. There remains the universal thought that all foreigners are human beings.
652 UN200: The human being sets out [to sea] so as not to leave an other out there and to subjugate to itself this immense, non-individualized element of the sea.

Spanish ingenuously, the Dutch with avarice. It was through the English, [UN201: who started from the thought of the human,] that the whole world first became connected – that is, the coastal land. The interior country is the closed country, the ignorant [country], either deserts or forests. All this is a worldwide interest. [UN201: World history shows the sides of the ethical whole]; world trade shows the side of connection between [mutually external] civil societies. At the same time, in civil society, this [connecting] is an inversion into an opposite: on the one hand, greed, on the other, all the [unifying effects] ascribable to greed. It is a higher moral necessity that intends human beings to dedicate themselves to [a material security] that they [at the same time] disdain [by going to sea].[653]

[149] The supersession of civil society is implicit in the fact that its concept is a limited, finite one. It is a stage that must transition to its truth. Civil society is the stage of appearance [where the dichotomy between the universal and the particular seems fixed]. It is the coming apart of the ethical, [UN201: both of whose moments, subjective self-consciousness and the universal, attain their respective right. Their unity is a relative one, and both moments merge [[in the corporation]]].

[C. 2. The Corporation]

In civil society, everyone is an end for himself. His understanding looks around for the means [of satisfying his interests]. His particularity is his end. [However,] this raising of self to end-status[654] turns round into [service for] the general interest, [UN201: such that, in satisfying himself, each also works for the generality]. As also an end [for the Police], the general [interest] is merely the abstract or external generality. [It is] the external order of the Police. On the one hand, the general interest that is self-consciously an end and particular self-interest are here separated. [On the other hand,] these two extremes are each self-consciously nugatory [without the other].[655] Their truth is their unity. Therefore, the Concept surpasses its self-externality [in civil society].

---

653 UN201: At the same time, by exposing its profit and property to danger, civil society transcends its principle. The urge to profit turns into its opposite, bravery. If morality raises a cry that men expose themselves to the peril of the sea from love of lucre, then opposed to this is the higher moral necessity that leads human beings to disdain their subsistence.

654 Translator: *Sich-selbst-zum-Zweck-Erheben*.

655 Translator: Separated from particular self-interest, the general interest is once again particular; separated from concern for the general interest, the satisfaction of particular self-interest is insecure.

At first, the unity is one that emerges still within civil society itself. It is in the interest of the particular individual that its [welfare] interest not remain uncertain [and that it] not remain merely an interest of the particular individual. It should be something secure, something removed from uncertainty.[656] On the one hand, the securing of subsistence such that it is not abandoned to chance seems at first blush to fall to the Police. However, the Police [cares] only for the general interest. If the interest of the particular individual is to be secured, [concern for welfare] must be attentive to the individual's specific [situation].[657] An essential part of this concern is mutual trust, [because otherwise] the poor are shamed in front of those who are not poor.

Now, since a tailored type of concern is necessary, in order to effectuate it, those who are enclosed [within a particular branch of society] must take on this concern.[658] They then care for these particular interests to the fullest extent. Since, with this, the particular no longer inverts into the [abstract] general, the ethical [fusion of the general and particular that we saw in the family] returns at this point to civil society.[659] Here, accordingly, it is posited that, precisely by [individuals'] giving up their interest in selfishness, the corporation [in which the satisfaction of their particular interests is assured] can enter.

The corporation is thus the second stage of ethical life. The family is the first in the form of love. The second, however, no longer rests on [150] love alone; rather, it has the independence of the subject as its principle.[660] On the one hand, these are independent persons, and on the other, they have a common interest. This they disentangle from selfishness. They thereby have a common interest in and through which they have their existence. They are active for themselves, but without selfishness. This is thus the family that has disintegrated, [but whose] unity now returns as a self-conscious purpose, [UN203: and indeed, within civil society itself].

---

656 UN202: The interest of the particular individual should not be a selfish interest, but should rather become something secure and generally recognized as a right; it should have objective reality.
657 UN202: Concern for the particular requires [attention to] particular interests, specific information, understanding of the particular [situation].
658 UN202: Only those who live in the particular [situation] can assume the task of caring for the particular individual.
659 UN202: ... [albeit] within its particularistic purposes [and organizations]. Those who put a particular interest first no longer care for themselves as isolated individuals.
660 UN202: The corporation is also an ethical society, but one that no longer has nature as its basis, as the family does.

This unity, however, is at a higher level, the level of the known. The vast work of civil society divides into particular branches that differentiate themselves and form their [respective] purposes into a common purpose, the purpose of the corporation. These are, first of all, the security of subsistence. Each individual has to provide for this through his own activity, but [without the corporation] this activity always remains a mere possibility [of employment], not a reality. Inasmuch as the corporation takes the place of the family, and since the particular individual as such is its proximate end, [UN203: it is responsible for the care of individuals where, and to the extent that, the powers of the family are insufficient]. So, it has to concern itself with the education of [UN203: its members' children]. The cooperative society has also to care for [its members'] children who have lost their parents as well as for those [members] who, through misfortune, have fallen into poverty. It has [also] to ensure that enough is done to meet general [societal] needs. Products must be of a proper quality. This is a duty owed to the rest of civil society. The other members [of civil society] cannot inspect [production]. It is the duty of the cooperative to care for the impeccable quality of work and therefore to ensure that those who have learned the work are certified. [Furthermore, the corporation] has the authority to secure the admission of the necessary number of members. Since only a certain number can be employed, it falls to the corporation to determine the number.

Against all this, modern times have raised [the principle of] self-reliance, the self-reliance of the particular individual. Everyone wants to stand on his own feet. It is said that everyone can freely chase what he can, whatever pleases him.[661] At this viewpoint, it is forgotten that [in civil society] subsistence [or] acquisition is not something done in isolation, that it rather relates to the broader society. This is how everyone abandons himself to chance. Thus, reasonableness consists in this, that [subsistence] not [151] remain a matter of chance, that it rather, for starters, be lasting, and [secondly,] that it not be contingent but fixed, so that, if someone comes back from illness, etc., he will be helped.[662] Everyone has a claim that civil society have concern for him. If he says he wants to rely on himself, then he is, on the one hand, correct and, on

---

661 UN203: It is seen as an absolute wrong to hinder someone from seeking what he likes and from applying the powers that nature gave him as he pleases.
662 UN204: This is accomplished in a true and purposeful way in the cooperative society. In civil society, the individual should have not only the possibility [of subsistence] but also the reality.

the other hand, incorrect. [Making a living] is always dependent on external circumstances. Everything is [exposed to] chance. It is therefore baseless to want to rely only on oneself.

The other thing is the interest of ethical life [that] the individual not remain in [a state of] selfishness. He should, while [looking after himself,] also assume care for a common interest. In this ethical whole, in this sphere, he is more advanced than [he was] in mere isolation. For him, this is the substantial [ground of his reality].[663] Here, with ethical life in view, we come closer to the specific form [of ethics] that we call honour.[664] [This form] arises for the following reason. In the family, what the individual is [immediately], he is [essentially].[665] In civil society, [by contrast,] reflection into self is at the same time reflection in the other. What I am (skilful, rich, talented) I am not only for myself [in my own estimation]; rather, I have my reality essentially through the [recognition of the] other. I am dependent on the other.[666] What I am for myself I am essentially through the reflection and perception of others; this perception should be something solid and objective, [and] this is honour. Our concept of honour did not appear in the ancient world. Honour is an image [of someone]. In civil society, what someone is, is [dependent] also on the perception of the other (partly on [one's] work, partly on [others'] opinion [of one's work]).[667] [Honour] requires recognition. Honour presupposes a distinction between what one is and what one ought to be.

What emerges in civil society is the isolated business. Trades are specialized; everyone has his particular [occupation]. [Yet] it is through civil society that business first has a solid being. [UN204: All the singular enterprises in civil society first acquire their meaning as links in a chain. What someone is proficient at has its sense, not immediately or in isolation; a mediated consideration is involved therein.] Now, honour is just such a mediated image. With the ancients, [UN205: someone was honoured directly for his wealth, his deeds, his ancestors]. If someone

---

663 UN204: Emergent here is the substantial, authentic ethical life, the unification of the particular and the general purpose.
664 UN204: [The corporation's] specific form [of ethical life] manifests itself in civil society in what we call honour.
665 Translator: In the family, there is no distinction between what the individual is and what he ought to become.
666 UN204: ... not only in a natural way, but I am also dependent on the opinion of another.
667 UN204: In civil society, an individual's achieving his purpose requires being recognized, and this recognition is an essential aspect of his reality. In civil society, what someone is and what he ought to be are not determined immediately together.

distinguished himself, he was honoured. [The honour lay in the objective fact of the matter, not in the opinions of others; by contrast, in civil society, honour] is essentially in the imagination. No further attention is paid to the objective reality. What someone puts forth is essentially cognizable in the reception thereof; it is what [others] think of it. The dimension of universality is just for that reason a [general] perception.

We saw that education [to the universal] is the [152] result of society.[668] What I do is at first something idiosyncratic. I must put the stamp of universality on it, so that in what [I] do there is not only something instinctive but something formed. The universal must become a habit in the most natural way – that is what constitutes the sphere of education. Honour is a reflection of education.[669] I recognize him whom I honour, not as a particular individual, but as an [instance of] something general [e.g., a physician, an ambassador]. This is modern honour, and it is a necessary phase. It may seem dishonest or false to treat a man (e.g., obedience, service) according to his estate [rather than according to his specific character]. But it is neither insulting nor reverential; rather, it is just the recognition [of his training]. The basis for it is that I relate to the individual as to something general. The solidness of people [and] courtesy [in treating them as somebodies] have their seat here. In law, the human being is merely an abstract person, and in civil society, the human being is a concrete person, but also something general. Since the [individual] in the corporation is also something general, and since the corporation cares only for general things, the corporation is the final requirement[670] of civil society. He who belongs to such a cooperative society has his honour therein; he is a member. He now cares not only for his own but also for a common good.[671]

The agricultural estate as such forms no corporation in the strict sense. This is because [farming] must be a self-contained business.

---

668 UN205: Education in general consists in the universal's manifesting itself in the immediately particular. The human being thus exhibits a difference from the animal in every feature; in everything he does [there is] a characteristic of humanity. This universal must become a habit. The most educated man is the least complicated. The uneducated man takes indirect routes to everything and often does things completely divergent from what he meant to do.
669 UN205: ... [signifying] that I am recognized and that in the conduct of individuals towards each other, this recognition is expressed.
670 UN205: determination.
671 UN206: The fact that his particular profession has its point in the whole, and the fact that he cares not only for his own ends but also for a community constitute his honour.

However, in the agricultural estate, the family is the central moment; and each [family] relies on its private property. Farming has more independence from individuals [than manufacturing]. [UN206: Accordingly, it is primarily the various industries that form corporations.] Then, commonalities [within an industry] again constitute a community. The corporation thus contains the ethical moment [of civil society] and the moment of honour. In England, there is great wealth next to great poverty and a rabble, and this is in large part the result of the loose ties of its corporations.[672] If individuals in a state are directed to living only for themselves, being recognized doesn't much matter to them. Thus, honour does not figure so much here.[673]

In the corporation, the corruption of wealth is eliminated. In [153] this context, the rich man is no longer an isolated individual [only] for himself. In the first place, he must think that he has the cooperative to thank for his earnings; [so] he won't be so haughty about what he has. He also has duties of care for the corporation, [the performance of which brings him honour].[674] With the Athenians, the richest had the duty to fund the games, and that was an honour for them. [UN207: Here a field was allotted to them, one where they applied their wealth to a public benefit.] The family, on the one hand, and honour in the corporation [on the other], are the two moments around which civil society revolves. Where these [institutions] do not exist, there is the seed of disorganization.

The corporation marks the transition to the State.[675] In general, the truth of the limited is the concrete universal [in which the limited is

---

672 UN206: England famously suffers from a superabundance of wealth and poverty. One can assume that the main cause of this is that the corporations do not exist in an organic, well-ordered form. If everyone is active only for himself, the ethical element is lacking.

673 Translator: It is doubtful that Hegel said this. UN's version contradicts Ringier's on this point and accords better with Hegel's published remark in *Outlines*, para. 253. [UN206: A human being cannot be simply a private person. Only in having a general purpose does he present himself as something substantial and essential. If individuals are reduced to living in isolation, then they must necessarily have the ambition also to be recognized by others in their particular activity. First, they abandon themselves to pleasure; and then, secondly, they must show off to the world, and this leads to the luxury of the commercial estates, a necessary result of which is that they are not ethically employed for something general.]

674 UN207: He has at once duties within this circle [and], externally, the universal duties of legality. Here he is a somebody through the ways in which he uses his wealth for his cooperative.

675 UN207: [The corporation] is already a community, yet it still has a particularistic purpose. The truth of the particular is the concrete universal.

contained]. Many corporations bound together [UN207: externally] do not yet make a State. [In civil society,] the particular, limited interest [of the corporation] remains the essential thing [and the state is a means]. [UN207: What characterizes the State in the strict sense is the willing of the universal in the strict sense.] States have often developed from [smaller] communities. In our modern times, the only basis for bourgeois commonality has been legality and honour. However, the extension of the purpose [of the corporation] to the inherently and self-consciously universal purpose is what makes up the subject of the State. The substantial is also unified therein. [UN208: The particular purposes and interests appear against the substantiality of the State only as something subordinate. At the same time, this substantiality has its true existence in the full development of the particular individual.]

Accordingly, the State has for its purpose, content, [and] final end the substantial, spiritual unity. At the same time, it contains the full development of the form [of subjectivity]. The substantial has the family within itself. In accordance with its concept, the State arises from these two moments [of the family and civil society]. The concept of the State can be grasped only from [the inadequacy of] these moments [taken alone]. In this sense [in the order of demonstration] they come before [the State]; in existence [or in the order of nature] they come after. [The State] is prior to civil society, and the latter's development is the continuing education to its higher necessity [in the State]. Civil society must educate itself towards [the State].[676]

---

676 UN208: The State as such is always prior to civil society. The latter develops itself only within the State, and it can appear only within the entire unity [of public and private sectors] that the State is.

[Third Section]

[The State]

The State[677] has the ethical for its purpose. It is the reality of the [Ethical] Idea. [It is] the Ethical Idea that has arrived at the full development of its form. It is the Ethical as self-manifesting.[678] [By contrast,] [154] the family is the self-sensing. The Penates are lower gods. The Mind of a people is higher, that which knows itself.[679] In the *Antigone* of Sophocles, we see this opposition between [family] piety and the Idea of the [Greek] state, [UN208: between ethical life in the form of feeling and ethical life in the form of self-consciousness]. It is the ethical in both these forms that come into collision in *Antigone*. They must come together.[680] The collision is the revelation of their one-sidedness against each other. This is the tragedy of Antigone, who practises piety, and of Creon, who exercises state power.[681] Antigone invokes an eternal law whose origin is unknown. However, civic-mindedness calls for knowledge. Creon calls the [gods of the] family the lower gods. [UN208–9: With that is expressed something that remains internal, subjective.] Antigone wants to make things right for her father and brother. It is the

---

677 Translator: "State" is capitalized if it refers to the fully realized Ethical Idea. Where it refers to the patriarchal state of ancient Asia, or to the state-type (a truncated realization of the Ethical Idea) of ancient Greece, or to the feudal state, or to the state relative to civil society, or to the state in a generic sense encompassing all possible forms, it is not capitalized.
678 UN208: … as self-knowing.
679 UN208: Political virtue is not a virtue of feeling but a willing of the universal purpose insofar as it is thought and known.
680 Translator: because they require each other.
681 UN208: Because these are the most fundamental ethical powers, their movement against each other is the ultimate tragedy.

netherworldly, [an instinctive ethical obligation]. By contrast, clarity constitutes the form of the necessary Mind that exists as the state.[682]

Accordingly, the State is the ethical as something thought and known. It is foolish to say that one cannot know everything.[683] The State is precisely that which knows itself as the only true reality. Thought as [the seat of] the universal constitutes the essence of Mind. To say that the Mind [of the State] knows itself is just to say that it has its laws before it as its object, hence as something known and conceptual. In pronouncing its law, the State is a living entity, passing through circumstances where conclusive action must be taken. This is something deliberated on, something thought through.[684] Because knowledge is essential to a state, the patriarchal state is incomplete. It rules by the dictate of inherited habits [or] of oracles. The oracle, not knowledge, nor even natural impulse, has divine authority.

[In the true State,] it is not left to an individual [UN209: to inspire the people to enthusiasm]; rather, it is conscious [law-making and law-executing] actions that govern the whole. Nor can these be fossilized and inherited laws – such is the case with merely historical states (feudal states).[685] It is only with the emergence of civil [bourgeois] society from the feudal state, only with the formation of civil society, that the ancient [feudal regime] has become something merely rigid and dead.[686] The universal Mind thus becomes known and gives itself reality. This [Mind] can [155] be considered as something common [but in a special sense]; an association of individuals for the purpose of self-preservation [exists for something common, but it] is not yet a [true] State.[687] If one asks further what the highest development of spiritual individuality is, then [the answer is that] its highest right is

---

682 Creon: Did you know that an order had forbidden this? / Antigone: I knew. Could I help it? It was plain. (Sophocles, *Antigone*, line 448)
683 UN209: It is foolish to think that one can will what is just without much thinking. The State is precisely that which has the highest things not as something instinctual but as something known; only in this way is [the State] truly present.
684 UN209: That the State knows itself is shown in the fact that the State parcels out its institutions, its constitution, its laws as a determinate objective existence.
685 UN209: The reasons that count here are of a quite positive sort: this is the way it has been, and that is why it is valid now.
686 UN209 It is only with the emergence of civil society ... that the universal as such has made itself authoritative.
687 UN209: This [that the state's end is something common] holds true for what is said about the purposes of civil society as protection, mutual support, and the like. In all this, the point of view of self-interest is presupposed. The individual, the particular, is therewith always made the fundamental end.

to be in [a condition of] objective freedom, to act within a spiritual universality. This is just the State itself, the individual's inherent nature.[688] Individuals are united – why? In order that they be united.[689] This is what constitutes their ethicality.

So, the universal ethical Mind is the essence of the State. The ancients [pictured] this Mind in their gods. They viewed its essence as their essence. This Mind, because it is Spirit, is conscious of itself in [the patriotism of] individuals. They are the side of its knowledge [of itself as naturally authoritative]; their willing and mediation is that through which the [State's] Mind is realized. On their side, individuals have as their essential nature and purpose what [for the State] is a result, [namely, the State's self-realization]. The [State's Mind] is not something at rest, dead; [UN210: rather, it is perpetually created anew and posited in reality]. The State's justice is, on the one hand, an absolute justice as against [the opinion of] individuals, and, on the other hand, it is that through which individuals attain their absolute right. Nothing in heaven or on earth is higher than this [double-sided] Spirit.[690] In it, [individuals], too, have their highest right. In it, their substantial being has come to real existence.[691] For that reason, the highest duty is to become a member of a State. To be alone is to be nothing. The solitary man would be either a beast or a god, says Aristotle.[692] Accordingly, it is by no means a matter of mere preference whether to enter a State or not. A duty is what is objectively necessary for the individual, and the State is the individual's essential nature. Therefore, the individual has a duty to be in a State. The individual's particular will [ought to be imbued with] a knowledge of its true will. It [then] knows the truth [about its essential nature] and wills the truth. Only thus is it something ethical.

In what way states have arisen is a matter of external [contingent] existence; [UN210: this is of no concern to us here at all]. Whether the State emerged from a patriarchal condition, whether fear or trust drew people together – this has to do with [external] history [and is a matter of indifference].[693] What is rational [in the State] would be unknown if

---

688 UN210: The individual first has objective freedom in the State. That which the individual inherently is, he is in the State as a real, objective world present before him.
689 UN210: Thus, the union occurs not for particular purposes but for the sake of union itself.
690 UN210: ... than this justice.
691 UN210: They thrive therein to the highest mode of their existence.
692 Aristotle, *Politics* 1.2.1253a.
693 UN211: It can be that a state was founded through force and injustice; this is irrelevant for the Idea.

the Idea [of a State] contained nothing but what arose in this [particular] state. The most incomplete state contains a divine element in that one knows that one belongs to this [UN211: objective] whole. [156] It can be that people are unhappy in a state and yet the state holds together. However, this [discontent] concerns particular institutions, and, contrary to the [people's] consciousness, an inner power holds them together.

It would take us too far afield to go into the various theories [of state authority]. On the one hand, it is said that the state exists through divine authority. The authorities are appointed by God. On the other hand, it is said that the state is an institution of human choice. Both views are one-sided. The Idea of the State unites both principles. One is right to say that kings [UN211: and authorities] exist through God; for it is Spirit that is active in the [human] understanding.[694] This Spirit is something divine. Spirit makes itself objective in the form of institutions. [The claim] that individuals do this is also correct. The universal in the State is, however, divine in nature. It was because people said that we cannot grasp the Divine that the Divine was banished from the present, that it came to be viewed as a beyond.[695] [But] God is also present in a people. He is present in order to be known. The State and the authorities have authority as soon as the substantial stands over against individuals. The State and its institutions are divine, but the misunderstanding lies in saying that, because the Divine exists, its authority is like that of fate, that is, of the incomprehensible. This is how the divine authority of kings was once understood. What they command need not be rational; rather, it can be something incomprehensible that is blindly believed and obeyed. [This is] a system of passive obedience;[696] the way one thinks of God as a beyond that transcends reason is also the way one thinks [about kings] in this case. [The king] is not divine by virtue of being above reason. What lies above reason is the unreasonable.

[UN211: On the other hand, it was proposed that the State is based merely on human choice.] Thus, it was assumed that a human sociability drive [UN212: led human beings to union]. This is a trivial view. If one understands [the pull of authority] as a drive, then one understands

---

694 UN211: ... for it is the objective Spirit that constitutes the active and effective force in the State. This Spirit is the Divine. Since the State is inherently rational, it is something divine.
695 UN211: Only in modern times, when it was said that one cannot know the truth, did it come to pass that the Divine was banished from the present and that reality was conceived as an aggregate of finite entities.
696 UN211: ... about which there was at one time a lengthy dispute in England.

it in the form of an instinct. The rational content [in this idea] is that the human being, as a mindful being, knows [its essential nature] and wills the universal. Not instinct but reasonableness brought human beings together. To be sure, this [reasonableness] is immanent in them, but it must [157] not remain in the form of [instinctual] immanence. It lies in the nature of universality, which is also [immanent] in individuals, to exist in a universal way. An abstract way [of stating this truth is to say] that the State rests on the will of individuals. The kernel of truth in this is that there is in human beings something immanent [UN212: whereby the State exists]. This, however, is their own essential nature that, in human beings, is realized in an objective way. It is another thing [to say that] the State is based on the atomistic will [on choice]. Certainly, the State is not external to the individual, whose own essential nature lies therein. When fear of a hero brought human beings together into a state, it seemed that an [external] power brought them together. But nothing is demanded of the human being that does not lie within him [to fulfil]. It is therefore only the appearance of state power that impels them to obey – [really,] it is something inward.[697]

It was mainly Rousseau who put forward the view that the state's basis is the will of individuals. [Thus,] if individuals want it otherwise, they have a complete right to that. Let their will as individuals be final.[698] [Rousseau] understood the state as [grounded in] a social contract. When from their free will two [persons] desire something in common, this is the ground of contract. Rousseau had the great merit of raising the will, and then the thought, the concept of freedom, to a [fundamental] principle [UN212: of the state].[699] The will is the mental world; the production [of this world] emanates from the will. If we say that the sociability drive is the basis for the state, then this is instinct, not will. The Concept is self-active only [as Will]. The State can be something conceptual only if it itself rests on the Concept. But where Rousseau went astray is in grasping the Will not as it is independently

---

[697] UN212: But even that which has the appearance of a quite external necessity is nevertheless our own inner nature, which drives us and compels us to obey it.
[698] Jean-Jacques Rousseau, *The Social Contract*, trans. G.D.H. Cole (London: Dent, 1968), bk. 3, chap. 18, p. 84: "I am here assuming what I think I have shown; that there is in the State no fundamental law that cannot be revoked, not excluding the social compact itself; for if all the citizens assembled of one accord to break the compact, it is impossible to doubt that it would be very legitimately broken."
[699] UN212–13: The sociability instinct is no thought. In this way, Rousseau laid the groundwork for thinking about the state. Thought about the [modern] state began with him.

[of the isolated individual,] but in its atomistic singularity [*Punktualisierung*], the way it comes forward in contract. Because of that, frightful consequences arose. Universal reason particularizes itself [in individuals]. The isolated individual as such is not the rational.[700]

Because the universal in and for itself is the essence of the State, the free will of the isolated individual is not the ultimate thing. From this there arose a great confusion. The concrete Spirit is the interpenetration [158] of the universal and the singular individual. The isolated individual [outside this unity] is mere subjectivity, something empty on its own. The free will (of the isolated individual) is lawless. What determines the content [of Right] is the Idea in its development, and this is independent of the opinion [UN213: and choice] of the individual. If the individual thought something different, then the universal need not worry about the individual but should rather hold him to his duty. The Will (freedom) is certainly the principle for the State's action, but it is not the principle of the isolated will. It was then said: if someone enters a contract, the [content of the] contract is something arbitrarily chosen; it can be this or that. But the essence of the State is that before which the arbitrary will disappears. To the extent that the human being cultivates himself into someone who knows and wills what is reasonable, he is not an isolated individual.

In recent times, it was also said that that the state should be based on religion, that this is the supreme directing principle of the state. If one says that religion is the ground of the state, then the [logical] relationship of the ground is introduced.[701] To be sure, religion is necessary for a people. But if one thinks and reasons from the ground [of a thing], then one can call anything a ground. In a legal or any other kind of reflection [on a subject], one side, which is in truth an essential side, can be made into the ground; and so, one can then arbitrarily regard anything in the action or object as the essential thing and determine it as the ground. In philosophy, however, one does not seek grounds of the thing, but rather the one substantial ground. And this is not only an essential moment [there are many essential moments]. [UN213: One

---

700 UN213: It is the Concept of freedom, the reasonable, universal, that constitutes the essence of the State. The self-interested individual has its right and validity only insofar as it accords with the independently existing universal. It is thus not the will of the isolated individual that is decisive here. On the one hand, Rousseau gave the impetus to true thinking about the State, but, on the other hand, he introduced confusion [in saying] that the individual and not the universal is to be considered as the prior thing.
701 Translator: See Hegel, *Science of Logic*, 402–7 (see n. 152).

can just as well say that] the family is the ground of the state or that the interest [UN213: or right or subsistence of individuals is].⁷⁰²

Further, as an association, religion too has property, and so it enters the domain of the State. Even more [does it do so] from the side of its teaching, especially insofar as it lays down principles of action, of the will. Determinations come forward that concern the universal as such in its relation to reality. In this way, [religion's] business of teaching also falls within the domain of the State. In crossing over into [this domain], it meets the State, and if both are on the right path, [159] their principles cannot contradict each other. [But it can also happen that] religion holds fast to its principle in its one-sided form [of inward subjectivity]. If, at this one-sided standpoint, that form becomes the essential thing, then one can come to believe that subjectivity is already enough [for rectitude, that] one can be judged only according to one's own conviction [of what is right].⁷⁰³ This extends even to the point where one says that one cannot know the truth [about what is right]. Particular world views, [it is said,] are the highest things and are to be respected as absolutes [by the State]. In this collision, the Church contradicts the State. The authority of conscience opposes the authority of the State.

Who is to decide? One can say that religion is the highest because it apprehends the all-encompassing Spirit. But [if it opposes the State, then] this is not the same all-encompassing Spirit that teaches [that religion is the highest]. The State, however, is that which thinks and knows [the all-encompassing Spirit felt by religion]. [By contrast,] the truth in religion takes the form [only] of feeling. The State [has the truth] in the form of knowledge. If religion steps forward into reality [e.g., with property], it must yield [to the State's regulation]; it must [UN221: give up its form of subjectivity] and accept the State's form of universality. The State thinks, knows, decides. One can say: I have my truth, and the State has its truth, and so [says] piety. No, there is only one truth, [and]

---

702 Translator: Here the Ringier manuscript breaks off for a few pages. We fill in the gap with UN's notes from the Henrich edition (pp. 213–20) in appendix 4.
703 Translator: This is probably an allusion to Wilhelm Martin de Wette, a theologian at the University of Berlin who, after the murder of the anti-nationalist writer August Kotzebue by the student Karl Sand, wrote to Sand's mother saying that her son's inner conviction of rectitude made his action right. On the letter's becoming public, the state removed de Wette from his post in the theology faculty, a dismissal of which Hegel approved (though he contributed to a secret fund for de Wette's financial support); see Terry Pinkard, *Hegel: A Biography* (Cambridge: Cambridge University Press, 2000), 445–6, 453.

that is the State's truth, and it should not be assassinated.[704] What religion recognizes as truth cannot oppose the State's truth.

The book learning according to which light consists of seven colours – whether one believes this sooner or later – this the State can let go. It can also leave [to religion] that one should not eat pork or whether fish is not also a meat. All this it can let go. Only religion must not contradict [the State's] principles. One can also argue over whether taxes should be laid on this or on that. There will always be controversies in the State [over means].[705] These are all particular devices. [But] regarding the basis of everything – that is a different matter because [this concerns what] is inherently and demonstrably true. Here the Church affects the State, and since [the State] is the knower and thinker, it must decide. And [where universal principles are concerned] it need not go lightly when someone thinks otherwise. [UN222: Nor can one object that these principles] have [160] to do only with beliefs. Such principles are precisely the basis of actions. [Whether the State is justified in outlawing religious expression] depends on whether the State can see it [UN222: as a mere opinion] or whether this [characterization] is to be considered a subterfuge. The State has to maintain itself against the Church. Its truths are not particular truths; they are divine truths. The State has to take notice of utterances of [purported] truth [UN222: that directly concern the State because] it is concerned that its members obey [its laws] not merely in ignorance but with knowledge and conviction.[706] The State has to see to it that knowledge of truth is not corrupted. Against this, it has to affirm the Idea [of Right]. It is the knower and therefore the decider. History shows that all improvements of religion were brought about by the state, because the need for thought and knowledge arises on its side.

Christ said: My Kingdom is not of this world.[707] This is to be taken in the sense that religion is inward and therefore must let the state stand

---

704 UN222–3: This truth is that the mind is free, that life and personal freedom must not be violated. [Translator: Hegel's choice of the word "assassinated" (*gemeuchelt*) is likely an allusion to the assassination of Kotzebue by Sand.]
705 UN222: In so concrete a whole as the State is, many controversies can arise with respect to the subsumption of the particular; but it is different with universal principles on which everything is based.
706 UN222: … because it is concerned that its power not be obeyed blindly, but rather that the conviction of individuals agrees with its commands. In any case, this has an even greater significance among an educated people, since here it is impossible to get by with a mere command.
707 John 18:36.

as it is. Actually, however, the Kingdom of Christ is of this world. The principle of the Christian religion has certainly reformed the world. [The idea] that personal freedom is an enforceable right has transformed the world, [UN222: and the principles of the Christian religion have become principles of the State]. These principles are products of the State and therefore of [public] truth. They are here [have force] in the State by virtue of knowledge, and it is only through narrow-mindedness that people refuse to believe that the truth of the State and of religion are one. If one opposes the State, one also opposes religion. The world (in the common expression) comes to be regarded as merely ephemeral and the State as a usurpation [of the Church]. The habit of declaiming about the world easily creeps in. An English bishop tells a story about a child who, having learned the Bible by heart, knew so much that he spoke against the vanity of the world before he had seen it. Discourses of that kind have occurred often enough.

The State is itself the manifestation of God. Religion has the form of feeling; in the State, [the same truth content] has the form of thought. In getting to know the State, we have to fight the prejudice [UN223: that the everyday that surrounds us is what matters]. Because we know individuals and their familiar ways, we easily imagine that we have a right [to inveigh] against [the world]. But these individual characters are not what matters; [what matters] are eternal laws. What individuals do in the State occurs in accordance with institutions. Christ said: seek [first] the Kingdom of God and [161] everything else will fall to you.[708] One must hold on to this tightly. If you go around talking without the substantial, you are as sounding brass.[709] You don't have to understand "fall to you" as if you had to be inert. It is not an accident; rather it takes a firmness of spirit and thought to become master of the subjectivity of will. It has cost centuries of blood to establish this institution [of the rule of laws].[710] The substantial Kingdom of God in religious form and the same [Kingdom] in the form of thought – to this one must hold fast. [When speaking about this Kingdom,] it is not my subjective fancies that should count [UN223: even if they are supported by biblical sayings]. All [subjectivity] falls away before the Kingdom of God.[711] These are the general aspects of the State's relationship to the Church.

---

708 Matt. 6:33.
709 1 Cor. 13:1.
710 UN223: It took the blood and sweat of nations to bring the rational, the substantial, to reality.
711 Translator: Here Hegel leaves no doubt that his rational State is a divine, not simply a human, State.

Accordingly, the State must let the Church be. It also has to ensure that religion is beneficial to the State. This fulfils a duty owed its subjects. The State has oversight over religion in order that piety not become polemical, that the subjective as such not be asserted [as a principle] against the objective. The Church itself enters the sphere of the State. It has property; [UN224: its individuals can commit crimes]. It thus comes within the jurisdiction of the State. Everywhere it intervenes in the State. The Church can also harm the State – for example, if it has too much real estate, so that there can't be as many owners as there could be.[712] The State has to regulate this side [of the Church's activity]. The State also has to adopt the family's interest in [a testator's] not bestowing too much on the Church to the family's detriment. Where the Church gets involved in education, it leaves cult behind [and] enters the domain of thought [where it UN224: falls within the purview of the State]. Indeed, one often sees that there are times when nothing is learned [in religious schools]. Learning demands a thoroughgoing specific freedom to proceed from concepts; [it demands] that one not be tied to historical forms. Freedom is, on the one hand, a formal principle, but it is, on the other hand, the true content. The truth is a self-enclosed [system] of determinations [of freedom].

Thinking has come to the Church from the secular side. It is only since the Reformation and from universities that [independent thought] has gained momentum.[713] However, fastening merely on the [State's] independence of the Church is hollow talk [UN224: behind which dishonest intentions are often hidden]. These two [162] powers cannot stand unconnected to each other. In our states, the Church has greater scope [for its beliefs] than in ancient Oriental ones. Our states have the great power to let particular beliefs go entirely their own way and yet to hold them together within the whole. In our times, we see Quakers, etc. who don't want to go to war. This is actually incompatible with the [principle of the] State, and yet the State [UN225: with its great strength] can accommodate them. They can be mere *bourgeois*, not *citoyens*. So too can various sects and religions stand within [one] State. Hence Jews.[714] The State is only properly constituted as

---

712 UN224: The interest of civil society can also be affected by donations to the Church. Because of large estates in dead hands [i.e., outside the market], the interest of civil society can be jeopardized. It becomes difficult for individuals to become property owners.
713 UN224: Universities first became independent of the Church and developed into what they are in Protestant countries.
714 UN225: The state can ... encompass several sects, not only Christian sects, but also Jews.

a State when [UN225: it has so broken away from the Church that] different confessions exist within it.⁷¹⁵ One might think that the citizens of one State must also have one religion. However, because the nature of the State is to vindicate the rational, the universal as such, it [UN225: obtains its true formation only by] disassociating itself from the form of love,⁷¹⁶ belief, etc. In Oriental states, state and church are one.

The [political]⁷¹⁷ State has for its object the universal as such. It does not have the welfare of the particular individual as its object, but rather the welfare of all as all. The welfare of the particular individual is the business of the corporations. Likewise, it is not for [the State as a political entity] to uphold property as a right of the particular individual; that is the task of the courts.⁷¹⁸ Its concern is the universal as such; so [UN225: the State has to be concerned with legislation], the setting up of courts, etc. The State has [to acquire] revenue and make expenditures. It has to manage the general wealth. On all sides, the universal interest has to be furthered, specified, realized through action.

We have now to consider the Idea of the State in three stages: (1) as an organism that relates itself to itself – [UN226: this is the object of] internal public law. (2) The State is a particular State and acts externally – [UN226: this is the object of] external public law. (3) The third is then that the State is contemplated [UN226: not as an immediate reality but] as it is inherently, as a universal Idea. [This is] the State as genus, the universal Spirit. This is the absolute power over individual states. The life of the universal Spirit presents itself in world history.

A. Internal Public Law⁷¹⁹

[163] We saw that, in the State, concrete freedom, the rational Will, is present. This rational universal is the Objective that is in and for itself. Over against it is the individual, particular will. The latter belongs to

---

715 UN225: The rational State emerges only in times when a fissure has occurred in the Church.
716 UN225: feeling.
717 Translator: In *Outlines*, para. 273, Hegel distinguishes the State as a political entity from the State as a whole. The political State is the side of the State that concerns itself only with universal matters – so the legislature, executive, criminal law courts, and the prince. The State as a whole includes families, the agricultural estate, corporations, and the adjudication of property disputes between private individuals.
718 Translator: The qualification "as a right of the particular individual" suggests that courts are outside the political State only when exercising jurisdiction over civil matters.
719 *Das innere Staatsrecht*.

the universal Will. It should be educated to recognize [the universal] and should be willing to accomplish it.[720] In that way, the State has come to its highest right; it is [the individual's] substantial being. What the individual otherwise wants to be is up to him, but he has his dignity in [the State]. He can lie on whatever [bed] he wants (collect insects, etc.). He can also think that this is the best thing for him, that this is what is [most] fitting for him, that this is his [UN226: ownmost] thing.[721] Of course, this is narrow-mindedness. To recognize this is a determination of philosophical thought. One [here] ascribes freedom [only] to one's particular [self]. This is, to be sure, a freedom, but a freedom that is formal [UN226: because its content is incongruent with its concept]. In the State, freedom exists in its truth. The human being has its highest freedom in the State. The only point of variance here is whether the individual knows this. If he knows it, then he knows that [in the State] he is free; if he doesn't, he obeys as a bondsman. He can regard [the State] as an external force and be wrathful towards it. Or he can instead flee into piety, into resignation; but for that he has only himself to blame [UN227: and remains always in complete dependence].[722] We saw this stage of civil society earlier. Here particular interests had their complete development.[723]

Public law is nothing other than the State's coming to [determinate] existence. To the constitution belong, first of all, the organs of the State [UN227: that will the universal as such], but the institutions of particularity [the family and corporations] also necessarily belong to it. When one speaks of the constitution, one often means the organization of the universal for itself. But the universal for itself is not something that must remain only for itself. Personal freedom is an essential element.

---

720 UN226: The [particular will] is substantial insofar as it accords with the universal Will, insofar as it knows and wills it.

721 UN226: It is common for people to regard only their particular opinions and activities as their ownmost and best thing. Human beings have their true dignity only in their universal rational nature. It is obtuseness to think that persistence in such particular activities is something essential and substantial and that these can exist without the universal.

722 Translator: This is likely a jab at Friedrich Schleiermacher, Hegel's colleague in Berlin, for whom the essence of religiosity is a feeling of absolute dependence; see Friedrich Schleiermacher, *The Christian Faith*, ed. H.R. Mackintosh and J.S. Stewart (Edinburgh: T&T Clark, 1976), proposition 4 and the following discussion (pp. 12–18).

723 UN227: Personal peculiarities and personal interests find their full flourishing in the spheres of the family and civil society. We also saw how those spheres pass over into the universal.

These institutions [of particularity] belong to the constitutional whole. It is thought that [the constitution] need only be set up at the top [of the State],[724] but particularity is something essential and basic. The essence of patriotism is that the individual burghers let their [particularistic] ends be grounded in [164] the universal. The patriotic sentiment has the more specific character that one knows that the particular can exist only in connection with the universal. We see this expressed in English patriotism. Everyone is honoured by the whole's existence. This political sentiment is the middle term [linking the public and the private]. It has for its content just this. Everyone knows that, by aiming at the universal [Good], he also aims at his particular [good]. In this sentiment, he can swing back and forth. [His activity] can have more the form of self-seeking [or of civic virtue], but both are intertwined.

What this involves in more detail is that the objective Will gains determinate existence. This must be ordered and determined in a definite manner. The Concept [of the free Will] differentiates itself within itself. The objective [constitutional order] must likewise differentiate itself.[725] This self-differentiation [of the constitution] is then just the existential reality [*Dasein*] of the rational [differentiation of the Concept]. When one speaks of a constitution, one must not [UN228: base it on] a purpose [to which the constitution is then instrumental], for example, the freedom of the individual [or] the welfare of a people. That is the first thought that comes to mind – that a universal power must be constituted [for the sake of a prior purpose]. [UN228: Then one finds that] this [power] can be abused. [The thought then follows that] we must devise checks [UN228: to prevent this universal power from becoming arbitrary]; one looks around for guarantees [against the abuse of power]. This idea proceeds from mistrust, but in general from the form of the negative. To one thing [UN228: the general Will] is set an opposite, [UN228: the particular will], for a reason [to check arbitrary power], and indeed as something external, as a negative. One is thus in the sphere of [instrumental] reasoning; one can come up with all sorts of clever possibilities for averting the damage. It is the understanding that proceeds in this way. So, it might appear that [because] a power [e.g., of the legislature] has become too great, a power [e.g., of the executive] has been opposed to it. In [historical] existence, things may

---

724 UN227: Were that the case, the particular would stand opposed to the universal as a crude heap.
725 UN228: The organization of the State should be nothing but an image of the rational differentiation of the Concept [of the free Will].

have occurred this way, but the main thing is that the Idea of the State must alone be present, and not as an enemy against another, but as a whole to which one belongs.[726] In a living organism, the liver, lungs, and stomach each has its particular function, but they are not hostile to each other. Each exists [through] the other.

One can the raise the question: who is to make a constitution for the State? [This question] seems to be quite obvious [UN229: and extremely important]. More closely considered, however, it is nonsensical. It assumes that there was no constitution existing beforehand. [UN229: Were that so, a people would be merely an abstract multitude.] However, as soon as human beings become rational, they do not at all exist as such a multitude. Human beings are not [beings of] [165] abstract understanding but of rational mind.[727] No one has to make a constitution out of a mere mass. How a mass gets along can be left to it.

So, one presupposes a constitution. One [then] asks: who should amend the constitution? The simple answer is that, [UN229: because a constitution already exists,] it should be amended according to the constitution. Really, the constitution is not made at all. It is not to be considered as having been made.[728] So many constitutions have passed away precisely because they were mere fabrications. Because a people is something intellectual, its Mind always develops. In nature, there are only tedious repetitions, but Mind as a whole is something self-developing.[729] If you look at a constitution over a period of twenty-five, fifty, or one hundred years, you will say that it has changed. What is constant is the particular problem [UN229: that requires a remedy]. The higher [stage] always manifests itself little by little, at first more as an anomaly, then as the custom.[730] The constitution is the substantial life of a people, [UN229: and all its relationships are immersed in it]; it cannot be changed in the way one would like to think. It belongs to its time. When a [new] concept has permeated all conceptions [*Vorstellungen*], the old has become a dead skin that is sloughed off without a great struggle.

---

726 UN228: The differences and determinations that come to light are moments of one Idea that are not hostile to each other.
727 UN229: ... and their relationship to each other is not an artifice; much more are human beings always an organized body.
728 UN229: The constitution must be something that implicitly and actually exists, something that transcends the sphere of artifice.
729 UN229: ... but a people that belongs to the world Spirit develops its constitution.
730 UN229: What slips in little by little and becomes customary later is made a law, and other things decay and are superseded.

A constitution is not to be given a priori – this is a bad thought. Napoleon wanted to give Spain a new constitution a priori, but this could not be done, even if it were so much better [than the old]. For [a constitution] to take hold, more is involved.[731] That constitution was too alien. The constitution is that wherein the people knows, wills, its gradual self-realization. This is a slow process.[732] It is this superficial thought [that one can make a constitution] that has brought so much mischief in recent times. For example, many have had thoughts about the unification of Germany. However, if you ask a Württemberger [or] a Bavarian if he wants [UN230: to belong to one Germany], he will not understand the question. What is set up a priori is mere superficiality.

In the Concept [of the State], there are two sides to be distinguished [the internal and the external]. A people is a whole. Its moments must develop themselves. In the State, the particular spheres must broaden out. [That is the internal side.] The State [also] presents itself [166] externally as an individual [a One or whole]. In this individuality, the State is posited as an ideality […][733]

[A. 1. The Internal Constitution for Itself]

[…] Furthermore, if one were to say that the powers [of the state] must hold bars [against each other], then they oppose each other externally. But then the unity of the whole is missing, and this [unity] precisely constitutes the essence of the State. The Mind of a people has a reality [in its constitutional powers]. If these powers are opposed to each other without unity, then the organism of the state does not work. Yet it must work [the state must function]. This necessity entails that unity must be manufactured. Here nothing formal helps [against extra-legal measures], nor do oaths [of office]. Nothing can happen but that one power throws the others overboard. [UN234: The history of the French Revolution provides the decisive example of this.] The legislative body made itself the government, and one committee administered everything. This was Robespierre's period of terror. After that, the

---

731 UN229: For a people to bear a new constitution, the people must already stand at a level of education that is suitable to this constitution.
732 UN230: The universal's making itself valid with such great richness [of detail] is a slow process that works itself out in a way that is, as it were, unconscious to the individual.
733 Translator: Here the Ringier manuscript leaves a gap, which we fill in with UN's notes from the Henrich edition (pp. 230–3) in appendix 5.

opposite occurred. [UN234: The five Directors stepped to the head of the executive.] The result was different. [When] the legislative power opposed the government, the government cleaned out the legislature and established unity. So it goes with such inventions.[734]

Fichte, too, devised such a contrivance. He wanted to establish an ephorate [to check the executive].[735] In simple states, it can be a matter of indifference whether there is a monarch or not – for example, in the Mosaic state. However, things have gone badly for this people. Spinoza said that God gave [the Jews] their constitution as a punishment for their sins in order to correct them.[736] Fichte considers it immaterial whether the [UN234: executive] is monarchical, democratic, or aristocratic. The ephorate was supposed to countervail and supervise it. The ephorate is supposed to [be able to] suspend everything, and so the executive power is forced to crawl to the cross.[737] This is a product of a half-baked understanding. The executive power must necessarily pack up this ephorate and scatter it.

[167] The entire State must necessarily have a unity. [UN234: The division of powers must not be what it is in Turkey or what it was in the feudal constitution. The division that exists there is a merely external one.] Observe that in Turkey, etc. the sultan has pashas and the latter in turn have subordinates. [But] these pashas have judicial and military power, and in [each of these] spheres they also combine the different powers. These misunderstandings [of what the division of powers is] must be supplanted.

The next question that comes to mind is whether one should compare constitutions and say which one is better. On this [topic] there can be a long discussion about all kinds of possibilities, [their advantages] and disadvantages. The main thing is that the classification [UN235: of constitutions as monarchical, aristocratic, or democratic] makes no sense for [modern] states. It has meaning only if the Idea [of the State] has not yet been understood.[738] The difference between monarchy, aristocracy,

---

[734] UN234: Where such an artifice is devised, the end is always that one power overthrows the other.

[735] Fichte, *Grundlage*, 171ff.; and *Foundations*, 151ff. (see n. 458).

[736] Translator: Actually, Spinoza says that God gave the Hebrews a defective constitution in order to exact vengeance for their worshipping the golden calf: Benedict de Spinoza, *A Theologico-political Treatise*, trans. R.H.M. Elwes (New York: Dover, 1951), 232–3.

[737] UN234: The ephorate that [Fichte] proposes is supposed, when it notices that the executive power has overstepped its legal boundary, immediately to pronounce an interdict over the country. It takes a homespun mind to concoct something like that. There must be courts in a country, and these will not be troubled by such an interdict. [Fichte, *Grundlage*, 172ff.; and *Foundations*, 151ff.]

[738] UN235: ... only if the State has not yet been understood [as a whole in which] each moment of the Idea becomes realized. [Translator: Hegel's State unites monarchical,

and democracy is suited only to the condition where [UN235: the powers have not yet been separated]. Should the exercise of [all] power be in the hands of one, several, or all? This question made sense and could still be asked in Greece. What the difference is about has been articulated especially by Montesquieu. He said that the principle of democracy is virtue, that of monarchy, honour.[739] [UN235: The statement that the principle of democracy is virtue] is true insofar as simplicity of custom is the first thing and, as in the family, the individual lives only in the ethos of the universal and the whole. This is what virtue meant in the Roman republic. One can say that virtue is also necessary in the monarchical and aristocratic [constitutions], but it is a further question whether it is their principle. In this regard, Montesquieu wrote that the absolute principle of democracy is that the willing of the universal remain paramount.

In the monarchical regime, virtue is a mere possibility.[740] By monarchy, Montesquieu understood only feudal monarchy [UN235: and of this he said that honour was the principle]; he knew no other [kind]. In any case, vassals and serfs have no share [in rule]. It is the nobility that makes up the state.[741] Here too Montesquieu was right [in saying] that the individual [under feudal monarchy] makes something of himself. The knight is not objectively a somebody [UN236: through belonging to an objective moment of the state]; rather, he is a somebody immediately [UN236: through birth]. To become a somebody also [UN236: in his own estimation], he must achieve this on his own. If he shows himself [worthy], he makes himself respected, and this is precisely honour. We [168] have seen beautiful and great [examples of] chivalry, especially in [medieval] Spain.[742] In Germany, it was present in a barbaric, crude form.

Montesquieu regarded aristocracy as the worst [constitution], and this is also true.[743] The patricians stand very close to the rest of the

---

aristocratic, and democratic elements. The power of resolution rests with the prince; the executive power is in the hands of an unelected meritocracy; the legislative power incorporates representatives of the organized many.]

739 Montesquieu, *Spirit of the Laws*, bk. 3, chaps. 3, 6.
740 UN235: In states where civil society has developed and where individuality as such blossoms on all sides – in this condition of higher vigour, virtue is, so to speak, [only] a possibility. Someone can be virtuous or not – this is more a matter of individual idiosyncrasy. With the ancients, we see great and splendid individuals coming forward only when the state breaks up. In [the modern] state, individuality comes to its full right [within the state.]
741 UN235: ... that sustains the monarchy.
742 UN236: Chivalry appeared in its most beautiful bloom in medieval Spain.
743 Montesquieu, *Spirit of the Laws*, bk. 8, chap. 5.

burghers in education and wealth. It is only the advantage of birth that gives them the government. Because their number is always large, [aristocracies can monopolize the government]. A monarch is motivated to allow others to administer his authority. Because in the aristocratic state, the patriciate can administer everything, hold all the offices, it engenders mistrust and hatred of all kinds.

Nothing is so silly as comparing different peoples [UN236: with regard to their constitutions], especially ancient and modern. Such a reasoning is the most superficial possible. Self-consciousness varies greatly among different peoples.[744] Greece lacked many concepts that we have – that the human being has worth just because he is a human being, etc.

With constitutions, much depends on whether a people is self-complete, independent, not only sovereign externally, but able to preserve this sovereignty. There can be various types of combination by which a state [UN236: that lacks the power to preserve its independence] can nevertheless endure. In such states, the constitution can be very imperfect. In such weak states, which, so to speak, eat political mercy bread [UN236: defective constitutions can survive]. We have, [for example,] particular constitutions in the states of Hamburg, Frankfurt, Switzerland. The preservation of these states' constitutions is not their doing; it is because of their surroundings that they remain independent.[745]

As for the details of [the rational] constitution, we see that the viewpoint of reflexive thinking, which sets two powers against each other, is inappropriate. We must raise ourselves to the standpoint of the Idea [UN237: and contemplate the rational as it is in and for itself] and not be hobbled by preconceived opinions. The moments of Reason must separate, [UN237: develop themselves independently,] and [then] be collected into a real unity. We have seen the separation [of moments] in a rational State in the family, civil society, and the State. The State is the universal, the ideal whole.[746]

[The first moment of the State is] the constituting of the universal as a universal, [and this] is the legislative power. The [second moment is] the [169] particular, [which] is nothing but the universal applied to the

---

744 UN236: Each people is an individuality; modern peoples are separated from ancient peoples by a tremendous gulf of time and education.
745 UN237: Such a state can remain at the stage of civil society. Whether the state really holds itself together by means of such constitutions one cannot say; it preserves itself only by means of other states.
746 UN237: The State has the universal for its purpose and is the ideality of its diverse spheres. In this universal, no determinations can exist other than its own.

particular.[747] The second [power corresponding to this moment] is the executive. The third [moment] is the singular as such, the subjectivity [of decision]; this is the princely [power] – the conclusion [of applying the universal to the particular]. The further thing is that each of these moments contains the other within itself; [each] in its determinateness is an image of the totality. In the legislative power, the executive is also active, as is the princely power.[748] [UN237: The same is true of the princely power and the executive.][749] These are the three powers that make up the State. This representation [of the Idea] is what we call *constitutional monarchy*.[750] Neither in the patriarchal state, nor in the Asiatic, nor in that of Dionysius of Syracuse, nor in the medieval feudal monarchy did the [constitutional] condition prevail that has developed only out of the contemporary situation: constitutional monarchy.[751] This is what Reason demands. One can prattle about a republic [or] about the feudal state as much as one likes, but it is not [the State conformable to] the rational Idea. It is constitutional monarchy that epitomizes modern times.[752] In no other constitution does freedom come into its right. This is the true organization of ethical life. Wishing back the feudal state is like wishing old age for a child.

A. THE PRINCELY POWER[753]

This is the first [power] that we consider because the Concept in its unity has its seat in subjectivity.[754] The first moment in this determination [of

---

747 UN237: The second is the entry of the particular so as to make it identical with the universal.
748 Translator: The executive presents bills to the legislative assembly for approval, and the prince gives royal assent.
749 Translator: The princely power of concluding decision presupposes the work of the legislature and the executive; the executive presupposes the universal it applies, and it requires the prince to will its judgments into force.
750 UN238: When we discuss monarchy, one must note well the kind of monarchy the discussion is about. One should not think here of ancient monarchy, to which aristocracy and democracy stand opposed.
751 UN238: Neither in the patriarchal nor in the Asiatic monarchy did a division of powers exist. Just as little is it found in feudal monarchy, which presents a condition that some foolish people wish back, while the struggle of the whole of modernity consists in purifying political life from feudal relationships.
752 UN238: Constitutional monarchy is the brainchild and work of the modern world. Here the substantial Idea has found its eternal form.
753 Translator: I translate *fürstliche Gewalt* as "princely" rather than "monarchical power" because Hegel's head of state does not monopolize domestic rule. Hegel, however, seems to treat "prince" and "monarch" as interchangeable terms.
754 UN238: The princely power is considered first because the existence of the Concept as subjectivity has its seat therein.

the princely power] is the sovereignty of the State. This [sovereignty] is, on the one hand, outward, on the other, inward. We have heard so much spoken about the people, about national character.[755] As soon as one speaks about the constitution, one no longer has this [indeterminate] aggregate in mind. In speaking about the constitution, one has to do with determination. A common view is that [the people] is separate from the princely power. A people without a [princely power] would remain a mere mass. When one hears the people spoken of in this way, one can already know in advance that one will get to hear a lot of raw drivel. The word *people* can [170] no longer be used [in the sense of a mass]; this concept now has determinateness.[756] Internal sovereignty is what we have [already] seen: the moment of substantial ideality, where the differentiated powers and spheres of private, [UN239: political and ethical] life are not independent, self-interested [agencies] but are rather grounded in the universal – have their root there. They are fluid members of a whole, and by virtue of that [alone] do they have their right, their rationality.

A further aspect of this [internal] sovereignty is that the various affairs of the State, the powers of the State, are not some kind of private property. If they were, they would be [the subject of] an individual right [UN239: in the manner of a private right]. They belong to the whole. [The powers] are assigned to individuals, [but] they are effective and valid [when exercised], not self-interestedly, but for the whole.[757] This is the attribute of modern states; this is the attribute that was missing from the feudal state. One can say that in [feudal] states where there is no constitution, the monarch is not sovereign – not even the state is [sovereign]. What needs to be done is carried out as an [exercise of] private ownership and not according to the concept of the State. Accordingly, the further aspect [of internal sovereignty] is that the powers [of the State] are not private property.[758]

---

755 UN238: "People" means the universal, still without more detailed determination, what the imagination envisions.
756 UN239: Rational cognition is just this, to understand in its determinateness what in the imagination is indeterminate.
757 UN239: The powers are merely allocated to individuals, and the individual has worth and dignity only insofar as he executes his office and his task properly.
758 Translator: The first-mentioned aspect of internal state sovereignty is that the State, not the indeterminate people, is sovereign; the second aspect is that the State's powers are not private property.

THE STATE   205

The second moment [of the concept of princely power][759] is that sovereignty is real as ideal subjectivity.[760] Subjectivity exists only for [UN239: as] a self. Subjectivity as such is precisely the "I." The "I" is the pure ideality wherein all difference is sublated. This ideality in its realization is subjectivity, which is a formal moment. To the truth of the Idea belongs not only subjectivity but also objectivity. In coming into existence, this second moment is necessarily individuality, and indeed existing individuality [e.g., George, Elizabeth]. The sovereignty of the State has its existence in this form of subjectivity, in a subject [UN240: in an individual] – a monarch. Constitutional monarchy is that [constitution] in which the different moments of the Concept separate. The organic [nature of the constitution] consists essentially in the unity of these [differentiated moments]. Subjectivity is the *This* as I, and that is the monarch. This, then, is a speculative thought. The certainty of this subjectivity [that I, George, am the Concept's "I"] is what forms the pinnacle that is necessarily the monarch.[761]

[171] Because the State is a Spirit – One – all particularities, evanescent [UN240: in themselves, are contained within it]. The correlate in nature is light, in which no turbidity is yet present. Likewise, all state powers are contained in [the State] as their source. They are fluid members, not [independently] subsistent, not rigid. The individuals through whom these powers are actuated have worth here, and exist through, [the office] that clothes them. Through the Idea, the offices are fixed, and the individual counts only by belonging to one of them. This ideality – in virtue of which the powers are related to a unity, [in virtue of which these powers] are not self-standing but are rather dependent, fluid members – constitutes the [internal] sovereignty of the State. With the feudal monarchy, sovereignty was not in the State because the [state] powers were all [private] property.

The third [moment of the princely power] is that this sovereignty exists only as a [personal] sovereign, freedom only as the freedom [of a subject], Will only as a person.[762] This ideality is just the for-itself of the

---

759 Translator: The first moment is the sovereignty of the State.
760 Translator: "as ideal subjectivity," i.e., as the subjectivity of decision belonging to the Idea of the State.
761 UN240: Constitutional monarchy contains the different moments of the Concept freely laid out. Its life consists essentially in the identity of these differences. The abstract, simple certainty [that I am the Concept's "I"], which is as yet without truth, appears as this ultimate pinnacle that is the monarch.
762 Translator: The second moment was that the State exists through subjectivity as an idea. The third moment is that this idea of subjectivity exists as a physical person.

ego. Heaviness exists not as heaviness, but only as a body. As weight exists directly as a body, so sovereignty exists directly as a subject. Therein lies the third [moment, namely] that sovereignty presents itself only as a This, exclusively as this [person]. That is therefore the true existence of subjectivity in the State. This constitutes the third determination in the concept of the sovereignty of the prince. That [and not the absorption of the State in the I] is sovereignty as the monarch.

There is talk about the sovereignty of the people. However, this talk is about another sense [of the people].[763] They say that the people as a people is the sovereign, but what they call the people is something indeterminate, [a mass]. This picture [of the people as an unstructured mass] has disappeared. [Even] when we speak of the animal organism, we necessarily come upon something structured; it has a head, an abdomen, a breast. In mucus animals, one can say there is also a sensibility, etc.[764] But it exists [explicitly] not in them but only in the muscle fibres of developed animals. Similarly, when one speaks of the people, the moment of mass ceases [to be relevant]. In the rational organism, specialization comes in. [In the rational organism of the State, there must be a special role for the special itself.] When I say "I," the I is the [UN241: special] itself.[765] This is therefore the moment of pure [172] subjectivity, which falls to the monarch. Qua formal, his self-certainty [of being only the State's moment of subjectivity] is the summit of decision-making. All unlocking of the not yet present begins with him. One can weigh reasons [for action] over and over; this does not yet begin [anything]. This plurality must be annulled, [UN241: vacillation terminated,] resolved, concluded. The monarch's signature signifies nothing further than that [the bill, the executive judgment] comes into existence: I will.

---

763 UN241: This [idea of the people] is valid only for the totality of peoples against each other. Thus, the French and English are sovereign against each other. By popular sovereignty, however, is also understood that the people as an aggregate are sovereign. But the picture of the people as an aggregate is here no longer the subject of discussion; rather [the people with] a definite structure and organization is. The mass, the aggregate, ends here, and the different moments of the Concept come to their distinctive existence.

764 UN241: Thus, we have in the animal world the different spheres of irritability and sensibility and reproduction, each having its own independent existence. All the more must that specialization enter when considering subjectivity, since this is the special itself. [Translator: See G.W.F. Hegel, *Encyclopaedia of the Philosophical Sciences, Philosophy of Nature*, para. 353.]

765 Translator: Ringier wrote *das Suchende* ("the seeker"), not *das Sondernde* ("the special"), but *das Suchende* does not make sense in context. UN wrote *das Sondernde*.

That the monarch is only one [UN241: μονος] likewise follows from this. [As subjectivity,] it is that which excludes [all others].

The concept of the monarch is a difficult one. Because the moment [of subjectivity] exists quite simply as a singularity, it is separate, [UN242: absolutely for itself]. Where this moment has not yet developed within the whole, it is still present as the particular [decision], but one that exists outside [the whole]. One is reminded of the states of antiquity. They might be democracies [or whatever], but the moment [of subjectivity] had not yet penetrated them. We see that in ancient states, this final will was not a distinctive moment of the state. Therefore, it lay outside [the state]. From this [circumstance] flowed the need for oracles. They had recourse to watching animals eating flies. A military commander who wanted to make a march slaughtered [an animal] beforehand. He had arranged everything else properly, but he would not presume to make the decision. This final "I will" was still lacking and was fetched from somewhere else, from an utterly low place. It did not fall within the sphere of the human because it is the self-specifying [*sich Sondernde*], and this had not yet found its place there. In modern times, when the human Mind has grasped its infinitude, [when it has understood] that the final decision also belongs to it, this ultimate pinnacle [of decision] must be placed inside the sphere of freedom.[766]

[Again,] the third moment is that the self of the whole State is one, one and final, immediate singularity. The infinite mediation that abstracts from everything cancels itself in this mediation.[767] [Nature is]

---

[766] UN242: The states of antiquity can be remembered here. In these states, namely in the Greek [states], whatever its constitution was, the moment of subjectivity did not yet have a free existence for itself. That moment thus fell outside these states, outside the sphere of human freedom. In the freest democracy, Athens, as in other states, the final decisive will appeared outside the state. For such final decisions, both private persons and the state had recourse to the oracle and the flight of birds. The military commander, after he had chosen his terrain according to his best judgment and had arranged everything, questioned the oracle, the entrails of animals, in order to receive the final decision. Before the battle of Plataea, Pausanius toiled for half a day investigating the entrails of animals. Likewise, the oracle was consulted when a colony was to be created. The decision was always fetched from outside. In ancient times, human self-consciousness had not yet comprehended its depth; it did not yet exist as self-certainty and as conscience.

[767] Translator: The infinite mediation is the unity-in-difference of the universal and the particular where the universal is confirmed in the particular and the particular is confirmed through the universal. This unity-in-difference abstracts from everything immediately given or natural. It is therefore *itself* cancelled as one-sidedly conceptual (but preserved as one moment of a whole) as it comes to existence in the natural individual through whom the unity-in-difference makes a decision.

the immediacy that simply relates to itself. Nature is. Being comes to it [from Spirit]. [In nature,] there is not yet mediation. Spirit comes to this immediacy in order to return to itself. The monarch is immediate individuality and therefore natural individuality. He is what he is by [173] birth. This Concept is entirely speculative. [In the prince,] the ideality of the whole exists as the opposite of itself, namely, as natural. This is the transition from Concept to existence – the same [transition] that occurred when we said that freedom must have existence [as] personal property. It occurs again in the so-called ontological proof of the existence of God, where one proceeds [to existence] from the Concept of God. That He is this abstract [immediacy] – this is the difficulty. Because of it, people in modern times, when the concept of philosophy went into decline, could not grasp this transition; here [is the wall where] the oxen stand on the mountain.[768] However, all comprehension of the infinite is based on this [transition]. So, the Concept exists in the monarch as self-conscious willing, insight, *immediate* certainty [of purity] – immediate certainty just because [the Concept] is determined [to self-conscious willing] through nature.

Because the concept of monarchy is so speculative, it constitutes something mystical that the [ordinary] understanding cannot grasp – majesty.[769] [Majesty belongs to] the decisive, ungrounded, abstract "I will" [that is uniquely at the same time a universal Will]. [It belongs to] a person who [as the Concept's person] is the most inward and for that reason the most external, [raised to his position] through nature, by birth. The understanding cannot grasp the majesty of the monarch. Therefore, one can say with justification that the understanding should not [try to] understand it. Only philosophy has the right to approach it. All other reasoning comes to nothing here, because it does not grasp the Concept, because it is not speculative. By comprehending monarchy speculatively, one stands in a free relationship to the monarch as to one essential moment of the [constitutional] whole. All other [justifications of monarchy stand] in an unfree [relation to it]. It can be a relationship of love, of trust, such that you honour, love, obey, fear [the monarch] –

---

768 Translator: This refers to a child's game similar to Mother, May I? The image is that of being frozen in one's tracks.
769 Translator: As the context makes clear, the concept of the monarch is "mystical" only to the ordinary understanding, for which the thought-mediated and the immediate are opposed and for which their unity is thus a logical contradiction. From the philosophical standpoint, there is nothing mystical here. The ideal unity-in-difference already implicitly contains determination and so is self-contradictory without concrete determination through a natural subject.

in the form of feeling. If the [ordinary] understanding then rationalizes [this feeling], it ruptures the relationship. [The subject's relation to the monarch] springs from love and trust, in which the rational Concept is really implicit, though only in the form of feeling, as when the person has faith in God. With the mere understanding comes a separation wall.

To be sure, one can engage here in [instrumental] reasoning, such as how essential it is to the welfare of a people that it have a monarch. With that [kind of reasoning], any *medius terminus* can be adopted as the ultimate one: [174] the people's welfare, peace, the freedom of the individual. Then, from these ends, you can reason further to reach this or that result, to understand this or that, because the viewpoints from which one proceeds are themselves very indeterminate. You can run such arguments, which are mere arguments of the understanding, beside which still others always stand open. The main thing, however, is that the understanding decides against monarchy, [for] the next [argument] it comes to is this: The monarch is an individual just like me, has no merit over anyone, is perhaps worse, or at least others have far more suitable qualities, and yet he is supposed to have this extraordinary privilege [UN244: in power and authority as well as in external honour and glory] merely through birth, a mere accident of nature, something intolerable to humans as spiritual beings and against which they fight, in order that the will might be what it ought to be – not appetitive, but thoughtful. And yet the monarch is supposed to have this character. Accordingly, the fortune of the entire people [hangs on a] contingency; it is irrational that the highest in the State not be the best, and so on to further possibilities.

That is the reasoning of the understanding – that the monarch is an individual person like others and nevertheless has this privilege that only intellect and character should give him. With that, the understanding believes itself to be justified in regarding the monarch as a victory for fortune and power. [The monarch] appears to it merely as a natural person, and indeed, as a negative thing when considered against what ought to be – namely, that the wisest and best rule. It must be conceded that the monarch is a natural [individual] and that the rational must rule. And so it seems contradictory [to what ought to be] that an individual is assigned to [the highest office] merely by accident. In that way, the understanding persists in this negative relation [to the monarchy], which negativity that can at the same time be tied to ill will and envy, and then it knows a host of other reinforcing reasons.

The solution lies in what has been said. The rational *should* rule. But the whole constitution is itself the realization of the rational; therefore, it is necessary that in this [UN245: rationality] there be one moment –

this ideality,⁷⁷⁰ subjectivity, This, and therewith the moment [175] of naturalness. Even this the rational must have within itself. As the powerful, the Concept, when it grasps, grasps even the opposite of itself; only thus is it concrete. If it did not encompass its other and know [the other] as its own, it would be merely the *abstract* understanding, sagacity etc. set against the natural and would remain with this opposition. The Concept knows [the natural], not as the negative of the conceptual, but as a moment thereof. So, when people argue about [monarchy], the concept of the speculative is usually missing. Only speculative philosophy has the right to apprehend what for the understanding is an enigma, the mystical,⁷⁷¹ in the concept of the monarch.

When it is said that the wisest should rule, and when it seems that the most natural thing is to choose a prince whom one trusts [for his wisdom], then one discusses the subject like a Stoic and an Epicurean. When they had to say what the reasonable [and] just [are], they remained with the merely formal and said only that [the reasonable and just are] what the sage does. People speak about wisdom and reasonableness in the same way here, as if they had their seat in a [person]. But there is nothing more boring than [hearing] what the Stoics tell about their sages and nothing more boring than [hearing about] the wise King Solomon, beside whom all others are unwise. The main thing is that reasonableness rule in the institution, not in a sage; this is the universal, objective reasonableness.⁷⁷²

Regarding the monarch, what is assigned to him is the subjective, the final decision, [UN245: the groundless I will,] and this, to begin with [and] on its own, is the formal moment, still without objectivity, without wisdom and reasonableness. What alone matters here is that he has this name and that he signs it, as the moment of final decision that ancient peoples fetched from the oracles. Completely superficial, therefore, are the [UN246: declamations]⁷⁷³ that the welfare of the entire people depends on the prince; superficial, [too,] are the great plans for the education of princes [as if they had to be wise]. If the constitution and laws of the people are rational, [the people's welfare] will take care of itself. What the monarch contributes substantively is not much. Besides, a prince is a child of his time, his people's representative. He therefore

---

770 UN245: identity.
771 UN245: the speculative.
772 UN245: Reasonableness, however, should exist as a developed system of institutions and not only in a subject. In the State, Reason is present in reality in an objective way.
773 Translator: Ringier wrote "declarations."

lives in [his time], its Mind, its images and concepts. If [176] various ideas circulate among a people, it seems very plausible that this or that [prince] will improve [on his own]. The government must be the last to adopt and implement these ideas of improvement.[774]

[UN246: That hereditary right determines who the prince is] is what is called legitimacy. This is a method [of succession] belonging to positive Right. [That the prince comes to the throne in this manner] is one of the most important determinations of the State's constitution. In Oriental kingdoms, [hereditary right] is not about [legitimacy]. A rational constitution can exist only if the legitimacy [of succession] is rightly determined [UN246: through nature]. Only then is the highest pinnacle [of the State] removed from the accidents of particularism. In Oriental[775] states, the prince stands over against the masses. There, everyone can imagine himself as something special, [UN247: and it is chance that rules].

It is natural to think that election is the required method [of choosing the head of state], because the entire people has an interest in whom to entrust the management of their welfare. It is for the entirety to determine in its own interest who will look after these affairs. In that case, it appears as though the ruler is the one to whom the people hand the assignment; the prince has the relation [to the people] of an authorized agent, a civil servant. If one asks about the history of advisory councils [or electoral colleges], one sees that this [institution] can readily occur, but with primitive peoples – so the German Empire, so Poland. Both have come to their end. However, longevity is not decisive [UN247: for the goodness of a constitution]. Germany, however, was never a state, never an empire; [it was always] something indefinite. As soon as [UN247: the old rudeness of custom and barbarism ended and] the self-consciousness of human freedom entered, it became clear that no constitution can be worse [UN247: than that of the German Empire. Poland offers the same spectacle]. Elective kingdoms are fated to have electoral capitulations whereby [the king-elect] submits [to conditions of assuming office]. [There is] also discretion.[776] To the extent that election takes place, particularistic opinion and outlook are made into a

---

774 UN246: The government must always be the last to adopt such ideas of improvement. For if a thought is really and objectively well founded, it must in addition have penetrated the individuals of a people beforehand and the other arrangements connected with it must have been put in place. This, however, does not happen right away. The government must let things [percolate] completely freely, so that, without doing violence to other branches connected to it, [an idea] can be changed.
775 UN246: despotic.
776 Translator: This perhaps refers to the fact that electors of the Holy Roman Empire had a discretion to vote for someone outside the dynasty of the previous emperor.

principle. Then particularism is let loose. In the electoral capitulations [of the Holy Roman Empire], the prince-electors and archbishops made more and more [privileges] into conditions until at the end, little was left [UN247: of state power and wealth]. It is then the particular will that is determinative.

It has been rightly argued that hereditary succession would control factionalism and breakdowns of the state. [Such factionalism] is almost inevitable [UN247: around settlements of the throne]. If a nation has a large [population], the voters are very numerous. In France, there were at one time five million voters. The consequence is that my voice [177] is insignificant relative to the five million. Many had the same feeling. [UN248: The thought that the individual's voice diminishes to utter insignificance brings with it the circumstance that few appear in the assemblies.] Those who do appear in the assembly are mostly the ones who [share] particular interests. They are parties – [collective] opinions [ranged] against each other. The opinions of others are for me something contingent. In their opinion lies their arbitrary will. This has the implication that they use power [to install their favourite]. Power is likewise something arbitrary. A ready-to-hand [recourse] against this arbitrariness is to compete with physical powers. Since the particularities are opposed to each other, [UN248: the inner arbitrariness appears directly as the arbitrariness of physical power.] These [two things, power and physical power,] lie right next to each other. Inevitably, it comes down to violence. Then something else happens. The emergent parties, since they differ with respect to [who should occupy] the highest pinnacle of state power, [implicitly] constitute different states relative to each other. They begin to form opposing states. There are then civil wars. It thus also comes to pass that foreigners must help [this or that side], for they are already two opposing states.[777] This was always the result of the right of electing [kings]. That is what happened in Germany. By a kick, the hollow shell fell completely apart.[778]

Where accession to the throne is given up to nature, it is taken away from ambition; and so enters the moment that is necessary [in the State]: the groundlessness of the decisional "I will." It is a contradiction if the power

---

777 UN248: This leads to wars that involve the deepest [issues]. Hence, the parties seek foreign assistance and draw [foreign powers] into their affairs.
778 UN248: In Germany, to be sure, it did not happen that the state came into foreign hands in this way. Through divine Providence, the whole dragged itself along until, by a kick to the rubbish heap, so to speak, the last hollow shell was cast aside without honour and without glory.

[of ultimate decision] is assigned through election.⁷⁷⁹ Saying that the prince is the highest official in the State is like saying "this rose is red." With that [predicate, the subject] is not exhausted. The prince is the [locus of] ultimate decision; therefore, he is not a transferee but rather an ungrounded.

It has been said: the princely power is divine authority; [UN249: so princes write] "by the grace of God." It is [indeed] the removal [of authority] from the arbitrary will [of men], and this can be called something divine. Only one must not think that by this is meant, [UN248: as it was by one party in England,] the complete arbitrariness of will with respect to the content [of the decision]. In general, the rational constitution is present in a state only if this [subjective] moment of the Idea is fixed. The other moments [the determination of Right in particular laws, the application of laws to particular cases] then likewise have their legitimacy.⁷⁸⁰ In the organic, one intestine is sustained by the other that [in turn] sustains it. In [178] an ancient feudal monarchy – in Turkey – there was a splitting [rather than an inner differentiation of powers]. By preserving himself, the pasha did not preserve the other [parts]; rather, he preserved only himself. But here [in a rational constitution], each is necessary to the preservation of the other. The rightful course in each sphere is limited by the powers' conducting themselves in accordance with their concept. The intuition is just this: each power can be satisfied in its own sphere only if the others are satisfied [in theirs].⁷⁸¹ What is stable is not the mass-like,⁷⁸² but rather that which

---

779 UN248: With hereditary monarchy, the prince first appears with the [specific] quality that [rightly] belongs to him – final, immediate subjectivity. It is therefore immediately a contradiction if this power to decide were something transferred by others. Frederick the Great called himself the first servant of the state, and this, to be sure, does him personal credit; but with that he did not express his [distinctive constitutional] quality. In the sovereignty, in the majesty, of the prince lies precisely the ultimate, groundless decision, and this is not something transferred, not something received from another.
780 UN249: Only if the moment of the princely power comes to its full right can the other state powers also preserve their rights in accordance with their concepts. Herein lies, on the one hand, the security of civil society and, on the other hand, the security of the throne and dynasty.
781 Translator: Only if the prince stays within the formality of decision are legislative and executive judgments protected against his particular will; only if the executive stays within law-application (does not legislate and does not will its own judgments into force) does legislation get approved by society's representatives as an expression of the universal Will and does the executive decision get purified through the prince as Law's decision; only if the legislature keeps to general legislation is the executive function carried out in accordance with laws applying equally to all and does the legislature's decision become purified through the prince as Law's decision.
782 Translator: "not the mass-like," i.e., not the mutual externality of the powers, as in a checks-and-balances constitution.

has the countervailing force within itself, as with a bridge or arch. This is one of the greatest [constitutional] advances: the fixedness of the succession so that the kingdom cannot be divided among the sons.

One often hears it said that the throne would be secure if the ruler knew how to win the love of the people. That [statement] is something indefinite and not even true. One has only to think of Louis XVI, [UN249: a thoroughly benevolent man brought by his subjects to the scaffold]. The Good is effective by its objective nature [whereas UN250: the saying reduces the Good to the subjective]. In despotisms, mind you, [the security of the ruler] does depend on love. So, too, in a democracy, whether or not injustices are perpetrated by the people against great individuals depends on [UN250: the subjectivity of the people]. In the rational constitution, the Good [is a quality of] the constitution, and subjectivity is [UN250: more or less] a matter of indifference.[783] In the rational constitution, it is not in the subjective as such that the Good has its seat [but in institutions]. This is not to say that it is a matter of indifference whether the subjects are good or bad.[784] The Good is in the institution[s], where it has its ultimate seat. [But] through the reasonableness of institutions, individuals will also become reasonable.[785] It is a peculiarity of virtue that it depends on free will. It is thus something higher than [UN250: virtue in the sense that Montesquieu raised to the principle of democracy[786]] in that it is not merely an immediate habit. It is virtue, after all, and [the virtue of] law-abidingness is a product of the free will, of reflection. The security of the throne rests on the reasonableness of the constitution. Because it is reasonable, it is venerated by persons.[787] The people feel its appropriateness instinctively. It is wrongheaded to say that people honour the prince out of fear and a servile sensibility; of such a thing fear and a servile sensibility would be incapable.

More detailed elaborations are really unsuited to sovereignty, [for] the monarch is the point of ultimate decision [hence of ultimate determinateness]. Everything that happens in a State happens [UN250:

---

783 UN250: Bad institutions, that is, their inadequacy to the Mind that had [historically] emerged, cost Louis XVI his life.
784 UN250: This does not mean that the constitution must be such that the state can exist even if all subjects are good-for-nothings.
785 Translator: So reasonable institutions, more than the character of the prince, inspire civic virtue and promote stability.
786 Translator: Ringier wrote "monarchy," but for Montesquieu, the principle of monarchy is honour, not virtue.
787 UN250: So, fear and love are not what the security of states essentially rests on.

in the name and] by virtue [179] of the monarch. Through a name, I differ from others and can say, "I am this." So, the name is [at the same time] a universal. The name is the imagination's sign [UN251: by which the individual is incorporated as an individual]. The monarch's name signifies this [particular] subjectivity. Judges speak in the name of the monarch even though he has nothing to do with them.[788] Furthermore, the monarch has to fill all posts – that is, the higher posts. The fact that an individual is tied to a public office is something contingent; [UN251: he has no right to it]. The connection [to the office] is the crucial thing. The objective condition [for holding office] is merit. There are many meritorious [individuals]; a large number of individuals can become qualified for most public posts. But the State does not wait for this or that individual. The fact that the individual attains his purposes by being appointed is [UN251: something external to the monarch's subjective decision and therefore something] accidental.

The sovereign has little involvement in the peaceful [life of the] State. Where it has to intervene is during an emergency, either a domestic or a foreign one. The whole is essentially entrusted to the sovereign as the State's [UN251: innermost][789] unity. It is this unity that bears the risk. If everything in the State runs in an orderly way, he should not, as we said, intervene. However, there can be cases where the monarch must intervene. The sovereign must intervene when [a matter] is badly judged. Frederick II chased away numerous councillors and sent them to Spandau.[790] That was a case where [a court] acted partially against a peasant in a way biased towards a nobleman. Then it was said that all

---

788 UN251: ... even though they are completely independent.
789 Translator: Taking UN's *innersten* over Ringier's *letzten*.
790 Translator: Hegel refers here to the case, famous in its day, of the millers Arnold, whose mill was put up for sale by their feudal lord to recoup their arrears of ground rent. The Arnolds complained that a dam constructed upstream for a fishpond had diminished their water supply, but the lord's own feudal court, headed by a magistrate apparently partial towards the lord, held against them. The millers eventually petitioned the king, who deplored the court's bias, held for the Arnolds, and sent to prison the judges who advised him that the case had been rightly decided on the law. These events inspired Frederick's Protocol of 11 December 1779, which contained the following sentence: "All men being equal before the law, if it is a prince complaining against a peasant, or vice versa, the prince is the same as the peasant before the law; and, on such occasions, pure justice must have its course, without regard of person." See Thomas Carlyle, *History of Friedrich the Second, Called Frederick the Great* (New York: Lovel, Coryell, 1858–65; Project Gutenberg, 2018), bk. 21, chap. 7, "Miller Arnold's Lawsuit," https://www.gutenberg.org/files/2121/2121-h/2121-h.htm#2H_4_0001.

[laws] were observed; but the court said that it could have held differently. Here, however, [the court] should not have spoken [as it did] – hence the acrimony. It is not about the formal but about the substance of the matter.[791] Admittedly, the monarch has the power to intervene here and there, and this revealed the large spirit of Frederick [the Great].

The right of pardon is also something that belongs to the ruler. [Pardon] goes *against* justice. Therefore, it is something unjust. However, it lies in [the nature of] Spirit to make un-happen what happened. So, the monarch can also have regard to the [UN251: inward] personality of the criminal.[792] The majesty of the monarch can forgive and make un-happen what happened.[793] It is left to the conscience of the monarch to use the pardon sparingly [UN252: so as not to obstruct the course of justice] and [180] not to forgive too much out of weakness. The highest moment is this ideality, this subjectivity.

It is when the State turns outward that the monarch's subjectivity comes to the fore.[794] The key concept in the princely power is the ideality that is present in the natural. It is the Mind of a people that differentiates itself in this way. It can occur to reflection to ask whether there is something in human beings that compels them to submit to a prince, or whether this is really to be considered a necessary evil.[795] [UN252: Kent says to King Lear:] "You have that in your countenance which I would fain call master."[796] [UN252: The question, therefore, is whether there is something in human beings generally that would like to recognize a master.] The answer lies in what has already been said. We must return to the concept of the human. [UN252: In its concept, the human being is free]; he should be a subject of law, [UN252: not of the subjective will of an individual]. [But Kent's speech reveals another side of the human, which] is none other than that as a real,

---

791 UN251: The same is true [with respect to] external state emergencies. The monarch, the conscience of the State, can encounter cases where forms can decide nothing. A limit cannot be specified here [by law], and this is something that must be self-legitimating.
792 UN251: The highest power of the State can, so to speak, see the inwardness of the criminal and acknowledge that the essence of the [criminal] deed, which is ascribable to the [abstract] will, is erased.
793 Translator: This repetition is also in UN's notes (252).
794 UN252: The identity of the State as such comes to reality in the State's external relations[s], where its general preservation is at stake. Reason allows the Will's extreme [determinacy], which appears as the princely power, to reach self-conscious existence.
795 UN252: ... or whether this is merely an external necessity.
796 *King Lear*, act 1, scene 4.

existing, particularity, the human being is after all a dependent being. The interdependence of particular interests [in international relations] is something else that lies outside him, the decision [concerning which] does not lie within him.[797] There enters here [the necessity of a free-standing] human decision, a subjective decision. [And this belongs to the monarch.] The monarch has a discretion only over eventualities [das Vorkommende], not over what is just. The deciding will is this subject.[798]

The formality of the decision is, [to begin with,] empty of content. However, it must have a content. Its content side belongs to a special body, a supreme advisory body, which brings forward eventualities [to the monarch]. The advisory body must bring this content before the monarch and also present the objective [considerations pertaining thereto]. This statutory [body of] advisors is [called] the ministry. It has to add [its view of] what is most advisable and lawful. Since these individuals have to do with the subjectivity of the monarch, it follows that their welfare [depends] entirely on the monarch's subjectivity.[799]

There is thus an indeterminacy here [in external affairs] as to whether the monarch heeds [the minister's] advice more or less. It all depends on the character of the monarch. With regard to [external affairs], the monarch can more or less govern by himself. Ordinary reasoning has odd ideas about this. On the one hand, it is common for princes not [sic] to rule by themselves,[800] but it is also dangerous when they do. It is safest if the ministers, who are and must be informed about the matter, can advise the prince.[801] The responsibility [for the content of the decision] then falls necessarily and exclusively on the minister. With regard to the [formal] subjectivity of the "I will," there is no [181] responsibility. The

---

797 Translator: "does not lie within him," because it is not a decision under a law that he can reflectively accept.
798 UN252: Laws and institutions are things that exist in and for themselves [objectively], and over these the monarch has no discretion [he must will into force the legislative or executive judgment]. He does have a discretion, however, over the [free-standing] particular [e.g., the making of treaties]. The deciding will in its true, Concept-adequate form is this subject.
799 UN253: … it follows that their appointment and dismissal must be left entirely to the monarch.
800 UN253: It can be considered essential that the prince rule by himself. But the self-rule of the monarch is also very dangerous.
801 UN253: It is therefore a mistake to view it as a weakness if a prince follows his ministers.

ultimate decision is the subjective [element], and there can be responsibility only for the objective [aspect of the decision]. In many countries this [ministerial] responsibility [to the legislature] has been introduced. This separation of the subjective from the objective [aspect of the decision] is a state of affairs [resulting from] a more advanced education and development.[802]

The third moment of the princely power is the universal in and for itself. These are the laws and the constitution. These are objectively [given to the prince]; the prince does not make them. The princely power presupposes the other powers of the State, as they presuppose it; for in an organic whole, nothing is isolated. In despotic constitutions, as in Turkey and the old Germany, the form of religion takes the place of the objective self-determination [of the Concept].[803]

B. THE EXECUTIVE POWER

The second power in the State is the *executive power* – the sphere of subsumption. This [power] has the task of leading the circle of civil life back to the universal. It is in this sphere that the universal and the particular collide. [UN254: The strong tendency of particular interests is to sink deeply into themselves, to become independent of the universal.] The [executive's] action maintains from the top down the connection between [self-interest] and the universal so that they become fluid with, not isolated from, each other. In this [executive] sphere, the particular interests [of society] are present before it and have their own [internal] management. Here particular [bodies] can also gain the right to decide [their own affairs]. [The executive power] also wants to make decisions [regarding particular interests], but only decisions concerning the universal are proper to it. Particularistic affairs can be [internally] managed in various ways. The authorities of private associations can be drawn from the cooperatives.[804] The human drive to do something for

---

802 UN253: Responsibility can fall on the minister alone. To be accountable means that an action must be in accordance with the constitution, with what is right, etc. This objective side [of the decision] belongs to the ministers. The majesty of the monarch is absolutely not responsible for government action. In many states the manner of the minister's responsibility is formally determined. The separation of the subjective and the objective shows itself in [the division between] the prince and the minister.
803 UN253: In despotic states, what is valid in and for itself is present chiefly as religion. In developed states, by contrast, it takes the form of rational thought.
804 UN254: The heads can be elected from the associates of the corporation ...

the universal is thereby given room for expression. It has here its local circle where it is at home [and UN254: for which specialist know-how and insight are sufficient].

Inasmuch as the [corporation's] officers apportion its business and attend to [its] management, the collective welfare [of the corporation] must here too be dealt with according to rules. Necessarily involved here is the influence of government representatives. Their occasional insights nestle easily into this sphere [because] [182] they are civil servants who deal with the lawful and the universal. The [private] sphere is where the universal and the particular affect each other, [yet UN254: private actors are inclined to follow their selfish interests]. It is the war of all against all; here the conflict between special interests [UN255: and between special interests and the universal] has its place. The corporation mind will easily know how to capture the universal Mind within its sphere. However, this corporation mind must not run to extreme selfishness. Precisely from [the corporation] there grows a burgher patriotism for the [larger] community.[805]

As was said, regard for special interests must not become an obsession. The chief concern of the corporation mind [UN255: during the Middle Ages] was to raise freedom [to a principle]. But then they became hardened and, [UN255: where the universal did not succeed in mastering them,] they splintered. So, for example, in Switzerland, cities separated from each other, and in Italy, this was the reason for the deterioration of [independence]. Machiavelli['s book *The Prince*] contains maxims for all constitutions on how the prince can come to power in order to transform the prince's power into a complete despotism. However, if you read the conclusion, you will see the solution: it is the expression of a high patriotism. He gives expression to the misery, the break-up, of his fatherland [and to the] profound sentiment that, if Italy is to become something, it must become united. This [for him] is the highest law. He then specifies means by which to end the fragmentation. In vain do people accuse him of promoting despotism; [for] when one reads *The History of* [*Florence and of the Affairs of*] *Italy*, one well understands the patriotic spirit of this great man. He laments the fact that there are so many petty lords in his fatherland. If Machiavelli provides stratagems for treachery, one must keep in mind that he wants them

---

805 Translator: This is an abrupt move. In these lectures, Hegel does not explain how the civic-mindedness of the corporation is to come about, but see *Outlines*, para. 289.

used against such brigands.⁸⁰⁶ The corporation mind [equated with particularism and petty despotism] then became precisely what was dreaded. The French Revolution smashed the corporations. In such small corporations there was no shortage of inept work, but this tendency, too, can be allowed to go on.⁸⁰⁷

[Regarding the organization of the] higher authorities, administration by individuals is the most effective, but when it comes to *decision-making*, collegial [administration] is necessary. The arbitrary will of the individual is thereby blunted. The affairs of the executive are so multifaceted that they fall into several [183] branches. [These branches] have to merge somewhere, and this makes for great difficulty and complexity in execution. It can easily happen that, if some temporary [exigency] must be dealt with quickly, because of the time, one has to choose shortcuts. There are some disadvantages to this fragmentation [of the executive] but on the other hand, they are minor.⁸⁰⁸

To the different departments belong individuals who carry out [the department's] business. [UN256: The objective moment here is that] they must [prove that they] have the qualifications for the subject matter, and once this is proved, no other obstacle may be placed before them.⁸⁰⁹ [UN256: The subjective side is that among several equally

---

806 UN255: Machiavelli, that great spirit, has, in his book about the prince, which many think contains secrets and maxims of despotism, emphasized that aspect [of disunity]. If you read especially the conclusion of that book, you obtain an insight into the whole; this conclusion contains an appeal that springs from a profound patriotic sentiment. Machiavelli expresses therein the misery of his fatherland, which has disintegrated into many principalities and local authorities that are constantly quarrelling and that then mainly provide a playground for foreigners. Machiavelli thus sets up the principle that the unity of the state is the highest law to which all others must yield, and he then specifies measures by which to attain this. One greatly misjudges Machiavelli if one believes that he wrote for the sake of despotism; rather, it is purely the deep feeling of a great spirit over the misfortune and misery of his fatherland that drove him. One has to read the history of Italy until the time of Machiavelli in order to understand why he wrote as he did. Most of the principalities of Italy arose because fortunate chieftains made a city or a district their private property. A large proportion of them were robbers and brigands, for whom no means of achieving dominance were too wicked. Accordingly, if Machiavelli also goes too far in the means he recommends, one must keep in mind the kind of people against whom he advises such means.
807 UN256: The more minor the matter [dealt with by the corporation], the more can [government] defer to the inclination to want to do something oneself.
808 UN256: The difficulty in the organization of executive authority lies in the fact that, at the point where the matter must be executed, it is concrete. In the middle, the business [of the State] must then be divided into its abstract branches, and at the top [these branches] must then be recombined.
809 UN256: Under this condition [of qualification], the way to public office must be open to every citizen.

qualified candidates, a particular individual is appointed.] That just this individual is tied to the State's business is an external [contingent] matter. As between several [candidates], it is often impossible to determine who should obtain [the post].[810] Here, therefore, there is always contingency. This contingency [of selection] belongs to the princely power once qualification has been demonstrated.

[UN257: The bureaucratic relationship has in it something of the nature of a contract.] There exists here a mutual assent: on the one side [the applicant's] acceptance and on the other [the prince's] choice. However, the relationship does not fall under the category of contract. If the individual manages the public business badly, he does not simply break a contract such that he need only render compensation; rather, he violates an objective duty and must on that account be penalized. The individual who is bound to his occupation through a sovereign act of appointment is directed to the fulfilment of duty. And because he rests his particular interest in [service to the State], the State owes him relief from concern for his subsistence. The civil servant, because he is a civil servant, is neither a client of the State nor a lackey of the State. He takes an oath, and the fulfilment of duty is the necessary and sufficient condition of his retaining public office. It must [therefore] lie within the discretion [*Willkür*] of the State to remove him from office. On this view [taken by itself], the civil servant would be taken on by the State temporarily. On the other hand, the civil servant fulfils a duty, and as long as he fulfils it, he is entitled to the security of his person for his entire life, [for] he has renounced other ways of acquisition. The State must retain the right to remove him [for cause], but as long as he is competent, he can expect to remain in office. [184] If the State sees that it made a mistake [in an appointment], then it is the State's fault. It must suffer for it and look after [the individual]. It is a different matter if [the civil servant] has committed an offence. The judgment then falls to be decided by the higher authorities.[811]

---

810 UN257: For most public business, no particular genius is required, and many individuals can qualify.

811 UN257: The decision as to whether the dismissal of the civil servant should or should not be a matter of free discretion has difficulties peculiar to it. A civil servant can, to be sure, consider his office as his property insofar as he has put his entire [life's] activity into the relationship; however, the State and service to it always remain the substantial thing. The [State] must therefore maintain the right to decide on the retention of office. If it sees that it has erred in the appointment of a civil servant, it always owes the individual some kind of compensation [for severance]. It is a different matter if an individual commits an offence in office. A court cannot decide on the manner of executing an office, but it can on a real crime.

With regard to individuals who have been appointed to public service, [a secure livelihood], besides being to their private benefit, is a condition of their qualification [for public service], provided they perform properly the business entrusted to them. In general, officials must be set up in such a way that they can subsist. Once in office, their private passions must recede.[812] This depends on the general level of cultivation and on the organization of the bureaucracy. An indication of the disinterestedness of officials is the size of the state. [UN258: Generally speaking, in a large state, personal passions cannot exert the influence over relationships with officials that they do in a small state.] Officials [in large states] have no families of great importance [that could influence them]. In their large aims, concerns, and networks of dependence, families oppose [hence check] each other. In imperial cities, it is easy to be watched closely or treated badly out of hatred.[813] In a large state this is not so easily done.

For members of the executive and for those who aspire to public service, a liberal education is necessary. This is a condition of their livelihood. They belong to the middle class.[814] [UN258: This class lives a life devoted to general knowledge, general viewpoints.] It requires a general education. The essential intelligence of a state rests on [UN258: the advanced education] and ideas of this class. The organization [of the State] must ensure that the power that this class gains through its [knowledge] does not become a means to an aristocracy over subordinates, as, indeed, used to be the case. It has often been found that officials and lawyers gain dominance through their knowledge of the legal process, etc., and that they tend to abuse it. Control from the top down does not completely help. [UN258: Institutions must have sufficient strength to form a solid wall against the arbitrary will and negligence of officials.]

---

812 UN258: Regarding the conduct of individual office-holders, it is necessary that they give effect to no personal passions and that, conversely, individuals pursue no personal passion with them.

813 Translator: An imperial city (*Reichsstadt*) was a city of the Holy Roman Empire subject, not to a local lord, but directly to the emperor. It was self-governing but usually dominated by an oligarchic dynasty.

814 Translator: In Hegel's usage, the term *middle class* (*Mittelstand*) denotes a sociological class (not an estate, which is a logical division of the Idea) of intelligentsia from which both the universal estate of civil servants and the members of the business estate are drawn. It is a middle class in the contingent sense that it has a status based on education and achievement that the peasantry lacks but that (in Hegel's time) was lower than the status of the landed aristocracy, whose honour came from economic independence making direct involvement in politics possible; see *Outlines*, para. 297.

C. THE LEGISLATIVE POWER

This is the power to set the laws that ought to have force as rules of decision. The laws are the universal relationships in the State. Besides these, there are also concrete governmental affairs and actions [UN259: so general that their determination also assumes the character of law-making]. [Some laws] are part of the constitution. The constitution lies outside the legislative power; [nevertheless], in the progressive development of legislation there is also a progressive development of the [185] constitution. Where there is no constitution, there is also no law-giving power. [UN259: Like the other powers,] the legislative power is by itself a totality [in which both the prince and the executive have a role]. The executive, which has oversight of the entirety, has its pinnacle in the prince, the monarchical element, to whom the highest decision falls. These all meet in the legislature, which is the advisory moment. The third element [in the legislature, besides the prince and the executive] is the estates' power. [UN259: That this power cannot exist independently and abstractly has already been remarked upon.][815]

The necessity for estates in a state[816] can be understood in many ways. The dominant view is that [estates] are a counterweight against the monarch. [UN259: The poverty of this view has already been noted.][817] To be sure, every organ in the body is something that limits and something that is limited. Very common, then, is the view that the princely power is only out to oppress, [UN259: whereas the people are presented as higher and more excellent]. [However,] corporations and local communities likewise have a tendency to immerse themselves in [their particular interests]. To say that the people are excellent is empty talk; everyone seeks his own interest. [UN260: Another point of view is that there is need for participation by the people's deputies because they know best what they need.] [However,] the people apart from the middle class [the intelligentsia] belong to the class of people who do not know what they want.[818] The people lack practical wisdom. The best thing one can say of a man is that he knows what he [truly] wants. France thought that it wanted now this, now that, but it soon became apparent that there was a truth of the matter.[819]

---

815 See, e.g., this translation, 199–200.
816 UN259: constitution.
817 See this translation, 197.
818 UN260: It takes deep insight to know what one wants; on the one hand, it takes scientific insight, on the other, great practical education.
819 UN260: In the French Revolution, there were only a few simple determinations that could be called the true content of the public will; this was the termination of feudal power and the rule of law.

What is inherently and actually universal, rational, beneficial, etc. can occur in monarchies without [the participation of] estates. But precisely because the universal is a universal, it is implied therein that it must be a totality and must come to existence in a universal manner. [UN260: This occurs through the participation of many from the general populace]. This is a determination inherent in the Idea [of Right]. One cannot say that the people know better [than trained civil servants and ministers of the Crown]. That is not true.[820] As far as insight is concerned, the ministries have always done best and still do. It is the character of modern times that everyone wants to see the truth for himself.[821] It is the formal moment [of assent] that should step forward in the estates. [UN261: The Athenians, the freest people of antiquity,] entrusted law-making to Solon. Later, however, self-consciousness demanded its right and ceased to believe everything [it was told]. What is in itself excellent can no doubt occur in the State [without the participation of the estates]. However, self-consciousness finds itself dissatisfied with that. It is not as if [law-making] is done better because of the estates; [186] and as far as their good will is concerned, this too is generally thrown aside, and selfishness very often exists.[822] [UN261: That said, it is a great and correct moment [[of public Right]] that government actions are subject to the scrutiny of the estates. In this way, the universal is validated as such.]

What are the bounds for the advice of the estates? Nothing more exact can be specified other than the general affairs of state. For example: the authorization of local communities and corporations. Corporations are independent, [but] are supervised by the government so as to accord with the laws of the whole. Criminal law is also an object for the estates' advice, as is the organization of government agencies. An object that many say could also be a matter for consultation [with the estates] is war and peace, and relationships with foreign [powers]. This is [from one point of view] the most general of state affairs [and so a suitable matter for the estates' advice]. However, [UN261: in its content] it is a

---

820 UN260: There is no question that men who have always been engaged in affairs of state understand what matters better than those who usually pursue particularistic ends.
821 UN260: By the way, the chief aspect of modernity is that the truth is valid not independently but only with the assent and knowledge of the individual. At first, people comport themselves to religion as to something revealed. Humanity can thereby settle down into a certain stage of cultivation; however, it has surpassed [that stage], and a demand has emerged for one's own insight and self-consciousness.
822 UN261: ... and still less can the superior will of the estates be asserted in their favour. Concerning whether or not they have a good will nothing general can be said.

quite distinct business, depending as it does on discrete contingencies. It involves a decision-making that is determined not so much in accordance with general principles as with sagacity. The general principles in play here can decide nothing [UN262: for particular cases]. The resolution of the matter belongs [UN262: by nature to the State's individuality, hence] to the princely power. An assembly of estates is least adept at something discrete. For this a very calm decision is required; therefore, a prince must decide. One would make a big mistake if one said that there would be fewer wars if the estates had a say over them.[823]

A principal object of the estates is taxation. This is a general affair of state that rests on general principles and belongs before the estates. Apportioning taxes properly requires a great deal of knowledge. One can adduce as a reason [for the estates' consent to taxation] that they then have a means by which to coerce the government. This [viewpoint] has been asserted especially in recent times and [UN262: initially seems very plausible]. It is, [however,] an entirely crude point of view. The State must endure; the estates cannot refuse taxes. And if they do, the government has the right to dismiss them. The thought has been that because private property owners have to relinquish something, their consent must be obtained [for taxation]. There is a misunderstanding here, because it is not a matter of discretion but rather a duty to give something [to the State], and, indeed, an objective, [UN263: not merely a positive,] duty. Taxes have no other purpose but to preserve the State, and this is an objectively necessary matter.

The consent of the estates is relevant to what was said earlier: that the [inherently] universal must also [187] come forward in the form of consciousness. The formal [moment] of their assent must also be there. A universal duty is thereby [constitutionally] fixed. [UN263: As for the practical effect of estate participation in taxation,] a principal object is that the needs [of the people] are thereby enquired into.[824] Everything [in the State] revolves mainly around finance. If finances are badly procured, the State is in great danger. At first sight, it looks sordid that

---

823 UN262: Some believe that there would be fewer wars if the estates decided on them; the truth is just the opposite. It is the same when the constitution of a people is such that the warlike [estate] is dominant in it. Precisely such a people is most embroiled in wars. Wars in which whole peoples take part usually turn into wars of conquest. Insofar as estates participate in financial affairs, they have an indirect influence on questions of war and peace.
824 UN263: With [the estates' participation in raising taxes] is connected both the [government's] checking of public needs and the [estates'] control over the lawful use of public taxes.

everything depends on money. In war, [the side that] bears up best is usually the one that has the most money. War is often a conflict between treasuries.

[UN263: The question arises why the main interest of the State has taken the form of money.] The first side [of the matter] concerns what one has to enjoy [from the State]: schools, court proceedings, etc. The second side concerns what one has to perform [for the State], and money is the most important thing around which this [performance] revolves. One could say that one can perform in a loftier way – for example, through patriotism. But this is a feeling, and one cannot do anything with a feeling. One must really perform, and what is performed is something specific. This could then be demanded in a specific form: you build a road, you be a teacher, you be a judge. The abstract possibility of every [kind of performance] is money. The State asks: who wants to do this [particular task]? In that way, room is left for free choice. The value of the specific performance is determined spontaneously [by the market], and the State, in needing one or the other, buys it and thus exacts fair services. What one does for the State is thus mediated through my free choice. This is the way services are performed. By means of money, services [to the State] can be performed in a completely fair way, mediated through my free choice.[825]

One can ask a further question. What should and must the estates do?[826] In general terms, the estates should make determinations for the universal [Good]. The estates must act mainly with the mindset [*Sinn*] of government. In the old Germany, it was otherwise. The feudal lord had the quality of a private property owner, and he entered the assembly as a private property owner with a mind to give as little as possible. [UN264: This is a conception that manifests itself in various ways even now.] It is essential that the estates stand together with the government

---

825 UN263: Through all of modernity runs [the theme] that the individual wants to be self-active. The State engages the particular individual in a free way by generally demanding only money and by transferring his [monetary] performance to those who are willing [to perform a concrete service]. What I take on credit from the State is thus thoroughly mediated through the free will of another. The State buys the particular [service] it needs, commissions a work for payment. Services [to the State] can thus be performed in a completely fair and uniform way.

826 UN264: What [specific] quality must the estates have? They are the particularity side of the State or what can be called the people. However, this particularity enters the universal. The mindset of the estates must in general be the mindset of the universal.

with the mindset of the universal. This is the bond of unity. [But] the second thing is [that their specific quality is] the mindset of particularity. They come to [lawgiving] also with this [specialized] know-how and sensibility, but this must be bound up with [188] the mindset of the universal.

What is more, we can ask who makes up the estates? The simple answer is: civil society, the private estate that belongs with the government.[827] The idea that first presents itself is that the entire multiplicity of individuals belongs to this [political] estate. One thereby imagines that we want to afford the individual qua individual a part in advising [government].[828] But the multitude of individuals is a mass, a mob, οἱ λολλοἱ. That is the atomistic point of view. The viewpoint of a mass is without effect;[829] a people must never appear as a mass. It is often the case that individuals are apathetic [UN265: about voting. This is currently evident in, for example, France.] If there are many of them, the vote of an individual is very insignificant.[830] The general rule is that the people must not appear [in the assembly] as a mass. As we become a community in the ethical sphere, the atomistic individual disappears. The atomistic individual counts only in abstract Right – in the family already [no longer]. Insofar as civil society appears [in the public sphere], it must appear as something organized.

Civil society is [composed of] the agricultural estate (family) and the business estate. In this connotation, estates can be understood by the name of [civil] estates. The political estates are the [legislative representatives of] the civil estates. Both are salient [in the State].[831] At one time, the [political estates] were called noble, spiritual, and bourgeois. The fact that the clerical estate has more or less disappeared as a [separate] estate stands to reason. As an estate, the clergy in council [*Rat*] would be like the fifth wheel [*Rad*] on a wagon. The

---

827 UN264: ... civil society in general, that which makes up the private estate *in contradistinction to* the government [translator's italics].
828 UN265: ... and one can then think that in a large State, it is too difficult for all individuals to assemble.
829 UN265: ... without worth.
830 UN265: ... and it turns out that it always takes a special interest for someone to attend that kind of election.
831 UN265: We use the expression "estates" in a double sense: on the one hand, as an estate in civil society, and, on the other, as a part of the legislature.

Church can only give advice; it cannot vote. Otherwise, it would be the apodictic.[832]

The subject matters of advice are those involving thought, [UN266: a form not constitutive of the Church's distinctiveness. There remain two estates]. One estate we have put forward is the agricultural estate, the estate of natural ethical life, the estate of families, [the estate] reliant on land. The fact that farmers, who are directly occupied with agriculture, are unable [UN266: to advise on affairs of state] is an accidental circumstance. [UN266: Having regard to the political constitution, some primal attributes of this estate turn out to be suitable for its political purpose.] This is the one estate whose basis is family life and land ownership. [The agricultural estate] thereby constitutes the stable, constant moment [of the State], the element that is removed from [labour and capital] mobility. That its independence be complete, it is necessary that this estate be independent of state wealth, [189] that it have its own, fixed possession in virtue of which it can manage without depending on payment and the gifts of patronage. It must also be removed from the insecurity of commerce and from the quest for profit. The merchant can know what is his and what is the other's. [UN266: Wealth that is torn apart in commercial relationships always remains dependent on external circumstances and the conduct of others.] So, trade and the pursuit of profit must be kept remote [from the agricultural estate]. Likewise, this estate must be independent of the favour of the crowd. [UN266: For all these reasons, its wealth] must be an [UN266: inalienable] patrimony, an entailed property, so that the accident of division among heirs also falls away. It is thus something stable, removed as well from personal caprice.

So that this estate might [UN266: for political purposes] possess a secure wealth, it bears the onerous imposition that its wealth cannot be divided among children even if they are loved equally, that it must

---

832 UN265: One might at first think that the clerical estate is necessary in order to give force to the true, godly, and free. Nevertheless, the Church has no political existence in the State; were it to vote as a Church, its voice would be apodictic, the voice of God, the voice of conscience. Where the Church is not the decision-maker, it has no place. [Translator: From the standpoint of the State, the idea is that the holding of a belief as an incontrovertible truth is incompatible with presence in a deliberative body, in which the vote is the culmination of debate and persuasion. From the standpoint of the Church, a truth held as incontrovertible has no place in a deliberative body, where it is one opinion and vote among others. So, the State should not want the Church represented in the legislature, and the Church should not want to be there.]

remain with the first born. This [restriction] disadvantages the rest, and it is a cruel burden on the heart of the father, who must love his children equally. All this follows from the proposition that the wealth [of this estate] must be secure, removed from external contingencies.[833] Wealth constitutes the [UN267: objective side of particularity, which can be regulated]. Inclinations, [by contrast,] can in no way be ordained [by law]. [UN267: In external independence lies the absolute possibility of internal independence.] It is in consideration of [internal independence] that these [legal] determinations [encumbering land] must be understood. One might think that this independence can be afforded by the lifelong enjoyment of a large pension. But that [again] falls into the realm of the contingent.[834] It is the estate [as a whole] for which this security is [legally] ordained. It thus occurs that one part [of the legislature] is determined by birth to be a member of the [political] estates. One can say that leaving this to birth is leaving [practical wisdom] to accident. But the purpose lies just in [political] necessity, and all other contingency [having to do with feelings of dependence and inner disposition] is thereby excised. Here too, therefore, [as with the prince,] nature must help in bringing forward something fixed and secure.[835]

The other estate element [the business estate] constitutes the mobile side of civil society. This [estate] cannot enter the advisory assembly en masse. The external reason is their number. The internal reason is that the work of civil society divides itself into an infinite plurality of abstract branches and that [UN267 the individuals caught up in them] are so dependent on others, while lacking the insight [UN267: needed for handling affairs of state]. They are [190] wont to lack the ruthlessness towards existence [that is sometimes needed of statesmen].[836] One cannot object that even individuals who are born poor or dependent can vault themselves to a greater independence of character. That is a mere possibility.

Civil society, then, presents itself [in the legislature] not at all as a mass but as something organized [UN268: into communities and

---

833 Translator: This estate must have a secure wealth so that it can have financial independence for disinterested public service.
834 UN267: In France, the senators were permitted the lifelong enjoyment of a large pension. But this always falls into the realm of contingency, and since the executive necessarily influences the distribution of senatorial positions, the possibility of all that dependence re-enters.
835 UN267: In this respect, too, human beings must take refuge in nature in order to secure something directly.
836 UN267: ... that is necessary in view of the vocation in question.

cooperatives]. If individuals entered [the legislature directly], work would leave [the private for the public sector]. There is no need for the entire corporation to appear [politically]; it is enough if a few [of its members] do so. And these few appear not as proxies but as representatives, as those who present the corps while being an individual member thereof.[837] So an individual is itself the genus, the universal. It is the [corporate] interest. Such estates are double-sided. [UN268: They are public-minded,] and they also have regard for their particular interests. [UN268: If the arrangement regarding deputies is that atomistic individuals elect them, then it is left completely to chance whether every interest receives its special voice.] But if the commercial estate, etc. sends off its deputies, then every interest has its voice. Justice requires that every interest have a vote. For this to occur, care must be taken that every interest obtains one.

There are still many details to consider. For the [qualifications of] deputies, much ado is made of their assets. [The thought is that] the property owner has the greatest interest in civil order. Whoever has nothing is better served by lawlessness. One can easily see, however, that there can be other guarantees [of a deputy's fitness for office] – for example, that persons have already administered offices [UN268: within their cooperatives and communities], etc. They then have expertise and practical abilities. Most importantly, they have demonstrated their proficiency in deeds.

The two estates are distinguished as fixed is distinguished from mobile. These institutions [of primogeniture, entailed estates, hereditary peerages] are established in order that the principle of stability be removed from the sphere of the changeable. Also cut off is the possibility of migration [from one estate to another]; for one cannot leave everything to preference. Preference is a disposition and can go one way or another. Merit and proficiency would then always depend on particularistic and arbitrary choice.[838] In order that the first estate achieve the perfection of

---

837 UN268: Their corporation, their cooperative, is itself present in them. In the same way, one recognizes the whole nation in a single member of a nation. In the representative, the corporation itself is present.

838 Translator: If the aristocracy could migrate to the business class, the existence of a private estate disinterestedly devoted to the common good would be left to chance; allowing members of the mobile estate to become peers would destroy the aristocracy's economic independence of the market that supports its leisure for political virtue. This, however, is obviously inconsistent with modernity's freedom of mobility and equality of opportunity and with Hegel's own critique of castes. What could replace this class rigidity without sacrificing its political benefits?

its nature, it must abandon [the principle of free mobility]. This is the estate of nobility [UN269: in the political sense]. Nobility in respect of political [virtue] needs no other privilege [than to participate directly in lawgiving]; and he shares this with [191] other [members of his estate]. If he has [other individual] privileges, these rest on the history of each state. They have no place in the concept of the political.[839]

Inasmuch as these estates introduce the aggregate [into the legislature], they initially step forward in opposition to the executive. This, however, is a non-rational relationship. The rational relationship is the closure by which these [extremes] show their unity, not through the process of [endless] struggle, but by remaining unified while being at the same time distinct. From its side, the princely power sends the executive to mediate [between the prince and the estates], but that [mediation] comes from one side only. The estates must likewise send a mediating element [from their side]. Negotiation is for the ministry, which is accountable [to the estates], and the prince [takes on only] the [formality of] decision. What the estates can send is nothing other than the first [the landed] estate.[840]

The reasonable [constitution thus] requires two chambers. [UN269: One chamber remains at the extreme [[of particularism]]; the other chamber forms the element of mediation.] The first estate is qualified to be the moment of mediation. In the first place, it shares the same rights with the [UN269: rest of] the private citizens [*Bürgern*], though it has to make more of a sacrifice. On the other hand, because [this estate] is for the conservation, persistence, and abidingness of what is, it also stands on the other side. The [political][841] State is the universal principle,

---

839 UN268: The first estate represents the abiding in general – being. Inasmuch as their property is fixed and inalienable, the members of this estate are firmly bound to the land to which they belong. They thereby make a hard sacrifice [of freedom] for their political position. The other estate is the estate of process, of changeability in general. Here it is always the principle of a particular personality that is active. The first estate corresponds to what is called nobility in the political sense. The vocation of this estate is to be devoted to the State in all manner of its relationships. With respect to politics, the nobleman needs no other titles and privileges. If he has other rights, these belong to positive, particular public law. These advantages do not lie within the concept of their political relationship.
840 UN269: This moment can be nothing other than one that contains within itself [both private and public dimensions], and this is the moment of universality, the first estate. [Translator: The landed estate belongs to the private sector, yet, like the civil servant's, its subsistence is secure, and like the prince's, its hereditary office gives it independence from special interests.]
841 See n. 717.

inherently and actually; the private citizen [embodies] the principle of particularism. So [the first estate] stands on both sides and therefore constitutes the middle term between the people and the [UN270: the princely power[842]].[843] Through this division [of the legislature] into two chambers, a rational relationship is established. This [relationship] is the essential [nature of the State].[844] A collateral consideration is that the same relationship enters [here] that exists between the different entities in the court system.[845] Since two chambers exist and the same [government] business is thought through in both, the resolution is more mature. This is very important for a large assembly. Nothing is easier in a large assembly than to make an uproar. So, [procedural] formalities are also needed, because nothing is as important as regulating the procedure for [conducting parliamentary] business – for example, by carrying it out in several sessions.[846]

The openness to the public of the estates' assembly is also often discussed. It has a risky side, which must be removed. [UN270: An estates' assembly ... can allow itself to be imposed upon and swayed by those in attendance.] The other side is that, through this publicity, [192] the many private citizens come to [political] insight; they can arrive at a knowledge of public affairs. They become acquainted with the points of view that have to be considered and with those that have to be rejected. Many also become familiar with the points of view that state [officials] have. They gain the capacity to judge matters of state rationally. [UN271: God does not give that to a person in his sleep, and a lot of perverse and useless things are argued at beer benches.] Only [by

---

842 Translator: taking UN's "princely power" over Ringier's "nobility." The first estate *is* the nobility.
843 UN270: It was said in the presence of an English peer that the House of Lords inclines more to the side of monarchy than to that of the people. Pointing to his children, this peer remarked that he always had a lower house around him.
844 UN270: In political terms, the nobility has a necessary place, and all declamation is to no avail. It is to be wished that those who are called to this political estate are satisfied with the arrangements that befit them. [Translator: This is another jab at the pro-Restoration aristocrats.]
845 Translator: Perhaps Hegel is thinking of the division between trial and appellate courts.
846 UN270: A large assembly is far more prone to making a decision on the spur of the moment than a single individual. Precisely for this reason, formalities are of the utmost importance, especially the rule that a motion should be made in several successive sessions. The most important thing is always that, by this means, opposition is mediated. If a chamber stands opposed to the princely power, the state is always exposed to the greatest danger. In France, the perniciousness of this relationship manifested itself in the clearest way.

observing legislative deliberations] do private citizens come to realize what great talents are involved in [holding] public office. At the same time, deputies gain a public stage of the highest honour, for [what they do] is very instructive; that is precisely why they can expect to be esteemed. [The many] hear discussed the interests that concern them.

One might, however, still perceive an imperfection in the fact that not every individual can express his opinion about [public matters effectively]. The expression *proxy* [*Stellvertreter*] assumes that [deputies] stand in the place of the individual. But this is an empty idea. If one adopts this view, then one thing is [still] absent: that individuals as such have expressed their judgment on the [public] interest.[847] What individuals [collectively] opine is called public opinion. This is where individuals have their judgment [counted]. This is something of the highest weight and influence. Even the executive and the prince stand in [the ambience of] this public opinion. Public opinion incorporates the disposition of the state [as a whole]. The result of the entire constitutional process, it contains the truest [understanding of the public interest]. It is what is called the healthy human understanding.[848]

[However, there is another side to public opinion].[849] The more idiosyncratic someone's product, the more admirable he thinks it is. As in poetry, so too in philosophy. Hence the proposition [of some philosophers]: that alone is true which one immediately perceives. This is also something original. [UN273: No peasant is so stupid as not to

---

[847] Translator: This may mean that, even on the atomistic view of representation, the deputy is the deputy of a district, not of an individual, and so the individual as such is never represented.

[848] UN271: It has already been observed that individuals as such do not come to expression, all the more because representatives are not their proxies. The expression and judgment of all in general is what is called public opinion. This is, as it were, a completion of the collective opinion that is expressed in the estates' assembly. Public opinion is something of great weight and great effectiveness. Everyone stands in [the ambience of] this public opinion – the estates, the executive, and the prince. Public opinion thus incorporates the substantial principles of justice; it is the disposition of the state, of the people as a whole, the result of an all-public things-considered [judgment]. It is, from this point of view, what is called the healthy human understanding in a people. The Chinese have an entirely different healthy human understanding than the English and the Germans. Fifty years ago, a Frenchman who was told about the position of the king of England would have found it entirely contrary to a healthy human understanding that a king should no longer have power.

[849] UN272: In public opinion there are also [the opinions of] discrete individuals who give expression to their idiosyncrasy and particularity. Because it is individuals in their particularity who express themselves, the public opinion in this huge mass of

know that one can err in one's first impressions and that in general what presents itself immediately is evanescent.] We have also seen this most recently in matters of state. Here, too, there is a conceit that all opinions other [than one's own] are mired in a swamp. [UN273: Such things are original because it does not occur to reasonable people to babble such trash.] It is therefore true that public opinion must be just as much scorned as respected. Thus, where one sees [UN273: a general] dissatisfaction, there is indeed a lack [UN273: that must be remedied]. However, if one probes the judgments [UN273: of public opinion as to the remedy] more closely, one sees that they were all wrong. Men who have done something great have always done it against public opinion. No [193] statesman should count on gratitude, [UN273: nor in general anyone who accomplishes something true]. Nevertheless, the truth [ultimately] prevails. [UN273: Despite the resistance of consciousness, we catch up to ourselves in the end.]

Interconnected with [public opinion] is what is called *freedom of the press*. We have already said that the best [discussion] will inevitably occur in the estates' [assembly], so that little [UN273: of importance] will be left for others. Freedom of the press is thus an extremely difficult subject.[850] [It] is a claim to a right to express one's thoughts – a formal right. If by a free press one means that one may say whatever one wants, then this is just like saying that freedom of action means that one can do whatever one wants. Only superficial thinking would want such a right. Laws cannot let the defamation of individuals go unpunished, and the same is true of [UN273: inciting] crimes against the State. All this [the State] cannot let go. Then also, the basic principles, the sacred bond [of the State] can be poisoned through teaching. The mob is easily swayed – for example, [by teaching] that people don't have to pay

---

utterances and conceptions of so many individuals is full of contradictions. If those who speak did not think they know better [than everyone else] how the matter lies, they would remain silent. Public opinion in that sense is one of the most difficult phenomena to understand, because it contains a direct contradiction. Public opinion is the completely nugatory and vain and, at the same time, the thoroughly substantial. The universal consciousness of a people is the voice of its god, and so the saying "Vox populi vox dei" is quite correct. Likewise, however, the opposite can also justifiably be said about the judgment and voice of the people. One can therefore say that public opinion must be respected, on the one hand, and disdained, on the other. Philosophers especially have in all times done the latter; likewise, no great statesman, no great prince has produced anything great who has not known how to scorn public opinion.

850 UN273: It is difficult to make laws for press freedom that are completely determinate.

taxes. It can happen that, by incessant poisonous ranting, the dignity of the government is lowered. Subjective civic feeling, which is an [essential] moment of the State, can be easily made to waver. This subject is very difficult [because lines are difficult to draw].[851]

The sciences remain safe against these [reservations concerning press freedom]. The sciences inhabit an element in which the State also lives. The element of the State is likewise thought. The State should place no hindrances on the sciences, still less should the Church, whose form is faith [UN274: and reason's subservience to faith. The Church can attach to obedience a number of works, etc. that intellectual enlightenment cannot tolerate.] However, the prohibition of [seditious] pamphlets is justified. The most severe punishment for these writings is scorn.[852] In England, they [relied on] this even though the strictest laws against [sedition] existed. However, when such opinions gave permission to deeds, they restrained them.[853] It is said, of course, that these are mere opinions, but such opinions poison dispositions. It is impossible to delineate something determinate concerning [punishable writing], because thoughts are so malleable that, with the most innocent words, something harmful can come out.[854] Here legislation is guided by the times.

[194] In democracies like Athens where [public] opinion is a [substantial] principle, if [subjective] opining becomes a pervasive condition, then the state dissolves and transitions into a monarchy or aristocracy. This is because the substantial exists here only in the form of subjective [patriotic] disposition. If this collapses into opining, then nothing more remains [of the substantial]. However, in a rational [constitutional] organization [UN275: where the rational and substantial are present in an objective way], opining is something external [to that organization] and inessential. At the same time, it is essential to the liberation of the

---

851 UN274: Certainly, an absolute boundary regarding what [speech] should and should not be considered criminal cannot be specified.
852 Translator: Ringier wrote *Vernichtung* (destruction), but UN's *Verachtung* (scorn, disdain) makes more sense in context.
853 UN274: In England, a lot of newspapers directed against the government come out daily. Every day they bring forward a host of grounds for ridicule against the government, but the government disdains them. Incidentally, English laws are by no means as lenient towards freedom of the press as we are accustomed to think. In England, too, the daily invective against the government engendered a vicious disposition among the rabble, and the government found it necessary to intervene.
854 UN274: Thought is something so malleable that one does not at all have to say something directly in order, through a combination [of words], to produce the intended effect.

particular individual [and] to the idealization of the existent. In opining, all that exists [immediately] is cancelled and becomes something ideal, [UN275: and this [[as the next Section explains]] is itself an objective determination of the State].

[A. 2. External Sovereignty][855]

In the way that we have [thus far] contemplated the rationality of the State, it is the peaceful coexistence of the particular spheres alongside each other. [In the State at peace,] ideality is only the form of their [inherent] cohesion; the [actual side-by-side] existence of the particular spheres is the chief moment. In the State at peace, the princely moment is more the formality of influencing and deciding. But that is only one way in which the rationality of the State exists. Inasmuch as the State is the Mind of a people, it is necessary that its ideality become real in the form of intention, in the [known] negativity of the particularistic spheres [within] the selfish unity of the whole. The [UN275: self-consciousness of the State] must appear as well in the form of a negation of the [isolated] particular by an opposed form. Just as in an organism, every member has its function, just as the blood is the centre of irritability in which all diversity of tissue is dissolved, so also do [the parts of the] State dissolve in this ideality. Just as the State lays out the reality of its moments, so must the ideality of the whole become real. In the State at peace, the particular is real [and] the universal is [only] the inner, inherent end of the external and changeable.

However, [the State] is also the negativity [of the self-subsistent particular spheres], the coming to reality of Spirit's relation to itself in its simple freedom. And so [the State] must stand against life, against the rights and property of individuals, and also as the power whereby the external spheres manifest their nullity. This is the second side of the State, where it pulls itself together and focuses on its negative unity. In this way, it has [195] sublated the difference [between public and private spheres] and it is precisely therewith a One [*Individuum*] in contrast to another One, simple ideality. Precisely in being [a One] inwardly, it reflexively [excludes] outwardly.[856] This is the moment of the State's independence, of its external sovereignty. Its independence is its honour. This [independence] is its highest law. Just as freedom, selfhood,

---

855 Translator: Angehrn, Bondeli, and Seelmann place this heading before the previous paragraph, but I think it goes better here.
856 UN276: In this moment, the State appears for the first time as genuine ideality.

self-relation are the highest things for Spirit, which is Spirit only as this cohesion, so the preservation of independence is the highest imperative and honour of peoples, an absolute duty for everyone. Everyone must contribute to [the State's] defence. And this is precisely a sacrifice whereby ideality comes to existence, in that the self-interested business of living exhibits itself as a nullity in the self-concentration of Spirit.[857] The moment of independence [vis-à-vis foreign states] is the province of the princely power. That moment gives reality to the princely power, [which internally is a mere formality]. The duty to defend [the State] constitutes the ethical element in war.

It is only from the viewpoint of the understanding that private citizens must defend the State for the sake of the security of life and property. If one considers the State merely as a civil society [the justification for which is the security of life and property], then [defending the State by risking life and property] is a perverse calculation – a contradiction. The ethical side of war lies in what has been said: [to show] that the immediacy of life, the external existence of freedom in property, and all particularistic purposes are contingent and surface things lacking objective rationality. Their superficiality, otherwise [the topic of] clichéd phrases spoken from pulpits, manifests itself existentially in war, in sacrifice and commitment to [the State]. The things that we allow ourselves to call unserious (the vanity of material goods), this ideality of the particular comes to existence in this sacrifice, which is part of the ethical and healthy Mind of peoples.[858] It keeps the movement of souls from the decay into which they fall as a result of permanent rest and perpetual peace. This ideality already comes to existence through the natural [process of dying], but this is a matter of nature. Here it is an end freely chosen by the individual.

[UN276: To consider in more detail how institutions must be arranged with a view to this moment would take us too far afield.] The main thing is that everyone has a duty to defend the fatherland, to treat the independence of the State as the ultimate end, and this occurs in the sacrifice [of life] for this ideality. On the one hand, it is a universal duty, on the other, a special vocation entrusted [in peacetime] to a particular estate, the estate of bravery. But when it is necessary, [196]

---

857 UN276: The [inner] fact that particular properties, particular lives, and particular businesses are insignificant comes here to existential reality.
858 UN276: It is necessary to the ethical health of peoples that everything particularistic be posited as vain, as ideal; otherwise, individuals would be enclosed in their selfishness and particularity.

everyone must contribute. [Military duty] is a special vocation where states stand in particular [diplomatic] relations and defend particular [claims]. However, if independence is threatened, all have a duty to step up. Then the other occupations of the State are put aside, and by gathering together the entire interior and turning it outward, the war inevitably becomes a war of conquest (thus the French in the [17]90s). It follows from this that the State must have a standing army.[859] [Readiness to die for the State] is a necessary element of the State that must also exist self-consciously as a particular estate and not be left to chance.

Here bravery has its place. [Absent the right purpose, bravery] is a formal [UN277: virtue] – exposing oneself to danger to life and loss of property. The true purpose is the defence of the State's independence. The robber is also brave [in the formal sense], as are duellers over petty causes; [UN277: but this bravery is not virtuous]. True bravery has the independence [UN277: of the State] for its purpose. This is an absolutely final, ethical end, [and] bravery is the means for achieving it. We have here the contradiction between complete negativity [of life and possessions] and complete positivity with respect to the content of the [brave] disposition; [or the contradiction of] a noble, free, and great-souled disposition that is at the same time a feeling of the nothingness of life-consciousness; [or] the opposition between complete self-alienation and dependence [on the one hand,] and the highest independence of self-consciousness, [on the other]. On one side, there is a dependence shown in subordination [to commanders], whereby one's own mind must be completely given up; on the other, there is the highest concentration and quickest presence of mind. Likewise, there is the opposition between action that is completely hostile and personal, and at the same time, completely indifferent towards those against whom one acts in so hostile a manner. In the modern form of warfare, it is precisely the case that, in hostilities, one does not act personally at all but rather shoots at the generality, out of which the bullet that hits you likewise comes. The way the ancients [fought] and the way youths fight especially as cavalrymen and free marksmen is not the authentic form [of warfare], but is rather the antithesis thereof.[860] One must also renounce glory, refrain

---

859 UN277: This is an important thought. If in every dispute between states the whole people are called to arms, the peace of states is destroyed, and the people becomes an aggressor. There must therefore be a particular estate and a standing army for war. This is necessary and much more rational than keeping the entire mass of people always under arms.
860 UN278: Youth wants to know itself as counting for something, so it likes to serve in the cavalry and in the volunteer corps.

[197] from acting in a personal way, from targeting anyone specifically [*auf das Korn nehmen*], and act instead only against the generality. An army is well organized if no one has a sense of his particular plans but rather acts only as a member of the regiment, of the whole, in which the individual does not will, do, or act out idiosyncrasies.

The [ideal] State is Spirit's work of art, but a greater one than Nature. What one must respect one must also understand, but [the State] must be [understood in light of] the Concept that captures true justice. It is a great course of study to learn about the State. The self-consciously straightforward unity is ready to hand as power.[861]

The next standpoint is that at which the state as a unit expresses itself in its external relations. The relation of state to state grounds an external public law.

[B. External Public Law][862]

Every state is a particular accomplishment of the Mind of a people. Independence is its priority. Therefore, no ethical union [of states] exists; rather union is merely an ought-to-be. The relations in which they stand are for that reason treaty relations. These treaties ought to be kept, but [this obligation] remains a mere ought [without reality]. States stand in a state of nature with respect to each other. In that condition, there is an alternation in the relationship between keeping and not keeping treaties. [UN279: There is no praetor between states. In his "Perpetual Peace," Kant presents the closure of a federation of states as a demand of reason.] A federation can be instituted, but it would rest on the particular disposition [of each state]. In any case, it is inherent in the individuality of states to be directed outward.[863]

The relationship between states is the natural province of the princely power. It is for the prince to make war and peace; this is not a matter for the estates. The estates have an indirect influence on these decisions

---

861 UN278: In general, the State is to be understood as the objective reality of freedom. In it, subjectivity also has a role to play. The State is thus a temple of Reason, Spirit's work of art, and so a much higher thing than Nature. At first, one imagines that the State is merely a conventional collection of particular laws. It is, to be sure, a right of self-consciousness to comprehend what one must acknowledge as authority; however, that which is to be comprehended can be grasped only through the Concept.
862 *Das äußere Staatsrecht*.
863 UN279: In any case, the demand [of reason] is that the ideality of the State be realized.

[UN279: through their approval of taxes] and because in a developed State it cannot occur to the [UN279: executive] to begin an [UN279: unpopular][864] war. The conduct of states towards each other is based on customs [UN279: and particular treaties]. [The situation] now is different from what it was in Greece. [UN279: In the Greek republics, it was still customary to kill captives; our customs on this are completely different, and in the disarmed soldier, the human being is always respected.] War must be conducted in a way that leaves the possibility for peace. Hence the law concerning respect for envoys. The murder of envoys is one of the greatest crimes against the law of peoples. War should not disrupt everything else. Trade and commerce [UN279: lie more in the middle].[865]

The relationship between peoples rests, then, on [198] treaties. The relationship among states – that they are particulars against each other – provides a theatre for great interests, great purposes, great virtues and talents. Within this relationship, war is the contingent moment in which the independence [UN280: of states] is [itself] exposed to contingency. [UN280: Above the particularity of individual states is the world Spirit that is free from all particularity.] The Mind of a people is a determinate Mind; particular states bring their particularizations [of the universal Spirit] into comparison with each other. From this dialectic of Minds [e.g., Persia and Greece, Greece and Rome, Rome and Germany] world history emerges.[866]

[C. World History]

World history is just the universal Spirit's judgment of particular [Minds]. Spirit is not something immediate; rather, it is what it does, and what it does is win consciousness of itself [as the Absolute]. Thus, world history is the third [division of the science of the State], with which we conclude.

To begin with, world history is the judgment [of civilizations] by the power of the universal world Spirit. But this power is not a blind fate; rather Spirit is Reason. What it does is rational. Its activity consists in

---

864 Translator: taking UN's *unpopulär* over Ringier's *antinational*.
865 UN279: War is not to be conducted against peaceful, universal institutions; thus, the administration of justice, lessons, and religious worship are not to be interrupted. Trade and commerce lie more in the middle, since they serve as the direct means to the conduct of war.
866 UN280: The universal Spirit has an absolute right against the particular Minds, and it vindicates that right in world history.

THE STATE 241

arriving at the self-consciousness of its freedom. The universal Spirit develops in world history in the following way. It grasps this [particular world formation] and, by understanding it, makes itself an object to itself. And, by making itself an object to itself, it supersedes itself. In understanding what it is, it transcends what it is.[867] It is the understanding and knowledge of itself. This [self-understanding], however, is [already] a higher stage; in this way, Spirit advances, and so it is not the monotonous repetition that Nature is. Spirit progresses. It has been debated whether we should ascribe perfectibility to human beings – whether we can see education [in history]. [The answer] is implied by what has already been said. [Spirit's] progress is nothing other than its reasonableness becoming self-known. In ordinary life this is what is called the plan of Providence. This is nothing other than Spirit's self-comprehension; this is its being. In knowing itself, Spirit is free.

The different stages through which the world Spirit passes are betokened by different peoples and states. Every [UN281: world-historical] people [199] expresses a moment of Spirit's general development. [UN281: It itself has no consciousness of what it is doing.] The people has its particular interests. Peoples batter each other over their particular interests. However, the interests [UN281: that are highest for each people] are particular in contrast to the universality of the world Spirit. The business of the latter is that the particular disappear.[868] Everything – great minds, dominant peoples – is subordinate. At the standpoint [of the world Spirit] all [UN281: considerations that count from other standpoints lose their peculiar significance]. We said that a world-historical people reflects a stage that Spirit has attained. That people is the dominant one, the one that asserts its right [UN281: against that of other peoples, which belong to an earlier stage]. The right of other peoples recedes; they are conquered. The one [that embodies the higher stage] becomes dominant.

Spirit manifests itself in particular peoples [and] this is accomplished in external reality. As a consequence [of existing in external reality,] peoples [*Völker*] have a natural side as [UN281: born] nations [*Nationen*]. Nations are natural. The principle they take on for the affairs of the

---

867 UN280: In grasping what it is, Spirit is no longer sunk therein but has rather become an object for itself. It is now [what it was before] and the knowledge of that object. This knowledge then becomes itself objectified. Spirit advances in this way, and [so] is not the monotonous repetition of one and the same law that Nature presents.
868 UN281: In this universality, all particularities recede into mere moments.

world Spirit is set for them by nature, [by their UN281: geographical, anthropological existence]. This principle of the world Spirit is the determining one underlying the entire development [of a people.] It is the soul of all the different sides [of a people's life]. All are expressions of one principle. [UN281: Because this principle is at the same time a natural principle,] a people can make an epoch only once, [UN282: for it is naturally tied to this one principle]. Other principles can also accompany [the fundamental one], but these would be something foreign.

Accordingly, the world Spirit passes from one people to another as carriers of its principles. By a principle's self-consciously emerging [in a people], that people becomes the dominant one; its right is the highest. Before [entering world history], it has to develop [its own internal] history to the highest bloom, and thereafter it has a [further] history. It begins in a childish condition, then [develops to] free, ethical self-consciousness, followed by decline. It can also adopt the higher principles [UN282: of later peoples], but they are not its own. When [the dominant people] has reached its height, the higher [principle] also makes itself known to it, but only as the negation of itself, only by way of its corruption and downfall. Now it becomes the plaything of foreign peoples. The fact that it deteriorates is no accident, however much [200] particularity and contingency also exercise their right. The essential destiny of a people is planted inside it.

In order to understand history, you must bring the Idea with you. Spirit manifests itself in world history, but to recognize it, you must bring along the eyes of Reason. The way you look at the world is the way the world looks back at you. If you look at it randomly, it will also appear to you in its greatest randomness. The field [of world history] is human interests, and that is why it appears to us as so paltry. On the one hand, we see a colourful bustle of various purposes, a play of [external] necessity, wherein purposes compete with and batter each other.[869] The secret of world history is then the inversion of necessity into the purpose of the Concept. We already saw this elsewhere [in the system of needs] – where a particularistic doing turned round into a doing for the universal. By giving [UN282: his particularistic aims] objective reality, the individual becomes something [a lawyer, a doctor] universal. In ordinary historiography, [the historian] views events in accordance with this external necessity. This [approach] bases everything on the welfare of the people, of the state. It explains outcomes in terms of passions,

---

869 UN282: We see a colourful bustle of various purposes, of noble and ignoble endeavours, a play of passions of all kinds, wherein powers check and batter each other.

circumstances, the condition of a people, the genius of individuals. This understanding is successful for its purpose, but unsuccessful in grasping the rational Idea [in history]. One has to know what Reason is and what its purpose is.

In world history, there are states, real folk-Minds, that come into relation with one another [and] that express thoughts in their activity and their laws. They are ethical wholes that contain ethicality in the form of laws. [UN283: These general laws oppose mere subjective opinion, the contingency of individuality.] The first general precondition [of world history] is that states exist; the coming-to-be of states comes before world history. That bare families become a state is the first thing – something that generally falls in a mythical period. This entire [pre-state] condition has been viewed as a paradisiacal, innocent, divine one. This is because the universal [UN283: of thought] and, on the other side, the reality of willing, acting, [UN283: and feeling] are in complete union, as with children. This union is [UN283: the starting point and] also the destination [of humanity]. But [the task] is to *attain* this union, not merely to have it in a natural way. [UN283: That first condition is still only a condition of immediate natural life.] The natural condition is [201] close to animalistic nature. The human being is what it is by producing itself from itself.[870] Mind is that which knows; mere sensation is animalistic. If one says, for example, that this is so lofty that it is inexpressible, one thinks that one has again said something lofty. But it is just subjective feeling that is expressed. [UN283: The genuinely rational must be capable of self-expression.] The animal is also in union with nature. The sleepwalker is too, although this is a lower condition.[871]

The first thing in history is the prehistorical. Germane here are the introduction of marriage and the introduction of agriculture.[872] These are the two foundations. Further particulars [of the state] must, at a minimum, be grounded in them. States [UN284: that have these elements] have a higher right in world history than people [without them, such as] nomads and cattle drivers. In world history, [states founded

---

[870] UN283: Spirit is [what it is] only as having brought forth the identity that it is inherently. The starting point is thus what must be completely abandoned.
[871] UN283: Even Schelling has partly presented the early natural condition of the human race as something excellent. However, that condition is quite comparable to the condition of somnambulism and sickness in general, where the human being falls into immediate union with nature.
[872] UN284: The individual must first be secured, especially through the introduction of marriage and agriculture … The founders of states were chiefly the heroes who introduced marriage and agriculture.

on marriage and agriculture] have a higher right and they realize that right.

If we contemplate the idea of Spirit in world history, we see that it must have four moments. The first form is that of the substantial Mind, where knowledge is still sunk in particulars.[873] The second stage is just the [individual's] knowledge of the substantial Mind; this is precisely the extrication of the for-itself[874] – no [longer] a drop in the sea – such that the relationship [of the individual to the substantial Mind] is a positive one [for the individual].[875] [The for-itself] remains within the substantial Mind, but it is at the same time an individuality. This is the realm of beauty. The third [stage] is the for-itself's grasp [of itself].[876] [The claim] that the substantial is in [the for-itself] is then the inversion [of the relation between Substance and individual]; this is the stage of universal[877] thought – the [for-itself's] grasp of essential being as itself – where the content enters into a negative relation with this for-itself.[878] The fourth [stage] is the one at which Reality is first established,[879] where Spirit exists for itself in thoughtful self-consciousness, in divine self-consciousness. The consciousness that this world is its [Spirit's] world and also a rational world – this is the highest point. Being in and for itself has authority [*gilt*] – that is [the human being's] self-knowledge; its Being is to know God as Spirit and in truth.[880]

The first [stage] is the Oriental realm, then the Greek realm, [then] the Roman realm, then the realm of Spirit's being in and for itself [UN285: that Christianity makes foundational, where God has revealed Himself] – the Germanic realm. These are the stages of world history. [202] The realization [of the principle of each stage] involves individuals. The individuals who stand at the pinnacle [of the age] are the world-historical individuals. [UN285: The true presentation would really be without individuals, but the ways of their time and of their people are reflected

---

[873] UN284: ... where the individual is still sunk in the substantial.
[874] Translator: individual self-consciousness.
[875] UN284: ... such that the relationship is something positive and the substantial Mind is presented through the individual.
[876] UN284: ... the grasping that the substantial is in the human mind itself.
[877] UN284: abstract.
[878] Translator: The content is expelled from the self.
[879] UN284: restored.
[880] UN284: The further step is then to make this ideality objective and so to re-establish Reality. Here is an inwardness that brings forth its world out of itself, and, indeed, a world as a Reality in and for itself. This is the highest point. The fourth stage is then self-knowledge. It means to revere God in Spirit and in truth. Therewith God is expressed as a thinking Substance.

also in world-historical individuals and their fates. This is especially shown in the characteristic ways their careers ended.] Cyrus stood at the pinnacle of the Persian realm. He died at the hand of his enemies. The most beautiful death was Alexander's. After he [UN285: avenged] the Greek world against the Oriental, he died of natural causes [UN285: in the bloom of youth and with full consciousness, within the circle of his friends and in the presence of his army]. Caesar, the Roman, died as the result of a plot, something premeditated – a great conspiracy that, however, brought forth nothing but a futile gesture [*einen Schlag ins Wasser*], an action without a result. Charlemagne died peacefully in old age [UN285: in a Christian way]. For us, Napoleon will be the individual who brought the ideas under which we live to outward reality.[881] [His end came] neither through a plot, nor by enemies, nor by natural causes, nor by all these things together, but rather because he ousted himself. He said, "Je suis l'ennemi de moi-même."[882]

[*C. 1. The Oriental Realm*]

We will consider more concrete characteristics only in general terms. The Oriental realm stems from a patriarchal condition. Although Oriental peoples have developed themselves, this condition nevertheless remains the same. In any case, they require a still higher development – [towards] cohesion.[883] The manner of government is utterly disciplinary. The minister[884] beats subordinates [UN286: with a bamboo rod] and so on down the line. Their chief religion is honour of ancestors. Their main enterprises are study and having descendants, [UN286: and these pray at the graves of their forefathers]. Here, humanity has not attained independence against animals, and just as little has it arrived at the independence of individuals. The state constitution and religion are not separate. The supreme ruler is also the god [UN286: or at least the high priest]. In this union, individual personality is totally

---

881 UN285: If we claim the honour of having lived through a world-historical epoch, Napoleon would be the individual to designate as the one through whom the thought of this epoch gave itself reality.
882 Translator: Henrich cites (UN329) Élie Faure, *Napoléon* (Paris: Éditions G. Crès et Cie, 1929), 197, for the following utterance by Napoleon: "Personne que moi n'est cause de ma chute. J'ai été mon principal ennemi, l'artisan de mes malheurs. J'ai voulu trop embarrasser."
883 UN285: [China] has a tremendous population that seems to amount to at least 150 million, and governing them demands highly developed arts and sciences.
884 UN286: first mandarin.

submerged.[885] The [wrongful] deed is not against a solid [person]. Their history is poesy. The Oriental realm does not have a differentiated life. For that reason, there is nothing stable, nothing solid in it. Its life turned outward is devastation and conquest, as if by floods. If there is peace, this is a [203] sinking into exhaustion, [UN286: which then incites another people to subjugate it]. In Oriental realms – in Persia – the beautiful view of nature has made its appearance.[886] In this way, Orientalism enriched the Greek world. In India there are 33,333[887] gods. [UN286: With them, the mixing of the spiritual and natural has risen to so high a degree that they have not developed into a rational organization.] They are the flower people, the abject people. They have a Brahma, but it has no temple. With the Jews and the Mohammedans, Orientalism raised itself to its highest pinnacle.

[C. 2. The Greek Realm]

[UN287: The next stage is the] knowledge of substantiality. Substantial life as foundation but fastened to beauty through the sublime.[888] The Greeks also began with subservience to nature. However, they put the Titans [the gods of UN287: natural powers] on their periphery. The new gods (the gods of consciousness) overthrew the Titans. They still have the former world view as mysteries – enigmatic but venerable. But [the old gods] were something completely different [from the new].[889] In the Greek Mind, the principle of personality,[890] individuality, came to the fore. Difference [between Substance and individuality] thus appeared, but in a naive way, so that the Greek Mind fell apart into [UN287: many particular individualities and their] particular gods.

---

885 UN286: In the Oriental view, the human being has not yet arrived at independent, legal personality.
886 UN286: In the Persian realm, the Oriental constitution has arrived at its most beautiful formation. The monarch is light, the sun of the state, and the princes surround him as stars.
887 UN286: 330,000 [Translator: The editors of Ringier's notes suggest (p. 244) that Hegel is here misquoting from memory James Mill's number of 330 million, given in his *The History of British India* (London: Baldwin, Cradock, and Joy, 1817), 1:200.]
888 UN287: The noisy, riotous Asiatic life is moderated, fastened to beauty through the sublime.
889 UN287: We have a great respect for Charlemagne and the Middle Ages, but we live in a completely different way. Likewise, the Greeks are not really serious about the mysteries.
890 Translator: Here, "personality" is meant in the sense of individuality, not of abstract personhood.

Also, the final decider is an oracle. [UN287: Concern for] need is not assigned to [the sphere of] freedom but is [considered] a slavish condition. [Greek life] is the life of beauty. Necessarily, however, it could not last [UN287: because it did not contain infinite opposition], and its decline came over it as a decay. The Greek realm attained its highest beauty in Athens. [UN287: Soon after, it appeared as Individuality in Alexander. With the death of Alexander, his empire did not disintegrate, for he had achieved his purpose, namely, to make Greek life dominant over Asian life.] And it is believed that, through Alexander's marching against the Orientals, the Oriental realm gave its sciences to the Greeks. [Alexander] was the second Achilles, the one who again gathered together the fragmented [Greek] nature. The first Achilles was immersed by his mother in the [river] Lethe; so too Alexander was immersed by Aristotle in the Lethe of speculative philosophy.[891]

[C. 3. The Roman Realm]

[204] The Greek Mind had to give way to bifurcation. The particular must oppose itself as one particular against another, [UN288: and the consciousness of particularity must come forward]. In the Roman world, we see, [on the one hand,] a union of noble lineages, on the other, the plebs.[892] With the Romans we see, [on the one hand,] these noble, pious families, on the other, civil personality. According to history, the Roman world arose from several [UN288: peoples],[893] an origin that is necessary for a world-historical people; it must carry opposition within itself right from the beginning. So, too, did the Germanic peoples; so many names crop up of peoples that intermingled.

With the Romans, accordingly, this inward opposition [between patricians and plebeians] appears. We see here the opposition between estates. With the Orientals [we see] castes, with the Greeks only freemen and slaves. The history of the Roman realm is just the mutual destruction[894] of the opposites and the emancipation of the plebeian principle, [UN288: for which the essential, determining, and dominant are not the natural Penates but rather free personality]. This opposition [between estates] was then knotted [at the top] in the abstraction of

---

891 UN287: ... in the pure element of thought.
892 UN288: With the Greeks, too, there were the Eumolpides, which, however, were merged with the rest of the people.
893 Translator: Ringier wrote "families," but "peoples" makes more sense of what follows.
894 UN288: inversion.

the state, not in a free life. And precisely this [UN288: obedience to the laws of the state] constituted Roman *virtus*. In Rome, we see the rigid subservience of private citizens [to the state]. Family life was also harsh [and] blighted, its inner life[895] sacrificed to service for the state. [UN288: At the same time, however, the higher dignities] stepped forward into reality, the matrons and the vestal virgins. This ethicality was limited to femininity; it was not present in the family.

In general, the abstraction of the state developed in the Roman state. On one side were aristocrats and a religious outlook, on the other plebeians and personal freedom. What [began in Rome as] a religious outlook [UN288: and the ethical power of the aristocracy] became superstition [UN288: and lawless power], while on the other side, personal freedom degenerated into [UN288: the depravity of] a rabble. That is how [Rome] broke up.[896] Individuals were reduced to mere private persons, as a result of which private law gained the development we see. They were [UN289: held together by] a Caesar, but a capricious and wild one. In this agony of the world, self-consciousness was driven back into itself; in the real [205] world, it found no cultivation. By being forced back into itself, self-consciousness grasped itself. There appeared the philosophies that precisely demonstrate this [retreat into self]: Scepticism, Stoicism, Epicureanism.

[C. 4. *The Germanic Realm*]

In this heartache, [self-consciousness] understood itself. It understood its pain, or it knew itself as that in which the opposition [between the universal and the particular] is contained [UN289: and in which totality therefore exists], and comprehended it. The idea of God's becoming human came to sight among peoples, the unity of the divine and human natures. By grasping its opposition, by knowing itself [as this opposition], self-consciousness is therewith precisely self-comprehension.[897] The awareness that the divine Self is at one with the human dawned on human beings. By taking hold of the [idea UN289: that the Divine is real and present], the human being is itself

---

895 UN288: family piety.
896 UN289: The whole thing ended in an abstract universality, where the folk deities of the various nations were brought together in a Pantheon and therewith demoted to particular gods.
897 UN289: Self-consciousness, by knowing itself as the opposition, is self-cohesion and thus self-comprehension as totality.

divine. [The task of carrying out this idea] was necessarily relayed to another people: the Germanic.[898]

The agony of the cross has now become the thing most revered. What was most scorned has become the most elevated.[899] The despised one has thus understood itself. It was for the Germanic people to carry out this principle. The principle is the reconciliation of God with the world. They are not alien to each other. This reconciliation was to become determinate, was to be made into a world formation. That reality conforms to the Concept – this is the principle of truth, [UN290: and this is freedom]. This truth was revealed to humanity. The Son has stepped forth, has united itself with God, and has thus become Spirit.[900]

However, this truth is not yet realized. [To begin with,] reality on its own is found as a secular realm. The world is not adequate to the truth. For that, great struggle and work are required. So, there was the [split] realm of the ecclesiastical and the worldly. The goal was to unite them. The secular realm arose from the North and, indeed, from the heart, from the [UN290: loyalty] relation of the free cooperative association. The relationship [based on] heart could not remain a sentimental one. The truth must come forward in the form of thought, [UN290: of universality, of law]. In accordance with the nature of things,[901] different estates emerged in the secular realm. These constituted the basic [constituent] principles of the Germanic principle. [In the corporation,] [206] particularity has adopted the form of the universal.[902] What Plato recognized in his *Republic* [that estates are divisions of universal Mind] has become realized in the Germanic [UN290: realm[903]].

The further development went as follows. On the one hand, the particular cooperative associations wrecked the unity of the state, [UN290: while on the other, state power gained predominance over particularisms. The former we see in Italy and also in Germany, the latter in Spain

---

898 UN289: This awareness, for which the breakdown of the Roman world prepared the ground, was not for the Romans to carry out; rather, [this task] was relayed to the Nordic principle of the Germanic people.
899 UN289: The cross, the symbol of contempt and lowliness, has thus been elevated to the principle of the world. Self-consciousness has come to the view that the beyond is also present. The contemptible, the human in general, has thus understood itself in its eternal being.
900 UN290: God is not grasped as Spirit if He is not grasped as the Trinity, as that which has returned to itself out of opposition.
901 UN290: In accordance with the determination of the Concept ...
902 UN290: Particular subjectivity developed from that sentimentality, but at the same time as something communal, as a cooperative association.
903 Translator: taking UN's *Reich* over Ringier's *Prinzip*.

and France]. [Meanwhile,] the ecclesiastical and secular realms battered each other. The ecclesiastical realm became worldly and thus degraded itself [UN290: to a realm of self-seeking and vice]. On the other side, the secular realm cultivated thought, [which] had to arise there. The further destiny was for the implicit [differentiation of estates] also to become something demanded, to be made determinate through thought.[904] The new era is nothing but the Germanic principle [of God's reconciliation with the world] assimilated to thought. [The demand of] the new era has been just this: reasonable argument, which requires that thought lay hold of itself. There is now nothing else to do but to understand what is ready to hand and, by doing so, to make it conform to thought. This is also the way of philosophy.[905]

Finit., 17 March 1820

---

904 UN291: The further destiny was this, that what was implicitly ready to hand, [namely,] the differentiation of political estates [spiritual, noble, bourgeois], now becomes determined through thought [as agricultural, business, and universal]. The differences had become partly ossified in positive law. The new era made determinate through thought what was implicitly reasonable and accomplished, and, at the same time, stripped the positive of its dust and rust. This is nothing but the foundational principle of philosophy, the free recognition of truth, stripped of the accidental.
905 UN291: This is the way of philosophy.

Appendix 1

UN51–4:

By contrast, the form of philosophy is, to be sure, also the form of the eternal, but in the form of pure thought, of the eternal in the pure element. Yet insofar as philosophy considers something intellectual, it [engenders] a separation, for [the Mind apprehended by thought] is something other than the Mind of the real [world]. The separation gains a more precise determination, one that we see when philosophy [first] emerges. It occurred when Mind in the form of thought stood over against the form of external reality. We see this emerge in Plato, Socrates, [and] Aristotle at the time when Greek life was declining and the world Spirit [was moving] to a higher consciousness of itself. In a duller way, we find this repeated in Rome, as the earlier, peculiarly Roman life ended and a different one [infused with Christianity] took shape. Descartes appeared because the Middle Ages were spent. The concentration of spiritual life [in thought] eventually arises where thought and reality are not yet one. When this concentration developed into a difference [between thought and reality], when individuals became free and the life of the state split apart, then the great [philosophical] minds emerged. Philosophy emerged as the self-sundering Spirit. When it painted its grey on grey, the divorce between body and soul had [already] occurred. Philosophy is not what causes the fracture; it has already occurred [and] philosophy is its symptom. How is this fracture to be understood? We could think that it is only an ideal [subjective] break, not a true one, that Spirit abandons the existing reality as a corpse [in order to bring into existence] a state of the world where free philosophy and the education of the world agree. On this view, philosophy would give up its supposed opposition [to the world], and this is its true goal. For in [philosophy] lies the moment of reconciliation; it ought to overcome the separation between the different [philosophic and worldly] consciousness[es].

Overview of Science

Our object is Right. This belongs to Spirit, and, indeed, to the side [of Spirit] that we call the Will. We enquire into the nature of the Will, of the thinking Will, that constitutes the starting point for Right. The desiring Spirit in its full compass wants to create Spirit as nature, as a present reality. By contrast, Right belongs to the Will. The Will is free because, at first something inward, it makes itself other, gives itself external reality. This is its freedom. The system of Right is nothing but the system of self-realizing freedom. Spirit is more or less an abstract Spirit;[906] the concrete is the many, the manifold in itself. The concrete falls out [of Spirit] in the result, not at the beginning. The result is that [Spirit] takes with it what it was earlier [but under] a higher purpose; it begins from the simple, not entirely concrete. The justice of the world Spirit is the resolution.

Let us compare our science [of Right] with the positive science [of law]. Positive law teaches us the viewpoint [from which] to determine what is right in these or those cases, whether this [particular] belongs to this or that [category]; it teaches how to judge an action. This viewpoint presents itself here as a means for [deciding] particular cases, one that constitutes the law for everyone. The reasonable presents itself as an instrument by which people arrange their affairs. The essential thing seems to be the affairs. What is here expressed only as a method is for us the essence [of the matter]; for us what counts in situations and relationships is just the reasonable, albeit that Spirit does not satisfy its Concept therein.[907] The spiritual, which is here our only concern, is at home on a different level. There, we contemplate [in positive law] the glimmering of Spirit, the validity of the universal; we do not enquire into the utility [of rules], how peace, order, and possession are secured. For us, the reasonable is the first and essential point. From our point of view, where reasonableness is the purpose, particularistic purposes (lawyerly things) recede. Spirit ought to fulfil itself. Here we have the same interest as in religion, to live a spiritual life. Our devotional practice is to find Spirit in the institution[s] of the world, [to discern] the reconciliation of Spirit with the world. The infinite goodness of the Divine consists in this, that it reveals itself to individuals and leaves room for the right of particularity. Therein we find the [true place for the concept of] utility, where something is a means to an end. The individual makes

---

906 Translator: depending on the richness of its content at any stage of development.
907 Translator: in rules for contingent situations.

itself its end; this should be the absolute foundation of the positive science of law. Nevertheless, the positive science of law has developed a somewhat condescending tone towards the reasonable. We set forth the Right in its totality; to develop it is our progress. The application to particulars does not belong to our philosophical science of Right. Fully developed, [this science] will gain the same comprehensiveness as the positive science of law. However, application is a matter for the understanding, which orders the particular under the universal, not for philosophical enquiry.

Appendix 2

UN150–3:

At this stage, individuals appear only as private persons, as bourgeois. The right of the particular will is what people are especially wont to understand by freedom. [They think that] civil liberty in [the pursuit of] inclination, in freedom of choice, in the exercise of one's skill, etc. ought not to be limited. This right of particularity does not exist in the patriarchal relationship. It is entirely foreign to Oriental life. This sphere emerges primarily in modern states. In calling this freedom, one is on the one hand correct, because it is [indeed] freedom, but only the freedom of the particular [will]; on the other hand, it is not known that this freedom is also the utmost dependency. The particular [will] has a content that is not a content of freedom. Necessity and freedom are here in conflict with each other; one always turns into the other. Freedom becomes necessity and dependency, and this again becomes freedom.

However, precisely for that reason, this freedom is not true freedom. Self-seeking, in satisfying itself, simultaneously gives itself up and effects the opposite of itself – the general. This turnabout, this dialectic, is the rational, the transition of one into the other. While private persons seek their purposes, this is at once mediated by the turnabout into the general, and individuals are thereby compelled to concern themselves with the general. In this way, the awareness dawns that particular interests can be protected and satisfied only through the general [interest]. For the consciousness [immersed in] particular ends, the purpose of the relationship [between the individual and society] is different from the one [grasped by] rational knowledge. Here [for the bourgeois] the particular [interest] is the end, and the general is merely a means. The form of universality as such is not aimed at. For rational knowledge, the universal is the end and the particular is merely a means.[908]

The glimmering of the reasonable shows itself in this sphere [of civil society]. The putting aside of idiosyncrasy in the generality occurs as a necessary effect. This is the reconciling element in this sphere. If, on the one hand, we regard the contemptibility or at least the [moral] indifference of particular ends as ignoble, on the other hand, the general [interest] is also brought about by [satisfying] them. This, in general, is the process by which the particular [will] is educated[909] to the universal, by which the ground is prepared for an ethical purpose. In order that the inherent and self-conscious purpose not be a mere figment of thought, it must be grounded in the particular [willing of individuals]. This ground must, as best it can, be raised to the form of universality. This second sphere is in general the sphere of [the particular will's] external reality. It is thus the stage of [its] objectification. We have here, on the one hand, the reality [that the particular will gives itself], and this is just the will and opinion of individuals. In order that this be a fitting element for the existence of ethical freedom, the will must not remain a natural will; it must rather become something universal.

There are thus the following three stages to consider:

1 The system of needs and their satisfaction, whereby these [satisfactions] are mediated through the work of the individual and through the work of all other individuals and by the satisfaction of their needs. Individuals must thus give themselves the form of universality.
2 The emergence therein of the substantial universal. In the system of needs, the universal stands out only as a form,[910] but it also goes further, retreating to its ground in justice, and indeed no longer in a merely abstract Right, but rather in the self-objectifying Right, or the administration of justice.
3 The totality of the first two moments; the comprehensive provision for the particular. This can only be an external concern, an external

---

908 Translator: It is doubtful that Hegel posed this simplistic contrast between the standpoint of the bourgeois understanding and that of rational knowledge. From the latter standpoint, the universal and the particular are each means for the other, and so both are ends.
909 Translator: reading *gebildet* instead of *eingebildet*.
910 Translator: Perhaps exchange value is meant.

[to the private sector] regime that has been portrayed by Fichte and others as the need-state, also as the state's police [power].[911]

[A. The System of Needs]

The system of needs emanates from the person in its complete particularity. This is really what we call "the human being." So, basically, we're here speaking about human beings for the first time.[912] The satisfaction of the individual is here mediated; his activity consists in translating his subjective [ends] into objective reality. In that the human being relates itself to others, it is, on one side, dependent on them. The satisfaction of needs becomes more and more systematic. The needs and the means of satisfying them create [socio-economic] clusters [*Massen*] that have an effect on each other. A [causal] necessity and systematization emerge. The contemplation of all this is the object of a particular science – political economy. This, to be sure, is, on the one hand, an external, empirical science, but at the same time there is something higher here, and the presentation of the laws of commerce is an important science that has originated only in recent times. Accordingly, as human beings, we have general needs, like the animal. At the same time, the human being distinguishes itself from animals. The latter have only a quite limited set of needs and of means for satisfying them. The multiplicity of needs is not a bad thing, not a misfortune; rather, it issues only from the rational [nature of human beings].

---

[911] Fichte, *Grundlage*, 291ff.; and *Foundations*, 254ff. (see note 458).
[912] Translator: Abstract Right is based on the person, morality on the subject.

Appendix 3

UN196–8:

Earlier we considered the right of necessity as connected with a momentary need. Here, need no longer has this merely momentary character. With this emergence of poverty, the power of the particular [will] against the [legal] reality of freedom comes to existence. Implied in this is that the infinite judgment of the criminal is brought about.[913] To be sure, crime can be punished, but this punishment is contingent. In the unification of the Substance in its full extent, there is a unification of [the legal and welfare sides of] objective Right in general. [But] just as, on the one hand, poverty is the root of vulgarity, of disrespect for Right, so, on the other hand, does the attitude of vulgarity likewise appear in wealth.[914] The rich man considers everything as being for sale to him, because he is conscious of himself as the power of the particularity of self-consciousness. Thus, wealth can lead to the same mockery [of Right] and shamelessness to which the poor rabble descend. The disposition of the master of slaves is the same as that of the slave. The master knows himself as the power of freedom, just as the slave knows himself as the realization of [another's] freedom. [Each represents one isolated

---

913 See this translation, 48.
914 Translator: In the unified political order, there is a harmony of both aspects of Right – of abstract Right and the right of individual welfare. In civil society, however, these two sides of Right stand opposed. The public entitlement to welfare opposes a private right of property indifferent to welfare. Abstract Right is enforced even to the point at which some have a stake in property and others do not. As a consequence, abstract Right loses its universality for both rich and poor. With that result, the personifications of each side of objective Right – the propertied man standing on his right and the propertyless man demanding welfare – show moral decay. The propertyless are indolent and lawless, while the propertied behave like privileged masters.

moment] of the Idea. Because the master thinks of himself as the master of another's freedom, the substantial in his disposition disappears. We have here a bad conscience, not only as something inward, but as a recognized reality.[915]

These two sides, poverty and wealth, thus constitute the ruination of civil society. [This is because] there is a demand that all be secure in their existence. The first remedy is to give directly to those physically incapable [of work]. As far as aid to the truly [working] poor is concerned, one can believe at first that they must also be given direct handouts through a tax on the rich. Thus, in England, a poor tax of nine to ten million pounds is paid. However, this aid only exacerbates the evil.[916] As regards the [unemployed] rabble, one might believe that they must be subdued by disciplinary means, but this would offend the essential rights of the citizen. The lack of work is, as was observed, a major cause of poverty. In a prosperous culture, there is always overpopulation [relative to jobs]. If the poor are given the opportunity to work, the quantity of goods is thereby increased. But it is precisely the superfluity of goods [relative to purchasing power] that brought about unemployment [in the first place].[917] If the goods are sold more cheaply, businesses are ruined. Were the rich directly to support the poor, then they would have less to spend on needs, and so another class would suffer as a result.[918] As well, the direct support of the poor gives rise to their complete degeneration. Those who have nothing have a right to assistance, [but] in this way, the self-esteem [shown in] wanting to live by one's diligence and work disappears. Because of this right [to assistance], the shamelessness that we see in England eventuates. Wherever in England no poor taxes exist, the poor are still civilized and inclined to work.

In view of [its creating] poverty, civil society forever lacks [sufficient] wealth. We have already spoken about direct [transfers of] assets and direct support. The other kind of asset is the opportunity to work; but civil society does not even have this to offer the poor. What is being achieved on a large scale by aid to the masses must be studied in places

---

915 Translator: With the reappearance of mastery and servitude, civil society is at odds with its own concept of equality of freedom. Hence bad conscience is an objective feature of the social world.
916 Translator: Aid exacerbates the evil because handouts encourage idleness and undermine self-esteem; see *Outlines*, para. 245.
917 See n. 641.
918 Cf. Thomas Malthus, *An Essay on the Principle of Population* (London: J. Johnson, 1798), 25–6, http://www.esp.org/books/malthus/population/malthus.pdf.

where, as in England, masses appear. One cannot speak right now about religious institutions as a way of remedying the evil of poverty. Religious works can do nothing against the immediate nature and necessity of the thing. There must be help for people for the most urgent needs, [yet] in general, civil society lacks the wealth to remedy poverty. It can find help only in an asset that is not its own; this other kind of asset is [foreign] real estate. It does not have [enough land] internally, and so it must instead look around for someone else's. With this is given the necessity for colonization. In all peoples, at various stages, the need for colonization arises. One finds this need even in agricultural and livestock-breeding peoples. Sometimes, such peoples merely long for the pleasures of more developed peoples. Such was the case with the migrations from middle Asia to India and also within Europe. The general, higher principle is that peoples reach a condition where [some] townspeople can no longer live in a satisfactory manner. Colonies must be formed [by settlers] on the loose[919] [from bondage], as with the Greeks. The [poor] must at least be given the beginning of a free, civic condition. In modern times, colonies were put in a special relationship to the motherland such that they were not allowed to trade with any other country.

---

919 *auf einem freien Fuß*.

Appendix 4

UN213–20:

All these[920] are essential moments without which the State cannot exist, [but none is the ground].

When religion is spoken of as the basis of the state, one thinks one has said the ultimate thing [about the state], but this is the ultimate thing only for the understanding. Religion is the contemplation of absolute Spirit, which is in every respect the all-encompassing Idea. The Spirit, as it exists in the State, is a determinate Spirit. Since the human being, as an individual mind, must arrive at a vision of its absolute essence, religion is inherently and actually an absolute necessity, quite apart from any connection to the State. But religion is also necessary in connection with the State. For [individual] subjectivity, the State has its ultimate and highest confirmation in religion. The subjective [conscience] can, as we have seen,[921] set itself up against the universal; it can find a pretext for everything, consider every [duty] in the form of something limited [in its obligatoriness] and rise above it. In religion, by contrast, the individual casts aside all these excuses, because it self-consciously comports itself to the all-embracing. If State institutions, etc., are thought of as grounded in the all-embracing, then they are protected against the arbitrary will of the subject. The subject no longer has an authority to set against [the State]. In the State so considered, religion is also a necessity; the divine Spirit, the rational Spirit should reveal itself in State institutions. Whatever the State undertakes should be done and determined in the spirit of truth.

---

920 Translator: "These" refers to the possible grounds of the State mentioned in the previous sentence (see this translation, 190–1) – namely, the family, or the right or subsistence of the individual.
921 Translator: in the Section on Conscience; see this translation, 85ff.

The Spirit, however, is not something merely inward; rather it depends on its revelation. In this respect, the religious principle differs from the principle of the State, not so much in its content but much more in its form. If we consider the phenomenon [of religion] in light of the relationship between religion and the State, it can immediately seem suspicious that it is as much the oppressors as the oppressed who are the chief advocates of religion. We have seen tyrannies that have referred the people to religion. There, the relationship [between religion and the state] seems to be this: in the state, anything goes; in religion, one receives compensation. We are remitted here to heaven, to a beyond. In times of misery and distress, people are so often referred to religion. It is said of religion that piety should have little to do with worldly affairs; when struck on one cheek, it should extend the other. Indifference and passivity towards [the tyrant's] arbitrary will is thus demanded. Further, we have seen that, while religion relates itself to absolute Being, the form in which the latter is an object of religion is the form of feeling and, in respect of cognition, the form of belief. Rational knowledge and knowledge from the Concept are therewith removed and even definitely excluded. With that is justified a belief that surrenders itself in everything and that accepts everything as sent by God. This is a disposition that can be quite welcome to those who want to rule in the state with injustice, arbitrariness, and brute force.

Furthermore, religion has an external existence. Cult is bound up with an external practice; for that, it requires a command structure. This structure is necessarily in the hands of human beings. There are commandments regarding what is to be believed. Thus, what is [believed under these commands] occurs for the Divine and stems from the Divine. It has the highest authority, and nothing should contravene it. Human authority is strictly banished from [these commands]. Every deviation in attitude, imagination, opinion, and action is a deviation from the Infinite, an infinite crime. Because it is the Divine that commands and for whom one should act, the relationship thereto is either a relationship of fear for one's singularity, and nothing can counter this fear, or it is a relationship of love, within which a surrender laying claim to all self-consciousness, all judgment, and all freedom is likewise demanded. Inasmuch as religious and ecclesiastical commandments have divine authority, so also, according to this point of view, does the Church have the character of an authority against which nothing can stand. Religion is thus in the hands of human beings who, in the name of God, enjoin what they desire [backed by] the most fearsome, all-crushing power. One's own will, one's own freedom, must not oppose such a theocracy. It could have come to the point where human beings become so humiliated that, from the moral point of view, they become thoroughly degraded. In this way, we have seen human beings humiliated more harshly and more severely than they ever were by the state. These are consequential aspects that the religious standpoint has had when made the ultimate commanding authority. These consequences should alert us at the start to the need to consider more closely the meaning of the demand that religion be the foundation of the state.

Religiosity has been described as the consciousness of the Absolute. In this consciousness lies the highest freedom. The individual is here with its essential being; it has returned to its true substantiality. But that elevation is only an elevation in the soul, in subjectivity. The State is itself this [absolute] Spirit, but one that unfolds into reality, [that does not remain] a merely subjective thing; it is thus the stepping out of the merely inward, out of subjectivity. This stepping out involves differentiation, and then these differences must be led back to their universality – that is, they must be expressed as law. If we take God as the self-concentrated Spirit and finitude as its disintegration, then the mediator between both is the law, the universal, the conceptual. This is the manifestation of God. There are other manifestations of God; this, however, is [God's] entrance into reality. The State has to lay out its Idea in limbs that are particular spheres whose function is comprehended in law – that is, in a universal. Religion [by contrast] remains within subjectivity. Were the content of religion developed, this itself would be the organization of the State. Reality can exist only through the universal, through the law. Therefore, one cannot wish that, instead of the State, there should be only religiosity among people. That would be like saying that the gelatin, the animal lymph, contains the whole animal, so [is something] whose development the animal does not need.

The rational Idea manifests itself in religion and in the State in different ways; in religion, in a subjective way. Religion stays at devotion; it does not advance to knowledge. What occurs in the State is something thoughtful, a universal. In the physical world, the human being passes over into sleep, into this union with the spirit of nature.[922] It is the same in the spiritual [world]; the concentration of Spirit in the soul, in feeling, is religiosity. So, in general, the religious standpoint has the form of an envelope of subjectivity against the Idea unfolded in the objective world.

---

[922] Translator: See Hegel, *Encyclopaedia of the Philosophical Sciences, Philosophy of Mind*, para. 398.

If religion wants to have force in a form counter to objectivity, counter to the State, then those inverted phenomena[923] come about. To begin with, religion manifests itself here as something negative; it is idealistic against the systematization of the different spheres and determinations [of the State]. If the religious principle asserts itself in that [negative] way, it becomes fanaticism; this can contain an exalted content, but the fanaticism consists in [taking] that negative direction. Herewith all existing differences [of institutions and estates] are destroyed. We have seen this orientation arise at various times in history. In the sixteenth century, it showed itself in the Anabaptists of Münster, who introduced roughly the same condition that the fanaticism of abstract freedom strove to bring about in France under Robespierre. Likewise, it was pious Presbyterians sitting in Parliament who led Charles I to the scaffold. Cromwell then chased away this Parliament and re-established at least the beginning of a lawful life. We seek the Lord, they say; [but] the Lord has never been here and will never come. If, therefore, they are not to remain in idle contemplation, they must transcend the merely negative [standpoint]. The will, in willing something, must determine itself as law. Who, then, will grasp these determinations? The ones who seek the Lord, those pious people, those who subjectively opine, those who opine and will their particularistic [beliefs]. Then comes the frightful crossing over to consciousness, to objectivity.

Those who keep themselves in mere subjectivity have also therewith abandoned thinking. They cannot, and know not how to, speak and govern in the form of universality. To that pertains the prodigious work of the thinking Spirit. The merely inward subjectivity, be it ever so beautiful, remains confined to arbitrary willing and particularistic opining, never reaching truth. If, then, a decision is made from a knowing of that kind, it is the arbitrary will that decides, non-universal thinking and willing, [the outcome of which is] the absurd and the abominable. When it is said that one must obey God rather than men, the question is precisely: what does God command? Who knows this? Those who conduct themselves in a merely subjective way do not know. The Divine certainly reveals itself, but in a universal and intellectual way. What God truly reveals and commands becomes humanly understood, and for it to be truly understood, it must take the form of universality. But then it is law. The instruction that flows from the religious standpoint also proceeds to general principles; they speak about righteousness and

---

923 Translator: "those inverted phenomena" wherein humanity's salvation becomes its humiliation and degradation.

laws, but they remain at a superficial generality. If one were to proceed to further determination, one would precisely go over to the domain of the State. In their generality, the sayings of religion do not contain the determinateness needed to govern the world. Thus, the Ten Commandments doubtless contain true rational imperatives, but they do not suffice for a criminal code. One cannot govern the world with the proverbs of Solomon, though they contain what is excellent.

One must have an exact awareness of all this if one wants to speak about the State's relation to religion. It is [a sign of] the weakness of the times that it has fled back to piety.[924] This piety is not naive, simple piety; rather, it is characterized by hostility and polemics. A need has arisen to relate with insight and knowledge to what ought to be respected as an objective reality. This kind of piety is not the way to that [goal]. To understand the State, one must undertake to control one's opining through the labour of study and reflection. This [labour] cannot be brushed aside with biblical sayings. Godliness is doubtless beneficial for all things, but it is not beneficial in lieu of all things. Since the State precisely contains universality, by giving up thinking, one has hidden behind religion with shallowness and with indignation at not having been heard. No one has known how to oppose authority with anything but another authority of the subjective will.

To the extent that religion is one-sidedly enforced against the State, it itself goes unrecognized [by the State]. It must, however, have its place and temple in the State; it must be a Church. It is an essential form of Spirit. Right away [*unmittelbar*], religion, too, needs an externalization; it has a ritual, a teaching, and the like. Work related to the rest of civil life must be interrupted [for worship]. Sunday is thus one of the greatest institutions we owe to Christianity.

---

924 Translator: It is likely that Hegel has Friedrich Schleiermacher in mind as the representative of the standpoint of piety that he criticizes in this and the following remarks. For the tense relationship between Hegel and Schleiermacher, see Richard Crouter, "Hegel and Schleiermacher at Berlin: A Many-Sided Debate," *Journal of the American Academy of Religion* 48, no. 1 (March 1980): 19–43; and Pinkard, *Hegel*, 445–7.

Appendix 5

UN230–3:

The idea of the constitution is to be understood through the Concept. A people, a State, is a whole. This entails, first, that in this unity of the State, where the universal should be fixed and active, its moments develop and the subordinate spheres likewise expand; this is the peaceful State. The second thing is that the differentiated spheres are posited as simply ideal [parts of a whole] and that the State presents itself as an individuality.[925] These two sides[926] are now to be considered.

It is inherent in the Idea that each moment of the Concept is free for itself as an autonomous sphere, an autonomous power, and that at the same time this moment comes to sight only as existing through the whole. Similarly, in the solar system we see the planets as free individualities that at the same time revolve around the sun, whose law is also its own. That the State differentiates itself within itself has the effect, first, that it is something internally at peace, something internally boundless. Whatever is not thus self-differentiated exists in the mode of immediacy and is therefore externally dependent. The chemical [element] is not such an internal totality. In that such differences exist [within the State], they must themselves be totalities. In that way, the whole comes to its completion and is satisfied within itself. In that each moment is thus a whole, it has the soul of the whole within itself; [it] is thus itself righteous and conformable to the Concept. Each organ in the living organism is thus a system unto itself; in the other, it has the mirror of itself. With the division of labour, we see how the whole becomes something self-complete through each part's performing its own work.

---

925 Translator: as an individuality in relation to other states.
926 Translator: the internal and the external.

The different powers of the State must be separate; this is to be understood in the sense just elaborated. In recent times, people have glimpsed in the separation of powers the guarantee of freedom. More generally, this is an idea belonging to modernity. The State is a real intellectuality only if it differentiates itself within itself, so that the differences are not stunted but are completely self-developed. Thus, we know how in Greek art, one artist was a poet, another a painter, the third a sculptor. The idea underlying these different elements is a circle of gods, each complete in itself, one and the same Mind discernible in all. This is the great freedom of the modern Mind – to come to its utter antithesis and freely to release its opposite without jealousy.

In an empirical way, which is the way this subject has been treated, people have rightly found [in the separation of powers] a guarantee of freedom. However, it is more than a guarantee,[927] for in this way, the Idea is realized. This theory was developed especially in France, but more in the style of the understanding. It has been said that without such a separation of powers, the arbitrary will would rule; it is easy to see that this [statement] is well founded. The union of judicial and legislative powers would lead to mere arbitrariness of will.[928] There would be no justice, for by justice, at least of the formal kind, we mean that the individual is treated according to a general rule. In the judicial [power] itself, the same differences appear; the declaration of law [for the judge] and the judgment in the particular case [for the jury] appear as different moments. If the police and judicial powers were in the same hands, one could likewise say that freedom would be imperilled.[929] Moreover, administrative and judicial powers have also been separated.

The separation [of powers] has now become a more or less universal insight, just as there are determinations of the Concept that gradually enter consciousness as necessary. This differentiation [of powers] has also been made in history, but here in a more external, accidental way.

---

927 Translator: It is more than a man-made device for checking the tyranny of a particular will.
928 Translator: If judges make law, then laws are framed with reference to the particularities of a case. They then undergeneralize, with the result that those similarly situated with respect to the reason of the law are not treated alike. If the legislator applies its own law to a case, then the individual is judged by the person of the legislator rather than under a free-standing and impersonal law.
929 Translator: If judicial cases were treated as internal security or administrative cases, the procedural protections for the individual provided by courts would be imperilled. If administrative decisions required court-like procedures, the freedom-promoting function of the Police would be hampered.

Thus, we know that the emperor once wandered around Germany, setting up his seat here and there and adjudicating himself. That the emperor subsequently ceased to adjudicate came about at first in a quite incidental way. It then became customary, however, for particular judges to adjudicate, and then this custom became recognized as something necessary. Now we view it as a tyranny if the prince himself dispenses justice to a criminal, [or] if he wants to meddle in private matters. Nevertheless, it is implicit in the concept of a prince that he has the supreme judicial power, about which more will be said later.[930]

In the Middle Ages, princes divided their lands among their sons. This [practice], which looks so much like private property, is quite unsuited to the concept of a State. This custom came to an end, not because it was recognized as conceptually repugnant, but at first only for the sake of the ruling family. A further important advance [was made] when that which originally appeared as the private property of the prince became state property.

With the separation of powers arose the distorted view that it was merely a check [on power]. So, it was said: the princely power always strives after despotism; the judge would like to be a legislator, etc. It then seemed that a separation must be fixed in order that he who would like to [expand his power] could not do so. There is a certain *Schadenfreude* associated with this [view] and, at the same time, a self-satisfaction with the cleverness that has arranged [the machinery of checks and balances] so well. The powers appear as dams against currents – at any rate, as something that is there merely to prevent a greater evil. With such a subjective viewpoint one can often be right about particular cases, because inclinations can be good, but also bad. With such ideas, [however,] consciousness is always filled with negativity.[931] This is a disposition partly characteristic of the mob. The correct view is that each member is on its own a necessary and distinctive moment, one that is differentiated in accordance with the nature of the Concept. When each sphere develops independently, each is satisfied within itself, and then further desires fall completely away. A well-organized court would find itself greatly burdened if it had to perform administrative functions at the same time.

---

930 Translator: The prince has the supreme judicial power only in the sense that all government powers, though exercised by bodies independent of the prince, are exercised in the prince's name.
931 Translator: "with negativity," i.e., with distrust.

Index

absolute Spirit, 260, 262
abstract Right: xlvi, li, 3, 13, 17–60; in civil society, 157–67, 255; colliding with welfare, 73–4; contrasted to moral standpoint, 63, 98; delegitimation of by poverty, xlvi, 257; as right of force, 51; unity of and morality, 101, 108–9; unity of and welfare, 75
action: and *Absicht*, lix; conscientious, 82–6; criminal, 52, 56; of the educated man, 95–8; fear of, 94–6; responsibility for, 64–7, 98; self-limitation in, 77; specific to morality, 62
administration of justice, 150–67
agricultural estate, 146–8, 182–3, 195, 227–9
agriculture, li, 33, 146–8, 228, 243–4
Alexander, 77, 245, 247
America, 175
Anabaptists, 263
Antigone, 96, 121, 185–6
Aristides, 72, 77
aristocracy, xxxi, 200–2, 203, 222, 230, 235, 248
Aristotle, 107, 175n637, 187, 247, 251
Athena, 92n318, 96n329, 107n368, 108

Athens, xvii, 107–8, 207n766, 235, 247

Beccaria, Cesare, 57, 57n190
Blackstone, William, 153n548
Bonaparte, Napoleon, 71n249, 154nn550–1, 199, 245
bravery/courage, 36–7, 77, 107, 154, 177, 178n653, 237–8
business estate, 148–9, 222n814, 227, 229

Caesar, Julius, 72, 77, 88, 245
Campe, Joachim Heinrich, 137, 138n486
capital: xl, xliii, 142–4; of business estate, 148; excess of, 176n641; in institutions, 170–1
Carlsbad Decrees, ix, xii, xiv, xxin28, xxiii, xxxii
charity, 143
Charlemagne, 245, 246n889
child/children: corporation's duty to, 180; education of, 112, 128–9; inheritance by, 130–1; marriage of, 118; responsibility of, 67, 83; society's duty to, 172
China/Chinese, lviii, 233n848, 245n883

chivalry, 71, 159, 201
Christianity, xli, 18, 244, 251, 264
church and state, 191–5, 228, 235, 260–4
civil society: xliii, xlvi, 110, 130, 132–84, 186, 255; in legislature, 227, 229; poverty as ruination of, 258–9
colonization, xlvii, 175–6, 259
Concept: 149, 242, 249, 261, 265, 267; of the ethical, 104, 109, 115–16, 121, 125, 128, 133; of freedom, xxxiv, 75, 98, 197n725; of the Good, 83, 102; in monarchy, 203, 205, 208–10; of Right, xv, xxiii, 3–4, 14–15, 46–7, 58
conscience: absent in antiquity, 207n766; as ethical, 111, 126; as evil, xxiii, 86–91; as formal, 90–1, 100; inalienability of, 34; in legal process, 164; of monarch, 216; religious, 191; right of, 63, 84–91
constitution: xxix, xxxi, xxxvii–xxxix, 4, 195–236; British, xxxix, 153; checks-and-balances, xxix, 267; feudal, xxvi, 200, 226; Greek and Roman, 107; organic, xxx–xxxix; post-revolutionary, xxxix–xl
contract: li–lvi, 20, 38–45; breach of, 51; emphyteutic, 30; exchange, 44–5; formal, 40, 43; and marriage, 40; and performance, 41–2; and political obligation, 40, 189–90; and promise, 42; real, 40, 43; Roman real, 41; of servitude, 34
corporation: xlii, xliii, xlviii–l, 178–84, 195, 249; and executive, 218n804, 219–20; and legislature, 223–4, 230
court: 56, 60n202, 159–67, 195, 267; of equity, 161; medieval, 160n585, 161n587, 166n610; Roman, 163
Creuzer, George Friedrich, 147

crime: in civil society, 158–9; and conscience, 84–9; consequences of, 66–7; as differentiated by externals, 52; intentional coercion as, 47n148, 71n248; as negative infinite judgment, 48, 52; punishment of, 54–9; as self-nullifying, 50–4
Cyrus, 245

death penalty, 57, 58n195
democracy: xxxi, 106n364, 201, 203n750, 214; industrial, xlviii, li
Descartes, René, 251
De Wette, Wilhelm Martin, xiii, 191n703
division of powers, 200, 202–3
divorce, 117–18
duties: 13, 51, 77–81, 85, 91; in abstract Right, 19; collisions of, 95–8; to corporation, 183; in ethical life, 108–9, 149; of parents, 128; of society, 171–5, 180, 259

education: 11, 13, 105, 182; of business estate, 148; of children, 128–9; of executive, 222; in history, 241; of judges, 166; through labour, 142–3; of princes, 210–11; to State, 184; through system of needs, 150–1; through travel, 177
electoral capitulation, 211–12
England/Britain: censorship in, 235; constitutionalism in, xxxiv; crime in, 60; customary law in, 153; formalism in, 157; jury in, 165; poor taxes in, 258–9; unemployment in, 173, 183
entailed estates, 230
Epicureanism, 248
equality: 18, 27, 39; inequality, 27, 144

equity, 73, 161
estates: 102, 117, 143, 145–9; assembly of, 223–33, 240; of bravery, 237–9; Germanic, 249–50; Roman, 247
Ethical Idea, xviii–xix, xxiv–xxv, xlviii, 37, 141, 185
ethical life: 37, 63, 101–10; in civil society, 133, 135, 150n537; in corporation, 179–84; in family, 111–32; Greek, 6, 102–3, 105–8, 185–6; modern, 7, 14, 110; in State, 203
ethics: 34, 78–80; of honour, 181–3
evil: in civil society, 135; of conscience, xxiii, 86–7, 90–1, 94; inherent in reflection, 89–90
exchange value: as aim of production, 142; determinants of, 144; fraud as to, 49; meaning of, 31; property in, lii, liv–lv, 39n127, 41, 45
executive, xxviii–xxx, xxxii–xxxiii, xxxv–xxxviii, 203, 218–23, 231, 233, 240

family: in agricultural estate, 147, 183; in *Antigone*, 96, 185–6; corporation as second, 179, 181; as immediate ethical substance, 111–33; in Plato, 7; in Rome, 170, 248
feudalism: xxvi, 223n819; constitution under, 200, 226; contract under, 31; courts under, 159; laws under, 186; monarch under, 201, 203, 205, 213; property under, 30–3, 154n554; state under, 204
Feuerbach, Paul Johann Anselm, 55n183
force, 20, 25, 50–2

Fichte, Johann Gottlieb: on contractual obligation, 42; his ephorate, 200; his formalism, 91; on inheritance, 130; on moral longing, 77; on the murderer at the door, 97; his need-state, xxxi, xlviii, 170, 256
France: as modern state, xxi; its political instability, 223, 232n846; under Robespierre, 263; separation of powers in, 266; state sovereignty in, 249–50; its voter apathy, 227; why revolutionary, xxix–xxx
Frederick the Great, 153, 213n779, 215n790
freedom of the press, 234–6
free will: 10, 12–13, 17; in action, 68; in contract, 39; and division of powers, 197; in marriage, 125n442; in property, 21–3; in Rousseau, 189–90; and service to state, 226
French Revolution, xxvi–xxx, l, 15n45, 64, 71n249, 199, 220, 223n819
Friedrich Wilhelm III, xxxiv

general Will: lviii; abstractness of, 172; constitutional protection for, 197; in contract, 38; in crime, 54, 56n186–7, 60, 158n577; education to, 150–1; in innocent wrong, 49; in morality, 61, 63, 78, 80–1
Germanic realm, xxxix, 244, 248
Germany: chivalry in, 201; its reformism, xxix; relation of philosophy to, xx–xxi; the Restoration in, ix, xiii, xliii; its unpreparedness for unity, 199, 211–12, 226; as world-historical people, 248–50

Goethe, Johann Wolfgang von, 77, 88, 112n384, 175
Good: as actual, 101–2, 214; and evil, 86–91; indeterminacy of, 86–7; as ought-to-be, 14, 61, 76, 78, 81–2, 100; as subjectively specified, 84–8, 94, 100

habit, 107, 140–1, 182, 186, 214
Haller, Carl Ludwig von, 159
Haym, Rudolf, xxxix
Henrich, Dieter, xi, xxxiv, 21n66, 70n247, 120n416, 245n882
Hercules, 106
hereditary succession, xxxiv, 211–13
heroes, 51, 59n199, 72, 96, 106, 127, 189, 243n872
Homer, 6n10, 92, 126n447, 175n637
honour: of ancestors, 245; of deputies, 233; of the great man, 72; of knights, 201; as principle of monarchy, 201; professional, xlix, 149, 181–4; in punishment, 57; of the state, 236–7
hypocrisy, 93, 97

Idea: xvii, xl, xlii, lvii, 5–6, 8, 14, 18, 51, 167, 185, 187n693, 258, 260; in the constitution, 203, 205, 213, 265–6; in the family, 111; of freedom, 61, 75, 98, 101; of the Good, 75–6, 81–2; in history, 242–3; of Right, xviin21, lviii, 3, 53, 192, 224; of the State, 185, 188, 195, 198, 200, 202, 262
Ilting, Karl-Heinz, xiii, xiv, xxix
imperial cities, 222
India, 18, 146, 158n578, 177, 246, 259
inheritance, 130–2
intention: and crime, 14, 47n148, 63n221, 71n248, 164; as determining the Good, 85–100;
to own, 24; and responsibility, 62, 64–7, 71, 828; as *Vorsatz*, lviii–lix
international trade, xlvii, 173, 176–8
irony, 91–3

Jacobi, Friedrich Heinrich, 22n71, 70, 90–1
Jesus, 90
Jews, 158n578, 194, 200, 246
judgment: xxxv–xxxvi, 47; of courts, 162–5; infinite in negative form, 48, 52; infinite in positive form, 48; ironic, 92–3; moralistic, 71–3; simply negative, 47; of world Spirit, 240
Justinian, 153

Kant, Immanuel: xxii, liv; his formalism, 80–2, 91, 100; on marriage, 40; as originator of threat theory, 55; on perpetual peace, 239
King Lear, 216
Kotzebue, August von, xiii, 191n703, 192n704

labour: 139–42; division of, 139, 141–2; as form of capital, 143, 167; theory of value, 144
law, 152–9
legal positivism, xxi–xxv
legislature, 200, 202–3, 223–36, 266
love: 71, 111–14; in antiquity, 120–1; and lust, 116; marital, 119–20; in modernity, 71, 120; passionate, 119; Platonic, 115
Lucian of Samosata, 132
Luther, Martin, 154n551, 154n553
luxury, 135, 137–9, 143, 183n673

Machiavelli, Niccolò, xx, 219–20
Malthus, Thomas Robert, xlvii, 176n642

man and woman, 121–4
marriage: 112–26; of blood relatives, 125; monogamy, 124–5; sex in, 114–16
Marx, Karl, xliii
mechanization, xliv, 141–2, 173
Metternich, Klemens von, xiii, xxi
Middle Ages, xli, 13, 15n45, 166n610, 219, 246n889, 251, 267
middle class, 222, 223
millers Arnold, 215n790
Mind: of an epoch, 7; of a family, 107, 112; Greek, 6–7, 108, 246–7; human, 207, 244n876; of a people, xxvii, 9, 185, 198–9, 216, 239, 240; substantial, 121, 244
modernity, xlv, xlix, l, 71, 120, 203n751, 224n821, 226n825, 266
Mohammedans, 246
monarchy: ancient, xxxi, 200–1, 203nn750–1; constitutional, xxx–xxxix, 203, 205, 208–10; feudal, 201, 205, 213; Prussia's, xxxiv; Turkey's, xxxi, 200, 213, 218
money, 31, 44, 145, 148, 226
Montesquieu, Baron de, 55, 157, 201, 214
morality: and ethics, 78–80; in the extended sense, 61–100; in society, 168; in the strict sense, 75–100

Napoleonic Code, xxvii, 154
nation: 132, 241–2; effect of trade on, 176–7
Niemeyer, August Hermann, 95
nomadic peoples, 147, 244

Odysseus, 175
Oedipus, 65
oracle, 71n247, 103, 186, 207, 210, 247
Orestes, 90, 91n312, 96n329

Oriental realm, 244, 245–6, 247
overproduction, xlvii, 176, 258

pardon, 56, 216
parents: 118; death of, 130; duty of, 128, 172; testamentary power of, 131
Penates, 111, 185, 247
perpetual peace, 237, 239
Persia, 240, 245, 246
person (personality), 17–20, 21–5, 34, 151
philosophy, xl–xlii, 3–9, 14, 250, 251
plagiarism, 35
Plato, xviii, xxviii, xli, 4–7, 26, 32, 115, 136, 249, 251
Platonic love, 115
play theory of education, 129
Police, 167–73, 178–9, 256, 266
political economy, 256
poverty, xliii, xlv–xlvii, 143, 173–6, 183, 257–9
primogeniture, 127n448, 230
princely power: xxx–xxxix, 203–18, 221, 267; in foreign affairs, 225, 237, 239; in the legislature, 223, 231–2
property: 21–37; alienation of, 34–7; as basis of system of needs, 150; in civil society, 157–8; of family, 126–7; intellectual, 35–6; in war, 236–7
Protestantism, 102
public law: internal, 195–236; external, 239–40
public opinion, 233–5
purpose: as *Absicht*, lviii–lx; and welfare, 68–74

Quakers, 84–5, 194

rabble, xlv–xlvi, 173, 175, 183, 235n853, 248, 257–8
rectitude, 77, 106, 149, 191

Reformation, xxviii–xxix, 194, 263
Rehberg, August Wilhelm, 25
Reign of Terror, xxvii, xxviii, 199
religion: 8–9, 34, 70, 102, 107–8, 136, 174, 190–5, 252, 260–4; in despotisms, 218; Oriental, 245
republicanism, xxix–xxx, xxxviii, 203
responsibility: 61, 64–7; of children, 83; of Crown ministers, xxxii–xxxiii, 217–18; of the insane, 83
retribution: 51–60; as punishment, 60; as revenge, 59–60; in society, 155, 158–60
right of insight: in ethical life, 102; in the legal process, 162, 164–7; in morality, 14, 69–70; in the political process, 224, 232, 264
right of necessity, 73–4, 257
Robespierre, Maximilien, xxvii, 199
Roman law: of contract, 41, 43; of family, 117, 127n448, 129, 132n466; of insolvency, 74; of property, 28, 33
Roman realm, 244, 247–8
Romanticism, 71, 120–1
Rousseau, Jean-Jacques, 40, 135n477, 189, 190n700

Scepticism, 248
Schelling, Friedrich Wilhelm Joseph, 115, 243n871
Schiller, Friedrich, 124nn436–7
Schlegel, Friedrich von, 91n314, 92, 119n410
Schleiermacher, Friedrich, 196n722, 264n924
sea travel, 175–8
sexual connection, 40, 113, 116
slavery, 18, 21, 26, 31, 130, 150, 257–8
Smith, Adam, 141
Socrates, xli, 87n300, 91, 99n344, 106n363, 251

Solomon, 210, 264
Solon, 224
Song of the Cid, 123
Sophocles, 6n10, 185
sovereignty: of Ethical Idea, xxiv–xxv; external, 236–9; of general will, xxix, 189; internal, 199–236; popular, 206; princely power as representing, 204
Spain, 199, 201, 249
Sparta, 6, 7n12, 81, 126n447
Spinoza, Baruch, 200
Spirit: xli, lvii, 4, 7n16, 9, 17n47, 105, 116, 119, 187–8, 190; in monarchy, 208, 216; as object of religion, 191, 249, 260–1; as object of science, 252, 263; as a State, 191, 205, 236–7, 239, 260, 262, 266; as the universal State, 195, 240–4, 251–2
State: as external power, 169–70, 178, 255–6; feudal, 186, 203, 204; Greek, 185–6, 246–7; Idea of, 185–239; Oriental, 245–6; patriarchal, 135–6, 151, 171n625, 186, 203, 254; Platonic, 4–7, 136; Roman, 247–8
state of nature, xvi, 17, 26, 49, 51, 59, 135, 239
St. Crispin, 85
Stoicism, 15n45, 248
suicide, 36–7, 90
system of needs, xlii, xliv, 136–49, 150, 167, 255–6

taxation, 225–6
Ten Commandments, 264
Thucydides, 70
trial by jury, xxi, 165–6, 266
Turkey, xxxi, 200, 213, 218
Twelve Tables, 130n456, 153n547

universal estate, 145, 149

vestal virgin, 114n391, 248
virtue: 77–8, 107, 125; of the ancients, 106; of bravery, 238; monkish, 72; political, 185n679, 214, 231; as principle of democracy, 201

war, 26, 27n87, 224, 225n823, 226, 237–8, 239–40
Wartburg Festival, xxvii, 154n550
wealth: 127, 143; accumulation of, 173; of family, 126–7; testamentary disposition of, 131–2
welfare: in collision with Right, 73, 257; of the family, 120; of moral subject, 61–2, 68–74; as object of corporation, 178–81, 195, 219; as object of Police, 167–73; as realized freedom, 75–7, 81
Wieland, Christoph Martin, 115
world history: 6, 178, 195, 240–50; world-historical individuals, 244–5; world-historical peoples, 241–2
wrong: 20, 46–60; criminal, 50–60; fraudulent, 49; against the Idea, 51; innocent, 48–9; poverty as, xlv–xlvi, 174–5; revenge as, 59–60; subordinating freedom to welfare as, 73

Milton Keynes UK
Ingram Content Group UK Ltd.
UKHW011539190923
428971UK00018B/163/J